Contemporary Approaches in Humanities

Hasan Arslan / Mehmet Ali Içbay /
Günther Löschnigg / Rasim Yılmaz (eds.)

Contemporary Approaches in Humanities

Business, Law

PETER LANG
EDITION

Bibliographic Information published by the Deutsche Nationalbibliothek
The Deutsche Nationalbibliothek lists this publication in the Deutsche Nationalbibliografie; detailed bibliographic data is available in the internet at http://dnb.d-nb.de.

This book is the scholar work of International Association of Social Science Research (IASSR). It is also printed with the financial support from IASSR. The papers are first reviewed by the independent reviewers, and then proof-read and edited by the editors. The opinions and views expressed in articles are not necessarily those of this volume's editors.

ISBN 978-3-631-68107-7 (Print)
E-ISBN 978-3-653-07231-0 (E-Book)
E-ISBN 978-3-631-69827-3 (EPUB)
E-ISBN 978-3-631-69828-0 (MOBI)
DOI 10.3726/978-3-653-07231-0

Peter Lang Edition is an Imprint of Peter Lang GmbH.

Peter Lang – Frankfurt am Main · Bern · Bruxelles · New York · Oxford · Warszawa · Wien

This publication has been peer reviewed.

www.peterlang.com

Table of Contents

Foreword

The book **'Contemporary Approaches in Humanities on Business and law'** gives a comprehensive and multiple perspective to the fields of business, economics, law and social sciences. Academic teaching staff, researchers, teachers, social workers, politicians, students and all other related persons will get significant benefits from constructional knowledge to experiemental applications from this book. The book is classified into two chapters and each chapter provides different perspectives and case studies through several papers in order to make more clear and understandable the theory and practices.

The first chapter is dedicated to **Business**. Işık Altunal discusses policies related to financial instruments'recognition about Borsa Istanbul (BIST) banking sector. The author tries to determine the disclosure degree of the acounting policy related to financial instruments of the firms listed in banking sector in the BIST index. An empirical study of the determinants of impulse buying in Algeria was written by Nadira Bessouh and Belkacem Ferouani. The authors outline the effect of the atmospheric variables inside the store as well as that of the product on impulse buying. The title of Ayşegül Uçkun's paper is the impact of the Shale Gas Revolution to the Russia-EU Energy Dialogue. The author tries to answer the question of how the shale gas revolution changes the balance among energy market. Yasin Barut takes a particular case related to the automotive supply industry in Izmir. He debates on the effect of emotional intelligence and organizational learning on automotive supply industry. Sevgin Batuk Turan underlines the effect of career planning on work engagement and the mediator role of perceived organizational support and the role of career planning in creating a strong relationship between the organization and the employee. Another paper is related to the relation between social and self-leadership with social network analysis. Şafak Baysal discusses the impact of social capital on multiple aspects of organizational life. Kamil Bircan, Güneş Açelya Sipahi and Batuhan Çullu present the evaluation of the supply chain solutions in low carbon development in their paper. Handan Cam and Busra Tosunoglu draw attention upon the effects of an accounting information system on the institutionalisation level of enterprises and the authors develop and tested a model in their research paper. Mucahit Cayin's study tries to indicate an assessment of commercial relations between Turkey and the organization of the Black Sea Economic Cooperation which Turkey played a leading role in its establishment. The paper on the Energy Source Selection by Fuzzy Moora and Fuzy AHP Method in a Textile Firm by Arzu Organ and Engin Yalçın underlines the importance of the best energy source election while determining gradation of alternatives. Gonca Gezer carries out a research related to Social Movement Unionism in Turkey: Yatagan Resistance Case. The author is looking for the effects of the economic and social conditions on the progress and the strength of the unions. The study carried out by Hakan Er discusses Pricing Efficiency of a Failed Futures Contract. Results indicate that the futures trading exhibited persistent underpricing. Esra Ciğerci, with their paper entitled the Relationship between Market Oriented Approach and Supply Chain Management within the Scope of Evolving Competition Concept debates developments in the economic, technological and social areas. Aslı Yenipazarlı and Mustafa Çelik try to answer the question of Does Higher Economic Freedom Lead to Higher Foreign Direct Investment in Emerging Market Economy? It seems that foreign direct investments (FDI), provide long-term capital inflows into the economy, and bring their technology, management information, innovation, and create employment. Bekim Berisha and Bernard Berisha examine the Impact of External Auditing on the Quality of Financial Statements of Limited Liability Companies in Kosovo. The empirical basis of the study is on data collected from all licensed auditors in Kosovo, who have performed financial audits in Kosovo LLC's, in the period of 2004–2010. Another research paper was written by Utku Altunöz who presents Validation of Feldstein-Horioka Hypothesis for the Turkish Economy. The author examines the validity of the Feldstein-Horioka hypothesis for Turkey by using the ARDL bound test covering the period between 1980 and 2013. K. Burcu Öngen Bilir, Mustafa Aytaç and Necmi Gürsakal carry out a research on Analyzing Turkey's Coal Mining Disaster Data (1983–2014) with Poisson Change-Point Models. The authors underline theoretical foundations of change point models and MCMC. Özgür Emre Koç and Mustafa Taytak's study of Regulatory Government Approach Application of Independent Administrative Authorities and Turkey as Policy Implementers. The authors attempt to articulate public sector regulations. Neslihan Koç presents a study of Tax Expenditues in Turkey: Problems and Evaluations. The author state that a set of problems will create in the budget or the tax burden created for the taxpayers. Ersin Karaman, Mahmut Ensar Göktaş, Murat Can Aktaş, Hilal Çalışır, Ayşegül İşci and Sümeyra Demir, with their paper entitled City Usability Evaluation: A Case from the Erzurum Municipality. The authors discuss the concept of usability from a different point of view. Cansu Tayaksi and Birce Dobrucalı argue her paper on Eliminating Muda and Increasing Level of Service in Airports: A New Model Using iBeacon Technology. The authors state that it is crucial to reduce waste and increase the level of service (LOS) in order to reach that goal and survive in a highly competitive environment, such as airport operating industry. Bekim Berisha and Bernard Berisha examine Value Relevance of Accounting Information in Kosovo. The authors argue on the value relevance of accounting information in pre and post-periods of the International Financial Reporting Standards (IFRS) implementation using the regression and portfolio approaches for sample of the Kosovo companies. Hasan Türedi and Duygu Celayir's papers present Evaluation of Corporate Sustainability Reports in terms of Assurance Services. The authors argue that sustainability has gained more attention especially amongst the business world, and social and economic actors in recent years. Ersin Yavuz argues the Implications of Governance Ratios over Five Frangible Countries. The author focuses on the fragile five countries in both economical and governance ways. Nesrin Ada and Aslı Ercan examine the Management Paradigm in Family Business in Turkey. The authors state that family businesses have been integrated with one's own business culture and are transmitted from generation to generation. Bünyamin Bacak, Ebru Kanyılmaz and Ali Şahin Örnek's paper present a Study about Job Search Behaviour of Unemployed Individuals with Higher Education Degree: the Case of Canakkale Province. The author states that many people work in jobs that are below their qualifications and they do not like their jobs and have the intention to find new jobs while they are actively working. Katarzyna Wierzbicka discusses the High Risk Capital as a Form of Financing Innovative Activity-Poland in Central and Eastern Europe. The author states that an increasingly important role in their creating and disseminating is played by small and medium-sized enterprises in the modern economy.

The second chapter contains papers in **Law Studies.** The paper on the Measure of Quickness of Judging in Turkish Courts by Adil Korkmaz argues that the average periods of trials in Turkish courts are highly long and they have no up or down trends except within the administrative cases. Another research paper was written by Volkan Çelik on the Peremptory Term in the Civil Procedure Law. The paper states that one of the purposes of civil procedure law is to provide the provision of a subjective right violated regarding private law via courts. Fatmagül Kale Özçelik examines the Right to Free Elections in Terms of the European Court of Human Rights and Turkish Constitutional Law. The author states that the right to free elections is one of the most important rights in the realisation of effective political democracy regarded as the common heritage by The European Court of Human Rights. In fact, it remains important as a single political right regulated by the Convention. Hakan Karakehya focuses on Information, Power and Law. The paper argues that one needs to know to get power, and surveillance to get to know. In order to be in power and ensure its continuity, those who are in power who need information and thus surveillance often use law as a means in this respect. Nurdan Orbay Ortaç and Belin Köroğlu Ölmez draw attention upon the Reflection of the Directive 2011/7 of EU on Turkish Commercial Code. The paper articulates that the protection of the weak one is preferred on the basis of the principle that freedom of contract will not be valid between the people and enterprises which are not equivalent in negotiation power and position.

Hasan Arslan

Chapter I
Business

Işik Altunal*

Policies Related to Financial Instruments' Recognition: A Research for Borsa Istanbul (Bist) Banking Sector

Abstract The purpose of the study is to determine the disclosure degree of the accounting policy related to financial instruments of the firms listed in banking sector in the BIST index, and put forward the factors effecting accounting policy related to financial instruments.

In the study, according to requirements of financial instruments standard, an accounting policy disclosure index related to financial instruments has been developed to determine the disclosure degree of the accounting policy, and a disclosure degree has been determined according to whether the firms in the financial sector explain the statement in the developed index or not. Discriminant analysis and logistic regression have been used to determine which one of these factors effect the accounting policy.

Keywords: Financial Instrument, Accounting Policy, Banking Sector

Jel Classification: M41

Introduction

Accounting policy chosen by enterprises has an important effect on activity outcomes and performances of enterprises. Therefore, knowing the factors effecting to be determined the policies of enterprises, is important. In this study, financial instrument standards are taken into consideration to determine the factors effecting accounting policy.

Determining what the degree of explaining accounting policy of enterprises in banking sector related to financial instruments is and which factors effects determining accounting policy related to financial instrument, constitutes the main problem of the study. With the aim of finding a solution to the main problems of the study, the 2014 annual activity reports of the enterprises in the Borsa Istanbul (BIST) banking sector are observed.

The aim of being banking sector to the study is to be used the financial instruments more in proportion to other sectors, and the importance of financial instruments in this study is more in proportion to other sectors. In this study, very

* Dumlupınar University, Department of Business Administration, isik.altunal@dpu.edu.tr

careful accounting is done. The average disclosure degree within this disclosure index is 87.5%. The range of scores for the disclosure index varies from 78.3% to 100%. However, this result is not thought to be good for the banks using these financial instruments. H1, H2 and H6 hypotheses are found to be meaningful. According to this, it is found, as the size, marked value, and profitability of the banks increase, the level of disclosure will also increase.

The Concept of Financial Instruments

A financial instrument is any contract that gives rise to a financial asset of one entity and the financial liability or equity instrument of another entity (IAS 32, paragraph 11). According to this definition, financial instruments are comprehended to compose of financial assets, financial liabilities, and financial instruments related to equity.

Financial assets can be expressed as financial instruments related to another enterprise's equity such as bankroll, equity share, interest share not related to consolidation, and limited enterprise shares. As for financial liabilities, they express all the liabilities bringing about a compulsion for paying cash. Thus, a bill of exchange and treasury stock become financial liabilities in terms of exporting enterprises. Additionally, trade liabilities, bills of debt, credits, accrues related to purchase of goods and services which will be paid cash, debt instruments being exported, and privileged equity share, are evaluated within financial liability (Mısırlıoğlu, 2008). Equity instruments are instruments that evidence a residual interest in the assets of an entity after deducting all of its liabilities (Epstein & Mirza, 2005).

Examples of equity instruments include non-puttable ordinary shares, some puttable instruments, some instruments that impose on the entity an obligation to deliver to another party a pro rata share of the net assets of the entity only on liquidation, some types of preference shares and warrants or written call options that allow the holder to subscribe for or purchase a fixed number of non-puttable ordinary shares in the issuing entity in exchange for a fixed amount of cash or another financial asset (IAS 32, AG13).

The Standard IAS 32 defines compound financial instrument as a non-derivative financial instrument that, from the issuer's perspective, contains both a liability and an equity component (Simtion & Luca, 2011).

Table 1 summarises the IAS 39's classification requirements and provides examples of financial assets and financial liabilities in the different categories.

Table 1: Classification requirements and provides examples of financial instruments

Category	Classification requirements	Examples
Financial assets are fair value through profit or loss	Financial assets that are either held for trading or electively designated into the category	Derivative assets and investments in debt and equity securities that are held in a trading portfolio
Available for sale financial assets	Financial assets that are either electively designated into the category or do not fall into any other category	Investment in debt and equity securities that do not fall into any other category
Held to maturity investments	Quoted financial assets with fixed or determinable payments for which the entity has an intent and ability to hold to maturity	Investment in quoted debt securities for which the entity has an intent and ability to hold to maturity.
Loans and receivables	Unquoted financial assets with fixed or determinable payments	Accounts receivable, notes receivable, loan assets, and investments in unquoted debt securities.
Financial liabilities at fair value through profit or loss	Financial liabilities that are either held for trading or electively designated into the category	Derivative liabilities and other trading liabilities
Financial liabilities at amortised cost	All financial assets with fixed or determinable payments	Accounts receivable, notes receivable, loan assets, and investment in unquoted debt securities

Reference: Mirza, Holt & Orrell, 2006

Previous Literature

Table 2 summarises the studies showing the type of statistical analysis conducted, the explanatory variables adopted, and the empirical results.

Table 2: Recent Empirical Studies On The Determinants Of Accounting Choices Based On Firm's Characteristics

Authors	Abd-Elsalam & Weetman, 2003	Glaum & Street, 2003	Chalmers & Godfrey, 2004	Lopes & Rodrigues, 2007	Malaquias & Lemes, 2013	Birt, Rankin & Song, 2013	Sevim & Altunal, 2015
Method	Multiple regression/ Wilcoxon-Mann-Whitney	Sample/ Multiple regression	Chi-square /Multiple regression	Sample/ Multiple regression	Panel Data analysis	Sample regression	Discriminant analysis/ logistic regression
Scope of the study	Egypt firms	Germany Firms	Australian firms	Portuguese firms	Brazilian firms	Australian firms	Turkey firms
Independent Variables							
Size		0	+	+	Y	+	0
Industry	Y/0		Y	-	+		-
Auditor Type	Y/0	Y	Y/0	+		+	0
Listing Status	Y/0	Y		Y			0
Multinationality				0			0
Profitability	0					-/+	
Leverage	-/0			0		+	+
Ownership Structure, Market Value	Y/0			0			
Corporate Governance				0	-		
Reputation Cost			Y				
Length of time to report					+		

Notes: Y statistically significant relationship; + positive relationship; – negative relationship; 0 no relationship

The Factors Effecting Recognition Policy of Financial Instruments: A Research For Banking Sector BIST

The Aim of Research

Two main purposes are determined in the study:

- To determine what degree banks in business in the İstanbul Stock Exchange banking sector conduct proper reporting to the financial instrument standards,
- To determine the factors effecting the policies, enterprises in financial sector adopt while reporting the financial instruments.

The Method of the Research

The analysis of the disclosure level of financial instruments in the selected reports was based on the disclosure index used previously by Lopes and Rodrigues (2007) applied to Portuguese companies listed on the Lisbon Stock Exchange.

In the study, the 2014 annual reports of 17 enterprises in the BİST banking sector are observed. In the study, explaining index of the accounting policies related to financial instruments is determined as the dependent variable, and size of enterprise, profitability situation of enterprise, the degree of institution management, the situation of being domestic or foreign enterprise, and market controls of enterprise, the factors which will effect the policies in the index, are determined as the independent variables. In this study, the relation between dependent variable and these five independent variables are observed. According to these expressions, the dependent variable is expressed in the Table 3.

Table 3: Explaining Index Of The Accounting Policies Related To Financial Instruments

Disclosure Index	**Score (If Disclosed)**
Accounting Policies	
Held for trading securities	1
Held-to-maturity securities	1
Loans and receivables originated by the enterprise	1
Available for sale financial assets	1
Held for trading liabilities	1
Other Financial liabilities	1
Trade date vs settlement date	1
Fair Values and Market Values	

Disclosure Index	**Score (If Disclosed)**
Measurement Method	1
Significant assumptions	1
Fair Value changes in Available for sale financial assets	1
Amount recognised in equity	1
Amount removed from equity	1
Unability of reliability in measurement	
Financial assets description	1
Their carrying amount	1
Explanation of the reason	1
Range of estimates within which the fair value is likely to lie	1
Securitisation and repurchase agreements	
Accounting policy	1
Nature and extent	1
Collateral	1
Whether the financial assets have been derecognised	1
Information about the key assumption used in calculating the fair value of new and retained interests	1
Derivatives – Accounting Policies	
Risk management policy, including hedging policy	1
Objectives of holding or issuing derivatives	1
Accounting policies and methods adopted	1
Monitoring and controlling policy	1
Financial controls	1
Derivatives – Risks	
Segregation by risk categories	1
Principal, stated value, face value, notional value	1
Maturity	1
Weighted average/effective interest rate	1
Derivatives – Hedging	
Hedging description	1
Accounting method	1
Financial instruments designated as hedging instruments	1
Fair values	1
Nature of risks being hedged	1
Future Transactions hedging	

Disclosure Index	Score (If Disclosed)
The period in which forecasted transactions are expected to occur	1
The period they are expected to enter in income	1
Cash – Flow Hedging	
The amount recognised in equity	1
The amount removed from equity and recognised in income	1
The amount removed from equity and added to initial measurement of the acquisition cost	1
Derivatives – Fair Value	
Fair Value	1
Method adopted	1
Significant assumptions	1
Average fair value during the year	1
Interest rate risk	
Future changes in interest rate	1
Maturity dates	1
Credit Risk	
Counterparties identification	1
Maximum amount of credit risk exposure	1
Significant concentration of credit risk	1
Collateral	
Terms and conditions	1
Carrying amount and fair value	1
Other	
Impairments losses	1
Total interest income and total interest expense (separately)	1
In AFS, realised and unrealised gains/losses (separately)	1
Total Score	**54**

Reference: Lopes and Rodrigues, 2007
Explaining Degree Index = (Total Explaining Value)\54

Thus, the total explaining value of enterprise, explaining all the items, will become 54. As for explaining degree index, it will be 1. The meaning of this; explaining degree of accounting policy related with financial instrument of this enterprise, is 100%, and it is found, this result explains all the policies in the index. So, the results will be between 0% and 100%.

The Hypothesis of the Research

This analysis is based on a list of categories, covering all the items that allow us to identify the existence of disclosure required by the IAS 32, IAS 39 and IFRS 7. The hypothesis of the research is as follows:

H_1: The larger companies are expected to have higher levels of disclosure than smaller companies.

H_2: It is expected that the companies having a larger marked value as compared to the companies having smaller marked value will have higher levels of disclosure.

H_3: The degree of disclosure is predicted to be higher the more the company relies on equity markets.

H_4: It is expected that the disclosure level of companies having more corporate governance degree will be higher.

H_5: It is expected that the domestic companies will have a higher level of disclosure compared to foreign companies.

H_6: It is expected that the companies having more profits will have a higher level of disclosure.

Results

In this study, very careful accounting is done. The estimation results for the linear models with total assets as a proxy for size are reported in Table 3. The average disclosure degree within this disclosure index is 87.5%. The range of scores for disclosure index varies from 78.3 to 100%. Three hypotheses are statistically validated. Three are total assets, marketing value, and profitability.

The first is H_1 that relates the company size to disclosure level. As predicted, the sign of the coefficient is positive. There are also significant relationships among market price, profitability, and the level of disclosure.

All the hypotheses and their results are shown in the table below.

Table 4: OLS Simple Regressions

Hypothesis	Variables	Coefficient	T-Statistic	The Results of Relation
1	Natural log of total assets	0.50	1.815**	+
2	Natural log of the market price of the company	0.55	2.095**	+
3	The proportion of equity held by outsiders	0.042	0.455	0
4	Corporate Governance Degree	0.048	0.239	0
5	Country of Origin	-0.036	-8.78	0
6	Natural log of net profit	0.036	2.350*	+

Note: *Significant at 5%, **significant at 10%, One tailed tests

Conclusions

It is important to determine to what degree the banks report to be in accordance to Turkey Accounting Standards as full-compatible to the international accounting standards, report in terms of being in accordance to the international accounting standards. Additionally, determining the degree of policies explained by enterprises in the financial sector and factors effecting the policies they explained, are important in terms of first independent supervisors making judgements about an enterprise and then investors.

An explaining degree is determined by being given "1 and 0" to the expressions in accounting policies explaining index related to financial instruments developed in the literature according to the explaining situation of enterprises.

In the study, the level of disclosure is found as 87.5%. However, this result is not thought to be good for the banks using these financial instruments. H1, H2 and H6 hypotheses are found to be meaningful. According to this, it is found that as the size, marked value, and profitability of the banks increases, the level of disclosure will also increase. This study will be expected to contribute to the literature, as it is a study intended to determine the level of disclosure related to financial instruments, to reveal the factors effecting the policies related to financial instruments, and to determine the conformity with other standards.

References

Abd-Elsalam, O.H. & Weetman, P. (2003). Introducing International Accounting Standards To An Emerging Capital Market: Relative Familiarity And Language

Effect In Egypt. *Journal of International Accounting, Auditing And Taxation.* 12(1), 63–84.

Birt, J., Rankin, M. & Song, L.C. (2013). Derivatives Use and Financial İnstrument Disclosure In The Extractives Industry. *Accounting and Finance.* 53(1), 55–83.

Chalmers, K. & Godfrey, J.M. (2004). Reputation Costs: The Impetus For Voluntary Derivative Financial Instrument Reporting. *Accounting, Organizations and Society.* 29(2), 95–125.

Glaum, M. & Street, D.L. (2003). Compliance with the Disclosure Requirements of Germany's New Market: IAS Versus US GAAP. *Journal of International Financial Management and Accounting.* 14(1), 64–100.

International Accounting Standards (IAS) 32, Financial Instruments: Presentation, http://ec.europa.eu/internal_market/accounting/docs/consolidated/ias32_en.pdf.

Epstein, B.J. & Mirza, A. A. (2005). *Interpretation and Application of International Accounting and Financial Reporting Standards.* America: Published by Wiley. pp. 89.

Linsmeir, T.J. (2011). Financial Reporting and Financial Crises: The Case for Measuring Financial Instruments at Fair Value in the Financial Statements. *Accounting Horizons.* 25(2), 410–425.

Lopes, P. T. & Rodrigues, L. L. (2007). Accounting For Financial Instruments: An Analysis Of The Determinants Of Disclosure In The Portuguese Stock Exchange. *The International Journal of Accounting.* 42(1), 25–56.

Malaquias, R. F. & Lemes, S. (2013). Disclosure of financial instruments according to International Accounting Standards: Empirical Evidence From Brazilian Companies. *Brazilian Business Review.* 10(4), 82–107.

Mısırlıoğlu, İ. U. (2008) Türkiye Muhasebe Standartları'na Göre Finansal Araçların Muhasebeleştirilmesi. *Mali Çözüm Dergisi.* 86.

Mirza, A.A., Holt, G.J. & Orrell, M. (2006). *International Financial Reporting Standards, Workbook and Guide,* Published by John Wiley: New Jersey.

Sevim, Ş. & Altunal, I. (2015). Finansal Araçların Muhasebeleştirme Politikalarına Etki Eden Faktörler: BIST Mali Sektörde Bir Araştırma, *The World of Accounting Science.* 17(4), 821–844.

Simtion, D. & Luca, R. (2011). Compound Financial Instruments. *Lucrari Ştiintifice Seria I.* 13(3). 307–355.

International Accounting Standards (IAS) 32, Financial Instruments: Presentation, http://ec.europa.eu/internal_market/accounting/docs/consolidated/ias32_en.pdf.

Dr. Nadira Bessouh* & Dr. Belkacem Ferouani**

An Empirical Study of the Determinants of Impulse Buying in Algeria

Abstract This paper aims at testing, on a sample of 385 Algerian buyers, the effect of the atmospheric variables inside the store as well as that of the product on impulse buying. These variables may distort the consumer's purchase decision at the point-of-sale and lead to impulse buying. The collection of data was carried out by means of a self-administered questionnaire at the store's exit. When the necessary analyses were done, the results confirmed the existence of a significant relationship between these variables and impulse buying. Based on these results, among the main managerial implications, managers at points of sale should choose experience as a differentiation, using various techniques and combining several types of strategies to get an experiential offer and thus cause an emotional and functional impulsive purchase.

Keywords: *Algerian shoppers, impulse buying, shopping environment, Product.*

1. Introduction

The buying behaviour of Algerian consumers has experienced remarkable changes; their consumption habits are changing as well. Today the Algerian consumer prefers shopping at malls, not only to do the shopping but also to have fun and spend some time with family or friends. Similarly, today the avalanche of products, large number of points of sale, development of new recreational activities and changing lifestyles of people encourage impulse buying. Algerian consumers are concerned by this iconic disease of modernity. Today's consumers are not the consumers of yesterday. Before, their purchase was well calculated, controlled and thoughtful, as the economic environment (socialism) did not allow for freedom of purchase. Nowadays, the emergence of the liberal economy and the large opening of foreign markets are generating new forms of distribution and new methods of sale; the new business landscape has experienced the rapid development of retail trade at the expense of traditional trade. Commercial temptations are everywhere (new products, prices, sales promotion, methods of payment, etc); this encourages the consumer's impulsivity by all means. For this reason, the present research

* The Preparatory School of Economics, Business Studies and Management Science, Tlemcen-Algeria. E-mail: bessouh_nadira@yahoo.fr

** Department of Management Science, Tlemcen-Algeria. E-mail: ferouani_bel@yahoo.fr

study aims to research the impulsive purchase of Algerian consumers. It has become one of the main concerns of many retailers, producers and researchers too. Indeed, given the large share of impulse purchase in turnovers, all companies seek to promote it. The real essence of an impulse purchase is to be unplanned, and only occurs once inside the store. The environment of the place of sale and its various components (variables of atmosphere, merchandising, and mix-marketing) are the triggering elements for this irresistible urge to buy something that was not previously planned to be bought (Rook, 1987). Indeed, previous research on impulse buying was mainly interested in the question of "*how to make the consumer come out of a store, having bought more than expected?*" (Giraud, 2002). Keeping this objective in mind, we try to answer the question

"***What are the determinants of impulsive purchase of Algerian consumers?***"
The following two research hypotheses can thus be established:

H1: Situational factors, and more precisely the atmosphere at the point-of-sale, have a positive impact on impulse buying.
H2: The product and its characteristics create the impulse to buy. Therefore, this study aims to find the variables, related to the environment at the point-of-sale, that contribute to impulsive buying of Algerian consumers. In the first section of this paper, our theoretical approach to impulse buying is presented; in the second part, the factors that trigger impulse purchase are explained; then our methodology of field study, on 385 impulsive consumers, is described in the third section. Finally, in the fourth section, the results of our investigation are given, thus validating our research hypotheses.

2. Literature Review

2.1 Impulse Buying

When the concept of impulse buying is discovered for the first time, whether in psychology or marketing, complexity seems appropriate. Indeed, studying impulsive buying encounters a major problem with its own definition. Impulse buying has often been viewed as an excessive action which is attributed to a deficit in cognitive resources and an inability to control oneself. In this context, impulse buying has a pejorative meaning (which corresponds to a totally irrational behaviour). Nevertheless, the analysis of impulse buying, in a purely cognitive perspective, does not take into account the complexity of the phenomenon. Indeed, if we assume that *individual rationality* can be limited by emotion, then impulsive buying behaviour can no longer be considered as pathological, but rather as a natural aspect of human behaviour; this constitutes the main contribution of the analysis of impulse buying, in an emotional perspective, when introducing the concept of impulse. D'Antoni and Shenson (1973) were the first to define impulsive purchase according to the time criterion and to the amount of information needed to make a decision. For them, impulse buying "*is a purchase for which the information elements obtained and the time actually needed by a consumer to make a decision are significantly small compared to the time normally used by the same person to make such a decision.*" This definition exhibits the rapid nature of a decision, as well as the relatively short time that leads to making impulse purchase.

Figure 1: d'antoni and shenson model (1973)

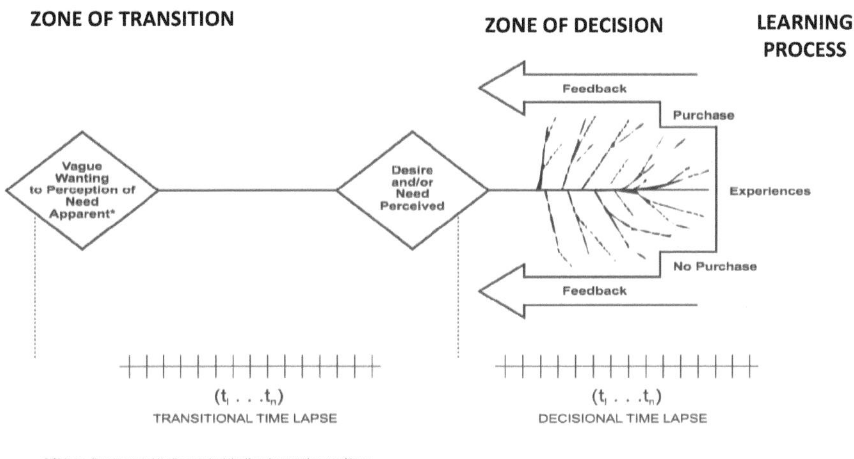

Rook (1987) showed that impulse buying is "*an instantaneous and powerful desire that pushes the individual to buy something immediately.*" This confirms the one proposed by Piron (1991), which reveals the importance of being exposed to a stimulus that triggers the process of decision, and consequently the decision-making. Some impulse purchases may be viewed as compensatory behaviours in which the individual seeks to get rid of an undesirable mood, or on the contrary, as behaviours of congratulation, comfort, or a particularly pleasant mood to search for good sensation (Giraud, 2002). According to Zhou and Wong (2003), impulse buying can cause three fundamental sources of influence, namely emotional influences, influences related to situational factors and demographic predictions, and those linked to the display at the point-of-sale.

3. The Impact of Point of Sale Environment on Impulsive Buying Completion

The influence of store environmental variables devoted significant attention to the analysis of the consumer shopping behaviour. The concept of "atmospherics" was first introduced by Kotler (1973), where a store's atmosphere is defined as the effort to design buying environments to produce specific emotional effects in the buyer that enhance purchase opportunity. Atmosphere refers to the visual display of merchandise, the ease of mobility within the store, piped in music, colour, decorative features and lighting all bundled together in one environment (Thang and Tan, 2003). In correspondence with the earlier studies (Donovan & Rossister 1982; Westbrook & black 1985; Sherman, Mathur & Smith 1997), Thang and Tan (2003) verified in their study on customers' store preferences that the linkage between the emotive response of consumers and the physical aspects of the store (s) exists. Subsequently, they suggested that pleasant store atmospheres providing comfort and gratification that advance consumers' sense of wellbeing within the environment ultimately augment the quality of their visits and hence increase consumers' preferences for the stores. The environment response model of Greenland and McGoldrick (1994), mapping the influences of the shop environment on its visitors, distinguishes three stages in the user reaction in shop and service environments: a cognitive, an emotional, and a conative stage. This model can be applied for atmosphere research as well, since atmosphere can be seen as a key component of the shop environment.

Figure 2: Environment response model of Greenland and Mcgoldrick (1994)

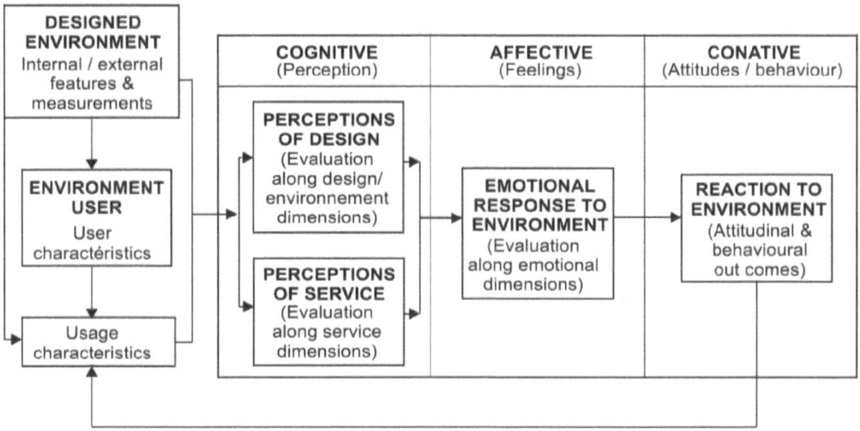

4. The Impact of Situational Factors on Impulsive Buying

Obviously, buying a product on impulse is particular to the point of sale. There is a feeling of closeness to the product; "it appeals us," in some way. Since the early works on the hedonistic shopping experience (Holbrook and Hirschman, 1982; Holbrook, 1986; Ladwein, 2002), various studies have been conducted in retail outlets (products or services, general or specialised), or in shopping centres (Rieunier *et al.*, 2002). The literature strongly emphasises the influence of the situation on the consumer's behaviour, which has now become a full-fledged research field. It emphasises the notion of time, the determination of roles, and previous states of the individual, the factors specific to a place and to an observation period. So the situation corresponds to "*all external factors to the individual and to the stimuli-objects, gathered in one place and at the same time, to which the consumer reacts*" (Petrof, 1999). It is therefore possible to operationally define a set of several stimuli whose specific combination (the situation) causes a certain type of behaviour. The influence of the situation on the buying process was highlighted in the 1970s by the American researcher Russel Belk. A rich literature has existed from that moment, but most of it focuses only on some situational components such as crowd, lighting, anxiety levels, etc., instead of considering the entire context. The situational approach opens an intermediate track, less ambitious, and probably more realistic (Dubois, 1996). Analysis of the effects of the situation on the buyer's behaviour allows the understanding of the scope of arbitrations, and particularly his search behaviour for product variety. Regarding impulse buying, it is often regarded as a response to the store stimuli. This approach has therefore placed emphasis on situational factors that trigger impulse buying.

5. The Interaction between Product-related Variables and Impulse Buying

The qualitative research on impulse buying suggests that the process that leads a consumer to make impulse purchases depends essentially on the product and the product-related variables. Some product categories are more likely to be bought on impulse than others; clothing seems more likely to be purchased impulsively than kitchen equipment. The reason given is that impulse buying is more often associated with pleasure, although today the marketing mix plays a key role in business success. However, the product itself, design, packaging, promotions, proximity, and price significantly influence the buyers to make impulse purchases. Stern (1962) speaks of "*impulse products,*" when he identifies nine product attributes that are likely to trigger impulse purchase: *low price, mass distribution, well exposed merchandise, marginal need for the product, free-service product, mass advertising, small size product, short lifetime, and ease of storage.* Our empirical investigation focuses on the factors that influence impulse purchases at points of sale.

6. The Empirical Study

6.1 Research Methodology

Empirical research methodology is based on a field survey; it corresponds to the validation of hypotheses on situational variables of the point of sale and products. The survey sampling method in the field is the ***in-situ*** method (convenience sampling). The sample size is set for 385 buyers that made impulse purchases. Moreover, the investigation is also carried out in specialised retail stores. The choice of specialised stores is justified by the fact that the atmospheric factors could have a significant impact on the consumer's behaviour for the main reason that the client goes there more for pleasure, as opposed to general stores and supermarkets where he goes rather because he has to (Rieunier, 2002). However, according to the literature on impulse buying, it was found that impulse purchase could cover a variety of products. For this reason, the following products were specified in this study: clothing (men & women), shoes (men & women), cosmetics, and children's toys. Our questionnaire was administered at the centre of the town of Tlemcen (Algeria), which consists of quite popular neighbourhoods and stores where people from different social classes go. These stores are selling environments where elements of ambience and design are manipulated in such a way as to influence the buyer's behaviour. The questionnaires were distributed during the summer holidays, and were then collected during the week, from 10am to 8pm. They were administered from June 04 to June 30, 2014. Data collection took place at the exit of the point of sale. The interviews were conducted face to face between the investigator and the respondent, to encourage spontaneous responses from the respondent and to put him in situations he has been through. Three main criteria were considered: age from 18 to 65, occupation, and gender.

6.2 Results of the Empirical Investigation

The first descriptive results of our investigation are presented, before processing any data, using the principal component analysis (PCA).

6.2.1 Determinants and variables that encourage impulse buying

It is first noted that Algerian buyers make a significant number of impulse purchases (65.25%). All four stores, selected for the survey, sell the following products: clothing, cosmetics, shoes, and children's toys. It was noted that the products purchased on impulse were cosmetics (36%), then clothes (27%), shoes (21%), and finally children's toys (16%). Impulse purchase varies by gender; i.e. cosmetics, clothing, children's toys for women, clothing, and shoes for men.

Table 1: The products that are likely to be purchased on impulse in the four selected specialty stores of the survey

Product bought on impulse	*Clothings*	*Cosmetics*	*Shoes*	*Children's toys*
Percentages (%)	26.49	36.36	20.78	16.36

It is noted that, as far as for the determinants of selected products purchased on impulse, the Algerian buyer is largely attracted by bargains (low price, promotion, and rebate) and then by the emotional gratification he gets from the products which trigger love at first sight in the consumer who is looking for fun, in order to break the daily monotony.

Table 2: Determinants of choice of products bought on the basis of impulse

Determinants	Bargain (low prices)	Emotional gratification	Searching for fun
Percentages (%)	37.00	32.75	29.88

The variables that encourage impulse buying are: low price (16.62%), promotions (14.55%), interior design (11.43%), quality product (11.17%), and special events [wedding, birthday, celebration of Aïd (7.27%)].

Table 3: Impulse buying Variables

Variables	%
Low price	16.62
Quality product	11.17
Interior design of the store	11.43
Ease of finding items	2.34
Wide range of choices	5.19
Good entertainment in the store	6.23
Crowd in point of sale or not	1.56
Music	2.08
New developments	14.55
Availability of Fashion products	4.94
Good brand product	3.38
Faster checkout	2.86
Warm welcome	5.45
Special events (wedding, birthday, feast of Aïd)	7.27
Colours of objects	2.34
Lighting	2.59
Total	100%

6.2.2 *Influence of the shopping environment and product on impulse purchase completion*

From these percentages, it is easy to see that the shopping environment and product prompt shoppers to make an impulse buy. So, the shopping environment can be a source of stimulation for the visitor to the store.

Table 4: Impact of the shopping environment and product on impulse purchase completion

Impulse purchase completion	Related to the shopping	Related to the environment Product	Related to the shopping environment and Product	Other
Percentages (%)	29.61	26.49	34.02	9.87

6.2.3 *Effects of the shopping environment and characteristics of the product on triggering impulse buying*

This table shows that the aesthetic and hedonic characteristics related to the products and to the situation, are more likely to arouse buying impulses and help make the transition to impulse buying. Some of these are the emotional/affective characteristics of the product, design, aesthetic characteristics of the product, ease of purchase and payment; will for immediate pleasure, shopping environment, promotion, bargains, and special events (feast, sales, etc).

Table 5: Effects of situational variables and characteristics of the product on triggering impulse buying

	Motivates my impulses	*Restrains my impulses*	*Motivates my impulse purchase*	*Restrains my impulse purchase*	*Neutral*
Emotional/affective characteristics of the product	**59**	**43**	**191**	**38**	**54**
Physical/objective features of the product	**56**	-	**63**	-	**266**
Design/aesthetic characteristics of the product	**137**	**40**	**180**	**20**	**8**
Ease of purchase and payment	**102**	-	**152**	-	**131**
Will for immediate pleasure	**122**	**82**	**134**	**15**	**32**
Buying environment / ambience, atmosphere	**141**	**39**	**178**	**18**	**9**
Influence of sellers	**64**	**103**	**88**	**79**	**51**
Familiarity with the store	**86**	**47**	**168**	**34**	**50**
Promotion/bargain	**136**	**20**	**191**	**30**	**8**
Frequent renewal of the offer	**108**	**31**	**164**	**82**	-
Use of smells, colors, lights	**121**	**64**	**139**	**50**	**11**
Special event (feast, sales, etc.)	**180**	-	**205**	-	-

The descriptive analysis of the investigation, which enabled us to determine the highest percentages associated with the different categories of variables, was presented first, and then the two proposed hypotheses were tested; a solution to our problem was to be found.

6.3 Testing of Hypotheses about Situational Variables of the Point of Sale and Product

6.3.1 The impact of situational variables of the point of sale on impulse purchases

The effects of situational variables on making an impulse purchase (Q2) are assessed and represented by Q21, Q22, Q23, and Q24; these are the *atmosphere in the store*, its *design*, the *presence of the crowd* and finally the *familiarity with the store*. By performing a principal component analysis (PCA), there was also an attempt to explain the effects of these variables on impulsive buyers. As presented in Figure 3, two variables have a direct impact on impulsive buying completion, i.e. the *atmosphere at the point of sale* (Q21) and *familiarity with the store* (Q24). The results indicate that perception of a pleasant ambience at the point of sale has a significant positive impact on cognitive reactions (the desire to return to the store, purchase intentions and impulse purchase completion) and affective reactions (the mood) of customers.

Figure 3: Graphical representation of PCA on situational factors

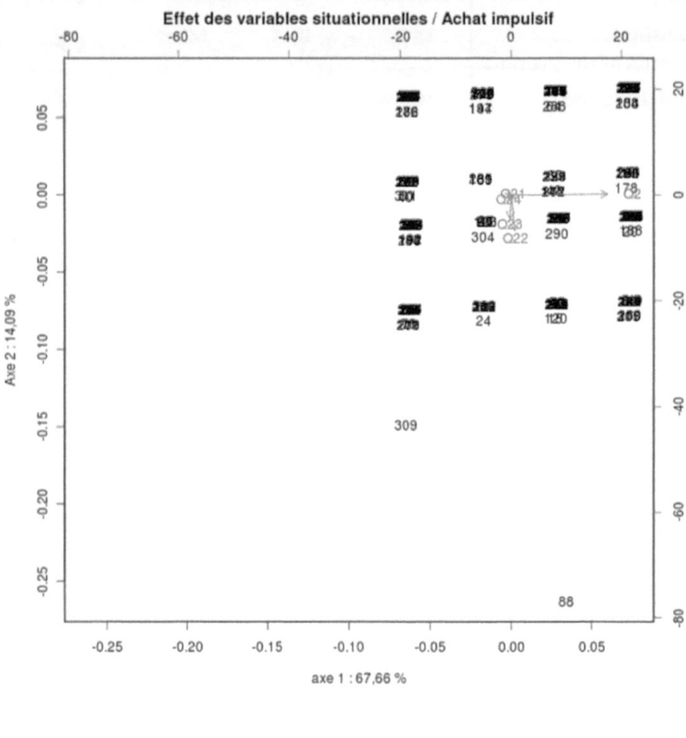

6.3.2 *Assessing the impact of the product-related factor on achieving impulsive purchase*

The principal component analysis enables us to draw out some main findings about the following variables:

1. Design and aesthetic characteristics of the product are more important than the objective features in an impulse purchase.
2. Buying environment /ambience /atmosphere.
3. Familiarity with the store.
4. Promotion/bargain.

Having a strong impact on impulse buying completion, these variables which elicit impulse buying correspond to the most intense attractive emotions that a consumer may experience at the point of sale. These controllable factors play a strategic role in the development of impulse purchases at the point of sale. As for the other factors, which are far from the mapping centre, it may be noted that they are not very important in the eyes of our consumers. If we consider the example of the factor '*influence on sellers*,' most interviewed respondents do not like the seller's involvement at the moment of their purchases. It can be concluded that the aesthetic aspect of the product as well as all related variables have a very positive influence on the behaviour of buyers. To know what the effects of the product on achieving impulse buying are, a number of acronyms were used to make them visible on the perceptual map.

Table 6: Acronyms related to situational variables and products

Acronym used	***Signification***
CEAP	Emotional/affective characteristics of the product
Cph	Physical/objective features of the product
Design	Design and aesthetic characteristics of the product
Facil	Ease of purchase and payment
Envie	Will for immediate pleasure
ENVA	Buying environment/ambience/atmosphere
Infv	Influence of sellers
Famil	Familiarity with the store
Prom	Promotion/bargain
Renv	Frequent renewal of the offer
Reco	Use of smells, colours, lights
Occa	Special event (celebration, sales …)

Figure 4: Graphical representation of PCA relative to the product and to the factors that motivate/restrain impulse buying

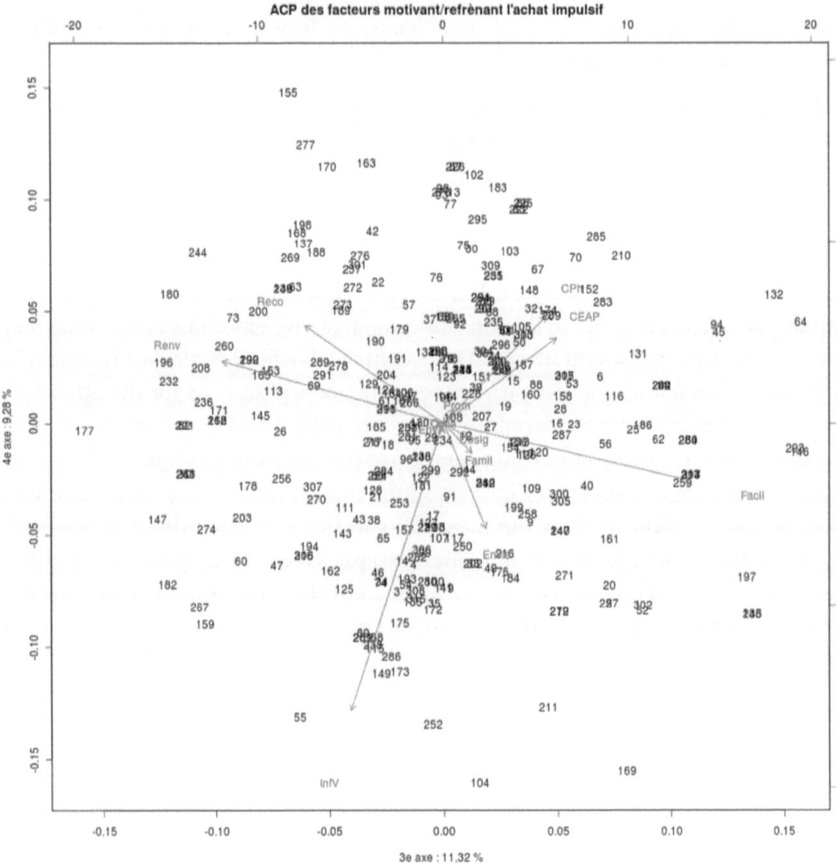

7. Conclusion

Now that the main results of our research are identified, it is possible to confirm that the atmospheric factors (such as decor, atmosphere, music, and lighting) do influence the Algerian consumers and urge them to make impulse purchases. In this context, managers should pay more attention to this aspect, for instance integrating all five senses (sight, hearing, smell, taste, and touch) to differentiate products of various competitors and create a sense of value in the consumer's mind. However, certain products, more than others, encourage impulse buying. In our study, 65.25% of impulsively-purchased products are mainly clothing and cosmetics. Impulse buying of Algerian consumers depends essentially on the product, on its class, symbolic meaning and price. Indeed, it would be interesting to focus on the symbolic meaning of a product in order to create a memorable experience.

Finally, among other characteristics of the product, the variable of *low price* can describe an impulse purchase. Results of the present research show that the lower the price, the more the consumer will buy impulsively. This can be explained by the fact that a small price creates an impulse in the consumer who feels attracted by the idea of a financial advantage, and thus can realise some savings on products. From a practical standpoint, this study allows marketers at points of sale to provide entertainment and pleasure to the consumer. Actually, even if the purpose of shopping is not to buy but look for good bargains, followers engaged in these practices still end up buying.

References

D'Antoni J.S. & Shenson H.L, (1973), Impulse Buying Revisited: A Behavioral Typology, Journal of Retailing, 49,1, p. 63–73.

Belk R.W. (1975), Situational Variables and Consumer Behavior, Journal of Consumer Research, 2, p. 157–164.

Dubois, B, (1996), « Marketing situationnel pour consommateurs caméléons », Revue Française de Gestion, n° 110, septembre–octobre, p. 83–89.

Donvan R.J, Rossiter J.R, (1982), Store atmosphere: an environmental psychology approach, Journal of Retailing, 58, p. 34–57.

Giraud M. (2002), « Les achats impulsifs en hypermarché : segmentation des acheteurs », XVIII ème Congrès International de l'Association Française de Marketing-Lille, 101–128.

Greenland S.J., Mc Goldrick P.J, (1994)," Atmospherics, Attitude and Behavior: Modeling the Impact of Designed Space", the International Review of Retail, Distribution and Consumer Research, Vol. 1, (1994) p. 1–16.

Holbrook M.B., (1999). Consumer value: a framework for analysis and research. London: Routledge.

Holbrook M.B. & Hirschman E.C. (1982).The Experiential Aspects of Consumption: Consumer Fantasies Feelings and Fun, Journal of Consumer Research, 9, 2, 132–140.

Kotler P. (1974), Atmospherics as a marketing tool, Journal of Retailing, 48. 64.

Ladwein R. (2003) ; « Le comportement du consommateur et de l'acheteur », 2ème édition. Paris. Economica.

Mehrabian A. & Russel J. (1974). An approach to environmental psychology Cambridge.

Petrof J.V. (1999). Comportement du consommateur et marketing 5e edition, Les presses de l'université Laval, Sainte-Foy.

Piron F. (1991), « Defining Impulse Purchasing », Advances in Consumer Research, 18, 509–514.

Rieunier S. (2002), Le marketing sensoriel du point de vente, Edition Dunod, Paris.

Rook D.W. (1987), "The buying impulse", Journal of Consumer Research, vol. 14, September, pp. 189–199.

Sherman, E., Mathur, A. And Smith, R.B. (1997), Store environment and consumer purchase behaviour : Mediating role of consumer emotions. Psychology and Marketing. Vol. 14 N°4, pp. 361–79.

Stern H. (1962), "The significance of impulsive buying today", Journal of Marketing, 26, 253–295.

Thang, D.C.L. & Tan, B.L. (2003), Linking Consumer Perception to Preference of Retail Stores: An Empirical Assessment of the Multi-Attributes of Store Image. Journal of Retailing and Consumer Services 10(4), 193–200.

Westbrook, R.A. & Black, W.C. (1985). A Motivation Based Shopper Typoligy. Journal of Retailing 61(Spring), 78–103.

Ayşegül Uçkun*

The Impact of the Shale Gas Revolution to the Russia-EU Energy Dialogue is the Balance of Power Changing?

Shale gas is one of the non-conventional energy resources and it is seen as a game changer in international energy markets and energy policies. The shale gas revolution has changed the energy outlook particularly for the United States of America (US) and the rest of the world. In this respect, it is expected to affect Russia's power to a certain extent since it uses natural gas as a lever in international relations. Because of the fact that the main export market of Russian natural gas is the European Union (EU), the EU is really important for Russia in the energy market. On the other hand, one of the main aims of the EU's energy policy is to ensure security of supply. Therefore, the EU wants to reduce the dependency rate on natural gas to Russia. Shale gas is one of the most basic solutions for the EU. However, shale gas production in the EU cannot be developed because the geological structure is not feasible enough for the production, there are environmental concerns, regulation of property rights contains strict rules, etc. Therefore, the EU has to find a different solution and this solution is given to the EU by the US. After the shale gas revolution, while the power of the US in gas market begins to increase, the market share of the Russia with the EU takes a turn for the worse. This study addresses the question of how the shale gas revolution changes the balance among energy markets and which conditions that affect Russia-EU energy dialogue.

Keywords: Shale Gas Revolution, Russia, European Union, Energy Balances

Introduction

Energy, which is a basic unit of our civilisation, is a determining factor in the improvement of people's welfare and country's economy for balanced growth. In this context, the importance of energy is increasing because of the fact that it is a basic stimulus of all economic activities and is a source of economic and social development. Regarding the use of energy resources in history, it is observed that there is an age of different energy sources at different times. The first resource used as an energy resource was wood and at that time, the leading force was the United Kingdom (UK). In other words, the UK played the role of global hegemon (most powerful actor). Later, coal which is nicknamed "King" emerged with the

* Department of Energy Management, University of KTO Karatay, Konya, Turkey. Mail: aysegul.uckun@karatay.edu.tr

Industrial Revolution and took the place of wood as a new energy resource. With industrialisation, steam machines had been used. The UK continued its role as the leading force because the UK provided coal from its colonies. At the end of 1880s, with the discovery of oil which is nicknamed "Black Gold," the balance of power changed and the United States of America (US) has become the leading force.

Today, it is estimated that shale gas will become the leading source of energy and the US will become the leading force. As the reason for this, it is stated that the shale gas revolution has occurred in the US and the US, the largest natural gas producer as of 2014, affects not only the US market but also the markets all over the world. In this context, this study has analysed the impact of the shale gas revolution to the Russia-European Union (EU) energy dialogue. Besides, this study has addressed the question of how shale gas revolution change the balance among energy markets and which conditions that affect Russia-EU energy dialogue.

Unconventional Energy Resources: Shale Gas

Shale gas is natural gas that is found within fine-grained sedimentary rocks. The origin of shale gas is the same as all hydrocarbons such as coal, gas, and oil (Ratner & Tiemann, 2015). In other words, chemically there is no difference between shale gas and natural gas that is produced by conventional methods. Shale gas is generally in the depth on the surface and in the compact and low permeability rocks. In this respect, shale gas is among the unconventional energy resources.

Figure 1: Unconventional Resources

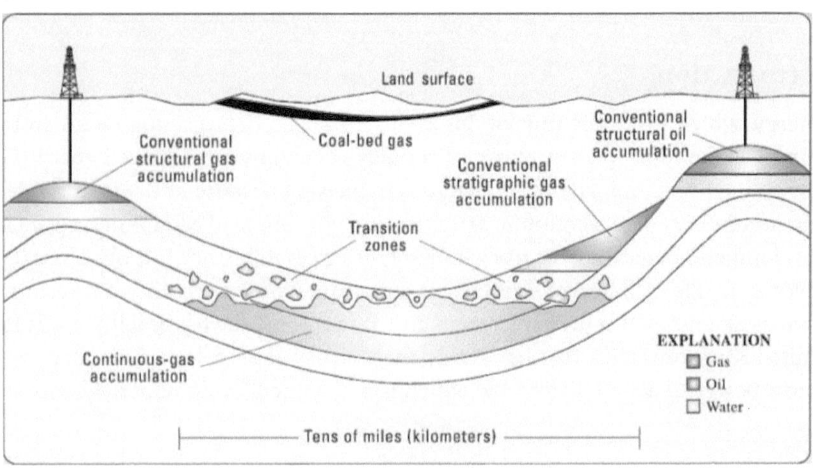

Source: Modified from US Geological Survey Fact Sheet 0113-01.

Shale gas is a natural gas that is found trapped within shale formations, i.e. shale gas is natural gas. The only difference from conventional natural gas is its location and extraction methods. Shale gas is in deeper than conventional natural gas. While conventional natural gas is extracted by the method of vertical drilling, shale gas has to be extracted by a new method because it is trapped in deep shale formations. Horizontal drilling and hydraulic fracturing techniques have been developed for this purpose.

Figure 2: Horizontal Drilling and Hydraulic Fracturing

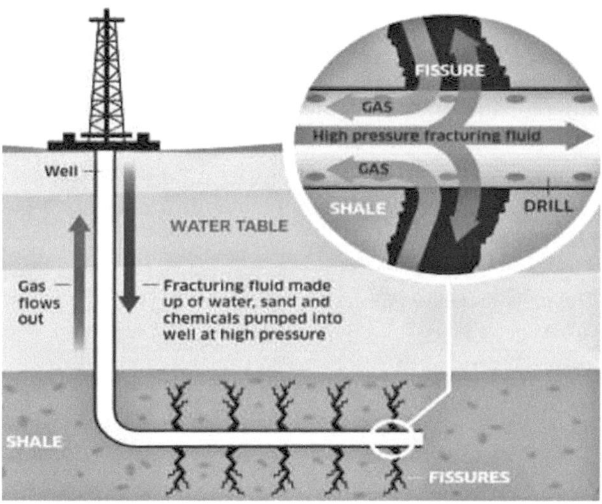

Source: http://www.lwvnyc.org/images/hydrofracking-how%20it%20works.jpg.

Horizontal drilling and hydraulic fracturing techniques were tried for the first time in 1998 in Texas (Howarth, Ingraffea & Engelder, 2011). The development of this technology in the US has been realised as a result of a 60-year study and conducting fracture simulations in more than 200000 wells (Tollefson, 2013). Economically, the first extraction of shale gas was realised in Barnett shale formation in the US in 2003 (Rivard et al., 2014).

Shale Gas Revolution

Shale gas is revolutionary. While economically recoverable reserves of natural gas has accepted approximately 60 years before shale gas reserves, economically recoverable reserves of natural gas has increased up to 250 years by the presence of shale gas reserves (Sevim, 2014). At present, countries such as the US, Canada, Australia, and China are producing shale gas in different amounts. The largest reserves are estimated in China, the largest production is done in the US. While Russia was the largest natural gas producer in 2008, the largest natural gas producer in 2014 is the US (BP, 2015). Approximately 47% of the US natural gas production comes from shale gas. The US was the importing country of natural gas before shale gas, however, with the production of shale gas, it is expected that the US will become an exporting country of natural gas. Therefore, shale gas is regarded as a game changer in the international energy markets.

Impacts of Shale Gas on the International Energy Markets

Shale gas is among unconventional energy resources and it is seen as a game changer in terms of international energy markets and energy policies. It is expected that the balance of power will change with putting shale gas on the market. Shale gas production in the world shows a large increase especially in North America (the US, Canada).

Figure 3: The Countries that have Potential for Shale Gas

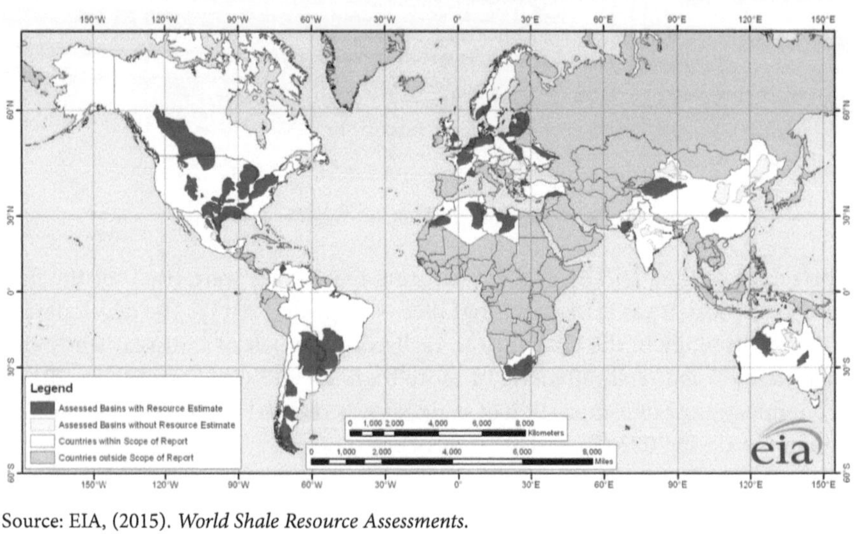

Source: EIA, (2015). *World Shale Resource Assessments.*

As shown in Figure 3, shale gas reserves are located in many parts of the world. Nevertheless, the centre of the shale gas revolution is the US. A large number of wells have to be drilled in order to achieve success in shale gas production. By the end of 2010, a total of 15467 wells have been drilled in the world and only five of the ten thousand of these total wells have been drilled outside of the North America. This case shows that the technology of shale gas production is a new technology for the countries outside of the North America (Çalışkan, 2014).

Table 1: Reserves of Shale Gas (Tcm)

COUNTRY	SHALE GAS
CHINA	33.5
ARGENTINA	24.1
ALGERIA	21.2
USA	19.9
CANADA	17.2
MEXICO	16.3
AUSTRALIA	13.1
SOUTH AFRICA	11.7
RUSSIA	8.5
LIBYA	8.2
BRASIL	7.3
TURKEY	1.8
WORLD TOTAL	218.9

Source: EIA, (2013). *International Energy Statistics-June 13.*

Increasing of conventional gas production in the US, then beginning of a slight start in China and in the EU, will create strategic challenges for existing gas exporters. Russia ranks 9th in the world reserves of shale gas. The first three countries are China, Argentina, and Algeria in terms of reserves of shale gas (Kropatcheva, 2014).

Chart 1: Shale Gas Production

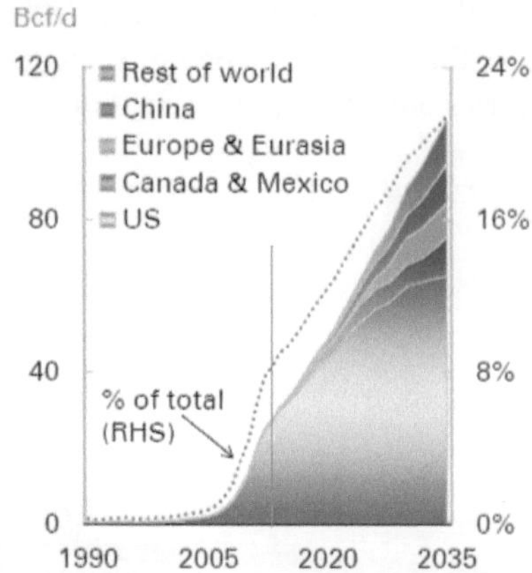

Source: BP Energy Outlook 2035, (2014).

It is estimated that total gas production of the US that was 610 billion m^3 in 2010 will rise to 820 billion m^3 in 2035. Also, it is expected that the share of shale gas in total gas production that was 23% in 2010 will rise to 45% in 2035 (IEA, 2012).

North America has a command of shale gas production due to holding about 99% of shale gas production until 2016. It is expected that North America will hold 70% of shale gas production in 2035. China is also among prominent countries with respect to supply of shale gas because of holding 13% of the total reserves of shale gas. It is estimated that China and North America will hold about 81% of the supply of shale gas in 2035 (BP, 2014).

Increasing of shale gas production has led to positive developments in the US economy. In the early 2000s, 200000 new jobs were created in the US with the start of the economically extraction of shale gas for the first time in the US (Jenner & Lamadrid, 2013). The US has experienced a decline in natural gas prices primarily because of the abundance of the shale gas supply. In this regard, improvements have occurred with a decline in natural gas prices for the petrochemical industries that use ethane as an input contained in natural gas. Petrochemical industries in Europe have turned towards the US and it has led to an increase in capacity of 30–40% in the US petrochemical industry between the years of 2012 and 2014 (Spencer, Sartor & Mathieu, 2014). Global-scale affect is that dependency of the US on natural gas to the Middle East has decreased with the increase of shale gas production. Another affect is the reduction of coal consumption in the US. With the reduction of coal consumption, the US has begun to export coal and annual export has increased by approximately $50 million (Bazilian et al., 2014). In light of all this information, the shale gas revolution has serious contribution to the US economy and it has broken the power of Russia in the international energy market.

Impacts of Shale Gas on the Russia-EU Energy Dialogue

The US is expected to become a net exporter of natural gas in 2018 rather than net importer due to shale gas production. In 2016, it is estimated that the US will become a net exporter of LNG (liquefied natural gas). Changeover of the US from importer to exporter is one of the factors that plays a role in changing the world's energy balance. Therefore, the shale gas revolution can be an obstacle for Russia's policies and power. Russia is one of the world's largest energy suppliers, transporters, and consumers so Russia is both an important actor and an energy factor because its choices and policies affect other countries. Also, "Russia is a threatening actor using energy as a weapon." According to a realist perspective by explaining the use of energy as a foreign policy tool, changes in the international system will affect the power of the country. The shale gas revolution is a factor that has significant changes in global power relations. This situation will affect the power of Russia in energy market and energy policies of Russia (Kropatcheva, 2014). Besides, the recovery of LNG market, that is widely used in global scale and does not require a pipeline, poses a serious threat to the Gazprom (a state company of Russia) and therefore Russia's interests in Europe (Sevim, 2014).

Russia is very active particularly in the natural gas market. Due to the EU's dependence on Russia's natural gas, Russia has power over the EU. Russia is the largest exporter country of the EU accounting for 30% of EU's overall gas imports (Gazprom, 2014). However, the shale gas revolution in the US as an external global factor has begun to penetrate into the relation between Russia and the EU.

The EU keeps shale gas on its agenda to reduce the dependence on Russia but the EU's energy sector falls behind in production of shale gas in comparison with the US. There are a number of reasons for this situation: stronger environmental concerns about shale gas production in Europe than in the US, less favourable geological structure in the EU than the US for the production of shale gas, stricter property rights regulations in the EU and more intensively populated land, and so on (Kropatcheva, 2014). When looking at Europe on the basis of shale gas reserves, the countries considered to have the largest shale gas reserves are Norway, Ukraine, Sweden, Denmark, England, Poland, and France. Nevertheless, still it cannot be make large-scale production of unconventional gas in Europe. In the current situation, the EU is the world's second largest regional gas market. Accordingly, the EU has well-structured pipelines and storage network though not as developed as in the US. In addition, when compared to North America, natural gas prices are very high in EU. For this reason, the EU is feeling insecure about its energy dependence on Russia.

Graph 1: Gazprom's Share in the European Gas Market (%)

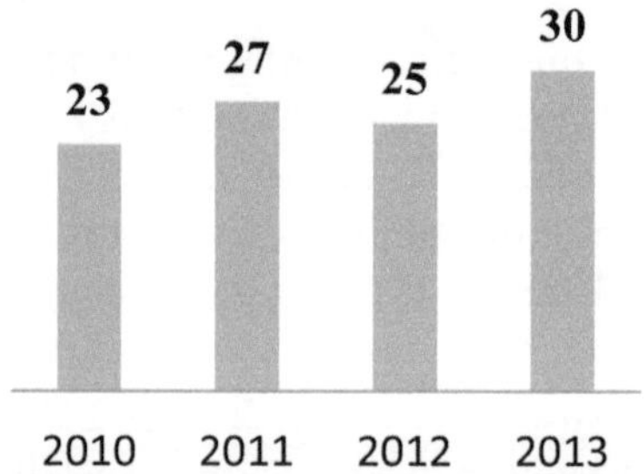

Source: Gazprom, (2013). *Annual Report.*

This graph shows what percentage of Europe's natural gas comes from Gazprom. According to the graph, Gazprom's share in the European gas market changed from 2010 to 2013. In 2013, Gazprom's share in the European gas market was 30%. It means that there was interdependence between the EU and Russia on energy trade.

The shale gas revolution has begun to affect the relationship between the EU and Russia significantly. The pressure of Gazprom on the EU has begun to decrease because the EU's demand for Russian gas has begun to decrease. There are several reasons for this situation. The first reason is the global financial and economic crisis experienced in 2008. Another reason is that with the reduction of US's demand for imported LNG (with increment of shale gas production); LNG exported by North Africa, Qatar and other countries in the Persian Gulf has become available to the EU. This gas is US $100 per 1000 m^3 in these countries while the price of natural gas in Russia is US $304.2 per 1000 m^3 in 2013 (Gazprom, 2015). For this reason, price in these countries is cheaper than Russia for the EU. The other reason is that the consumption of natural gas has begun to increase in the US with the beginning of the production of shale gas and therefore, the consumption of coal is reduced. More coal production has begun to be exported to the EU. In 2012, US coal exports to the EU increased by 49% (Kropatcheva, 2014).

All these events have begun to pose an obstacle of power for Russia in the international energy market. First, the energy market of Russia has faced more competition. In 2010, the US increased the production of shale gas and therefore consumption of gas also has increased. "Just at this time, Qatar has put into operation new export capacity for the supply of LNG to the US market." Consequently, redundant Qatari gas to the US went to Europe, thus spot prices reduced and then "counterparties of the Russian company 'Gazprom' began to demand the revision of prices and long-term contracts." In addition, with the increase of gas production in the US, consumption of coal has started to decrease. The oversupply of coal has directed to the EU, bringing down the price of Russian gas. The EU has maintained the production of coal which is less efficient but cheaper. Therefore, Gazprom has to compete with coal suppliers (Grinkevich, 2016). Secondly, the growing of trade of LNG because of the shale gas revolution in the US and the development of the technology that will convert shale gas to LNG has begun to undermine the power of Russia in the energy market. Because the LNG trade reduces gas imports carried by pipelines and it is expected that the demand for Russian gas will decrease since Russia has conducted export of gas mostly by pipelines. Therefore, the growth of LNG trade is seen as a serious challenge for Russia. An oversupply of LNG will create a downward pressure on gas prices across the globe. As a result, it is estimated that decreasing gas prices in the EU will lead to serious financial difficulties for Russia (Kropatcheva, 2014).

Discussion

The emergence of shale gas has had a significant impact on international energy markets; therefore shale gas is revolutionary. Accordingly, the fundamental question is whether the balance of power between Russia and the EU will change or not.

The EU wants to ensure their security of supply because the EU's dependency rate is almost 53%. In order to ensure security of supply, it is required to move towards diversification, by country of origin, and/or by energy sources (Uçkun, 2015). The EU imports gas primarily by pipeline supplies from Russia (largest gas exporting country to the EU), Norway, and Algeria. Therefore, the EU tries to diversify its energy sources and also the EU wants to reduce the dependency rate to Russia. For this reason, the EU had pinned high hopes on shale gas production, especially in Poland. Nevertheless, shale gas production in the EU cannot be developed because the geological structure is not feasible enough for the production, there are environmental concerns, regulation of property rights contains strict rules, etc. However, there is a strong relationship between Russia and the EU in terms of energy. Although the power of Russia in the international energy market has begun to decrease with the shale gas revolution, the EU remains the key market for Russian export gas supplies.

Europe is one of Gazprom's three core gas markets but its gas demand dropped in 2014. While gas demand of the EU was 540.3 bcm (billion cubic metres) of gas in 2013, this demand decreased to 486.0 bcm in 2014. In other words, European countries consumed 54.3 bcm less than in 2013 (decrease of 10.1%). One of the causes of the reduction in demand is the displacement of natural gas with coal in power generation. However, although with decreasing export supplies in 2014, Gazprom has maintained its share of the European gas market. Besides, in the long-term, "potential build-up of Russian gas supplies to the European market includes slowdown in the nuclear sector, wider use of natural gas in the transport sector, and the emergence of new consumer segments (i.e. bunker fuel sector)" (Gazprom, 2014). Therefore, Gazprom will sustain being the largest supplier of gas to the EU with the share of almost 30% in the long-term.

Conclusion

Shale gas is seen as a game changer in terms of international energy markets and energy policies. It is observed that the emergence of shale gas does not affect the balance of power between Russia and the EU, especially in terms of percentage of gas trade and despite decreasing export supplies in 2014. Gazprom has maintained its share of the European gas market. On the other hand, the US should also be taken into consideration in the balance of power between Russia and the EU to understand the impact of shale gas. Because the shale gas revolution in the US as an external global factor has begun to penetrate into the relationship between Russia and the EU. One of the reasons shale gas is a game changer is the changeover of the US from importer to exporter. While Russia was the largest natural gas producer in 2008, the largest natural gas producer in 2014 is the US. Additionally, while a positive contribution of shale gas to the US economy, the emergence of shale gas affects the Russian economy negatively. While the EU decreases the demand of natural gas imported by Russia, it increases the demand of coal imported by the US. The EU consumed 54.3 bcm of gas less than in 2013 because one of the reasons of the reduction in demand is the displacement of natural gas with coal in power generation. The EU prefers to consume coal because coal imported from the US is cheaper than natural gas imported from Russia, and also the EU wants to reduce the energy dependence on Russia to ensure for a security of supply. The EU remains dependent on Russia, but Russia's power over the EU is shrinking. The important point is that the shale gas revolution has become important challenge for Russian power, so that "Russia is not aiming at power maximization, but at sustaining its current position and preventing more losses of the global influence and revenues needed for an assertive foreign policy" (Kropatcheva, 2014).

References

Bazilian, M. et al. (2014). Ensuring Benefits from North American Shale Gas Development: Towards a Research Agenda. *Journal of Unconventional Oil and Gas Resources*. 7, 71–74.

BP, (2014). *Energy Outlook 2035*.

BP, (2015). *Statistical Review of World Energy*.

Çalışkan, M. (2014). Enerji İhtiyacının Karşılanmasında Yeni Yöntem Olarak Kaya Gazının İncelenmesi. *Wise Man Center for Strategic Studies*. 221–231.

EIA, (2010). *What is shale gas and why is it important?* Retrieved December 31, 2015, from http://dnr.louisiana.gov/assets/TAD/reports/about_shale_gas.pdf.

Gazprom, (2014). *Gazprom Annual Report 2014*.

Gazprom, (2015). *About Gazprom/Marketing: Europe*. Retrieved December 9, 2015, from http://www.gazprom.com/about/marketing/europe/.

Grinkevich, V. (2016). *Shale Revolution is Already Irreversible*. Open Economy. Retrieved January 12, 2016, from http://opec.ru/1791125.html.

Howarth, R.W., Ingraffea, A. & Engelder, T. (2011). Natural Gas: Should Fracking stop? *Nature*. 477, 271–275.

International Energy Agency, (2012). *World Energy Outlook: Golden Rules for a Golden Age of Gas*.

Jenner, S. & Lamadrid, A.J. (2013). Shale Gas vs. Coal: Policy Implications from Environmental Impact Comparisons of Shale Gas, Conventional Gas and Coal on Air, Water and Land in the United States. *Energy Policy*. 53, 442–453.

Kropatcheva, E. (2014). He Who Has the Pipeline Calls the Tune? Russia's Energy Power against the Background of the Shale Revolutions. *Energy Policy*. 66, 1–10.

Ratner, M., & Tieman, M. (2015). An Overview of Unconventional Oil and Natural Gas: Resources and Federal Actions. *Congressional Research Service*.

Rivard, C. et al. (2014). An Overview of Canadian Shale Gas Production and Environmental Concerns. *International Journal of Coal Geology*. 126(1), 64–76.

Sevim, C. (2014). Kaya (Şeyl) Gazının Uluslararası Enerji Politikalarına Etkileri. *Ege Stratejik Araştırmalar Dergisi*. 5(1), 49–64.

Spencer, T., Sartor, O., & Mathieu, M. (2014). Unconventional Wisdom: An Economic Analysis of US Shale Gas and Implications for the EU. *Institut du développement durable et des relations internationales (IDDRI)*. No. 02/14.

Tollefson, J. (2013). China Slow to Tap Shale-Gas Bonanza. *Nature*. 494, 294.

Uçkun, A. (2015). Arz Güvenliği ve İklim Değişikliği Açısından Nükleer Enerji Bir Zorunluluk Mudur? *Energy & Diplomacy*. 1(4), 46–72.

Ass. Prof. Arzu Organ*

The Energy Source Selection by Fuzzy Moora and Fuzzy AHP Method in a Textile Firm

1. Introduction

The energy source selection has become increasingly more important. It is blatant that this topic will increase its importance in the next years. In this paper, the best energy source selection has been carried out by fuzzy AHP and fuzzy MOORA. In the phase of determining criteria, fuzzy AHP was used, while determining gradation of alternatives, fuzzy MOORA was used.

Keywords: Multi-criteria decision making, Fuzzy AHP, Fuzzy MOORA, Energy

1.1 Fuzzy Sets and Fuzzy Numbers

The fuzzy set concept was firstly introduced by Zadeh in 1965. To him the fuzzy set is a cluster of goals ranging between 0 and 1. (Zadeh, 1965: 338).

1.2 Fuzzy AHP

The analytic hierarchy process (AHP) method, introduced by Saaty, aims to simplify the solution of the multi-attribute, multi-person, and multi-period structural problems.

The AHP is a popular method for solving multi criteria analysis (MA) problems involving qualitative data. However, this method is often criticised due to its use of an unbalanced scale of judgements and its inability to adequately handle the inherent uncertainty and imprecision of the pairwise comparison process. This paper presents a fuzzy approach for tackling qualitative MA problems in a simple and straightforward manner. As a result, effective decisions can be made based on adequate modeling of the uncertainty and imprecision in human behaviour (Deng, 1999: 215).

The fuzzy AHP method is used to determine criteria weights in the study, and is carried out as follows:

Step 1: Construct pairwise comparison matrices among all the elements/criteria in the dimensions of the hierarchy system.

* Research Assistant Engin Yalçın

$$\begin{bmatrix} 1 & \tilde{a}_{12} & \dots & \tilde{a}_{1n} \\ \tilde{a} & 1 & \dots & \tilde{a}_{2n} \\ . & . & & . \\ . & . & & . \\ . & . & & . \\ \tilde{a}_{n1} & \tilde{a}_{n2} & \dots & 1 \end{bmatrix} = \begin{bmatrix} 1 & \tilde{a}_{12} & \dots & \tilde{a}_{1n} \\ 1/\tilde{a}_{12} & 1 & \dots & \tilde{a}_{2n} \\ . & . & & . \\ . & . & & . \\ . & . & & . \\ 1/\tilde{a}_{1n} & 1/\tilde{a}_{2n} & \dots & 1 \end{bmatrix} \quad (1)$$

$$\tilde{a}_{ij} = \begin{cases} \tilde{1},\tilde{3},\tilde{5},\tilde{7},\tilde{9} \; i \; kriteri \; j \; kriterine \; göre \; daha \; önemlidir. \\ 1, i = j \\ \tilde{1}^{-1},\tilde{3}^{-1},\tilde{5}^{-1},\tilde{7}^{-1},\tilde{9}^{-1} \; i \; kriteri \; j \; kriterine \; göre \text{ daha az önemlidir.} \end{cases} \quad (2)$$

Decision makers used the fuzzy five level scale to evaluate criteria.

Table 1: The Linguistic Assessment Variables and its Corresponding Scale in Terms of Triangular Fuzzy Numbers

Linguistic Variable	Triangular Fuzzy Scale	Triangular Fuzzy Reciprocal Scale
Equal	(1,1,1)	(1/1, 1/1, 1/1)
Moderate	(2,3,4)	(1/4, 1/3, 1/2)
Strong	(4,5,6)	(1/6, 1/5, 1/4)
Very Strong	(6,7,8)	(1/8, 1/7, 1/6)
Extremely Preferred	(8,9,9)	(1/9, 1/9, 1/8)

Step 2: To use the geometric mean technique to define the fuzzy geometric mean and fuzzy weights of each criterion by Buckley as follows:

$$\tilde{r}_i = (\tilde{a}_{i1} \otimes \dots \otimes \tilde{a}_{ij} \otimes \dots .\tilde{a}_{in})^{\frac{1}{n}} \quad (3)$$

$$\tilde{w}_i = \tilde{r}_i \otimes [\tilde{r}_1 \oplus \dots .\tilde{r}_i \oplus \dots \oplus \tilde{r}_n]^{-1} \quad (4)$$

Step 3: The result of the fuzzy synthetic decision reached by each alternative is a fuzzy number. The procedure of defuzzification is to find the Best Nonfuzzy Performance value (BNP). To utilise the Center of Area (COA) method to find BNP is a simple and practical method.

$$\text{BNP}_{\text{wi}} = \frac{(U_{wi} - L_{wi}) \oplus (M_{wi} - L_{wi})}{3} \oplus L_i; \; \text{i} = 1,2,\dots\dots,\text{n} \quad (5)$$

Lwi, *Mwi*, and *Uwi* values are triangular fuzzy numbers and respectively represent the lower, middle, and upper values in the equation (Kiris, Ustun: 2010, 332).

1.3 Fuzzy MOORA

MOORA is a multiobjective optimisation by ratio analysis technique firstly used by Brauers and Zavadskas (2006).

Table 2 shows that comparative performance of some MCDM techniques with regard to computational time, simplicity, mathematical calculations, stability, and information type (Brauers ve Zavadskas, 2012).

Table 2: Comparative Performance of MCDM Techniques

MCDM Techniques	Computational Time	Simplicity	Mathematical Calculation	Stability	Information Type
MOORA	Very Less	Very Simple	Min.	Good	Quantitative
AHP	Very High	Very Critical	Max.	Poor	Mixed
TOPSIS	Moderate	Moderately Critical	Moderate	Medium	Quantitative
VIKOR	Less	Simple	Moderate	Medium	Quantitative
ELECTRE	High	Moderately Critical	Moderate	Medium	Mixed
PROMETHEE	High	Moderately Critical	Moderate	Medium	Mixed

Fuzzy MOORA, used in the evaluation and ranking of the alternatives, was carried out in the following stages.

Step 1: Based on the expert opinions of the decision makers, develop the fuzzy decision matrix in which each criterion value is measured by using triangular membership function (Vatansever ve Uluköy, 2013: 283).

$$\begin{bmatrix} \left[x_{11}^{\,l}, x_{11}^{\,m}, x_{11}^{\,n}\right] & \left[x_{12}^{\,l}, x_{12}^{\,m}, x_{12}^{\,n}\right]\ldots & \left[x_{1n}^{\,l}, x_{1n}^{\,m}, x_{1n}^{\,n}\right] \\ \left[x_{21}^{\,l}, x_{21}^{\,m}, x_{21}^{\,n}\right] & \left[x_{22}^{\,l}, x_{22}^{\,m}, x_{22}^{\,n}\right]\ldots & \left[x_{2n}^{\,l}, x_{2n}^{\,m}, x_{2n}^{\,n}\right] \\ \cdots\cdots\cdots & \cdots\cdots\cdots & \cdots\cdots\cdots \\ \left[x_{m1}^{\,l}, x_{m1}^{\,m}, x_{m1}^{\,n}\right] & \left[x_{m2}^{\,l}, x_{m2}^{\,m}, x_{m2}^{\,n}\right] & \left[x_{m2}^{\,l}, x_{m2}^{\,m}, x_{m2}^{\,n}\right] \end{bmatrix} \tag{6}$$

Table 3: Linguistic Variables Used in Evaluating the Alternatives

Linguistic Variables	**Triangular Fuzzy Numbers**
Very Weak	(0, 0, 1)
Weak	(0, 1, 3)
Moderate Weak	(1, 3, 5)
Moderate	(3, 5, 7)
Moderate Good	(5, 7, 9)
Good	(7, 9, 10)
Very Good	(9, 10, 10)

Step 2: Normalise the fuzzy decision matrix using vector normalisation procedure.

$$\mathrm{r}_{\mathrm{ij}}^{\mathrm{l}} = \frac{\overset{l}{x}_{ij}}{\sqrt{[\sum_{i=1}^{m}[(\overset{l}{x}_{ij})^2 + (\overset{m}{x}_{ij})^2 + (\overset{n}{x}_{ij})^2]}} \tag{7}$$

$$\mathrm{r}_{\mathrm{ij}}^{\mathrm{m}} = \frac{\overset{m}{x}_{ij}}{\sqrt{\sum_{i=1}^{m}((\overset{l}{x}_{ij})^2 + (\overset{m}{x}_{ij}) + (\overset{n}{x}_{ij})]}} \tag{8}$$

$$\mathrm{r}_{\mathrm{ij}}^{\mathrm{n}} = \frac{\overset{n}{x}_{ij}}{\sqrt{\sum_{i=1}^{m}(\overset{l}{x}_{ij})^2 + (\overset{m}{x}_{ij})^2 + (\overset{n}{x}_{ij})^2}} \tag{9}$$

Step 3: Determine the weighted normalised fuzzy decision matrix employing the following equations;

$$\overset{l}{v}_{ij} = \mathrm{w}_{\mathrm{j}} \cdot \overset{l}{r}_{ij} \tag{10}$$

$$\overset{m}{v}_{ij} = \mathrm{w}_{\mathrm{j}} \cdot \overset{m}{r}_{ij} \tag{11}$$

$$\overset{n}{v}_{ij} = \mathrm{w}_{\mathrm{j}} \cdot \overset{n}{r}_{ij} \tag{12}$$

Step 4: Calculate the overall ratings of beneficial and non-beneficial criteria, the overall ratings of an alternative for lower, middle and upper values of the triangular membership function are computed as follows for benefit criteria,

$$s_i^{+l} = \sum_{j=1}^{n} v_{ij}^{\ l} \mid j \in J^{\max} \tag{13}$$

$$s_i^{+m} = \sum_{j=1}^{n} v_{ij}^{\ m} \mid j \in J^{\max} \tag{14}$$

$$s_i^{+n} = \sum_{j=1}^{n} v_{ij}^{\ n} \mid j \in J^{\max} \tag{15}$$

For non-benefit criteria;

$$s_i^{-l} = \sum_{j=1}^{n} v_{ij}^{\ l} \mid j \in J^{\max} \tag{16}$$

$$s_i^{-m} = \sum_{j=1}^{n} v_{ij}^{\ m} \mid j \in J^{\max} \tag{17}$$

$$s_i^{-n} = \sum_{j=1}^{n} v_{ij}^{\ n} \mid j \in J^{\max}$$

Step 5: Determine the overall performance index (S_i) for each alternative. For this, the defuzzified values of the overall ratings for beneficial and non-beneficial criteria for each alternative are computed using the vertex method as follows:

$$S_i(s_i^{+}, s_i^{-}) = \sqrt{\frac{1}{3}[(s_i^{+l} - s_i^{-l})^2 + (s_i^{+m} - s_i^{-m})^2 + (s_i^{+n} - s_i^{-n})]} \tag{18}$$

Step 6: Based on the descending values of overall performance index, rank the alternatives from the best to worst. The alternative with the highest overall performance index is the most favourable choice (Karande and Chakraborty, 2012)

2. Application

Our aim is to provide proper energy resource for business. Fuzzy pairwise comparision matrix is as in Table 4.

Table 4: The Fuzzy Pairwise Comparison Matrix of Criteria

	Eco friendly level	Cost	Attainability	Calorific Value	Machinability
Eco friendly level	1,00 1,00 1,00	0,11 0,11 0,125	0,125 0,142 0,166	0,16 0,20 0,25	0,125 0,142 0,166
Cost	8,00 9,00 9,00	1,00 1,00 1,00	1,00 1,00 1,00	1,00 1,00 1,00	0,11 0,11 0,12
Attainability	6,00 7,00 8,00	1,00 1,00 1,00	1,00 1,00 1,00	4,00 5,00 6,00	1,00 1,000 1,000
Calorific Value	4,00 5,00 6,00	1,00 1,00 1,00	0,16 0,20 0,25	1,00 1,00 1,00	0,25 0,33 0,50
Machinability	6,00 7,00 8,00	8,00 9,00 9,00	1,00 1,00 1,00	2,00 3,00 4,00	1,00 1,00 1,00

Fuzzy weights are obtained for each criteria group by using equation 3

$$\tilde{r}_1 = (\tilde{a}_{11} \otimes \tilde{a}_{12} \otimes \tilde{a}_{13} \otimes \tilde{a}_{14} \otimes \tilde{a}_{15})^{\frac{1}{5}}$$

$$\tilde{r}_1 = (1*0{,}11*0{,}125\ldots*0{,}125)^{\frac{1}{5}}, (1*0{,}11*0{,}142\ldots*0{,}142)^{\frac{1}{5}},$$

$$(1*0{,}125*0{,}166\ldots0{,}16)^{\frac{1}{5}}$$

$$\tilde{r}_1 = (0{,}1940,\ 0{,}2135,\ 0{,}2437)$$

$$\tilde{r}_2 = (0{,}976,\ 0{,}997,\ 1{,}023)$$

$$\tilde{r}_3 = (1{,}888,\ 2{,}036,\ 2{,}168)$$

$$\tilde{r}_4 = (0{,}693,\ 0{,}802,\ 0{,}944)$$

$$\tilde{r}_5 = (2{,}491,\ 2{,}852,\ 3{,}103)$$

Criteria weights are calculated by using equation 4,

$$\tilde{W}_1 = \tilde{r}_1 \otimes (\tilde{r}_1 \oplus \tilde{r}_2 \oplus \tilde{r}_3 \oplus \tilde{r}_4 \oplus \tilde{r}_5)^{-1}$$

$$= (0.1940,0.2135,0.2437) \otimes \begin{pmatrix} 1/(0.2437 \oplus 1.023 \oplus \ldots \oplus 3.103 \\ 1/(0.2135 \oplus 0.997 \oplus \ldots \oplus 2.852 \\ 1/(0.1940 \oplus 0.976 \oplus \ldots \oplus 2.491 \end{pmatrix}$$

$$= (0{,}1940,\ 0{,}2135,\ 0{,}2437) \otimes (0{,}133,\ 0{,}144,\ 0{,}160)$$

$$= (0{,}0258,\ 0{,}0307,\ 0{,}0389)$$

$$\tilde{W}_2 = (0{,}1298,\ 0{,}1405,\ 0{,}1636)$$

$\tilde{W}_3 = (0{,}2511,\ 0{,}2931,\ 0{,}3468)$

$\tilde{W}_4 = (0.0921,\ 0{,}1154,\ 0{,}1510)$

$\tilde{W}_5 = (0{,}3313,\ 0{,}4106,\ 0{,}4964)$

Best non-fuzzy performance values are obtained from defuzzifying fuzzy criteria weights with Center of Area (COA) method by using equation 5,

$$\mathrm{BNP}_{\mathrm{w1}} = \frac{(U_{wi} - L_{wi}) \oplus (M_{wi} - L_{wi})}{3} \oplus L_i$$

$$\mathrm{BNP}_{\mathrm{w1}} = \frac{(0{,}0389 - 0{,}0258) \oplus (0{,}0307 - 0{,}0258)}{3} \oplus 0{,}0258$$

$\mathrm{BNP}_{\mathrm{w1}} = 0{,}0318$

$\mathrm{BNP}_{\mathrm{w2}} = 0{,}1446$

$\mathrm{BNP}_{\mathrm{w3}} = 0{,}0710$

$\mathrm{BNP}_{\mathrm{w4}} = 0{,}01195$

$\mathrm{BNP}_{\mathrm{w5}} = 0{,}4127$

Fuzzy decision matrix about energy selection is formed in line with the opinion of decision makers, shown in table 5.

Table 5: Fuzzy Decision Matrix

	Eco friendly level	**Cost**	**Attainability**	**Calorific Value**	**Machinability**
Coal	0,00 0,00 1,00	9,00 10,00 10,00	9,00 10,00 10,00	7,00 9,00 10,00	3,00 5,00 7,00
Natural Gas	5,00 7,00 9,00	7,00 9,00 10,00	7,00 9,00 10,00	3,00 5,00 7,00	7,00 9,00 10,00
Diesel Fuel	0,00 1,00 3,00	0,00 1,00 3,00	7,00 9,00 10,00	7,00 9,00 10,00	7,00 9,00 10,00
Electricity	9,00 10,00 10,00	7,00 9,00 10,00	5,00 7,00 9,00	0,00 1,00 3,00	0,00 1,00 3,00

Normalised fuzzy decision matrix is obtained from the vector normalisation process by usingequations 6,7,8.

Table 6: Normalised Fuzzy Decision Matrix

	Eco friendly level	Cost	Attainability	Calorific Value	Machinability
Coal	0,0000 0,0000 1,0000	0,5369 0,5965 0,5965	0,5369 0,5965 0,5965	0,4616 0,5934 0,6594	0,3293 0,5488 0,7683
Natural Gas	0,4616 0,5934 0,6594	0,4616 0,5934 0,6594	0,4616 0,5934 0,6594	0,3293 0,5488 0,7683	0,4616 0,5934 0,6594
Diesel Fuel	0,0000 0,3162 0,9487	0,0000 0,3162 0,9487	0,4616 0,5934 0,6594	0,4616 0,5934 0,6594	0,4616 0,5934 0,6594
Electricity	0,5369 0,5965 0,5965	0,4616 0,5934 0,6594	0,4016 0,5623 0,7229	0,0000 0,3162 0,9487	0,0000 0,3162 0,9487

Weighted normalised fuzzy decision matrix is obtained by calculating weights obtained from fuzzy AHP, and normalising fuzzy decision matrix components, using equations 9, 10, and 11.

Table 7: Weighted Normalise Fuzzy Decision Matrix

	Eco friendly level	Cost	Attainability	Calorific Value	Machinability
Coal	0,0000 0,0000 0,0318	0,0776 0,0863 0,0863	0,0381 0,0424 0,0424	0,0055 0,0071 0,0079	0,1359 0,2265 0,3171
Natural Gas	0,0147 0,0189 0,0210	0,0667 0,0858 0,0953	0,0328 0,0421 0,0468	0,0039 0,0066 0,0092	0,1905 0,2449 0,2721
Diesel Fuel	0,0000 0,0101 0,0302	0,0000 0,0457 0,1372	0,0328 0,0421 0,0468	0,0055 0,0071 0,0079	0,1905 0,2449 0,2721
Electricity	0,0171 0,0190 0,0190	0,0667 0,0858 0,0953	0,0285 0,0399 0,0513	0,0000 0,0038 0,0113	0,0000 0,1305 0,3915

Each alternative ranks are obtained with regard to benefit and non-benefit criteria using equations 12–17, and finally performance scores are obtained in equation 18.

3. Conclusion

Diesel fuel is the best resource businesses can select.

	S+	S-	S	Ranking
Coal	0,1795 0,2759 0,3991	0,0776 0,0863 0,0863	0,2193	4
Natural Gas	0,2419 0,3125 0,3491	0,0667 0,0858 0,0953	0,2209	3
Diesel Fuel	0,2288 0,3042 0,3570	0,0000 0,0000 0,1446	0,2516	1
Electricity	0,0456 0,1932 0,4732	0,0667 0,0858 0,0953	0,2271	2

4. Reference List

Brauers W.K.M., Zavadskas E.K., (2006). "The MOORA Method and its application to Privatization in a Transition Economy" *Control and Cybernetics* Vol: 35 pp. 445–469.

Brauers, W.K.M. and Zavadskas, E.K. (2012). Robustness of Multimoora: A Method for Multi-Objective Optimization. Informatica, 23, 1, 1–25.

Deng H., (1999). "Multicriteria Analysis with Fuzzy Pairwise Comparision" *International Journal of Approximate Reasoning* Vol: 21 pp. 215–231.

KiriS S., Ustun O., (2010) "Fuzzy MCDM Approach of Stocks Evaluation and Portfolio Selection" International Conference 24th Mini EURO Conference pp. 330–336.

Vatansever, K., Uluköy M., (2013). "Kurumsal Kaynak Planlaması Sistemlerinin Bulanık AHP ve Bulanık MOORA Yöntemleriyle Seçimi: Üretim Sektöründe Bir Uygulama" *CBÜ Sosyal Bilimler Dergisi* Cilt: 11 Sayı: 2 s. 274–293.

Zadeh L.A. "Fuzzy Sets" (1965). *Information and Control* Vol: 8 pp. 335–358.

Gonca Gezer*

Social Movement Unionism in Turkey: Yatağan Resistance Case[1]

1. Introduction

Increasing effects of globalisation and neoliberalism worldwide, from the 1980s to the present has created important consequences on unions as well as on economic, social, and political spheres of life. The positive economic and social conditions before 1980 presented an opportunity for the progress and the strength of the unions; however, after the 1980s new conditions led to the loss of the ability of organisations and powers of unions. The growth period, which projects the state intervention in economic life, welfare state policies, and industrial relations that had supported the economic and social power of unions, lost its influence with the changes after 1980. Thus, a new period that had an impact on the union movement began. Indeed, the effects which were created by globalisation on work conditions such as flexibility in labour process, privatisation, the changing structure of labour force, unemployment, growth of the informal sector and new understandings of management in firms led to a considerable decrease in organised power of labour and social power of unions.

Although the current situation of unions creates a pessimistic scene, some experiences of union movement throughout the world bring hope that unions will be a social power again. Especially unions of the third world with an eclectic understanding which combines social struggle and class struggle became a considerable power which challenges neoliberal policies and they also became a dominant social power that plays a crucial role for all dimensions of social life. This new union understanding that is named the social movement unionism created important consequences on workers movement by including different social groups alongside the workers into the class struggle and also politicising these groups against neoliberalism.

In South Africa, Brazil, Philippines and South Korea, social movement unionism appeared as a different movement that fill their agenda with the problems of

---

* goncagezer@hotmail.com

1 This study is partly produced from the PHD thesis "Social Movement Unionism and Reflections on Turkey."

the poor in their societies, militant, autonomous, and with high class consciousness. In these countries, unions link the working conditions with the condition of the country. Furthermore, beside the wages, worker healthcare and safety in workplaces that are related with the working conditions, unions put democracy, civil rights, gender discrimination and ethnic discrimination on their agendas (Scipes, 1992: 123). This way, unions are not considering workplace problems out of social life and include two sides in an integrated approach.

Unions with their militant understanding, which is not limited to wage and working conditions, see some other topics such as transportation, housing, education and health as main topics of union struggle. Accordingly, they can mobilise different social groups too (Doğruer, 2004). Thanks to this understanding, social movement unionism does not limit itself with only workers and it can communicate with a larger population. In this way, the unionist movement was supported by the whole society. As a result, unions had a more massive impact by uniting unionist struggle and social struggle.

The consequences created by global and neoliberalist policies, especially in the 2000s in Turkey, led to a rise in various worker movements. These movements that resisted neoliberal policies and authoritarian sanctions on workers has special importance since they increased social opposition and social sensitivity as well as union power. Both the ideological perspective against the neoliberal policies and the dynamism that it created among society are different from the former movements and these current movements has been discussed in the context of social movement unionism which began to enter the agenda of the labour movement in many countries. The purpose of this study is to investigate the Yatağan Resistance which came out of the reaction against neoliberal policies, in terms of social movement unionism.

2. The Concept of Social Movement Unionism

The concept of social movement unionism was used first by Peter Waterman in 1984. Then, Eddie Webster used this concept to define the union movement in South Africa (Pillay, 2013: 11). By considering the conceptualisations of Rob Lambert and Webster, the movement was defined as "New Labor Internationalism" (Lambert and Webster, 2011: 337). In recent years, social movement unionism became a popular concept for studies of worker movements in South Africa, Brazil, South Korea, and Philippines. More recently, this concept has been seen as ideal for unions that want to regain its political and economic power by researchers and activists (Noyes, 2009).

While Waterman was defining social movement unionism, he defended to create a new theory which is based on collaboration of new social movements and worker movements (Waterman, 2008: 303). According to Waterman, a new worker movement is needed for an alternative world. He says that worker movements are the basis for collaboration of other social movements and this movement is the power that will change the world. Moreover, the organisation, that is the core for social collaboration and will put worker class into action, is social movement unionism. Unlike Waterman, Webster and Lampert do not emphasise the theory of "social movement." They tend to combine social movement unionism and political unionism and use this concept under some restrictions that refer to unions in authoritarian regimes; such as, South Korea, Philippines, Brazil, and South Africa in the 1980s. They tried to show how workplace struggles and social struggles can unite; in other words, how the economic and social face of unionism can be handled together while independency of unions is being held (Pillay, 2013: 11).

According to Kim Scipes, uniting workplace struggle and political struggle is the point that makes social movement unionism unique. Social movement unionism exceeds the distinction of economic and political struggles, which is accepted by the pragmatic and Leninist unionism (Scipes, 1992: 133). According to Kim Moody, in the first place, the social union movement should have an internationalist identity. Only with this identity, can unions embrace the variety of worker classes. Thus, the power of class can be maximised by them (Moody, 2002: 437). According to Moody, the active participation of members is another feature of social movement unionism. Unions play an active role in the political sphere by mobilising its members and making democracy active by using elections and coalitions, and also mass protests in the streets. In addition, like other authors, Moody states the importance of social coalitions and emphasises that these coalitions should be strong and permanent rather than temporary coalitions.

The reason for not defining social movement unionism in a certain way comes from different socio-economic and cultural structures of different countries as well as different perspectives of authors who are interested in worker movement. However, the fact that authors begin their conceptualisation with the "South Africa" example and properties of union movements are determined by same union examples makes it possible to create a common theoretical frame. The academic studies which are related to social movement unionism and union practices show that social movement unionism progressed parallel to new social movements and also shows that the aim of movements is to be embraced by the whole society. In this sense, social movement unionism is a political movement as much as a union movement. It is able to develop tools for the fight against globalisation as well as the local agenda; thereby it is able to move the union struggle to a universal dimension. By this approach, unions not only protect the interests of the workers but also they become a social power and focus on to the aim of "social change."

3. Yatağan Resistance

Yatağan Resistance, which holds an important place for the struggle against privatisation, began against the attempt of the privatisation of coal mining and the thermal plant of the Yatağan district of the Muğla province in the 1990s and continued with different forms of struggles till today. It was one of the longest worker struggles of Turkey and the Turkish union movement gained a crucial experience since it was support by the people and mobilised local awareness (Çelik, 2012: 122–123).

The Spring Protests carried out in 1989 had a significant effect on the Yatağan workers. Collective bargaining negotiations and protests rising from these in 1989, with the effect of union management, made workers actively support the protests. During the Spring Protests, thousands of plant workers and miners poured into the streets for the first time. In this way, with the Spring Protests, the Yatağan workers gained experience as well as a serious union movement began at the Yatağan (Şahin Güngör, 2012: 135–136). Alongside the Spring Protests, the gains of Türkiye Enerji, Su ve Gaz İşçileri Sendikası (Tes-İş) involving the working conditions of workers in 1987 played an important role for increasing the confidence of the workers to form a union themselves (Soğancı, 2012: 149). The Yatağan movement started in 1989 and continued in the 1990s with lots of protests like food boycotts, getting collective permissions, hunger strikes, and marches.

The struggle against the privatisation process first started in 1994 with the 90 days stay of execution for the production of Yatağan Thermal Plant given by the Aydın District Administrative Court. After this execution, two thirds of workers decided to take a paid vacation and then unpaid time off. This decision mobilised the threatened workers and they organised protests that lasted ten days under the leadership of Yatağan branch of Tes-İş Union. In a short time, these protests worked and after ten days, with the decision of the Cabinet, Thermal Plant started production again (Şahin Güngör, 2012: 138–139). This success against the closure of the plant brought an increase of self-confidence and motivation to the workers (Soğancı, 2012: 152).

In 1996, the Yatağan-Yeniköy-Kemerköy Thermal Plants and mines of Yatağan and Milas which were providing fuel for these plants were put out to tender with their reserves and equipments. An aggregate corporation consisting of four domestic and foreign companies received the tender but officers of the company who came to Yatağan in 1997 and 2000 could not enter the plant because of the public resistance. As a result of the judicial process initiated by the unions, the transfer process was stopped (Bekem, 2012: 159).

The privatisation attempt of mines together with thermal plants evoked the miners of Yatağan with thermal plant workers. Therefore, the Yatağan resistance became a common struggle of thermal plant workers attached to the Tes-İş Union and mineworkers attached to the Maden-İş Union (Soğancı, 2012: 147).

In 2003, thermal plants were included in re-privatisation process by the decision of High the Board of Privatization. In 2010, City Group-Master Advisory-Oyak Investment and Scoin Advisory consortium, which received the advisory tender of Department of Energy in 2009, came to Yatağan with a 20 member committee. As in previous years, after the resistance of the Yatağan workers and locals, this committee had to leave the town (Bekem, 2012: 159).

In 2012, lignite fields covered by the Mining Law number 2840 were closely concerned with the decision "according to the law dated 24.11.1994 and numbered 4046 named Implementation of the Law on Privatization, it is privatized by the Privatization Administration Presidency" which was legislated and this legislation provided convenience for the firms in Yatağan (Bekem, 2012: 159). With this privatisation agenda again, workers resisted for 447 days in 2013. After the tender of enterprises, the entrance of the plant was closed and privatisations were tried to be prevented. But this resistance was a failure and on December 6 2014, the Tes-İş and Maden-İş Unions and their employers agreed on the 4C status. This agreement ensured the protection of existing benefits of workers and the Yatağan resistance was ended by the unions (http://www.sendika.org/2014/12/yatagan-direnis-4-c-anlasmasi-ile-sonlandirildi/).

From the 1990s until the end of 2014, the privatisation process did not end well for the workers. The Yatağan resistance is a symbol of one of the most unyielding struggles of the working class of Turkey. The Yatağan resistance, by exceeding the limits of thermal plants and mines, became a struggle of local people and it has led the people to adopt a political stance against privatisation that are part of neoliberal policies. Along with the dynamism it created, it also revealed an experience that was quite similar with social movement unionism with its way of organising in Turkey.

With the Yatağan resistance, the efforts of union branches about mobilising local communities have turned into social mobilisation. There have been several examples that can be considered unique in terms of social solidarity. For example, when the arrivals of the representatives of companies were learned, municipality and mosque speakers were used to call people to support. Announcements were made for people who are in Muğla to return back to Yatağan, since some locals of Yatağan were thought to be in Muğla. Also, imams of the district were making speeches against privatisation in their evening gatherings and Friday khutbahs in order to include people with the struggle (Şahin Güngör, 2012: 145). In this sense, resistance was a successful example of social movement unionism in terms of its support from local people and the pioneer status of unions.

The years 1996 to 2001 is an important process of gaining experience of union struggle by protests and actions including workers and their families, local authorities, professional chambers, artisan organisations, and the people of Yatağan as a whole. The most important feature that separates the Yatağan resistance from other worker resistances was that the decisiveness started from the workplaces which could be moved to local social relations. On the other hand, the most substantial factor of this success was the decisive and systematic efforts of two branches of unions (Şahin Güngör, 2012: 142).

"Workers Councils" which emerged during the struggle against the closure of thermal plant led to an experience that all workers were part of the decision making processes. In all activities and actions that are performed, they acted in accordance with the decisions of these councils. From the banners that were carried to the slogans that were shouted, every worker was a part of and an organiser of the process (Soğancı, 2012: 152). This experience that was created by the Tes-İş and Maden-İş is an example of social movement unionisms' understanding of grassroots democracy depending upon workplace committees.

Even if the Yatağan Resistance had various deficiencies when it comes to its limitation to locality, since it was not able to be moved to the national level, it is similar to social movement unionism with its many features. In this sense, being a resistance shown against the privatisation as a result of neoliberal policies, including masses to the union struggle, using grassroots democracy efficiently and making unions the centre and organiser of the social opposition, the Yatağan Resistance can be evaluated as an example of social movement unionism.

4. Objective, Scope and Method of the Study

Objective of the study is to investigate the Yatağan resistance in terms of social movement unionism. The aim is to find out the similarities between the Yatağan resistance and social movement unionism by analysing the data obtained during the study. Discussions were limited with the union branch presidents since the Yatağan resistance was organised under the leadership of union branches. Top organisations which the unions were attached were not included since protests were made without the leadership of these confederations.

Qualitative research techniques were used for the field research and in-depth interviews were conducted by asking semi-structured questions. In order to compare different interviews, every interviewee was asked identically formed questions. The interview form had eleven questions so general frames could be formed by these basic questions. Apart from these questions, for the purpose of getting more detail, some additional questions were also asked.

The researcher conducted these interviews by making appointments with participants. Before the meetings, every interviewee was given a form that had general information about social movement unionism and after stating the aim of the interviews the questions were asked. A tape recorder was used for these interviews with the permission of the participants. The first meeting was with the Maden-İş Yatağan Branch Vice President. The meeting was in the Yatağan branch of the Maden-İş union and it lasted about one and a half hours. The second meeting was with the Tes-İş Yatağan Chairperson of the Branch who was leading the Yatağan resistance together with the management of the Maden-İş Yatağan Branch. The meeting was in the Tes-İş Yatağan Branch and lasted about two hours. Also, due to their leadership to the Yatağan resistance, the former Yatağan branch presidents of Tes-İş and Maden-İş were interviewed. The meeting with the former Tes-İş president was in the Tes-İş Biga Branch and lasted about one and a half hours. The meeting with the former Maden-İş branch president was an online interview and lasted about an hour and fifteen minutes.

5. Findings of the Study

According to the information obtained from the analysis of the data, opinions of the unionists were investigated by dividing them into themes. While forming the themes, literature on social movement unionism was put to use and the main features of social movement unionism were considered. These themes consist of the opinions on mass struggle, cooperation with social movements, political unionism, class consciousness, and organisational structure and function.

Views on the Mass Struggle

During all the meetings, unionists stressed that protests were owned by different parts of the community and they were transformed into mass struggles. Having a mass struggle characteristic is among the main features of social movement unionism for union movements. The opinions of unionists are as follows:

- Maden-İş Branch Vice President: "*The struggle of working class is very different here. We had the power of gathering everyone with a whistle for our protests and activities. Places of everyone were confiscated for the coal fields here. Everyone gave these expropriated fields with the taught 'state will give my children job opportunities'. With the privatization of the mine, young, old, women, men, artisans, peasants… everyone set their heart on this struggle."*

- Tes-İş Yatağan Branch President: *"At first, we said 'These KİTs (Public Economic Enterprise) are the wealth of the country. They exist with the taxes of peasants, artisans, citizens'. We did not take this road just for our bread. We told people this. All local people stepped into action. Everyone stood behind us, struggled with us. Workers, peasants, artisans, they were standing by with us, at all of our actions."*
- Maden-İş Yatağan Branch Former President: *"There, workers, peasants and locals chased a social case. They looked after public establishments forming the backbone of the economy of the Republic. Resistance was organized like knitting. In this process, we did not sign any act that aimed at the destruction of the public support. Our resistance increased since it got support from everyone. We handed over a huge legacy which will pave the way for tomorrow."*
- Tes-İş Yatağan Branch Former President: *"Protests were not made only by workers. Families of the workers and locals were get involved. Half of our population was women and children. For example, while the number of our members was 2000, our number in meetings was around 4000–5000. Children grew with slogans, their childhood was like that."*

Views on the Cooperation with Social Movements

During the meetings, all unionists emphasised that they acted in cooperation with other social movements or organisations. Also, the managers of Tes-İş and Maden-İş expressed that during the resistance, they were in cooperation and this cooperation was crucial for the existence of the resistance. This aspect of the movement shows parallelism with the understanding of social movement unionism which put the cooperation with social movements at its base. The opinions of unionists are as follows:

- Maden-İş Yatağan Branch Vice President: *"All the unions supported us. Especially Petrol-İş union never left us alone. It was a moral support. Lots of unions supported us also in Ankara. Lots of organization supported us from Association of Kemalist Thought to Chambers of Agriculture, from Craftsman's Associations to Pir Sultan Abdal Association. The biggest support was from CHP and İşçi Partisi. Afterwards, we supported them as well. We did not leave alone those who did not leave us alone. It is an example of pacta sunt servanda (agreements must be kept)…The harmonious actions of Tes-İş and Maden-İş unions had an important role for the strengthening of the movement. If two unions was not in a solidarity there, this resistance could not have advanced this far."*

- Tes-İş Yatağan Branch President: *"Throughout the resistance, there was a huge support from civil society organizations, from political parties and from professional chambers. DİSK and other unions attached to DİSK showed great support. HDP and Ülkü Ocakları were side by side for these protests. Likewise, ÖDP and İşçi Partisi was able to walk together. Youth was also side by side. It was for the first time in Turkey…We did not carry separate flags as Tes-İş and Maden-İş. We carried the same banner as Tes-İş and Maden-İş Branches."*
- Maden-İş Yatağan Branch Former President: *"Throughout the protests, there were students who were always with us. With our unionist discipline, they were with us because of the unifying power of the labor since they were the working class of the future. We had a beautiful synergy. There was no one who did not support us during the resistance. We heard that even the local administrators of AKP did not want these privatizations but they could not do anything since these were the government policy. Besides AKP, every organization supported us institutionally. Political parties came to our resistance tents in crowds. Even some of them went hunger strike with us. They took care of the needs of workers."*
- Tes-İş Yatağan Branch Former President: *"There was a labor platform which consisted of Türk-İş, DİSK, TMMOB and I guess Hak-İş. They were taking crucial decisions locally and nationally. In this process, there were important protests in Ankara. We could take 1200–1300 people to these meetings as Yatağan Branch. We went there with 40–50 busses and we were the most dynamic group there…We had established a union cooperation attached to Türk-İş in Muğla. There were 12–13 branches. We did periodical meetings with these branches in every 15 days. We were getting their support. Unions attached to DİSK and KESK were also involved in our activities. Also TMMOB, Türk Tabipler Odası and Bar gave their support. They were coming whenever we needed help. Political parties gave critical support from time to time. For instance, we were going to CHP, ÖDP, TKP and İşçi Partisi. We established a functioning that since our field was small, all the managers of political parties were among us… We carried out all of our activities with Maden-İş. With Maden-İş, we were like one branch. There were some contradictions and problems from time to time, but we always acted together. This is significant."*

Views on Political Unionism

There are two main sub-themes when interviews with the unionists were investigated. First of these themes was about the 'views on the political demands' of the protests and second was about the 'transformation of the political attitude of the mass.' All of the unionists stressed both of these themes and they pointed out the importance of these for the gain of the resistance. Both of these themes show parallelism with the social movement unionisms' political unionism understanding.

- Maden-İş Yatağan Branch Vice President: "*Class struggle is not only for your own interests. It is for social interests. First of all, this should be told and proved to the workers. We proved this with our stance in the protests. For this reason, people who were annoyed by this situation took our side. The opinion of the person who fights for the labor is to be with the policy that defends the labor. We tried to express this as much as we could. But while doing this, we did not exercise pressure over political preferences of people. This would not be ethical. (…) There were people who got mad to us because of this. But when we said 'this government is taking our bread, it wants to sell our profit-making workplaces. That's why we need to resist to the government also', they agreed with us.*"
- Tes-İş Yatağan Branch Vice President: "*We did not take this road for only our bread. The situation which all of our friends in Turkey fell is obvious as a result of the privatizations and pro-capitalist policies. (…) We started this resistance for the interests of our country. We continued it not only for ourselves but Turkey also. We told our friends that: today there is a political power and we resist against this power. We insisted this and at the last elections we saw that people who had said to be a part of that political party voted for other political parties and opinions. People who were praising the political power before cannot praise them now. The effect of this really reflected to the polls. Existing political party in power could only be the third party here in the elections. This change was inevitable. This situation reflected from worker to his/her partner and from him/her to their child.*"
- Maden-İş Yatağan Branch Former President: "*When it came to the transfer of workplaces, workers learned that this work was about political struggle. Because, the cake was distributed where? In the parliament. We told as much as we could that whether this cake was distributed to workers or capitalists and what should workers do. Workers agreed on to interfere to this distribution process.*"
- Tes-İş Yatağan Branch Former President: "*People saw how existing rights would be lost after the privatizations. SEKA was privatized, milk factories, feed factories were privatized right under our noses. Thus, they saw the need to move for the public interests. They became more conscious. If there was a political structure that embraces them in Turkey, they would fight. I know lots of people like that. During the resistance, political choices of workers changed. This can be seen by comparing the percentage of votes with the past. Interestingly, all the*

workers who were hired in the ANAP period (their political tendencies were also in that direction), were involved in this resistance."

Views on Class Consciousness

During the interviews, all unionists remarked positive opinions about the effect of the resistance on the development of consciousnesses of workers.

- Maden-İş Yatağan Branch Vice President: *"Most of our friends forced to be retired during the privatization process so we were here with our young friends. They learned class consciousness, being a worker, union, being organized through this resistance. Above all, everyone learned to resist, to struggle and to stick up here. We do not have a friend who did not experience tear gas, rubber bullet, batons and fight against the police. Everyone comprehended to risk everything for the class struggle. In this sense, this resistance was a great experience for the settlement of the class consciousness."*
- Tes-İş Yatağan Branch President: *"Our friends saw what we could accomplish if we unite with this resistance. By this way, they realized the class consciousness. They saw what working class can do if they could interlock with unity and togetherness. Now, they are supporting every class struggle and they see these resistances as if these are their own. It is an important gain."*
- Maden-İş Yatağan Branch Former President: *"Yatağan workers had a crucial tradition of struggle. Each new worker has reached class consciousness more rapidly with the channel of their brothers from the tradition of struggle. We saw and lived this. This will continue as long as this tradition of struggle continues. Yatağan workers have a crucial place with their class consciousness in Turkey."*
- Tes-İş Yatağan Branch Former President: *"People who were only worried about their insurances and without consciousness got proletariat. They realized that they were a class. That was not like that before. The idea of shared problems, interests and solutions and 'we can do it together' jogged our friends, partners and children's memory. The idea of belonging a union got stronger. These are I think really important successes and outcomes."*

Views on Organisational Structure and Functioning

During all the interviews with unionists, they stressed that at the start and during the protests, members actively participated with the decision making processes and none of the decisions were made without asking their opinions.

- Maden-İş Yatağan Branch Vice President: *"During the resistance, most of the suggestions of workers were evaluated and applied. We were always open to their advices. Workers were saying 'do this' and we were doing it. We never said 'no'. We tried to apply decisions that are made, whether they were true or false. We built committees before the starting the resistance and we made them operational quickly. We made worked out about what we could do against privatizations in this committees. We applied the decisions that were taken by these committees after, with a selfless manner, during the resistance."*

- Tes-İş Yatağan Branch President: "*We made till today since we heard the voice of the base. The worker usually does not know about a decision when it is given from above. But if you apply the decision of the workers, then everyone knows about it and self control would be possible. In this case, no one says 'I will not go' when his/her friends would go to a protest. Besides self control, he/she feels a pressure. This made the base to feel an ownership about the actions and achieved success. We took all the decisions with the workplace committees during the resistance. We assigned representatives to the head of committees of ten people. We gave missions to the committees and wanted information about their missions. They presented information with files to us. System worked in this way. Resistance have grown and formed by this process.*"
- Maden-İş Yatağan Branch Former President: "*We included all the workers to the decisions that were made. Workers knew what we knew. We were always transparent with our resistance and actions to our worker friends. Tes-İş and Maden-İş both included the workers to all the stages of the resistance. By this way, resistance was enlarged and came to this point. We applied all the decisions by the committees and by discussing with workers. From Ankara protests to sudden protests, even press conferences were made by making decisions together through these committees.*"
- Tes-İş Yatağan Branch Former President: "*All the decisions made during resistance were unanimous. We did not take decisions of our own. We just agreed on the demands of the base. We internalized this process and we did not make these in terms of tactics. Conditions we lived in already convinced us. During the resistance, all the decisions were made in the worker committees. We gave importance to people from all political views, regions and titles being in these committees. Committees were open to everyone. Those who wanted to sabotage were blocked by our friends. By this way, decisions were everyone's decisions. We told these decisions to workers during entrances and exits of the workplaces. Decisions were voted by the workers and taken by consensus.*"

6. Conclusion

The data obtained from the interviews were classified according to their themes and investigated comparatively during the evaluation. Considering the results obtained from field research, the Yatağan Resistance was determined to fit all the themes of social movement unionism. In this context, it can be said that the Yatağan Resistance is a working class struggle which is an example of social movement unionism.

All interviewed unionists stated that resistance became a mass movement with the support of different sectors and they were in social solidarity with different social movements in a similar way with social movement unionism. In addition, all the unionists stated that during the resistance, political demands were at the forefront and political attitudes of protesters were transformed. In this way, it was stressed that resistance also carried a political character. Also it is seen that unionists were in consensus about the resistances' contribution to the development of class consciousness and solidarity. The opinions about the organisational functioning were that workers actively participate in decision-making process and workplace committees were used effectively. In this sense, the Yatağan Resistance shows similarities with the understanding of grassroots democracy of social movement unionism.

However, unlike other examples of social movement unionism in other countries, the Yatağan Resistance was limited in its impact on Turkey's union movement. The reason lies behind the fact that the socio-economic structure of Turkey and the basic characteristics of union movement were far from the conditions necessary for the strengthening of social movement unionism. The limited understanding of freedom about working conditions, the weakness of class consciousness and culture of organising, the strength of pragmatic approach in unions, failure of the unions to mobilise society, the weakness of social movements and the indifference of unions to these movements and some other factors had a negative impact on social movement unionism to becoming a strong alternative.

References

Bekem, Murat (2012). "Yatağan Özelleştirme Süreci", Sosyal Haklar Ulusal Sempozyumu IV Bildiriler Kitabı, Petrol İş Yayını 117, pp. 159–161.

Çelik, Aziz (2012). "Türkiye'de 2000'li Yıllarda Grevler ve Grev Dışı Eylemler: Çalışma Hayatında 'Pax Romana' mı?", Sosyal Haklar Sempozyumu IV Bildiriler Kitabı, pp. 107–133.

Doğruer, A. Can (2004). "Toplumsal Hareket Sendikacılığı Tartışmaları Üzerine Birkaç Hatırlatma ve Bir Örnek", http://www.sendika.org/2004/10/toplumsal-hareket-sendikaciligi-tartismalari-uzerine-birkac-hatirlatma-ve-bir-ornek-a-can-dogruer/, (Retrieved on: 29.06.2014), http://www.sendika.org/2014/12/yatagan-direnis-4-c-anlasmasi-ile-sonlandirildi/, (Retrived on: 28.02.2015).

Lambert, Rob & Webster Eddie (2011). "Southern Unionism and the New Labour Internationalism", Antipode, Vol: 33, Issue: 3, (July 2001), pp. 337–362, http://onlinelibrary.wiley.com/doi/10.1111/1467-8330.00188/pdf, (Retrieved on: 19.09.2014).

Moody, Kim (2002). "Towards an International Social Movement Unionism", Industrial Relations: Labour Markets, Labour Process and Trade Unionism, Ed: John E. Kelly, Routgedle.

Noyes, Matt (2009). "Business Unionism and its discontents: reflections on 'Social Movement Unionism' and the Union Leadership in the U.S.", The Center for Transnational Labor Studies, http://www.re.rollingearth.org/?q=node/148, (Retrieved on: 10.06.2014).

Pillay, Devan (2013). "Between Social Movement and Political Unionism: COSATU and Democratic Politics in South Africa", Rethinking Development and Inequality 2, pp. 10–27, http://rdi.andir-south.org/index.php/rdi/article/view/9, (Retrieved on: 04.07.2014).

Robinson, Ian (2000). "Neoliberal Restructuring and U.S. Unions: Toward Social Movement Unionism?", Critical Sociology, Vol. 26, No:1–2, pp. 109–138, http://www-personal.umich.edu/~eian/Critical_Sociology.pdf, (Retrieved on: 01.07.2014).

Scipes, Kim (1992). "Social Movement Unionism and the Kilusang Mayo Uno", Kasarinlan: Philippine Journal of Third World Studies, Vol: 7, pp. 121–162, http://journals.upd.edu.ph/index.php/kasarinlan/article/view/1393/pdf_38, (Retrieved on: 21.08.2014).

Soğancı, Erol (2012). "12 Eylül Sonrasının En Parlak Deneyimlerinden Biri olarak Yatağan Direnişi: Eylül 1987-Ocak 2006", Sosyal Haklar Ulusal Sempozyumu IV Bildiriler Kitabı, Petrol İş Yayını 117, pp. 147–158.

Şahin Güngör, Özlem (2012). "Yatağan Direnişini Başarıya Taşıyan Etkenler", Sosyal Haklar Ulusal Sempozyumu IV Bildiriler Kitabı, Petrol İş Yayını 117, pp. 133–146.

Waterman, Peter (2006), "Union Organisations, Social Movements and the Augean Stables of Global Governance", CSGR Working Paper, 211/06, pp. 1–38, http://wrap.warwick.ac.uk/1895/1/WRAP_Waterman_wp21106.pdf, (Retrieved on: 28.06.2014).

Waterman, Peter (2008). "Social Movement Unionism in Question: Contribution to a Symposium", Employee Responsibilities and Rights Journal, Vol: 20, Issue 4, pp. 303–308, http://link.springer.com/article/10.1007%2Fs10672-008-9093-z, (Retrieved on: 18.09.2014).

Elmas Akin[1]

Evaluation of the Development Plans between the Years 1963 and 2018 in Turkey

Abstract *Planning, which means to determine the way in advance, has occured throughout history. The planning process, which includes elements such as determining current sources and evaluating options, is also important because of decreasing inequities and correcting imbalances.*

After World War II, planning was set as one of the development method. After experiences of economical plans, in 1961, the State Planning Organization (SPO) was founded and made planning more formal in Turkey. Development plans, which have continued with the Development Ministry that was founded in 2011, are important documents for determining social policies.

In this article, aims and achievements of the development plans were discussed with a descriptive analysis of the qualitative method used in this research, evaluated with social work view and suggestions offered in light of the literature research studies for Turkey.

Keywords: *Planning, Development Plants, Social Policy, Turkey.*

Introduction

Planning is an important function of the management process that provides a pre-determined road map and to evaluate current options to achieve a goal. While basic components of planning are goal, duration, and method, its basic principles can be arrayed as openness, consistency, and flexibility. Beydemir (2006) states that the planning process is defined as "setting goals to reduce inequalities in the redistribution of social residual and eliminate this alienation and to mobilize the society and social resources in the context with these goals." Planning can be observed across all areas of business, sectors, cities, regions, nationwide, and internationally. Development plans have been confected to achieve economic and social goals in terms of determined development goals for the entire country or merely a region. Ways of worldwide searching of national development after World War II and increasing concern on developmentalist methods have designated discussion axis over development/ underdevelopment. In the context of

1 Research Assistant, KTO Karatay University, Faculty of Social and Human Sciences, Department of Social Work, E-mail: elmas.akin@karatay.edu.tr

these issues by determining planning as a development method, 'development' and 'planning' have been embraced often together (Beydemir, 2006).

Turkey has made much progress with the process that begun with the five-year development plan. The state has been charged with performing development plans via the 41st article of the constitution of 1961, the state planning organization was founded due to development plans that covers five-year periods via Law no. 91 that entered into force on September 30 1960. The Republic of Turkey Ministry of Development was founded in 2011 instead of State Planning Organization.

Development Plans

In this section, development plans are discussed with the axis of social services and are evaluated with the descriptive analysis technique[2].

First Five-Year Development Plan 1963–1967

Development of public services, one of the goals of the first five-year development plan is that highlighted principles in this context can be arrayed as increasing the area of services, accessing services on the basis of equality of opportunity and social justice, eliminating inequalities in accessing services across the regions, promoting voluntary participation of citizens in services, and providing efficiency of public institutions. The objective of social service in the plan is expressed as eliminating irregularity and defect among many environments, and moreover the importance of voluntary institutions' supports and inability of trained human capital are highlighted in the plan. The goals of the plan in the context with social service are figured as

> *"helping to implement the program of population planning and solve social issues that emerged poor neighborhood of cities, providing elderly care, work orientation for disabled people, the prisoners and society and individual welfare in terms of similar social issues. Caring and growing of children in need of protection, preventing juvenile delinquency, solving problems of mal adjusted and retarded children, preventing abuse of child labor, supporting child welfare would be handled as main issues" (SPO, 1963)*

Precautions in accordance with aforesaid objectives includes maximising voluntary savings instead of public resources about accessing services, founding of the 'Coordination Council' among public authorities and the 'Social Service

---

2 Descriptive analysis is a qualitative method that present obtained data by editing and evaluating for readers as systematically in order to take photography of interviewed or observed individuals' views in a striking way (Yıldırım and Şimşek, 2013, p. 256).

Institution' for executing funds on a single source. Planned investment for addressed services within objectives and precautions are reviewed under three categories as, children in need of protection, home care for elderly people, and rehabilitation centres. Planned five-year investment amount for aforementioned services was 29800 Turkish Liras (SPO, 1963).

Second Five-Year Development Plan 1968–1972

The scope of social welfare services is stated in the plan as (SPO, 1967):

> *"Social welfare services would be public programs that implemented about the issues as social assistance for elderly and poor people, child welfare, young welfare, family care, care for unemployed people due to physical or mental disability, medical and social rehabilitation, work orientation, crime and services related crime, leisure time activities with the aim of providing essential safe environment to develop individuals in social life and thus, empowering them to copy with social problems."*

The request of the founding of the juvenile court as a solution of increasing juvenile delinquency by migration is uttered and secondary school education for children in juvenile detention centres are characterised within the report. The following statement is used for disabled children within the report (SPO, 1967):

> "There were 62630 children with mentally retarded and physically disabled «defective children» in our country in 1955. In response to this need, 5 schools for the deaf and 2 schools for the blind, where educated 1465 children, were founded in 1966. The issue of retarded children has an important place in respect of child welfare in our country. On this topic, 1768 children are educated in 95 classrooms. However, pedagogic problems are visible due to being these classrooms in primary schools."

Number of in need of elderly people was 928723 in 1960. There were only twelve poor houses connected with municipalities and there was only the one elderly people home of Health Ministry with a 200- person capacity presented services for these people (SPO, 1967). Although presenting services for many applicant groups such as those drug addicted and women faced with social problems was a necessity, the lack of any services for these target groups was mentioned; and also only municipalities and voluntary institutions presented services for poor families and military families. Staff were considered to be educated in girls' technical high schools as 'allied social work personnel.'

Third Five-Year Development Plan 1973–1977

Long term objectives of the plan can be listed as: enhancing life standards, industrialisation, decreasing dependence on outsourcing, solving unemployment problem, and reforming income distribution (SPO, 1972). Social services were performed with different foci in different units within the period of the plan. Ministry of national education, ministry of health and social assistance, ministry of public works and housing, ministry of interior and ministry of justice were performed services related with children in need of protection, delinquent children, disaster-victims, immigrants (SPO, 1972).

The number of children in need of protection between the years 1967–1971 can be examined in Table 1 (SPO, 1972):

Table 1: Number of in Need of Children as to years between 1967–1971

	Number of Facility		Number of Care Given Children			
Years	Children's Home	Orphanage	Children's Home	Orphanage	Society for the Protection of Children	Foster Family
1967	15	79	1433	10613	716	105
1968	16	83	1473	11415	704	112
1969	17	84	1833	11734	758	124
1970	17	87	1930	12286	600	131
1971	17	87	1877	12332	578	135

The Social Services Agency that would provide coordination of social assistance and welfare services in 1972 still had not been established, this led to a dilemma between services. Studies on the rehabilitation of disabled people were conducted by the Ankara Rehabilitation Center in 1963 as stated in the report and it was observed that the expression 'disabled' was used instead of 'detective individuals' approach. Long-term development direction of social services was designated with the founding of the Social Services Agency; it was agreed to determine ratings of need as objectively and to provide support assistance according to these ratings.

Fourth Five-Year Development Plan 1979–1983

Although the grwoth rate for the third development plan period was determined at 7.4%, it actualised as 6.5% respectively (SPO, 1979). The oil crises at the international level is expressed as the reason for that in the report. As to the perspective of social services, an inclusive institution that coordinates all services was still not available in the mentioned plan period and it was observed that nursery services for children with working mothers were still not presented. Although there were 1.5 million children in need of protection in the age group of 0–6, only 3030 children could possess services in 21 carehomes. While there were 2.2 million children in need of protection in the age group 7–18, only 15002 children were presented services in 93 orphanages in 1977 (SPO, 1979).

While in the academic year 1975, 586 students, who were in the age group 0–19 and blind, were involved, almost 40000 students were in need of this program (SPO, 1979). Programs for deaf involved 2454 people in 13 institutions in 1975. In this period, the number of people in need of these services was 46450 in the age group 0–19 and the scope of such a service was so narrow. An institution related with retarded children that was considered to be founded by the Ministry of Health and Social Assistance would provide essential care for 500 children in 1977. 8747 students in special classes under the Ministry of National Education were educated, as related with retarded but educable children in 1977 (SPO, 1979). Children, who had been named as 'defective children' in previous five-year development plans, were expressed as 'blind, deaf and retarded children' in the fourth five-year development plan. Aforementioned statistical data was designated disabled children and the rate of disabled adults was reported within the plan as that individuals, who were in the age group 65 and over, had a rate as 4.5% to the total population in 1977. 494280 individuals of 1.9 million of this group were in need of care and rehabilitation, however the lack of institutions that presented services for this group was observed (SPO, 1979).

The law, which projected to assign for elderly people that over of the age of 65, needy and disabled people, passaged into law in 1977 and 780000 people had the opportunity to benefit from this law (SPO, 1979). Social Services and Child Protection Agency was conveyed to the Ministry of Health and Social Assistance in 1981, thus this Agency has obtained a qualification as a public institution. Other factors that determine structures of the services and socio-cultural construction more of basic fields of social services are that: by examining the plan in the framework with tenement, although 1.2 million unit tenements were aimed to be producted, 978361 unit tenements were built and the deficit of thereof was met by shanty houses. It was reported in the plan that various problems such as electric, water system, etc. were observed due to the lack of infrastructure of shanty houses and many objectives were highlighted to eliminate these problems.

Considering education levels, the rate of literate people was 62% in 1975. The rate of individuals, who were in the age of primary school and had the opportunity of education was 87.5% between the years 1977–1978. It was realised that one million children, who were in the age of primary school, lacked opportunities for education. In addition to that, excessive capacity of high school, İmam Hatip schools and Commercial High schools, which building is easy or do not need any investment and also can be opened in assigned and rental buildings, has occurred. The curriculum of education in technical schools was not at the required level of modernised industry and lacked available means to self education principles (SPO, 1979). As the plan is handled in terms of employment, while 2286000 individuals were constituted of domestic surplus labour in 1978, problems of unemployment and lack of institution in the field of health sustained.

Fifth Five-Year Development Plan 1985–1989

The access to services within the fifth development plan is expressed as (SPO, 1984):

> "Accessing social services are based on eliminating material, spiritual and social problems and meeting needs of individuals and families, prevention of social problems and helping to solve thereof, enhancing life standards." Individuals that possess preferential right of social service are expressed as 'children in need of protection, disabled and elderly people in need of protection' and unmet needs are highlighted.

Enhancing quality and quantity of institutions that provide social, psychological and cultural improvements of children in need of protection, arranging laws to expedite the employment of children, who grew in these institutions, are involved among the objectives of the plan. Similarly, it is aimed to increase quality and quantity of institutions in services for disabled and elderly people and expressed to provide coordination between all institutions. The objective of the plan is to increase social assistances to maximum capacity and announce the reached assistance to the people in need to the public according to principle of voluntary sharing of social assistance. 'Encouragement of charities, which has an important place in social assistance, as to charity law and culture' is a project that took part within the plan. It is highlighted that the need of guidance in shantytown and metropolitan and these services should be presented by integrating social work principles, furthermore expressed to open new business fields for individuals within prisons and juvenile detention centres, being advisor for enhancing efficiency in production obtained from work dorms in terms of making occupational theraphy and necessity of possessing services that provide socialisation of prisoners after the conviction. Besides, the importance of preschool education is stated due to participation of women in economical life and it is mentioned the need to enhance the quality and quantity of aforesaid institutions in this direction.

Sixth Five-Year Development Plan 1990–1994

Examining the plan in the context with population policies, the following statement attracted attention, "it is estimated that high rate of infant mortality that is incompatible with our country's social and economical development level will decrease by the precautions in the period of sixth plan and 81 thousand of 1,7 million babies will die before completing one age." For the first time, such a title as 'Family-Woman-Child' has a place in this plan. In the context with this title, the protection of family because of its holistic structure that conserved national and spiritual values is emphasised. Protective and preventive quality of social services and assistance programs are cared, rational use of resources in assistances is expressed and 'family' focused view is based on transmitting all services. "These services will be organized by aiming with view of care within the family instead of institution care as possible as. It will place importance on social integrity in the event of making institution care" (SPO, 1989). The view of using family support mechanisms instead of increasing quality and quantity of institutions as mentioned in previous plans is observed as understood with said statement.

It is expressed that 'local executive and people' should play more roles in arrangement of social services and assistances, encouragement of charities and entrepreneurship of private sector would be enhanced to find nursing home, rehabilitation centres are stated. The following statement that "alcolism, prostitution, infectious diseases related with prostitution, coping with bad habits and social rehabilitation implementation related with protection of ex-convicts would be generalized effectively" (SPO, 1989). Otherwise, 'prostitution and its results' are emphasised for the first time.

Seventh Five-Year Development Plan 1996–2000

The published period of the plan was a period of observing the currency of unemployment – almost 120 million persons – all over the world, increasing immigration due to unemployment and occurring social exclusion because of increasing immigration. The literacy rate, according to data from 1990, for men was 88.8%, for women was 72% and for the total population was 80.5%. The literacy rate for particularly women was low and 28% of the women were illiterate. The emphasis on providing equality of women and men several times and the thought of enhancing quality and quantity of insitutions that support the family was mentioned in addition to supporting the individual besides the family.

Holistic precautions that protect children from exploitation and bad habits, prevent pushing them into crime; improvement of protective and preventive services for children that possess criminal tendency, eloped and under risk factors on the street, reintroducing children that turn to crime and perpetrator to society are objectives of the plan. Moreover, from the principle of that the ideal environment for child's care and growth is family forth many projects were discussed about family protective precautions, implementations of foster-family and adoption, promoting institution care (SPO, 1995). Providing the participation of children that are out of the education system in thereof and to attend in occupational education, laying emphasis on solutions of the problems about health, social security and occupational education, providing essential environment for children to leave working life in the long term are the other objectives (SPO, 1995). Another objective mentioned within the plan to protect women and children are these: creating child observation and admittance centres that are prescribed in Law no. 2253, separating children from adult prisoners by creating child retention centres and observation houses, implementing the principle of union of goods between couple for savings during the marriage process, providing shared responsibilities in the family and the participation of women in social life equally (SPO, 1995). Furthermore, as one of the objectives of seventh five-year development plan was to legislate Social Security Basic Law to determine basic principles of social security, social assistance, and services.

Eighth Five-Year Development Plan 2001–2005

This plan contains a 'Long Term Strategy' that involves the years 2001–2023 and the five-year development plan that includes the years 2001–2005. The growth rate of the Gross National Product was 7.0 was determined for development and this rate was 3.7 between the years 1996–1999 (SPO, 2000). Literacy rate of men was 94.2% and 77.4% for women and it was reached to 85.7% for the whole population (SPO, 2000).

As a result of the Marmara and Düzce earthquakes in 1999, 18373 persons died and 48901 persons were injured. 93010 tenements and 15165 workplaces were ruined or heavily damaged. 104440 tenements, 16120 workplaces were moderately damaged. 113283 tenements and 14656 workplaces suffered mild damaged (SPO, 2000). For this reason, the transformation from prefabricated tenements to permanent tenements was aimed for within the eighth five-year development plan. Increasing welfare is connected with the improvement of science and technology for the first time. As the plan is examined in terms of women and children that are handled among vulnerable groups, increasing the literacy rate, enhancing compulsory education to eight years are assumed as affirmative developments for women. Additionally, employment opportunities of women is searched in the framework with the Employment Education Program by Employment Agency and organised skill courses. The 153rd article of the law no. 4248 Civil Law was altered in 1997 and women are entitled to use their maiden names. A centre was founded by General Directorate on the Status and Problems of Women to direct women to income-generating activities, entrepreneurship, and evaluate hand work. Directorates on the Status of Women within 13 Governorships were founded with the aim of enhancing effectiveness of women oriented services and presenting services for large masses (SPO, 2000).

The United Nations Convention on the Rights of the Child came into force in 1995 and implementation, following and coordination of the convention were classified as the objectives of the plan. It was estimated that three million children were disabled by the year of 1999 and 32542 children attended 904 schools by the Ministry of National Education. Medical studies aimed at preventing disabled births due to preventive causes are within the scope of the plan. 76 Kindergarten and 97 orphanages within Social Services and Child Protection Agency presented services for 16595 children in need of protection, 421 children were placed alongside families and 1730 children were adopted (SPO, 2000). The Branch Office of Protection for Little was created in 25 metrapolitans, named as the Department of Child in other cities within the General Directoriate of Security. The number of juvenile courts reached to six and two prisons for juveniles were created (SPO, 2000). Welfare-enhancing services for children were mentioned as generally within the plan and also it was particularly emphasised that censorship for the publications of studying on violence, sexuality and drug abuse should be applied. Law no. 4320 on the Protection of the Family entered into force in 1998 to prevent violence within the family (SPO, 2000). The plan consisted of many objectives such as assistance for poor families and consulting services due to education expenditures. 28 Community Centres were created by 1999 (SPO, 2000). It was highlighted that social assistane for Marmara, Bolu and Düzce earthquake survivors was provided and the importance of the need for social services and assistance agencies was highlighted. The following enhancements were created: Administration Office for Disabled People was established by Decree Law No. 571 in 1997, the ILO Contract No. 159 about Occupational Rehabilitation and Employment of Disabled People was confirmed in 1999 (SPO, 2000).

Ninth Development Plan 2007–2013

The Ministry of Family and Social Policies and the Ministry of Development were established in 2011. Economical and social development axis of the plan are expressed as:

1. Enhancing competitive advantage
2. Increasing employment rate
3. Empowering human development and social interdependence

4. Providing regional development
5. Enhancing quality and effectiveness in public services

The vision in the framework with ninth development plan long term strategy (2001–2023) is expressed as "a Turkey is that enhancing in stability, sharing income more fairly, possessing competitive advantage on the global scale, transforming to knowledge society, completed adaptation process for membership to European Union" (SPO, 2006). The employment rate annually increased by 0.4% in the period of 2001–2005 and the unemployment rate was 10.3% by 2005 (SPO, 2006). While the rate of increase of the Gross National Product is labeled as the rate of development within the plan, the Gross Domestic Product is often used thereof. While the population growth rate was 1.41% in 2000, it decreased to the level of 1.26% in 2005. By the same period, the age group of 15–64 that was the working age population and over the age of 65 elderly people population remained respectively as increasing from 64.7% to 65% and from 5.4% to 5.9% (SPO, 2006). While the share of the richest 20% group from annual revenue was approximately 9.5 fold to the poorest 20% group in 2002, this share fell to the level of 8.1 fold in 2003 and 7.7 fold in 2004 (SPO, 2006). It was highlighted within the plan exam focused educational structure was not reached to the expected aim and caused the decreasing quality of education and 15 new public universities were founded in 2006. When examined the data of health within the plan, the number of persons per doctor was 792 in 2000, this number decreased to 715 in 2005. This was quite below the average of the European Union that was 288 within the same period (SPO, 2006).

The poverty rate was 26.96% in 2002, 28.12% in 2003, and 25.60% in 2004. 24.8% of disabled people, who had chronic illnesses and 36.3% of other disabled people were illiterate during the period of the plan. Only one out of every five disabled people can participate in labour force due to many reasons such as causing limitation of activity by social life environment, being unable to create available working conditions, and limited demand for disabled labour force. The law no. 5378 as Law on People with Disabilities entered into force in 2005 that was aimed to provide participation of disabled people in society by enhancing health, education, employment, and access to social security. Although the rate of literate women between the years 2000–2004 increased from 76.2% to 80.6%, it was behind the rate of literate men. While the employment rate among women was 22.3%, it was 64.8% among men. Women, who employed free family employee in rural area, leave economical life because of lack of their skills as to job qualifications in urban area and social oppression that occurred by different environment, thusly they become clarified for many risk factors such as poverty and social exclusion (SPO, 2006). Turkey participated in the Community Action Programme to Combat Social Exclusion in 2003 as a part of the adaptation process to the European Union. The work on preparation of Social Inclusion Document was initiated within the period of this plan to determine current conditions and strategies about social exclusion as a part of this process. Social assistances are maintained as in – kind and financial aid and coordination of many sectors are emphasised to provide a more qualified assistance. It is expressed within the plan that home care services for elderly people are noticed.

The Tenth Development Plan 2014–2018

The tenth plan is generated in accordance with Vision 2023 targets within the frame of being human focused (Ministry of Develeopment, 2013). Planning is embraced under many titles as qualified person, empowered society, innovative production, steady increasing development, livable space, sustainable environment, and international collaboration for development. While the Gross Domestic Product between the years 2002–2006 was performed as 7.2%, it increased between the years 2007–2012 at 3.3% (Ministry of Develeopment, 2013). Such a statement in the objectives and policies of the plan is utilised as (Ministry of Development, 2013); "It becomes more of an issue to empower the most vulnerable groups of the society in the framework with reflecting development residual as fairly for every segments of society and enhance interdependency connections among different segments of society." In respect thereof the importance of empowerment and social inclusion is highlighted in terms of development. The unemployment rate that was increasing in the process of a global crisis was 10.2% in 2006 and this rate was observed as 9.2% with the increasing participation in labour in 2012. On the other hand, the population rate that had a daily income below $4.3 was 13.3% in 2006, as well as 2.8% in 2011 (Ministry of Development, 2013). While the share of the richest 20% group from annual revenue was approximately 8.1 fold to the poorest 20% group in 2006, this share fell to the level of seven fold in 2011 (Ministry of Development, 2013).

36 public and 41 private universities were founded within higher education in the period of the 9th Development Plan and number of universities reached 170 in the month of May in 2013. Thereby, access to higher education made important progress, however the need of increasing quality has still carried out (Ministry of Development, 2013). Objectives and viewpoints of education programs are shaped to implement a transformation program as decreasing school types, enhancing sportive, artistic and cultural activities in order to extend mental and physical growth and skills of students, possessing a curriculum that integrated with information and communication technologies, non-exam oriented, regarding individual differences.

The population has reached 75.6 million people at the end of 2012. While the population growth rate was 12.2 per thousand in 2006, it dropped to 12 per thousand in 2012. In this context, population policies exist to enhance the fertility rate. It is considered as important within the report that enhancing related programs such as tackling the lack of physical activity, tobacco abuse, and obesity. Regional social development programs particularly the Social Support Program within the scope of providing social inclusion in underdeveloped regions are performed (Ministry of Development, 2013). In the period of the Ninth Development Plan, women participation and effectiveness in economical life and decision making processes has been extended, the principle of positive discrimination oriented women is attached to the constitution, arrangements for the prevention of violence against women are fulfilled and a committee on equality of opportunity for women and men in the Turkish Grand National Assembly was established (Ministry of Development, 2013). The progressive parts of the report in terms of 'family and woman' currently are classified in the report as, particularly participation in employment and decision making mechanism, preventing violence, sustaining progress respecting education and health and enhancing effectiveness in practice in the matter of equality of opportunity for women and men. A sustained transition from the extended family to elementary family and alteration of relationship types among family members has been observed. In this sense, monitoring and guidance are needed for the solution of single parents' problems that generated as the result of divorce (Ministry of Development, 2013). Policies to apply have been designated as, generalising premarital education, enhancing woman employment, designing social and economical policies as completing each other, decrasing adverse effects of visual, audial and printed media on families, executing flexible working hours and kindergarten services for answering family and work life's purpose as integration, conducting of awareness studies concerning violence against woman by starting with male children. Considering the theme of child and youth, the population of Turkey consisted of 30% of the total population is children (below aged 18), 16.6% is young people (aged 15–24) as well. While 31.4% of the population in the age group 15–29 have attended education, 47.1% of it are a part of the labour sector, however 28.1% of this population are in neither education nor the labour sector (Ministry of Development, 2013). As a consequence of that, it is observed that the young population has a decreasing rate of participation in the labour force, insufficient basic skills, and an increasing unemployment rate. Current risk factors for children and young people can be listed as: socio-economical and regional inequalities, poverty, gender inequality, child marriage, delinquency, violence and sexual assault of children, disintegration of family, declination of belongingness and interdependency feelings, drug abuse such as cigarette, alcohol and narcotics, and internet addiction (Ministry of Development, 2013). Considered policies in the field of child and young people can be performed by various programs that systems of child welfare and justice should be coordinated and preventive and also possess risk monitoring and early warning systems; prevent the worst styles of child labour such as working at hard and dangerous tasks, at mobile and transient agricultural labourer; support applications to enhance young people in the fields of sport, culture, art, etc. (Ministry of Development, 2013).

Conclusion

The planning practice in Turkey consisted of three processes as the industry plans of the 1930s, Development Planning between the years 1960–1980, and Strategic Planning was observed with structural adaptation policies instead of development planning due to being eliminated of the power and integrity on political decision mechanism after 1980s. Ten Development Plans by 1963 up to the year 2018 were investigated and their objectives, current functions, social developments were expressed within the study. In the period between the years 1983–1985, lack of planning and caring of planning activities were observed within the examined plans.

Unexpected progresses that are not mentioned in the plans, often occurred especially in the last two planning periods and the concepts and services are entitled so diversified in each plan such as social welfare services, social services, social assistance, etc. It is considered that this confusion of concepts makes inroads on service integrity. Despite the fact that the labeling of disabled individuals as 'defective children, retarded children, disabled, etc.,' it can be assumed as normal as using language of that period, using such concepts reflect viewpoint for these disadvantage groups. While the Development Plans are important reports in terms of determining and implementing social politics, they represent the role of being a road map that possesses sources and objectives, ipso facto the necessity of analysing the Development Plans, being informed about social processes and policies reveal an important place for social work science and occupation that has a key role as "policy maker."

References

Beydemir, C. (2006). *1960–1980 Yılları Arası Beş Yıllık Kalkınma Planlarının İrdelenmesi*, Maltepe Üniversitesi Sosyal Bilimler Enstitüsü, İktisat Anabilim Dalı, Yüksek Lisans Tezi, İstanbul.

Demirayak, M. (2004). *Beş Yıllık Kalkınma Planları'nda Avrupa Birliği*, İstanbul Üniversitesi Sosyal Bilimler Enstitüsü Avrupa Topluluğu Anabilim Dalı, Yüksek Lisans Tezi, İstanbul.

Devlet Planlama Teşkilatı (1963). *Birinci Beş Yıllık Kalkınma Planı 1963–1967.* http://www.kalkinma.gov.tr/Pages/KalkinmaPlanlari.aspx adresinden 23.10.2014 tarihinde erişilmiştir.

Devlet Planlama Teşkilatı (1967). *İkinci Beş Yıllık Kalkınma Planı 1968–1972.* http://www.kalkinma.gov.tr/Pages/KalkinmaPlanlari.aspx adresinden 23.10.2014 tarihinde erişilmiştir.

Devlet Planlama Teşkilatı (1972). *Üçüncü Beş Yıllık Kalkınma Planı 1973–1977.* http://www.kalkinma.gov.tr/Pages/KalkinmaPlanlari.aspx adresinden 23.10.2014 tarihinde erişilmiştir.

Devlet Planlama Teşkilatı (1979). *Dördüncü Beş Yıllık Kalkınma Planı 1979–1983.* http://www.kalkinma.gov.tr/Pages/KalkinmaPlanlari.aspx adresinden 23.10.2014 tarihinde erişilmiştir.

Devlet Planlama Teşkilatı (1984). *Beşinci Beş Yıllık Kalkınma Planı 1985–1989.* http://www.kalkinma.gov.tr/Pages/KalkinmaPlanlari.aspx adresinden 23.10.2014 tarihinde erişilmiştir.

Devlet Planlama Teşkilatı (1989). *Altıncı Beş Yıllık Kalkınma Planı 1990–1994.* http://www.kalkinma.gov.tr/Pages/KalkinmaPlanlari.aspx adresinden 23.10.2014 tarihinde erişilmiştir.

Devlet Planlama Teşkilatı (1995). *Yedinci Beş Yıllık Kalkınma Planı 1996–2000.* http://www.kalkinma.gov.tr/Pages/KalkinmaPlanlari.aspx adresinden 23.10.2014 tarihinde erişilmiştir.

Devlet Planlama Teşkilatı (2000). *Sekizinci Beş Yıllık Kalkınma Planı 2001–2005.* http://www.kalkinma.gov.tr/Pages/KalkinmaPlanlari.aspx adresinden 23.10.2014 tarihinde erişilmiştir.

Devlet Planlama Teşkilatı (2006). *Dokuzuncu Kalkınma Planı 2007–2013.* http://www.kalkinma.gov.tr/Pages/KalkinmaPlanlari.aspx adresinden 23.10.2014 tarihinde erişilmiştir.

Eren, A. (2001). *Türk İktisat Tarihi*, Muğla Üniversitesi İktisadi ve İdari Bilimler Fakültesi Yayınları, Muğla.

İlkin, A. (1988). *Kalkınma ve Sanayi Ekonomisi*, İstanbul Üniversitesi Yayınları, İstanbul.

Kazgan, G. (2002). *Tanzimattan 21. Yüzyıla Türkiye Ekonomisi*, İstanbul Bilgi Üniversitesi Yayınları, İstanbul.

Korkmaz, A. (1995). *Kalkınma Planlarında Öngörülen Eğitim Hedeflerinin Gerçekleşme Düzeyi*, Gazi Üniversitesi Sosyal Bilimler Fakültesi Eğitim Yönetimi, Teftişi, Planlaması ve Ekonomisi Anabilim Dalı, Doktora Tezi, Ankara.

Kuruç, B. (1998). 1961 Anayasası ve Planlı Ekonomi, Kili, S. (ed.). (1998) *27 Mayıs Devrimi, Kurucu Meclis ve 1961 Anayasası*, Boyut Kitapları, İstanbul.

Osmanoğlu, A. (2009). *7–9 Kalkınma Planlarındaki Gelir Politikaları*, Marmara Üniversitesi Sosyal Bilimler Enstitüsü Maliye Anabilim Dalı, Yüksek Lisans Tezi, İstanbul.

Say, N. P. (2004). *Stratejik Çevresel Değerlendirmenin Beş Yıllık Kalkınma Planları ve Enerji Sektörü Örneğinde Araştırılması ve Bir Uygulama Modelinin Geliştirilmesi*, Çukurova Üniversitesi Fen Bilimleri Enstitüsü Peyzaj Mimarlığı Anabilim Dalı, Doktora Tezi, Adana.

Soyak, A. (2003). Türkiye'de iktisadi Planlama: DPT'ye İhtiyaç Var Mı?, *Doğuş Üniversitesi Dergisi*, 4 Temmuz 2003.

Taş, U. (2007). *Türkiye'de Kalkınma Planları Işığında Eğitimin Kalkınmadaki Rolü*, Osmangazi Üniversitesi Sosyal Bilimler Fakültesi İktisat Anabilim Dalı, Yüksek Lisans Tezi, Eskişehir.

Tekeli, İ., İlkin, S. (1981) *Savaş Sonrası Ortamında 1947 İktisadi Kalkınma Planı*, Odtü-Türkiye Belgesel Tarifi, Ankara.

Türkiye Cumhuriyeti Kalkınma Bakanlığı (2013). *Onuncu Kalkınma Planı 2014–2018*. http://www.kalkinma.gov.tr/Pages/KalkinmaPlanlari.aspx adresinden 23.10.2014 tarihinde erişilmiştir.

Yıldırım, A. ve Şimşek, H. (2013). *Sosyal Bilimlerde Nitel Araştırma Yöntemleri*, Dokuzuncu Baskı, Ankara: Seçkin Yayıncılık.

Yılmaz, F. (2009). *Türkiye'nin 1980 Sonrası İhracata Dayalı Sanayileşme Sürecinde Kalkınma Planlarında Yatırım Teşviklerinin Etkileri: İmalat Sanayi-Beyaz Eşya Sektörü Örneği*, Marmara Üniversitesi Sosyal Bilimler Fakültesi İktisat Anabilim Dalı, Doktora Tezi, İstanbul.

Hakan ER*

Pricing Efficiency of a Failed Futures Contract: A Transactions Data Analysis of the ISE 100 Futures

Abstract This paper investigates the efficiency of the stock index futures market and index arbitrage for delisted ISE 100 Turkish futures contracts by employing intraday transactions data. Results indicate that the futures trading exhibited persistent underpricing. Because of the limitations on short selling in the spot market, exploiting arbitrage opportunities from this persistent underpricing is highly unlikely. However, results also indicate that there are a considerable number of overpriced futures and the mean of arbitrage profits generated from short arbitrage positions are much higher than the mean of the profits generated from long arbitrage profits.

1. Introduction

Stock index derivatives such as futures, options, and options on futures on a stock index have become prominent in financial markets in a short space of time. Stock index futures contracts on the Standard and Poor (S-P) 500 Index was first introduced in the United States of America (U.S.A) in April 1982 by the Chicago Mercantile Exchange (CME). This was followed by the S-P 500 futures index options at the CME in January 1983. Trading in the S-P 500 index option contracts (SPX) was started by the Chicago Board of Trade (CBOT) in July 1983. The success of the index derivatives in the U.S.A led to early adoption and high trading volumes on stock price indices such as the FTSE-100, Nikkei, Hang Seng and others outside the U.S.A.

Stock index derivatives have gained phenomenal success primarily because they are ideal vehicles to hedge equity portfolios against market risk. Low transaction costs in the derivatives markets compare favourably with the higher costs in the cash market despite the computerisation of trades in baskets of stocks of the underlying stock index. Further, the cash market may have illiquidities in the availability of stocks which do not occur in index derivatives as typically delivery is cash settled rather than in the underlying index portfolio. Moreover, short sales

* Akdeniz University, Antalya/TURKEY, erhakan@akdeniz.edu.tr

which can be problematic on the spot-cash market for stocks is not so in the index derivatives market.

Academic interest accorded to the testing for no arbitrage price efficiency of derivatives markets is in part because of the practical significance that properly aligned cash and derivatives prices have for the conduct of hedging and the orderly functioning of these markets. Large misalignments in the prices of assets when combinations of a subset of these can replicate the payoffs of another could signal arbitrage profits which incentivise arbitrageurs to take profitable positions that work to drive the prices in to the equilibrium range.

One limitation of the existing empirical work is that it mostly relates to stock index futures contracts traded in developed countries. This results in a data snooping bias (see Leamer, 1983 and Lo & Mackinlay, 1990 for the details of data snooping phenomenon). Over the last two decades the number of exchanges and contracts traded in developing countries has grown dramatically. In this context, it is somewhat suprising that little research can be found on emerging markets where thinness in the market trading may be highly prevalent and thus has significant impact on the efficiency of the market. There is a growing amount of evidence that emerging markets are less liquid, less informationally efficient, and more volatile than mature markets. Therefore, it will be interesting to see the the pricing and arbitrage of stock index futures on emerging derivatives markets. As a rapidly developing emerging market, Turkey is well suited for this task.

Another interesting phenomenon observed in recently formed derivatives markets is that many new futures fail to attract and sustain a profitable level of trading volume and they are delisted within ten years of their introduction (Brorsen and Fofana, 2001). A considerable amount of research has tried to identify factors that contribute the failure of a derivative product. Observable variables like the size of the cash market, the volatility of the cash prices, market competition and hedging effectiveness are the factors commonly cited in the literature as the determinants of a futures contract's success or failure.

Many researchers attempted to provide theoretical explanations for the failure of the futures contracts and emphasised the importance of contract design. It is suggested that poorly designed contracts fail to attract investors' interest. An interesting observation about the success or failure of futures contracts is that if a new futures contract experiences initial popularity it is unlikely to fail subsequently. Moreover, it is difficult for a new futures contract to attract significant interest if there is already a contract traded in the market that effectively meets the demands of the investors (Economides & Siow, 1985). Even if the new contract is designed better than the existing one, the new contract will probably fade existence in a short space of time. This phenomenon is called the "first-mover effect."

A recent example of a failed stock index futures contract is the ISE 100 Stock Index Futures contract. The Turkish Derivatives Exchange (TurkDEX) started trading two stock index futures contracts on February 4, 2005: the ISE 30 Stock Index Futures Contract and the Istanbul Stock Exchange ISE 100 Stock Index Futures Contract. On August 5th 2013, the merger of the TurkDEX and the Borsa Istanbul Futures and Options Market (VIOP) was completed. Following the merger all futures and options contracts in Turkey started trading on the single platform of the VIOP. By this merger, the ISE 100 contracts, which have never attracted sufficient trading volume, were delisted. ISE 100 contract failed despite the fact that it was trading on an index which is broader-based than the underlying index of the ISE 30 contract. As both contracts started trading on the same day, no first-mover advantage is observed. Moreover, apart from the underlying index there was no design differences between these contracts and both were traded on the same platform. This is an interesting case worthy of investigation. This study contributes to the literature by analysing the pricing efficiency of this failed product.

This paper is organised as follows: The next section examines the relationship between index futures and underlying cash market. Section 3 gives a brief summary of empirical literature. Section 4 describes the data and methodology and the results. The last section concludes the paper.

2. Stock Index Futures Arbitrage

The linkage in prices between a spot index and a futures contract on it is maintained by arbitrage. If interest rates are nonstochastic and the dividends to be paid during the life of futures contract are certain, in the absance of the taxes and transaction cost, the no-arbitrage futures price will be given by the standard cost-of-carry model:

$$F_t = S_t e^{(r-q)\tau} \qquad (1)$$

where F_t is the futures price at time t, S_t is the underlying index level at time t, r is the risk-free rate at time t, q is the expected dividend yield and τ=(T-t) is the remaining time to maturity. Futures are "overpriced" if $F_t > S_t e^{(r-q)\tau}$, and "underpriced" if $F_t < S_t e^{(r-q)\tau}$.

An arbitrage opportunity arises when futures price deviates from its theoretical value in the absence of transaction costs. If $F_t > S_t e^{(r-q)\tau}$ an arbitrageur can sell the futures contract, borrow simultaneously an amount equal to S_t and use these funds to buy the constituents of spot index, carry this basket of stocks until the delivery date. On the delivery date, arbitrageur can use the stocks for the delivery of the futures and use proceeds from the futures delivery to pay back the debt. Arbitrageur will net $F_t - S_t e^{(r-q)\tau}$ at the delivery date as a result of this strategy.

If $F_t < S_t e^{(r-q)\tau}$, arbitrageur can buy the underpriced futures, short the constituents of the underlying index at the same time, and invest the proceeds from the short sale to an interest bearing riskless security. On the delivery date, arbitrageur will use the proceeds from the riskless security to pay for the delivery of the futures contract and use the delivered index to close its short sale position. Arbitrageur will net a profit of $F_t - S_t e^{(r-q)\tau}$. Although the stock index futures is cash settled, the net profit will be the same.

In the presence of transaction costs, actual futures prices might deviate from the fair price. However, arbitrage opportunities will only be available if the arbitrageur's net gain covers the transaction costs. Therefore, in the presence of the transaction costs the fair futures prices will fluctuate within a no-arbitrage band and arbitrage will only occur when prices move outside this band. With transaction costs an overpriced futures will provide an arbitrage opportunity if $F_t > S_t e^{(r-q)\tau} + TC$, and underpriced futures will provide an opportunity if $F_t < S_t e^{(r-q)\tau} - TC$. Therefore, as long as $S_t e^{(r-q)\tau} - TC < F_t < S_t e^{(r-q)\tau} + TC$, there will be no arbitrage opportunity. $S_t e^{(r-q)\tau} - TC$ and $S_t e^{(r-q)\tau} + TC$ are the lower and upper bounds for arbitrage. An arbitrage opportunity arises whenever the market price of the futures moves outside of this arbitrage-free-band. If the market price of the futures is above the upper bound, an arbitrageur can sell the futures and buy the spot at the same time. At maturity the arbitrageur will net $F_t - (S_t e^{(r-q)\tau} + TC)$. If the market price of the futures is below the lower bound, on the other hand, then the arbitrageur can short the spot and buy the "underpriced" futures and net $S_t e^{(r-q)\tau} - TC - F_t$ at maturity.

3. Literature Review

Early studies of stock index futures arbitrage used daily data and employed the cost of carry model. Many studies reported significant deviations from the cost-of-carry model prices. Cornell and French's (1983) study concluded that mispricing exists and attributed mispricing to tax timing option. Cornell (1985), however, showed that the tax timing option had nothing to do with mispricings and mispricings began to disappear as the futures contract matures. Modest and Sundaresan (1983) calculated no arbitrage bands for futures and found that prices fall within these bands. However, the transaction costs they used were much higher than institutions usually pay. Figlewski (1984) also reported deviations. However, approximately 70% of these arbitrage opportunities disappeared by the close of the following day. Figlewski (1984) also concluded that mispricing disappears with time as markets mature.

Saunders and Mahajan (1988) employ regression analysis to examine the pricing relationships between futures and cash for the S&P 500 and NYSE contracts. Their approach is different than the studies prior to theirs. Instead of analysing the levels of spot and futures prices, they analysed the first differences. This approach obviated the troublesome assumptions of deterministic interest rates and known dividend payments. Their analysis "failed to reject" the hypothesis that futures prices are efficient.

Brenner et al. (1990) analysed the three active futures contracts: the Nikkei Stock Average contracts traded on the Singapore International Monetary Exchange and the Osaka Securities Exchange and the Tokyo Stock Price Index contract traded on the Tokyo Stock Exchange and found that Japanese futures contracts exhibited persistent departures from their fair prices. However, they also concluded that as the markets matured, these deviations declined substantially.

Starting with the 1990s, thanks to the increasing availability of the intraday data, efficiency studies started using intraday data. Chung (1991) is one of the first examples of these studies which used intraday transactions data to analyse The Chicago Board of Trade's Major Market Index contracts and found that the size and frequency of arbitrage opportunities are substantially smaller than those reported by earlier studies that used daily data and have declined sharply with time. Yadav and Pope (1994) analysed FTSE-100 futures and suggested that exploitable arbitrage opportunities exist in these contracts. McMillan and Ulku (2009) investigated mispricing of ISE30 index futures in Turkey for a very short sample period. They found there most of the futures are underpriced; however, because of the difficulties in shorting the stocks these deviations do not provide arbitrage opportunities. However, there are persistent arbitrage opportunities for the overpriced futures.

Numerous other studies reported deviations from fair prices. However, studies employing intraday data found fewer arbitrage opportunities than the ones that employed daily data. This shows that using nonsynchronous closing prices of futures contracts and spot index may lead to a significant source of error.

The results of both group of studies using daily data and intraday data suggested that persistent mispricing exists in index futures market. One explanation suggested in the literature for this phenomenon is that there is a risk premium for index arbitrage. Another explanation is that there exist hidden costs or impediments to arbitrage not captured by the cost-of-carry model. If there are impediments like nontrivial transaction costs, the uptick rule in the stock market, the lack of arbitrage capital, and the position limits, etc., the true risk-free arbitrage will be difficult and mispricings will arise and persist.

4. Data, Methodology and Results

Trading in the ISE 100 index futures started on the TURKDEX on February 4, 2005. The TurkDEX has a fully electronic trading system which allows remote access. The contract has six delivery months: February, April, June, August, October and, December. The contract is settled by cash at the Exchange Delivery Settlement Price (EDSP). The EDSP is based on the average level of the ISE 100 Index in the last thirty minutes of trading on the Last Trading Day. Table 1 below summarises contract specifications:

The contract did not attract market interest during the course of its first six months. During this period there were trading days during which no transactions on the contract took place. However, from November 2005 onwards the trading volume increased dramatically. Therefore, data from the first eight months of 2005 were not included in the sample.

Table 1: ISE 100 Index Futures Contracts

Underlying Asset	ISE 100 Index
Contract Size	Value calculated by dividing the index value by 1000 and multplying the quotient by TRY 100 (ISE 100 index /1000)*100
Minimum Price Tick	Price tick is 0.025 which corresponds to TRY 2.5
Contract Months	February, April, June, August, December (Contracts with two different expiration months to nearest to the current month shall be traded concurrently)
Settlement Method	Cash Settement
Expiry date	Last business day of each contract month. In case domestic markets are closed for half day due to an official holiday, expiry date shall be the preceding business day.
Last Trading Day	Last business day of each contract month. In case domestic markets are closed for half day due to an official holiday, expiry date shall be the preceding business day.

The analysis uses intraday historical trade data on the ISE-100 index futures traded on the TurkDEX from November 1, 2005 to May 21, 2012. The sample yielded 25454 observations. Trade data were obtained from the TurkDEX. The trade data records contain time stamped transactions/trade price data with the following information: (i) trade number; (ii) security type; (iii) security short name; (iv) the price of the contract; (v) the quantity of the transaction; (vi) the total value of the transaction. The security short name field contains information about the delivery month of the futures contract. For example the last four digits of the code "101F_IX1001211" implies December 2011 delivery.

The futures data matched with the intraday spot index levels obtained from the Borsa Istanbul. The ISE 100 Index is a market capitalisation based index composed of the ISE2s top 100 capitalisation companies' stocks. The index is calculated every ten seconds during the trading hours. Every futures price in the sample matched with the index level which is calculated within a minute of the time stamp of futures contract. Therefore, each individual futures price is matched with six different index levels. This procedure yielded 117414 matches.

Each futures price further matched with daily risk free interest rates which were calculated from the ISE Government Debt Securities Price indices (ISE GDS 91, ISE GDS 273, and ISE GDS 365) and annual dividend yield data. The ISE GDS Index data and dividend yield data were also obtained from the Borsa Istanbul.

We first analyse the pricing efficiency of the futures contracts in the absence of the transaction costs. To this end, the following regression equation is run to test the spot-futures relationship.

$$F_t = \alpha + \beta\, S_t e^{r\tau} + \varepsilon_t. \qquad (2)$$

By construction the absence of arbitrage profit condition that the long(short) index futures and the opposite position viz. short (long) in the synthetic futures is risk free with zero return requires the two are perfectly negatively correlated. Thus, in the linear regression in (2) for market efficiency by the spot-futures arbitrage, the beta coefficient should not be statistically different from 1 and the intercept term should not be statistically different from zero. Table 2 summarises the regression results.

The regression yields α= -1580.88 with a t-statistic of 13.15 and β = 1.02119 with a t-statistic of 81.59. This indicates that α or mean mispricing is significantly different from zero and β is significantly different from 1. The regression equation reflects the pricing inefficiency in the absence of the transaction costs. Negative intercept implies that the mispricing is negative, i.e. the futures are generally underpriced.

Table 2: Regression Results

Multiple R	0.996224495
R Squared	0.992463245
Adjusted R^2	0.992463181
Standard Error	956.2974312
Number of Observations	117414

ANOVA

	df	*SS*	*MS*	*F*	*Significance of F*
Regression	1	1.41393E+13	1.41393E+13	15461175.42	0
Residual	117412	1.07374E+11	914504.7769		
Total	117413	1.42467E+13			

	Coeeficients	*Standard Error*	*t Stat*
Intercept	-1580.88	13.14987588	-120.2205
Theoretical Price	1.02119	0.000259708	81.59

We further investigate the futures-spot mispricing with transaction costs. The transaction costs for an arbitrage position involves the sum of bid–ask spreads in both the spot stock and index futures markets and commissions. Total round trip transaction costs estimated to range between 0.5 to 1% of both spot and futures. We investigated arbitrage opportunities for three transaction cost levels: 0.5, 0.75, and 1%.

Table 3: Transaction Costs as 0.5% of the Futures and Spot

Delivery Year	Time to Delivery	Total Number of Opportunities	Mean of all Arbitrage Profits	# of Short Arbitrage Opportunities	Mean of Short Arbitrage Profits	Standard Deviation of Arbitrage Profits	# of Long Arbitrage Opportunities	Mean of Long Arbitrage Profits	Standard Deviation of Arbitrage Profits
2005	< 30 Days	2032	7.10	0	-	-	2032	7.10	6.94
	30 to 60 Days	6781	19.31	0	-	-	6781	19.31	16.06
	> 60 Days	-	-	-	-	-	0	-	-
2006	< 30 Days	2503	33.76	72	43.65	45.99	2431	33.47	26.61
	30 to 60 Days	8822	55.35	132	30.60	21.12	8690	55.73	37.66
	> 60 Days	5099	61.21	36	449.10	171.44	5063	58.45	42.11
2007	< 30 Days	519	163.49	227	135.00	150.79	292	185.64	129.42
	30 to 60 Days	278	186.30	140	243.76	181.79	138	128.01	159.18
	> 60 Days	105	298.55	47	524.99	343.10	58	115.07	97.96
2008	< 30 Days	834	93.74	446	90.37	94.72	388	97.61	118.59
	30 to 60 Days	1127	135.24	978	142.85	187.49	149	85.31	57.94
	> 60 Days	415	260.95	273	317.67	213.22	142	151.89	132.98
2009	< 30 Days	2632	52.19	1351	39.84	47.29	1281	65.21	105.24
	30 to 60 Days	1472	60.48	1063	64.80	127.66	409	49.25	65.48
	> 60 Days	18	71.09	18	71.09	1.56	0	-	-

Delivery Year	Time to Delivery	Total Number of Opportunities	Mean of all Arbitrage Profits	# of Short Arbitrage Opportunities	Mean of Short Arbitrage Profits	Standard Deviation of Arbitrage Profits	# of Long Arbitrage Opportunities	Mean of Long Arbitrage Profits	Standard Deviation of Arbitrage Profits
2010	< 30 Days	1868	91.84	1067	109.60	156.73	801	68.18	68.70
	30 to 60 Days	1137	57.53	690	60.67	60.78	447	52.69	71.80
	> 60 Days	0	-	0	-	-	0	-	-
2011	< 30 Days	1504	57.27	923	49.64	49.98	581	69.38	86.19
	30 to 60 Days	1724	59.68	917	37.17	48.00	807	85.26	100.32
	> 60 Days	2920	93.16	2576	89.30	76.80	344	122.01	130.62
2012	< 30 Days	265	127.59	209	158.21	123.48	56	13.30	10.54
	30 to 60 Days	589	94.69	463	114.30	167.80	126	22.63	17.52
	> 60 Days	249	89.81	193	96.35	71.04	56	67.27	68.36

Table 4: Transaction Costs as 0.75% of the Futures and Spot

Delivery Year	Time to Delivery	Total Number of Opportunities	Mean of all Arbitrage Profits	# of Short Arbitrage Opportunities	Mean of Short Arbitrage Profits	Standard Deviation of Arbitrage Profits	# of Long Arbitrage Opportunities	Mean of Long Arbitrage Profits	Standard Deviation of Arbitrage Profits
	< 30 Days	33	26.38	-	-	-	33	26.38	22.73
2005	**30 to 60 Days**	2894	18.27	-	-	-	2894	18.27	11.90
	> 60 Days	-	-	-	-	-	0	-	-
	< 30 Days	1429	28.90	35	63.45	35.83	1394	28.04	25.17
2006	**30 to 60 Days**	6367	51.00	75	25.93	15.40	6292	51.30	29.15
	> 60 Days	3903	56.72	36	428.42	169.67	3867	53.26	37.70
	< 30 Days	416	177.10	176	145.91	154.11	240	199.98	110.43
2007	**30 to 60 Days**	252	179.80	130	236.23	177.09	122	119.67	162.74
	> 60 Days	87	335.11	47	501.23	342.41	40	139.92	78.19
	< 30 Days	608	107.88	358	92.22	95.22	250	130.32	121.48
2008	**30 to 60 Days**	1057	123.70	924	130.73	189.64	133	74.92	54.79
	> 60 Days	393	251.04	273	293.12	211.21	120	155.31	128.07
	< 30 Days	1698	58.05	760	43.95	52.18	938	69.47	114.61
2009	**30 to 60 Days**	752	90.19	486	108.81	165.62	266	56.15	72.13
	> 60 Days	18	52.26	18	52.26	1.56	0	-	-

Delivery Year	Time to Delivery	Total Number of Opportunities	Mean of all Arbitrage Profits	# of Short Arbitrage Opportunities	Mean of Short Arbitrage Profits	Standard Deviation of Arbitrage Profits	# of Long Arbitrage Opportunities	Mean of Long Arbitrage Profits	Standard Deviation of Arbitrage Profits
	< 30 Days	1154	110.83	654	140.92	175.78	500	71.48	67.84
2010	**30 to 60 Days**	675	60.71	405	65.58	58.86	270	53.41	82.41
	> 60 Days	0	-	0	-	-	0	-	-
	< 30 Days	793	67.85	480	55.06	49.06	313	87.46	93.25
2011	**30 to 60 Days**	794	84.34	338	49.07	56.56	456	110.49	106.00
	> 60 Days	2116	92.82	1894	85.55	73.32	222	154.82	127.64
	< 30 Days	177	153.04	174	155.65	115.88	3	1.68	0.80
2012	**30 to 60 Days**	302	144.40	271	158.95	189.74	31	17.21	12.84
	> 60 Days	217	72.67	192.00	68.68	69.88	25	103.35	51.06

Table 5: Transaction Costs as 1% of the Futures and Spot

Delivery Year	Time to Delivery	Total Number of Opportunities	Mean of all Arbitrage Profits	# of Short Arbitrage Opportunities	Mean of Short Arbitrage Profits	Standard Deviation of Arbitrage Profits	# of Long Arbitrage Opportunities	Mean of Long Arbitrage Profits	Standard Deviation of Arbitrage Profits
2005	< 30 Days	17	26.12	0	-	0	17	26.11891	15.96432215
	30 to 60 Days	1444	11.83	0	-	0	1444	11.83091281	7.15778476
	> 60 Days	0	-	0	-	0	0	0	0
2006	< 30 Days	776	25.52	35	43.76	35.92	741	24.65833873	23.01315105
	30 to 60 Days	5052	40.35	46	16.93	8.75	5006	40.56704165	21.47020884
	> 60 Days	3061	50.30	36	407.75	167.91	3025	46.05030315	33.30232104
2007	< 30 Days	401	159.06	162	132.83	155.57	239	176.842811	110.3550032
	30 to 60 Days	224	176.85	125	220.46	174.56	99	121.7885727	170.1819013
	> 60 Days	81	335.09	47	477.48	341.72	34	138.2567947	61.28548508
2008	< 30 Days	496	113.00	283	96.27	95.00	213	135.2203965	118.1715202
	30 to 60 Days	873	128.02	750	139.09	199.79	123	60.5270961	54.17899709
	> 60 Days	381	234.39	273	268.56	209.26	108	148.0203126	125.5882288

Delivery Year	Time to Delivery	Total Number of Opportunities	Mean of all Arbitrage Profits	# of Short Arbitrage Opportunities	Mean of Short Arbitrage Profits	Standard Deviation of Arbitrage Profits	# of Long Arbitrage Opportunities	Mean of Long Arbitrage Profits	Standard Deviation of Arbitrage Profits
2009	< 30 Days	1104	66.69	428	51.52	57.33	676	76.29263587	125.7376559
	30 to 60 Days	510	110.50	313	143.59	182.44	197	57.91983629	77.29774993
	> 60 Days	18	33.43	18	33.43	1.57	0	0	0
2010	< 30 Days	780	128.74	457	167.91	184.98	323	73.31058505	65.3954631
	30 to 60 Days	444	59.18	268	65.13	52.40	176	50.1212821	95.07406885
	> 60 Days	0	-	0	-	-	0	0	0
2011	< 30 Days	449	81.29	263	61.55	42.17	186	109.2059931	89.00891592
	30 to 60 Days	476	103.74	147	68.41	52.18	329	119.5248325	103.5095386
	> 60 Days	1688	83.27	1508	74.07	70.97	180	160.341015	120.6454184
2012	< 30 Days	152	145.57	152	145.57	108.81	0	0	0
	30 to 60 Days	216	169.81	210	174.55	196.71	6	4.06963	1.336967736
	> 60 Days	164	61.78	145	56.90	71.91	19	99.03132158	27.90720377

If either $F_t-(S_te^{(r-q)\tau}+TC)$ or $S_te^{(r-q)\tau}-TC-F_t$ is negative there is arbitrage opportunity. If $F_t-(S_te^{(r-q)\tau}+TC)$ is positive, there is a long arbitrage opportunity.[1] If $S_te^{(r-q)\tau}-TC-F_t$ is positive then there is a short arbitrage opportunity. Tables 3–5 show the summary of the arbitrage opportunities.

At the 0.5% TC level, there are 11821 short, 31072 long arbitrage opportunities. At the 0.5% TC level, the number of short arbitrage opportunities is 7726, and the number of long arbitrage opportunities is 18409. The numbers of short and long arbitrage opportunities at 1% TC level are 5666 and 13141 respectively. There are far more long arbitrage opportunities than short arbitrage opportunities at any transaction cost level.

However, the mean of the arbitrage profits are higher for short arbitrage opportunities. For example at the 1% TC level, the mean for short arbitrage is 116.51 TRY, the mean for the long arbitrage is 51.39 TRY (the mean of all opportunities is 71.01). When the constraints on short selling are considered, this result suggests that although there are more underpriced futures in the market, arbitrage profits are only possible for short arbitrage.

The figures in the tables also suggest that the mispricing is related with time to maturity of the futures contract. The number of mispricings are generally higher when there are 30–60 days to maturity. The trading volume increases as the delivery month approaches. There are more opportunities in months prior to delivery month than delivery months despite the fact that the volume is highest in delivery month.

The results also show that the market for the ISE-100 futures matured over time. 2007 and 2008 are crisis periods and trading volume decreased in these years, hence the number of arbitrage opportunities is limited in these years. However, the number of opportunities in years 2009, 2010, 2011 and 2012 are far less the number in 2005 and 2006.

5. Conclusions

In this article we find that in the delisted ISE-100 futures contract, there is substantial underpricing. However, because of the limitations on short selling in the spot market, exploiting arbitrage opportunities from underpricing is highly unlikely. However, although there are fewer overpriced futures, the mean of profits generated from short arbitrage positions are much higher. This suggests that this

1 We named arbitrage positions with respect to the position to be taken in the futures market. If the arbitrage opportunity requires a long position in the futures we have long arbitrage opportunity. If a short position in the futures is required there is a short arbitrage opportunity.

contract provided exploitable short arbitrage opportunities. These results are in line with many previous studies on other markets and futures contracts.

Pricing inefficiency and poor hedge performance provided by the futures are the most cited determinants of a futures contract's failure. Most of the other factors which have been thought to be important factors for the failure of futures contracts are not relevant to the failure of ISE-100 futures. Two almost identical futures started trading on the same day, on the same market and trade on the same platform. Therefore, probably one the reasons for the ISE-100 contract's low trading volume and eventual failure is its lack of price efficiency.

References

Brenner, M., Subrahmanyam, M. G., & Uno, J. (1990). Arbitrage opportunities in the Japanese stock and futures markets. *Financial Analysts Journal*, 14–24.

Brorsen, B. W., & Fofana, N. F. (2001). Success and failure of agricultural futures contracts. *Journal of Agribusiness*, *19*(2), 129–146.

Chung, Y. P. (1991). A transactions data test of stock index futures market efficiency and index arbitrage profitability. *The Journal of Finance*, *46*(5), 1791–1809.

Cornell, B. (1985). Taxes and the pricing of stock index futures: Empirical results. *Journal of Futures Markets*, *5*(1), 89–101.

Cornell, B., & French, K. R. (1983). The pricing of stock index futures.*Journal of Futures Markets*, *3*(1), 1–14.

Economides, N., & Siow, A. (1985). *Liquidity and the success of futures markets* (No. 118). Center for the Study of Futures Markets, Columbia Business School.

Figlewski, S. (1984). Explaining the early discounts on stock index futures: The case for disequilibrium. *Financial Analysts Journal*, *40*(4), 43–47.

Leamer, E. E. (1983). Let's take the con out of econometrics. *The American Economic Review*, *73*(1), 31–43.

Lo, A. W., & MacKinlay, A. C. (1990). Data-snooping biases in tests of financial asset pricing models. *Review of financial studies*, *3*(3), 431–467.

McMillan, D. G., & Ülkü, N. (2009). Persistent mispricing in a recently opened emerging index futures market: Arbitrageurs invited. *Journal of Futures Markets*, *29*(3), 218–243.

Modest, D. M., & Sundaresan, M. (1983). The relationship between spot and futures prices in stock index futures markets: Some preliminary evidence. *Journal of Futures Markets*, *3*(1), 15–41.

Saunders, E. M., & Mahajan, A. (1988). An empirical examination of composite stock index futures pricing. *Journal of Futures Markets, 8*(2), 211–228.

Yadav, P. K., & Pope, P. F. (1994). Stock index futures mispricing: profit opportunities or risk premia?. *Journal of Banking & Finance, 18*(5), 921–953.

Esra Ciğerci*

The Relationship between Market Oriented Approach and Supply Chain Management within the Scope of Evolving Competition Concept

1. Introduction

In today's world, developments in the economical, social, technological, etc. areas have not only led markets to become globalised, but also led competition to become more difficult and complicated. Efforts of change and development in businesses' merely traditional functions, for example in production, technology or quality, are not decent any more (Karahan and Varinli, 2002). Therefore, businesses have been facing the difficulty of finding and searching for different methods to develop effective strategies and to achieve competitive supremacy. The businesses that achieve supremacy both in the national and global fields depends upon the fact that they supply the increasing demands and desires of the customers in a different and economic way than their opponents do. As well, they can meet these demands and wishes and, more importantly, they create new demands and wishes too. This situation forces businesses to be more flexible, creative, and innovative (Papatya, 2006). The "Big fish eats little fish" concept, which was true for the competition once, has given place to the "Fast fish eats slow fish" concept. The businesses which are faster in terms of supplying the demands and wishes of the customers are now more successful than their opponents. Achieving this goal is only possible with a market oriented supply chain management.

2. Supply Chain Management Concept

Supply chain management has its roots in stock management studies of the 1950s. In addition, the supply chain management concept came out when Chrysler had turned the purchased material from raw material into a product, which is called material flow management. With the passing years, supply chain studies have turned into supply chain coordination problem analysis, modeling of integrating knowledge in supply chain, modeling the supply contracts and the demand

* Afyon Kocatepe University / Bayat Vocational School, ebilmez@aku.edu.tr

forecasts, and modeling the product design integration with supply chain management (Kağnıcıoğlu, 2007). Supply chain management refers to the coordination and integration of material, knowledge, and finance into a net which is formed of suppliers, producers, distributors, and customers (Lee, 2000). Supply chain management includes coordinating the products' flow from suppliers to manufacturers and from manufacturers to distributors within the chain and also sharing the information of sales-forecasting, sales-dates, promotions, etc. among all members of the chain (Yüksel, 2002). Accordingly, it is possible to say that the supply chain consists of an integrated operations row. Integrated Supply Chain Management is, on the other hand, defined as the management of all processes which are essential to providing value to customers by putting them in the centre. The most important objectives of integrated supply chain management are speeding up the product development studies, increasing the quality, minimising the costs of products, and meeting the needs of the market on time. The main reason of the Amazon.com and Dell's success, for example, is to gain a competitive advantage by carrying out integrated supply chain management perfectly. Apart from these companies, Ford Motor Company, Intel, Cisco and Whirlpool are also among the businesses that successfully implement integrated supply chain management (Johnson & Weinstein, 2004). The significance of supply chain management has increased after having find out the secret of success of all these companies. One of the reasons that increased this significance is that an effective coordination system reduces the cost in today's competitive environment (Chandra & Kumar, 2000). The fact that companies run in coordination with the suppliers and the customers and they carry out the supply chain management operations successfully helps not only in reducing the costs, but providing a competitive advantage as well. Forming an integrated supply chain is highly important to facilitate this coordination, especially for companies which are internationally in service.

3. Market Orientation Concept

Serving to customers was considered fairly enough for many years in order to gain a competitive advantage. However, globalisation-the new business fact of 21st century-has created global trade, new technologies, and converging customer needs. The changing market environment and the increasing constraints in this environment has changed the role of marketing. As a result, marketing needs to be designed as a philosophy that controls the whole organisation and a management function now. Not only serving to customers, but also having them by creating values has become important in the long term and the need of adopting this as a responsibility which spreads out the whole organisation has come out (Yüksel, 2007). So, this necessity has led the "Market Orientation" concept to come out and develop. Market orientation which has various definitions by different researchers can be described shortly as the, "implementation of modern marketing approach on the entire business" (Min, 2001). When the studies about market orientation are analysed, it is clearly seen that a new model of scale was developed in the studies by three groups of researchers (Kohli & Jaworski 1990; Jaworski & Kohli, 1993; Narver & Slater 1990; 1994; Deshpande, Farley & Webster, 1993) and that these studies has lead the other studies. Market Orientation, which is knowledge-based and which has market knowledge fundamentally, was analysed in different perspectives in the studies. For example, some of the studies (Akimova, 2000; Jaworski & Kohli, 1993; Avlonitis & Gounaris, 1997; Hooley & Beracs, 1997) brought market orientation an administrative perspective. Accordingly, market orientation is described as, "gathering all the information related to change in customers' current and future needs, delivering this information to all units in the organization and assigning and implementing the response to the market in accordance with this information." On the other hand, researchers (Baker & Sinkula; Deshpande, Farley & Webster, 1993; Pelham & Wilson, 1996) who take Narver and Slater's study (1990) have approached the subject in a cultural way. From the cultural perspective, market orientation is defined as, "adopting customer orientation and facilitating coordination in order to get competitive advantage by creating superior customer value." Reuekert (1992), on the other hand, who takes market orientation in a strategic perspective explains the concept as, "gathering information from customers, developing strategies by using these information in order to meet the customer needs and implementing the strategy that can meet the customer needs best." According to Reuekert's approach (1992), administrators should gather information from customers and interpret this information in order to be market oriented. In other words, a strategic approach requires one to determine the needs of customers and to develop proper strategies accordingly to satisfy the customers (Naktiyok, 2003). In their studies Deshpande, Farley and Webster (1993) described market orientation as, "a body of beliefs that puts the customer profits into uppermost." According to Deshpande, Farley and Webster (1993), Day (1994) and Sinkula's (1994) studies, describe market orientation as "creating customer value by taking all stakeholders into account in order to profit." According to all of these definitions, being customer-driven has been the most important part of market orientation. Still, in order to perform market orientation successfully, businesses have to take other stakeholders such as opponents and suppliers as well as customers into consideration, as stated in previous studies (Özer, Koçak & Çelik, 2006).

4. Supply Chain Management and Marketing

The fact that competition has increased and markets have become global has increased the options for customers on one side and has approached the products to the services in terms of performance on the other. Besides, buyers now have become active in markets where sellers once were effective (Karasu, 2006). Based upon these developments, there have been changes in the marketing management concept, as well. These changes in marketing management show signs of the importance that is given to the supply chain management studies. These signs can be outlined as (Dedeoğlu, 2001):

- The change in customer concept within supply chain,
- That the change concept between the buyers and the sellers giving its way to mutual interaction and relationship between all of the members in the value chain,
- Increasing efforts for holding the current customers rather than gaining new ones.

In today's world, businesses must offer the highest value to customers in order to gain a competitive advantage. In order to carry out this framework completely and as required, the business should have good relations with their suppliers and other resellers (Min & Mentzer, 2000). Businesses now structure themselves according to customers' expectations and constantly decrease delivery times. While fixed investments were considered as the most important part of the supply chain in the past, a customer oriented approach is seen as the heart of a competitive environment now. There are various subjects that need to be regarded to create a successful and customer oriented supply chain (Aydın, 2005):

- Receiving orders is only a part of the customer need. Businesses have to keep their promises by making the delivery according to the customer's choice of time and place, not according to the company.
- Timing is one of the most important factors that provides for a competitive advantage in the market. In order for the businesses to meet the needs of the customers right on time, a nonstop information and supply flow is vital in the supply chain.
- Cost is another significant factor. In order to reduce the cost of the last product, businesses should minimise their expenses.
- Reducing the length of time for the design process and the service quality are also important, because these reduce the length of time to meet the customer needs.

In this respect, it may be helpful for businesses to have a market oriented approach with the aim of creating, maintaining, and increasing the buyer-seller relations in the supply chain.

5. Creating Value Through Supply Chain

Today, supply chains are competing, not brands or businesses. Therefore, businesses now focus on the customer and value rather than product/service when they are creating their marketing strategies. With the increasing importance of distribution chains, supply chains have become the most effective means for creating the real value with regard to customers in order to apply marketing strategies.

5.1 The Value Concept and the Customer Value

The value concept on which there has been a debate for many years has many different meanings in the literature. These differences are the results of using this concept in various fields. The difference in using the value concept has reflected upon the management literature, as well. For instance, financiers asserted shareholder value, while environment theoreticians asserted interest groups value and marketers asserted customer value. The Value concept, which was formulised as functionality/cost and associated only with the price in the beginning, was later used together with the market orientation concept (Akyıldız & Tuna, 2007). The fact that customer value stands out in marketing stems from that the customer orientation is the fundamental component of market orientation (Slatter & Narver, 1995). Value, in Porter's (1999) definition is "the desire which makes customers make payment willingly for the products and services," it is pointed out that value is a body of benefits discerned by the customers (Akyıldız & Tuna, 2007). Accordingly, the value effects an individual's collaboration level, selective perception, and the power of interpreting the knowledge as well as determining his/her vision and playing an important role in choosing and deciding among alternatives, solving the problems and conflicts. Thus, values help individuals make a choice among behaviour patterns that reflect their interests, motivations, needs, desires, wishes, aims, and attitudes. Besides, values function as a standard which determine the ideal behaviour pattern and as an object or a situation which individuals try to obtain (Naktiyok, 2003).

5.2 Creating Customer Value within Supply Chain

When the materials are transferred from the suppliers to the final customers, they go through different phases and they are added values in this process. The aim of the supply chain is to maximise this value. The value created by the supply chain reflects the difference between the final product's value to the customer and the supply chain's effort of meeting the customer needs (Kağnıcıoğlu, 2007).

The value created by the members of the supply chain is reflected not only on the customers, but also on the other stakeholders within channel limits. For instance, in order to facilitate the flow of the products from the producers to final customers, a specific percentage of the retail price goes to the channel members. While the value presented to the customer at the end of distribution channel actions is between 25%–50%, the value created by advertisements is less then 3% and the value created by personal sales is less then 6% (Sudharshan, 1998). Sudharshan (1998) explained two different ways of creating customer value. Accordingly, businesses create values by either forming a cost advantage or providing more benefits to customers than their opponents do. These two options are also applicable for distribution channels.

Cost Advantage: The value created by costs in the distribution channel actions provides an opportunity with businesses and creates an advantage of competition. For example, Gallo-a wine producing company-has more of a cost advantage in distribution than its opponents by choosing supermarkets instead of local dealers that sell high cost drinks. However, Gallo had to concentrate on advertisements in order to attract the customers, after supermarkets started to become less effective than other local dealers that sell alcoholic drinks for the wine customers.

This led to a rapid impact and supermarkets agreed to collaborate with Gallo with less of a profit margin than their opponents. The cost advantage can be ensured through a scale economy that is a result of distributing lots of products through the same channel. For example, GE and Whirlpool have been able to reduce their distribution costs by offering a big-scaled range of products (fridges, washing machines, dish washers, etc.) to supermarkets (Sudharshan, 1998). Making profits from a cost advantage is much more possible for the companies producing standard products and for the sectors that are gradually changing.

Since environmental conditions are very unstable in global markets, this redounds on the customer needs and desires, which makes it difficult to gain a cost advantage for most businesses (Ülgen & Mirze, 2006).

Unique Customer Benefit: Through distribution actions customers may be provided with unique benefits which are generally high cost and hard to imitate by the opponents. For example, Hanes succeeded to provide favour to its customers with its women socks named L'Eggs. Hanes producing woman, men, and children clothes considerably developed the comfort in purchasing by creating a unique system for distributing socks to supermarkets. They were able to present more value both to the customers and the retailers through innovative packaging, displays, and a direct delivery program for supermarkets (Sudharshan, 1998). The mutual relationship among the channel members and information sharing is also an important point for creating value in the supply chain. Many companies see the suppliers and the local dealers with which they have business relations with every day as businesses that need to be negotiated and that are risky for information sharing.

In fact, specialties of these collaboration partners, powers and attitudes are important factors which considerably determine the quality of the product or the service offered to the final customer. The real competition is not the one with the collaboration partners, but with the other value chains. Thus, the strong link of the supply chain is definitely mistaken if it chooses this power not to improve the total strength of the chain, but to improve only its own (Yüksel, 2002). In this respect, the understanding of information sharing bringing suppliers competitive strength should be adopted first. Information sharing is limited among businesses in two aspects: (i) Information includes the operations only between two businesses, (ii) Information is shared among the businesses which have direct relations in the supply chain. The reason for this is that businesses usually think that information sharing causes them to lose their powers. This mentality causes problems for the information flow in the supply chain (Croom, Romano & Giannakis, 2000). On the other hand, not sharing some important information sets the members of the supply chain back from working coordinatively and meeting the markets rapidly, which decreases the value presented to the customers.

6. Supply Chain with Market Oriented Perspective

In order to increase their performances in competitive markets, businesses have turned towards relation-oriented marketing strategies by gradually drawing away from business-oriented marketing strategies. While business have multiple relations with various stakeholder groups such as suppliers and mediators on the one hand; they carry on their actions on the other (Winklhofer, Pressey & Tzokas, 2006). The degree of success that the business gain in competitive markets may change according to the importance they give their relations with these stakeholders. Therefore, supply chain managers spend much more time on building up relations with the suppliers and manage this relation than they do on buying products and services. The main reason for this is that the relations with the suppliers affect the quality of the product and the service that is presented to the customers (Wisner & Stanley, 2008).

The businesses which have constant communication with the suppliers, care about information sharing and which prefer working collaboratively with its supplier beyond a purchasing relation become much more successful. The significance of the relations with suppliers is also suggested through various studies. For example, Shin, Collier and Wilson (2000) studied the impacts of focusing on supplier relations on the performance of the suppliers and on the buyers' competitive supremacy. In the study, terms such as long-term relationships, collaboration, supplier's contribution to develop a new product, diminished supplier numbers and performance quality were among the important determinants. As a result of the study it was found that focusing on supplier relationships have a positive impact on supply chain performance.[2]

Kasouf and Celuch (1997) did research analysing the relationship of the original part producers in the automotive industry with their suppliers and assessed the importance of the relationship with the customers and the other companies in the industry. At the end of the study it was found that companies with strong supplier relations were more positive about their own smaller and industrial skills. It was also found that these companies see rapid technology change in a better way when compared to the other companies that have weak supplier relations. Yau et al. (2000), on the other hand, assessed supplier relations and the effects of this on business performance. 4000 businesses which are located in Honk Kong and China and have 50 or more employees were chosen for the study and 573 of these companies provided feedback. They searched the impact of market orientation in supplier-producer relationship and the contributions of this on business performance and they used four components for this study. These components are determined as trust, empathy, bonding, and reciprocity. It was seen that these components were important especially in the manufacturing sector and from these components the most significant element in terms of supplier-producer relations was trust.

In order to gain a competitive advantage in today's global markets, business which have understood the importance of the supply chain management have started to attach more importance to supplier relations. It is important to have good relations with the suppliers who play an important role especially in purchasing numbers. Toyota and Honda, as a good example of this, are known for their suppliers and their strong business values with their suppliers (Winklhofer et al., 2006). In highly competitive markets, businesses need to develop supply

---

2 (Also look: K. de Ruyter and M. Wetzels, "Determinants of a Relational Exchange Orientation in the Marketing-Manufacturing Interface: An Emprical Investigation", *Journal of Management Studies*, Vol. 37(2), 2000, sf. 257–276; K. Woo and C. Ennew, "Business-to-Business Relationship Quality: An IMP Interaction-Based Conceptualization and Measurement", *European Journal of Marketing*, Vol. 38 (9/10), 2004, sf. 1252–1271)

chain management processes which are ruled by market orientation, in order to become more flexible against constantly changing environmental conditions and to meet the customer needs and desires faster. In order to reach this aim they should try to find ways to strengthen the relations with the suppliers.

7. Market Orientation and Impact of Supplier Relations on Business Performance

Although many studies related to supplier relations exist in the literature, there are a limited number of studies which are related with market orientation and approach the subject from this perspective. In fact, many studies have clearly shown that market orientation has positive impacts on business profitability (Reukert, 1992; Slater and Narver, 1994; Webster, 1992), sales personnel (Siguaw, Brown and Widing, 1994), and business performance (Narver and Slater, 1990; Kohli and Jaworski, 1990; Jaworski and Kohli, 1993; Slater and Narver, 2000; Min, 2001; Blankson, 2006).

Narver and Slater (1990), who conducted one of the primary studies in this field, found that market orientation has a considerable impact on profitability. Other studies also support Narver and Slater's (1990) study by revealing that market orientation can create positive effects on business performance in different aspects. For example, there were also studies that suggest market orientation creates a positive effect on businesses' financial performance, such as profitability of the assets, sales and new product success, quality of the product and profitability in small businesses and successful product innovations (Siguaw et al., 1998).[3] Therefore, the potential effect of market orientation on channel relations cannot be overlooked. It is possible to say that businesses which are ruled by market orientation will be more successful in channel relations and they will perform better in the supply chain. In the studies, even if they were limited, the potential of achieving greater success through supply chain management that is integrated with market orientation was found. Indeed, a dual relationship can be discussed between market orientation and supply chain management. Market orientation helps companies build up strong relations with suppliers (Martin & Grbac, 2003). Besides, effective supply chain management can be a means for businesses to improve performance and develop market oriented actions, because an effective

3 (Also look: Kwaku Atuahene-Gima, "Market Orientation and Innovation", Journal of Business Research, Vol. 35, February 1996, 93–103; Alfred M. Pelham, David T. Wilson, "A Longitudinal Study of the Impact of Market Structure, Firm Structure, Strategy and Market orientation Culture on Dimensions of Small Firm Performance", Journal of the Academy of Marketing Science, Vol. 24 (1), 1996, 27–43)

supply chain supports all channel members to work in an integrated way and to conduct information sharing. Market oriented businesses are better at achieving this aim. In the conducted researches, this idea is supported. For example, Siguaw, Simpson and Baker (1998) conducted a well known study in this subject that explored the impacts of market orientation on channel performance. At the end of the study it was found that market orientation has direct and positive effects on trust, collaboration, and channel performance. In the study it was also revealed that market orientation has a positive impact on building and maintaining long term relationships with the customers and the suppliers. It was suggested that the market orientation of the supplier increases the market orientation and the performance of the distributor, and positively effects the attachment between the distributor and the customer (Siguaw et al., 1998). In the table below, the supplier and market orientation relationship is presented. Accordingly, gathering information about the suppliers, the customers and the opponents, as well as using this information in the most effective way are highly important in terms of supplier relations. However, gathering information is not merely enough to have an effective relationship with the suppliers. The gathered information needs to be shared with the other departments (marketing, manufacturing, etc) and then coordinated (Martin & Grbac, 2003).

Figure 1: Market Orientation in Business and The Impact of Supplier Relations on Business Performance

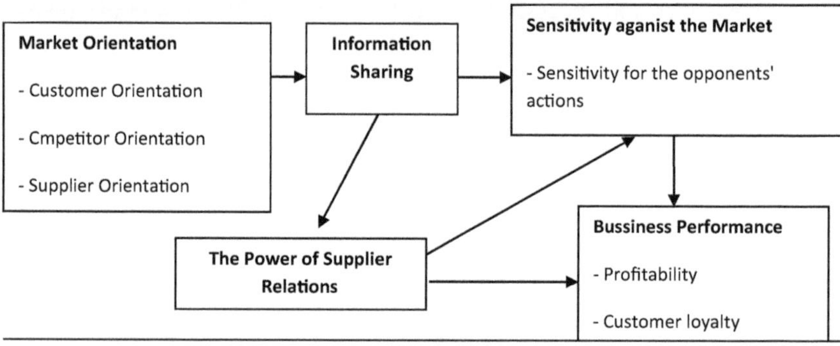

Reference: Adapted from Martin and Grbac, 2003: 26

Lambert and Cooper (2000), on the other hand, suggested that the variety of the information shared among the organisations and its frequency of updating have a strong impact on supplier relations. However, in other studies (Ganesan, 1994; Morgan & Hunts, 1994; Mohr, Fisher & Nevin, 1996; Sirdeshmukh,

Singh & Sabol, 2002), it was stated by emphasising the importance of finding the right partner in the supply chain that collaborating with a company, which does not share the same goals and purposes and has no attachment, causes only a waste of both time and effort. When successful examples are compared with the less successful or unsuccessful ones in terms of the supply chain, it was found that communication skills and information sharing are important factors for this success (Mason, Doyle & Wong., 2006). Having strong relations leads to harmony among the strategic partners and increases the ability to create and present values. Thus, the channel communication becomes an important element that enables the implementation of market orientation in the supply chain. Cost and price advantages that a supplier obtains naturally redound on the profitability. With an advantage of better understanding the customer needs a supplier that can develop more effective marketing and management abilities. In addition, the failure risk of the product presented by the supplier, who knows the needs of his producer well, reduces, and this effects the profitability of the supplier positively by redounding on the costs (Kalwani & Narayandas, 1995).

8. Conclusions and Suggestions

Within a supply chain, it is possible to say that the market orientation of the businesses are affected by sector aspects, competition level, and the stage that market orientation has in the chain. It is clearly seen that information sharing is highly needed to keep up-to-date and more importance is attached to supplier-producer collaboration to keep up with the change, especially in sectors such as automotive and electronics. Even though it is assessed positively that supplier-producer collaboration is seen in comparatively developing and innovating new products, much more is needed to gain a competitive advantage. For example, the collaboration among the members of the supply chain should be enhanced in two ways as both supplier-oriented and customer-oriented by concentrating on customer relations management and customer service management. It is also known that reducing the costs of the collaboration among the members of the supply chain, increasing the product quality and increasing the productivity and effectiveness of the supply chain as a whole is helpful. Thanks to information sharing of businesses that are market oriented in the supply chain, it came out that businesses can keep-up-to date faster, catch up with the changes more easily, become successful in finding new customers, and have long-term relationships. On the other hand, most of the businesses cannot fully perform the marketing as an organisation culture, since they do not lean towards information sharing. Because adequate information sharing cannot be performed, various difficulties are faced in providing coordination. As for the main reason of all these difficulties, it is considered that professional management incompetencies, especially in small and medium businesses, and also not applying the marketing concept as an organisation culture play an important role.

As a result, it is important that the managers perceive of the supply chain concept well, determine the privileges related to production and marketing, and make good decisions about the strategic shareholders. Systems need to be developed in order to follow market needs and the changes in demands should be controlled constantly. Open information sharing should be supported among the supply chain shareholders through focusing on customer relations management. To reach this aim, traditional management must be changed to be suitable for a modern management concept. Especially the significance of information sharing has a great importance in the modern management concept. Today's leading companies try to transport real-time information to the other customers as well. They take their customer relations to another dimension by transparenting their actions and provide integrated services in terms of customer loyalty. Therefore, market orientation can be used as an effective means for the supply chains to transform into the desired structure and to become a value chain.

References

Akimova, I. (2000). Development of Market Orientation and Competitiveness of Ukrainian Firms. *European Journal of Marketing, 34*(9/10), 1128–1148.

Akyıldız, M. ve Tuna O. (2007). Lojıstik Değer ve Ek Değer: Bir Odak Grup Çalışması. *Ege Akademik Bakış Dergisi*, Vol. 7 No. 2, 653–667.

Baker, W. E., & Sinkula, J. M. (1999). Learning Orientation, Market Orientation, and Innovation: Integrating and Extending Models of Organizational Performance. *Journal of Market-Focused Management*, *4*(4), 295–308.

Blankson, C.; Motwani, J. G. ve Levenburg, N. M. (2006). Understanding The Patterns of Market Orientation Among Small Businesses. *Marketing Intelligence & Planning*, Vol. 24, No. 6, 572–590.

Chandra, C ve Kumar, S. (2000). Supply Chain Management in Theory and Practice: A Passin Fad or Fundamental Change, *Industrial Management & Data Systems*, Vol. 100, No. 3, 100–114.

Croom, S.; Romano, P., Giannakis, M., (March 2000). Supply Chain Management: An Analytical Framework for Literature Review. *European Journal of Purchasing & Supply Management*, V.6(1), 67–83.

Day, G. S. (1994). The Capabilities of Market-Driven Organizations. *Journal of Marketing*, 58(4), 37–52.

Dedeoğlu, A. (2001). Pazarlama Bilimindeki Gelişmeler Işığında İnternet Ortamında Pazarlama ve Tüketici Eğilimleri Araştırması. *Doktora Tezi*, İzmir: Dokuz Eylül.

Deshpande, R., Farley, J.U., & Webster, F.E. (1993). Corporate Culture, Customer Orientation, and Innovativeness. *Journal of Marketing*, 57(1), 23–37.

Deshpande, R. (1999). *Developing A Market Orientation*, London: Sage Publication

Ganesan, S. (1994). Determinants of Long-Term Orientation in Buyer-Seller Relationships. *Journal of Marketing*, V.58(2), 1–19.

Gounaris, S. P., & Avlonitis, G. J. (1997, May). Company and Market Correlates of Marketing Orientation Development: An Empirical Investigation. In *26 EMAC Conference* (pp. 20–23).

Hooley, G., & Beracs, J. (1997). Marketing strategies for the 21st century: lessons from the top Hungarian companies. *Journal of Strategic Marketing*, *5*(3), 143–165.

Jaworski, B.J. ve Kohli, A. K. (July 1993). Market Orientation: Antecedents and Consequences. *Journal of Marketing*, Vol. 57, 53–70.

Johnson, W. C. ve Weinstein, A. (2004). *Superior Customer Value in the New Economy*, London: CRC Press.

Kağnıcıoğlu, C. H. (2007). *Tedarik Zinciri Yönetiminde Tedarikçi Seçimi*. Eskişehir: Anadolu Üniversitesi Yayınları, No. 1723.

Kalwani, M.U. ve Narayandas, N., (January 1995). Long-Term Manufacturer-Supplier Relationships: Do They Pay Off for Supplier Firms?, *Journal of Marketing*, Vol. 59, 1–16.

Karahan K. ve Varinli İ. (Ocak-Şubat 2002). Pazar Yönlülük ve Bankacılık Sektöründe Bir Uygulama. *Pazarlama Dünyası Dergisi*. Yıl:16, Sayı:91, 4–11.

Karasu, I. F. (2006). Tedarik Zinciri Yönetiminin Yapısı ve İşleyişi. *Eskişehir Anadolu Üniversitesi Sosyal Bilimler Enstitüsü Yayımlanmamış Y.Lisans Tezi.*

Kasouf, C. J. ve Celuch, K. G. (1997). Interfirm Relationships in the Supply Chain: the Small Supplier's View, *Industrial Marketing Management*, Vol. 26 (6), 475–486.

Kohli, A. K. ve Jaworski, Bernard J. (April 1990). Market Orientation: The Construct, Research Propositions, And Managerial İmplications. *Journal of Marketing*, Vol. 54 (2), 1–18.

Lambert, D. M.; Cooper, M. C. (2000). Issues in Supply Chain Management. *Industrial Marketing Managemet*, V.29, 65–83.

Lee, H. (Semtember/October 2000). Creating Value Though Supply Chain Integration. *Supply Chain Management Rewiev.*, V.4(4), 30–37.

Martin, J. H. ve Grbac, B. (2003). Using Supply Chain Management to Leverge A Firm's Market Orientation. *Industrial Marketing Management*, Vol. 32, 25–38.

Mason, K.; Doyle, P. ve Wong, V. (2006). Market Orientation and Quasi-Integration: Adding Value Through Relationships. *Industrial Marketing Management*, Vol. 35 (2), 140–155.

Mohr, J. J.; Fisher, R. J. ve Nevin, J. R. (1996). Collaborative Relationships: Moderating Effects of Integration and Control, *Journal of Marketing*, V.60(3), 103–115.

Morgan R. M. ve Hunts, S. D. (1994). The Commitment-Trust Theory of Relationship Marketing. *Journal of Marketing*, V.58(3), 20–38.

Min, S. (December 2001). A Market Orientation in Supply Chain Management. The University of Tennessee, Knoxville-Doktora Tezi.

Min, S. ve *Mentzer*, J. T. (2000). The Role of Marketing in Supply Chain Management. *International Journal of Physical Distribution & Logistics Management*, Vol. 30, Iss. 9, 765–787.

Naktiyok, A. (Ocak-Haziran 2003). Yönetici Değerleri ve Pazar Yönlülük Üzerine Bir Uygulama. *Erciyes Üniversitesi İktisadi ve İdari Bilimler Fakültesi Dergisi*, Sayı: 20, 95–116.

Narver, J. C. ve Slater, S. F. (October 1990). The Effect of a Market Orientation on Business Profitability. *Journal of Marketing*, V.54(4), 20–35.

Özer, A., Koçak, A. ve Çelik, O. (May 2006). Determinants of Market Orientation in Accounting Firms. *Marketing Intelligence & Planning*, Vol: 24, No: 6, 591–607.

Papatya, N. (Temmuz 2006). İşletmelerde Sıradışı Rekabet İçin Yenilikçi Pazarlama Yaklaşımı / Başarılı Bir Örgüt Modeli Gelişti. *Pazarlama Dünyası Dergisi*, Y. 20, S. 4, 42–46.

Pelham, A.M. and Wilson, D.T. (1996), A Longitudinal Study of the Impact of Market Structure, Firm Structure, Strategy and Market Orientation Culture on Dimension of Small Firm Performance, *Journal of the Academy of Marketing Science*, 27–43.

Reukert R. (1992). Developing a Market Orientation: An Organizational Strategy Perspective. *International Journal of Research in Marketing.* Vol: 9, No: 3, 225–245.

Shin, H.; Collier, D.A. ve Wilson, D.D. (2000). Supply Management Orientation and Supplier/buyer Performance. *Journal of Operations Management*, Vol. 18(3), 317–333.

Siguaw, J. A., Brown, G., & Widing, R. E. (1994). The Influence of the Market Orientation of the Firm on Sales Force Behavior and Attitudes. *Journal of Marketing Research*, 106–116.

Siguaw, J. A.; Simpson, P. M. ve Baker, T. L. (July 1998). Effects of Supplier Market Orientation on Distributor Market Orientation and the Channel Relationship: The Distributor Perspective. *Journal of Marketing*, Vol. 62, 99–111.

Sinkula, J. M. (1994). Market Information Processing and Organizational Learning. *The Journal of Marketing*, 35–45.

Sirdeshmukh, D.; Singh, J. ve Sabol, B. (2002). Consumer Trust, Value and Loyalty in Relational Exchanges. *Journal of Marketing*, V. 66(1), 15–37.

Slater, S. F., & Narver, J. C. (1994, March/April). Market Orientation, Customer Value, and Superior Performance. *Business Horizons*, 37, 22–28.

Slatter, S. F. ve Narver, J. C. (1995). Market Orientation, Customer Value and Superior Performance. *Journal of Marketing*, Vol. 59, 22–28.

Sudharshan, D. (1998). *Marketing Strategy-Relationships, Offerings, Timing & Resource Allocation*, Upper Saddle River, New Jersey: Prentice Hall.

Ülgen, H. ve Mirze, K. (2006). *İşletmelerde Stratejik Yönetim*. İstanbul: Literatür Yayıncılık.

Webster Jr, F. E. (1992). The changing role of marketing in the corporation. *The Journal of Marketing*, 1–17.

Winklhofer, H.; Pressey, A. ve Tzokas, N. (2006). A Cultural Perspective of Relationship Orientation: Using Organisational Culture to Support a Supply Relationship Orientation. *Journal of Marketing Management*, Vol. 22(1), 169–191.

Wisner, J. D. ve Stanley, L. L., (2008). *Process Management Creating Value along the Supply Chain*. USA: Thomson-South-Western.

Yau, O. H.M;. McFetridge, P. R.; Chow, R. P.M.; Lee, J. S.Y.; Sin, L.Y.M.; Tse, A.C.B. (2000). Is relationship marketing for everyone?. *European Journal of Marketing*, Vol. 34 Iss: 9/10, 1111–1127.

Yüksel, B. (2007). *İşletmelerde Pazar Yönlü Kültürel Değişim*. Bursa: Ekin Yayınevi.

Yüksel, H. (2002). Tedarik Zinciri Yönetiminde Bilgi Sistemlerinin Önemi. *Dokuz Eylül Üniversitesi Sosyal Bilimler Enstitüsü Dergisi*, Cillt 4, Sayı 3, 262–263.

Aslı Yenipazarlı[1] & Mustafa Çelik[2]

Does Higher Economic Freedom Lead to Higher Foreign Direct Investment in Emerging Market Economies?: Panel Data Analysis (1995–2013)

Abstract Foreign direct investments (FDI), provide long-term capital inflows into the economy, and bring their technology, management information, innovation, and create employment. FDI contribute to an increase in the economy's capacity. In this context, it is important to attract FDI for all groups of countries, both developed and developing countries in particular. In this study, it is aimed to identify the relationship between foreign direct investment and economic freedom which is one of the effective parameters of the international mobility of foreign direct investment. Twenty one emerging economies constituting the MSCI Emerging Market Index, which is one of the indexes of the Morgan Stanley Global Equity Indexes, are used as a sample. FDI data of those countries is accessed through the statistical database of UNCTAD, UNCTADSTAT. With regard to economic freedom scores of these countries, it has benefited from the Foundation of Heritage Index of Economic Freedom prepared since 1995. In the study covering the period of 1995–2013, yearly, the analyses are done with the method of balanced panel data in E-views program. A positive relationship between FDI and economic freedom has been identified in emerging economies. The analysis proved that higher economic freedom increases a country's ability to attract foreign direct investment. With the econometric model, a contribution has been made about economic freedom and foreign direct investment relationship where the literature about this subject is not so deep yet.

Keywords: Economic Freedom, Foreign Direct Investment, Emerging Market Economies, Panel Data Analysis.

Introduction

In a global world, foreign direct investments, as a part of capital movements have been studied in terms of their effects on economy, or in terms of factors attracting foreign direct investments into an economy. Foreign direct investments are long

---

1 Corresponding author. Assistant professor at Adnan Menderes University, Nazilli Faculty of Economics and Business Administrative Sciences, Department of Economics, İsabeyli, Aydın, Turkey. E-mail: ayenipazarli@adu.edu.tr

2 Lecturer at Celal Bayar University, Manisa, Turkey. E-mail: mustafacelikcbu@gmail.com.

term international capital movements aiming real investments. By means of these investments new employment opportunities emerge, and production knowledge and technology, also global work experience can be transferred.

Especially for developing countries, attracting foreign direct investments is related to different economic, political, legal and technological parameters such as; market size of the country, infrastructure facilities, population, natural resources, low level of labour cost, relatively low costs of factors of production, technological infrastructure, laws, etc. Economic freedom is to be complementary of such parameters by affecting foreign direct investment.

Economic freedom indicators identified in the Heritage Foundation Index are freedom to trade, freedom of investment, financial freedom, freedom of entrepreneurship, monetary freedom, fiscal freedom, government expenditures, property rights, and corruption. All these nine indicators are put into econometric analysis for their effects on foreign direct investments.

According to Gwartney et al. (2014: 1), the main components of economic freedom are personal choice, voluntary exchange coordinated by markets, freedom of entrance to the market, freedom to compete, protection of people, and properties against others. Economic freedom is related to freely choose, to act freely without harming other people (to buy freely or to sell, to save or to invest, etc.). If there is economic freedom in a country people decide how to act, what to produce or how to produce by themselves. Personal property rights will be the reason to freely choose and to use their time and facilities freely (Gwartney and Lawson, 2003: 405). A comprehensive meaning of economic freedom is a structure in which minimum government intervention to the market occurs, free market mechanism leads this structure which maximises personal welfare, and induces the dynamics of economic growth and development (Patry, 2009: 151, cited in Akıncı, Yüce and Yılmaz, 2014: 82).

FDI Stock Changes in the World

The World Investment Report of UNCTAD 2014 is a useful guide to analyse the trend and movements of world investments and their statistics. According to this report in 2013 FDI movement showed a positive 9% increase to 1.45 trillion dollars. This positive trend depends on the improvement in developing countries. The UNCTAD Report also emphasises the role of the instability or crisis in economic indicators on FDI negatively.

Figure 1: FDI Stock Trend In The World Of Country Groups Regarding To Their Development Levels (1995–2013 /million $)

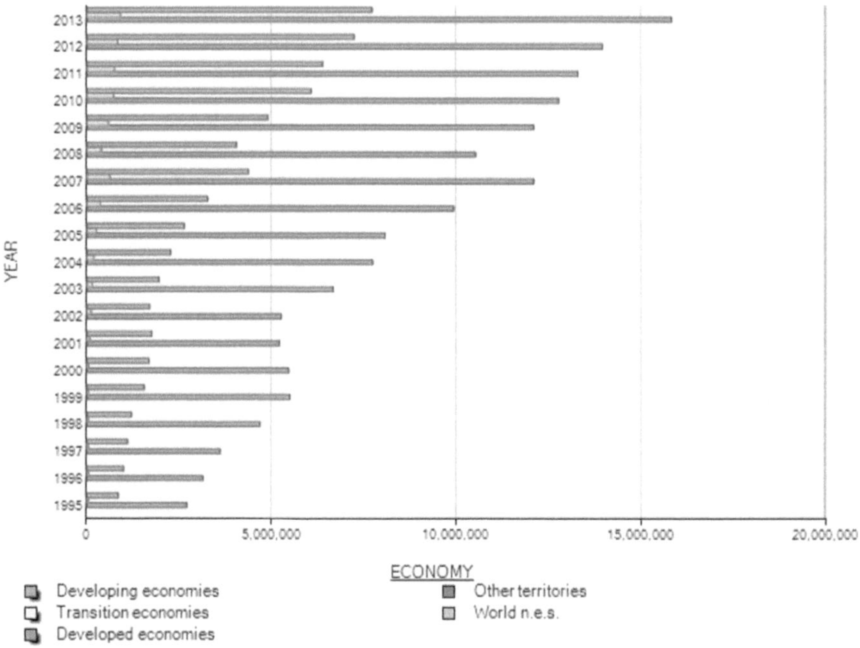

UNCTADSTAT, (2015). Inward & Outward Foreign Direct İnvestment Stock, Annual, 1995–2013. http://unctadstat.unctad.org/wds/TableViewer/tableView.aspx.

Figure 1 emphasises different FDI Stock levels of different country groups in the world. This figures out that mostly developed countries increased their levels of FDI Stock in the world. Second country group has been developing countries and then transition economies follow.

Literature

Bengoa and Sanchez-Rables (2003) studied 18 Latin American countries for the period of 1970–1999 to analyse the relationship of economic freedom, FDI, and economic growth. They found that the economic freedom level of the host country is the positive predictor of FDI of that country. Savaşan and Dursun (2006) divided countries into groups according to classification of the World Bank as low, low-medium, high-medium, countries with high income out of OECD and countries with high income of OECD. They analysed the correlation between economic freedom level and FDI. According to that study, there is a positive and significant correlation between economic freedom and FDI and also economic freedom level is higher in groups with high income than groups with low income. Among the country groups, the difference between FDI and GDP averages is statistically significant for the groups with high income, except for the groups with high income out of OECD and for the groups with high income of OECD. On the other hand, in the study of Pourshahabi et al. (2011) with the OECD countries, it has been found that there is a positive but not significant effect between two variables (from Türen et al., 2011: 11).

Ajide and Eregah (2014), including twelve ECOWAS countries, analysed the correlation between economic freedom components in 1995–2010 and FDI through the panel data method. They predicted the model via the random effects predictor. According to the results, financial freedom is the main variable in attracting FDI. Other main variables are business freedom and property rights. In our study, it is shown that FDI has a 1% significant effect on financial freedom, fiscal freedom and monetary freedom. It also has a 5% significant effect on government spending. Gökmen et al. (2011) studied the regression between economic freedom components and attracting FDI. In the study it is shown that economic freedom components have a 58.1% significant effect on FDI. Among those components, business freedom and labour employment freedom have been the most effective factor group on FDI. Second factor group is fiscal freedom, government spending, property rights, and the freedom from corruption. The most limited and the least effective factor group is trade freedom, monetary freedom, investment freedom, and financial freedom. Foreman (2007) concluded it is possible that FDI will be more interested in an economy in which property rights could be protected more strictly, government interference into the economy could be reduced, and there are policies which will activate foreign capital.

Data and Methodology

The test of the models using balanced panel data analysis method on the value of 21 emerging economies published by the Heritage Foundation between 1995–2013. Those 21 emerging economies are the ones in the Morgan Stanley Global Equity Indexes and MSCI Emerging Markets Index. Those emerging economies are are Brazil, Chile, China, Columbia, The Czech Republic, Egypt, Hungary, India, Indonesia, South Korea, Malaysia, Mexico, Morocco, Peru, The Philippines, Poland, Russia, South Africa, Taiwan, Thailand, and Turkey (MSCI, 2012: 1). The data about FDI have been reached through UNCTAD's database. The 1995–2013 period has been chosen because the data about economic freedom of those countries have been published completely only during that period.

Panel data have been described as "time series of cross-sections or cross-sectional data of time series" (Greene, 2003: 283, 284), which means that horizontal cross-sectional observations such as company, country, and household are also represented by time dimension (Baltagi, 2001: 1). Panel data models are classified as balanced and unbalanced according to the missing data in the panel. Because there is no missing data case in the balanced panel, there are the same number of observations for each horizontal section unit (Çalışkan, 2009: 129).

With the balanced panel data analysis, the effect of economic freedom on FDI has been analysed first and then the effects of each economic freedom components (property rights, financial freedom, business freedom, government spending, monetary freedom, fiscal freedom, trade freedom, investment freedom, freedom from corruption) on FDI (dependent variable). In the second model, the effects of all economic freedom components have been analysed on FDI with only one regression equation.

Econometrically 2 models are tested on variables of FDI and EKO.

Model 1: Equation of the relationship between FDI (foreign direct investment) and (EKO) overall economic freedom.

$$FDI = \alpha i + \beta_1 EKO + ei$$

FDI shows the ratio between the amount of the foreign direct investment stock and the GDP value of the country. It has been found through the data about foreign direct investment over gross domestic product. EKO stands for overall economic freedom value of the country. Economic freedom value is expressed by the overall economic freedom score in the **indices** of economic freedom which the Heritage Foundation has published since 1995. To obtain this value, the arithmetic mean of the index values of nine components (trade freedom, investment freedom, financial freedom, business freedom, monetary freedom, fiscal freedom, government spending, property rights, and the freedom from corruption) has been calculated.

Model 2: equation of the relationship between FDI and the components of economic freedom.

$$FDI = \alpha i + \beta_1 MUK + \beta_2 FIS + \beta_3 GIS + \beta_4 KAH + \beta_5 MAS + \beta_6 PAS + \beta_7 TIS + \beta_8 YAS + \beta_9 YOO + ei$$ [3]

3 FDI = FDI stock value / GDP, MUK = Property rights score, FIS = Financial freedom score, GIS = Business freedom score, KAH = Government spending score, MAS = Monetary freedom, PAS = Fiscal freedom, TIS = Trade freedom score, YAS = Investment freedom score, YOO = Freedom from corruption score.

Table 1: Stationarity Test – Panel Unit Root For FDI

FDI	Levin, Lin and Chu		Im, Pesaran and Shin W		ADF	
	Constant	Constant+ Trend	Constant	Constant+ Trend	Constant	Costant+ Trend
Level	-4,952*** (0,000)	-4,128*** (0,000)	-1,499* (0,067)	-3,082*** (0,001)	54,803* (0,089)	69,811*** (0,004)
1. Difference	-14,018 (0,000)	-11,643 (0,000)	-14,969 (0,000)	-13,450 (0,000)	264,760 (0,000)	206,846 (0,000)

For significance levels, "*", "**" and "***" represent 10%, 5% and 1% significance respectively.

Table 2: Panel Unit Root Test For Economic Freedom (EKO)

Economic freedom (EKO)	Levin, Lin, Chu		Im, Pesaran, Shin W		ADF	
	Constant	Constant+ Trend	Constant	Constant+ Trend	Constant	Constant+ Trend
Level	-4,410*** (0,000)	-2,518*** (0,0059)	-3,779*** (0,0001)	-2,426*** (0,0076)	77,841*** (0,0006)	69,243*** (0,0051)
1. Difference	-16,301 (0,000)	-15,798 (0,000)	-14,081 (0,000)	-12,237 (0,000)	243,729 (0,000)	194,073 (0,000)

For significance levels, "*", "**" and "***" represent 10%, 5% and 1% significance respectively.

The series are determined as stationary at their level values for constant + trend models with both FDI and EKO. SIC for the variables has been determined automatically.

Table 3: Panel Data Analysis With LSM, Fixed and Random Effects (Model 1)

Dependent variable (FDI)	LSM (Least Square Method)	Fixed effects	Random effects
C	-38,809 (-5,5709)[1] (0.000)[2]	-26,879 (-2,6307)[1] (0.0089)[2]	-28,5716 (-2,8502)[1] (0.0046)[2]
Economic freedom	1,048 (9,3511)[1] (0.000)[2]	0,8548 (5,1721)[1] (0.000)[2]	0,8822 (5,6829)[1] (0.000)[2]
R^2	0,1805	0,7123	0,0753
F_{test}	87,4435 (0.000)[2]	44,4516 (0.000)[2]	32,3584 (0.000)[2]
Hausman Test		0,2335 (0.6289)[2]	

[1]represents t values, [2]represents p values.

Three predictors (LSM, fixed effects, and random effects) have been used in the study. But F test and Hausman tests were used to determine which predictor is superior. Hausman test has been used to determine if the fixed effect method or random effect method will be suitable to predict the model. In Hausman test, a null hypothesis shows that random effect model is suitable and alternative hypothesis shows that fixed effects model is suitable.

According to Table 3, it is clear that regression equation obtained from LSM is significant and the fixed value and economic freedom parameters are also significant. Fixed effects model and random effects model are also significant. In both models, fixed value and economic freedom variable parameters are significant. It has been found that result of the Hausman test is 0,2335 and it is not statistically significant. Therefore, fixed effects can be avoided in the model. It has been found that random effects predictor is more consistent.

There is a positive correlation between economic freedom and FDI. One unit increase (decrease) in economic freedom variable means 0,88 unit increase(decrease) in FDI. Those findings are similar to the ones in the literature.

Model 2: $FDI = \alpha i + \beta_1 MUK + \beta_2 FIS + \beta_3 GIS + \beta_4 KAH + \beta_5 MAS + \beta_6 PAS + \beta_7 TIS + \beta_8 YAS + \beta_9 YOO + ei$

Pooled Least Squares method findings used to identify the relationship between economic freedom components (nine of them) and FDI are in Table 4.

Table 4: Pooled Least Squares For FDI and EKO

Dependent variable (FDI)	parameter	Standard error	t statistics	Probability
C	-44.585	8.2438	-5.4083	0.000***
Property rights	0.0634	0.1432	0.443	0.658
Financial freedom	0.2635	0.0513	5.1339	0.000***
Business freedom	0.1142	0.1525	0.7487	0.4545
Government spending	-0.3481	0.0415	-8.3689	0.000***
Fiscal freedom	0.6601	0.0946	6.9741	0.000***
Monetary freedom	0.2706	0.0576	4.6919	0.000***
Business freedom	0.0005	0.0003	1.5833	0.1142
Investment freedom	-0.088	0.1232	-0.7207	0.4715
Freedom from corruption	0.3586	0.0606	5.9156	0.000***
R^2	0.4331			
F_{test}	31.242 (0.000)			

For significance levels, "*", "**" and "***" represent 10%, 5% and 1% significance respectively.

The significance of the parameters in terms of the variables are analysed and property rights, business freedom, and investment freedom are not significant but financial freedom, government spending, fiscal freedom, monetary freedom and freedom from corruption are 1% significant.

Whereas FDI has a negative correlation with government spending, it has a positive correlation with financial freedom, fiscal freedom, monetary freedom and freedom from corruption. It means that if government spending increases, FDI will decrease and if the others increase, FDI will increase. One unit increase (decrease) in government spending causes 0,34 decrease (increase) in FDI. Moreover, as a result of the effect of independent variables on FDI, one unit increase (decrease) in financial freedom causes 0,26 unit increase(decrease), one unit increase (decrease) in fiscal freedom causes 0,66 unit increase(decrease), one unit increase (decrease) in monetary freedom causes 0,27 unit increase(decrease), one unit increase (decrease) in freedom from corruption_causes 0,35 unit increase(decrease).

Table 5: Random Effect Results

Dependent variable (FDI)	Coefficient	Standard Error	t statistics	Probability
C	-43.616	7.683	-5.677	0.000***
Property rights	0.0937	0.0815	1.1503	0.2507
Financial freedom	0.2054	0.0446	4.5975	0.000***
Business freedom	0.1428	0.0872	1.6368	0.1025
Government spending	-0.1302	0.055	-2.3667	0.0185**
Monetary freedom	0.6973	0.0698	9.9836	0.000***
Fiscal freedom	0.2764	0.040	6.9004	0.000***
Trade freedom	9.00E-05	0.0001	0.4854	0.6277
Investment freedom	-0.0582	0.0698	-0.8331	0.4053
Freedom from corruption	-0.0645	0.0618	-1.0438	0.2972
R^2	0,3582			
F_{test}	22.824 (0.000)			

In Table 5, the model is significant as a result of random effect analysis between FDI and nine economic freedom components. Financial freedom, fiscal freedom and monetary freedom are at 1% significant, government spending is at 5% significant. However, property rights, business freedom, investment freedom, and freedom form corruption_are not significant.

FDI has a positive correlation with financial freedom, fiscal freedom, and monetary freedom. It means that the increase in financial freedom, fiscal freedom, and monetary freedom causes an increase in FDI. There is a negative correlation between government spending and FDI. One unit increase (decrease) in financial freedom causes 0,20 unit increase (decrease) in FDI, one unit increase (decrease) in fiscal freedom causes 0,69 unit increase(decrease) in FDI, one unit increase (decrease) in monetary freedom causes 0,27 unit increase(decrease) in FDI and one unit increase (decrease) in government spending causes 0,13 unit increase(decrease) in FDI.

Table 6: Fixed Effect Results

Dependent variable (FDI)	Coefficient	Standard Error	t statistics	Probability
C	-43.861	7.4036	-5.9246	0.000***
Property rights	0.0964	0.0815	1.1822	0.2379
Financial freedom	0.1850	0.0457	4.0495	0.000***
Business freedom	0.1442	0.0872	1.6528	0.099*
Government spending	-0.0820	0.0588	-1.3954	0.1638
Monetary freedom	0.6925	0.0704	9.8244	0.000***
Fiscal freedom	0.2755	0.0404	6.8165	0.000***
Trade freedom	6.88E-05	0.0001	0.3705	0.7112
Investment freedom	-0.0608	0.0698	-0.870	0.3849
Freedom from corruption	-0.1088	0.0638	-1.7044	0.089*
R^2	0.8309			
F_{test}	58.976 (0.000)			
Hausman Test	16.601 (0.0553)			

Table 6 summarises the results of Fixed effects analysis. The model is significant as a result of fixed effect analysis between FDI and nine economic freedom components. As a result, financial freedom, fiscal freedom and monetary freedom are 1% significant, business freedom and the freedom from corruption are 10% significant. However, property rights, government spending, trade freedom, and investment freedom are not significant.

Whereas FDI has a negative correlation with the freedom from corruption, it has a positive correlation with financial freedom, business freedom, fiscal freedom and monetary freedom. It means that if the freedom from corruption increases,

FDI will decrease. The increase in financial freedom, business freedom, fiscal freedom and monetary freedom causes the increase in FDI.

In both models (Fixed effect and random effect), financial freedom, fiscal freedom, and monetary freedom are statistically significant. Besides, Hausman test score is 16,601 and it is not statistically significant. Therefore, there are not fixed effects in the model. It has been concluded that random effects predictor is more consistent.

Conclusion

This study not only analyses FDI in the globalised world and the environment in which those investments are but also finds out about the countries via economic freedom. In terms of the components of economic freedom, not only Turkey, but other countries which have emerging economies will attempt to improve freedom. With this study, those attempts have been determined. The analyses have shown that if the economic freedom level increases in a country, attractiveness for FDI will increase. It is also known that financial freedom, fiscal freedom, monetary freedom, and government spending are leading factors to make FDI choose that country. It means that an effective banking system without government interferences, financial environment, autonomous reserve bank, effective credit delivery system, strong capital market, foreign financial institutions have an effect on economic freedom of that country and this is vital for investors. Another issue is that, in terms of fiscal freedom, tax incidence such as direct or indirect taxes for the individuals, income tax, institutional taxes must be reasonable. This is also essential for the investors. Inflation, which is an indicator of the stability in economy, price stability and price control all show the monetary freedom aspect in economy and if the price control is achieved without outer interferences in countries, those countries are appealing for FDI. If the government spending does not cause budget deficit, foreign debt stock, and if it does not make individuals move away from market, and if it does not make the productivity decrease, FDI will eagerly try to find a way to invest in that country. Therefore, if the governments want to attract FDI in emerging economies, they need to make their investment environment better and make their countries appealing for FDI. They need to have a market which is independent from government interferences and decrease the uncertainty in economy with the help of low inflation and price stability. Financial environments need to have a liberal system running without government interferences and they need to stay alive in market conditions. They also need to take precautions so that public expenditures do not affect productivity in economy and individuals do not have troubles with excessive taxes.

Additionally, business freedom has a large positive effect on FDI. That variable shows the intensity of bureaucracy in starting a job, doing business, and flow. It is easier to do business with the help of business freedom so it is effective to make investors prefer to choose the country via FDI.

Attracting FDI is important not only for developing countries' economies but for developed countries' economies because of its positive economic effects. For future researches, it might be a good opportunity to analyse the correlation between economic freedom for each category (developed country, developing country, less developed country) and FDI.

References

Ajide, K.B. & Eregha, P.B. (2014). Economic Freedom And Foreign Direct Investment In Ecowas Countries: A Panel Data Analysis. *Applied Econometrics and International Development,* 14(2), 163–174.

Akıncı, M., Yüce, G. & Yılmaz, Ö. (2014). Effects of Economic Freedom on Economic Growth: Panel Data Analysisi. *Anadolu University, Journal of Social Sciences*, 14(2), 81–96.

Baltagi, B. (2001). *Econometric Analysis of Panel Data* (2. Edition). U.K.: John Wiley & Sons Ltd.

Bengoa, M. & Sanchez-Rables, B. (2003). Foreign direct investment, economic freedom and growth new evidence from Latin America. *European Journal of Political Economy*, 19: 529–545.

Celik, M. (2015). Economic Freedom a nd Foreign Direct Investments In Emerging Market Economies: Panel Data Analysis (1995–2013), *Adnan Menderes University, Institute of Social Sciences, Department of Economics,* Unpublished MA Thesis, Aydın, Turkey.

Çalışkan, Z. (2009). Health Expenditures In OECD Countries: Panel Data Analysis. *Erciyes University Journal of Faculty of Economics and Business Sciences*, 34, 117–137.

Foreman, K.V. (2007). Economic freedom and foreign direct ınvestment in developing countries, *The Journal of Developing Areas*, 41(1), 143–154.

Gökmen, Y., Türen, U. ve Dilek, H. (2012). The Relationship In The World Between Country Selection Of FDI and Economic Freedom Index. *Journal of Financial Politics & Economic Interpretations*, 49(568), 5–20.

Greene, W.H. (2003). *Econometric Analysis* (5. Edition). New York: Prentice Hall.

Gwartney, J. & Lawson, R. (2003). The concept and measurement of economic freedom. *European Journal of Political Economy*, 19, 405–430.

Gwartney, J., Lawson, R. & Hall, J. (2014). Economic freedom of the world 2014 annual report. Fraser Institute, Canada, http://www.fraserinstitute.org/uploadedFiles/fraser-ca/Content/research-news/research/publications/economic-freedom-of-the-world-2014.pdf.

Heritage Foundation (2013). 2013 Index of economic freedom – methodology. https://thf_media.s3.amazonaws.com/index/pdf/2013/methodology.pdf

MSCI (Morgan Stanley Capital Index), (2012), MSCI Emerging Markets Indicies, https://www.msci.com/resources/factsheets/index_fact_sheet/msci-emerging-markets-imi-usd-net.pdf.

Patry, W. (2009). *Moral Panics and the Copyright Wars.* New York: Oxford University

Pourshahabi, F., Mahmoudinia, D. & Soderjani, E. S. (2011). FDI, human capital, economic freedom and growth in OECD countries. *Research Journal of International Studies*, 19, 71–81.

Savaşan, F. ve Dursun, İ. (2006). Economic Freedom and Foreign direct Investments: A Statistical Survey. *Selçuk University, Faculty of Economics and Administrative Sciences, Journal of Social and Economic Research,* 12, 29–52.

Türen, U., Gökmen, Y., ve Dilek, H. (2011). The Effects on Knowledge and Information Technologies on Economic Freedom: A Global Study Regarding Countries. *Journal of Knowledge Economy and Management,* VI(II), http://beykon.org/dergi/2011/FALL/U.Turen.pdf.

Türker, O. (2009). Economic Liberalization and Economic Growth: Panel Data Analysis. *International Davraz Kongress*, Süleyman Demirel University, Isparta.

UNCTAD (2014). World Investment Report 2014: Investing in the SDGs: An action plan, http://unctad.org/en/publicationslibrary/wir2014_en.pdf.

UNCTADSTAT (2015). Inward & Outward Foreign Direct Investment Stock, Annual, 1995–2013. http://unctadstat.unctad.org/wds/TableViewer/tableView.aspx.

Prof. Ass. Dr. Bekim Berisha* & MSc. Bernard Berisha**

The Impact of External Auditing on the Quality of Financial Statements of Limited Liability Companies in Kosovo

Abstract This paper describes the importance of an external audit and its contribution on increasing the quality of financial statements of limited liability companies (LLC) for the period of 2004–2010 in Kosovo.

In the theoretical framework of the study, regularity on the audit of financial statements is designed to be a causal factor for the quality of financial statements, expressed through the types of audit opinions on the audited financial statements.

The empirical basis of the study is on data collected from all licensed auditors in Kosovo, who have performed financial audits in Kosovo LLC's, in the period of 2004–2010. The comparative method was used to determine differences in the quality of financial statements LLC's which audited its financial statements for the first time, compared with the LLC's that have performed the audit of its financial statements for a period longer than one year, classifying them according to the type of activity, annual turnover, and number of employees.

Surveys were used as the method for collecting and analysing necessary information. Our research is based on analysis of the quantitative values of the independent variables and type of opinion and recommendations contained within the audit report and management report. To ensure quality of the data, we have utilised the Critical Incident Technique (CIT). Using CIT it was possible to expand the number of areas related to the impact of the relevant factors on the quality of financial statements.

Identified areas provided a solid foundation to establish two basic dimensions for evaluating quality of financial reporting through comparison – type of opinion and recommendations.

We collected a total of 188 critical cases that were reviewed and classified them into twelve area dependent variables (dimensions that affect the quality financial statements) and two areas that are related to the independent variable (type audit opinion and recommendations of the auditor).

Keywords: external audit, audit impact on quality, corporate governance.

* University of Prizren, bekim_@hotmail.com
** College AAB Prishtina, bernard@qendra.org

1. Introduction

Kosovo after 1999 is characterised by the construction of a new socio-economic system and creating mechanisms for transition to a market economy. However, the period of transition is characterised by a series of problems and reluctance to accept the changes. Practices built and maintained for years are difficult to overcome, and the application of requirements of a market economy requires time, effort, and training of the largest possible number of people who are part of such a market economy.

Currently there are important changes occurring that evolve towards the creation of modern enterprise which changes aligned with market globalisation challenges, internationalisation of business, the development of information technologies and in particular the competitive economic environment.

To withstand all these changes, and be an active participant in these markets, for limited liability companies (LLC) in Kosovo, obviously it is important to unify the financial reporting system, and thus establish confidence in the financial statements on which decision makers base their decisions.

Recent studies (eg, Healy and Palepu, 2001; Bushman and Smith, 2001; Lambert, Leuze, and Verrecchia, 2005) suggest that enhanced financial reporting may have important economic implications in increasing the efficiency of investment.

Hence, the increase of reliability of financial reporting is of crucial importance.

Therefore, the aims of this study are to describe the importance of an external financial audit as part of external control and its contribution on increasing the quality of financial statements of limited liability companies (LLC) in Kosovo.

The study findings will be particularly important for enterprises, professional and state institutions and academic institutions from accounting and auditing in Kosovo and beyond.

2. Literature Review

By (Rodrigo S. Verdi, 2006), it is assumed that the highest quality of financial reporting can improve the efficiency of investment by reducing asymmetric information in two ways: (1) it reduces the asymmetry of information between the company and the investor, and so the firm lowers the cost of fundraising, and (2) it reduces the information asymmetry between investors and managers and thus reduces the cost of monitoring managers by shareholders.

Recent studies (eg, Healy and Palepu, 2001; Bushman and Smith, 2001; Lambert, Leuze, and Verrecchia, 2005) suggest that enhanced financial reporting may have important economic implications in increasing the efficiency of investment.

However, despite the theoretical underpinnings for such a link, there is little empirical evidence to support these claims. I assume that increasing the level of confidence in financial reports reached by raising the quality of financial statements.

Ongoing interactions with external events as well as within the enterprise are essential reasons for an analysis of the relationship and the importance of the quality of financial statements. The starting point in these reviews represent factors that influence management decisions.

To be confident in their decisions, the management and all those who make important decisions about the company want to raise the level of confidence in the company's financial statements.

One of the key functions of corporate governance is to ensure the quality of the financial reporting process. Levitt (1999) stated in a speech to directors "the link between company directors and financial reporting system never has been before so important."

Although it is common for government "good" corporate financial reporting leads to advanced, there is a deficiency on consensus on the elements that make up "the quality of financial reporting." In the US although the Blue Ribbon Committee (BRC) (1999) and Sarbanes-Oxley (2002) require auditors to discuss the quality of financial reporting methods and relevant, rather than just accepting them, the notion of quality of financial reporting. It remains a vague concept. Jonas and Blanchet (2000) believe that the auditors, audit committee members, and management are trying to define with precision "the quality of financial reporting."

Therefore, a mosaic of governance of LLC undoubtedly has a crucial role in an external audit of the financial statements as one of the factors that ensures decision makers that the financial statements are free from material misstatement and present a fair and honest financial position and performance of LLC in Kosovo.

3. Data and Research Methodology

Increasing the quality of financial reports in Kosovo should be approached with a modern and essential understanding of quality, in terms of the diversity and variety of the users' requirement features of financial statements.

Therefore, the quality of financial statements as measured by the external audit of LLC in Kosovo is fundamental in decision-making for investors, creditors, regulators of the profession, professional associations, universities, etc.

Obviously, we must emphasise the role of the external auditor, internal auditor, and the Board of Corporate Management, who together have responsibilities that directly impact on improving the quality of financial reports (Cohen J, Krishnamurthy D Wright A. 2004).

Research objectives are:

- **Increasing the quality of financial reports;**
  Which will detect and needs regular review of financial statements and consistent application of the recommendations of the auditors, and
- **Ensuring deciding.**
  Through regular auditing of financial reports, it provides participants in a market economy have greater reliability in process financial reporting.

The hypothesis of the study are:

X-1 = the more regular audits of the financial statements that are done, the greater are the opportunities for obtaining an unqualified opinion for financial statements
X-2 = the more regular audits of the financial statements that are done, there will be less recommendations for adjustments.

3.1 Research Methodology

Surveys were used as the methods and procedures for collecting and analysing necessary information. Our research is based on the analysis of quantitative values of the independent variables – type of opinion and recommendations contained within the audit report and management letter, to provide data quality, we have applied the method of Critical Incidents Technique (CIT).

It is evident that CIT has done a lot on development conceptual structure in cases where there was no theoretical base on certain phenomena (Walker and Truly, 1992) by the time they were used.

We have collected a total of 188 critical cases that were reviewed and classified into twelve areas of dependent variables (dimensions that influence the financial statements) and two areas that are referred as the independent variable (type of the audit opinion and recommendations of the auditor).

As part of our research we include all types of opinions that auditors could give during the auditing of a financial statement.

The types of audit opinions are divided into two main groups, mainly:

- Unmodified opinion, and
- Modified opinion.

As an independent variable that affects dependent variable – in the quality of financial statements, we have grouped recommendations into two identifying categories from which can be derived conclusion regarding the quality financial statements:

(a) The weaknesses of Internal control
(b) The number of recommendations

4. Results and Suggestions

Through questionnaires we received records of other areas that can affect the quality of Financial Statements (dependent variables). From twelve areas, respondents answered only on six of them.

Measuring their impact, we decided the type of opinion in relation to these areas, to prove if they affect the type of opinion:

- Board of Directors
- Composition of the Board of Directors,
- Users of the audit report
- Activity of LLC,
- Size LLC,
- Capital structure.

For the processing of statistical data, we used SPSS (Statistical Package for the Social Sciences).

Table 1: Overview of the type of opinion and recommendations by year

DESCRIPTION	QUANTITY							Total:	%							Total:
TYPE OF OPINION	Year -1	Year -2	Year -3	Year -4	Year -5	Year -6	Year -7		Year -1	Year -2	Year -3	Year -4	Year -5	Year -6	Year -7	
1) Unqualified opinion	2	6	8	13	17	24	27	97	2%	6%	8%	13%	18%	25%	28%	100%
2) Qualified opinion:																
a) Emphasis affairs without inpact at opinion																
- Other auditors	0	0	0	2	1	0	0	3				67%	33%			100%
- Going concern	1	1	0	0	0	0	0	2	50%	50%						100%
- Deviation from KAS/IAS	0	0	1	1	0	0	0	2			50%	50%				100%
- Lack of consistency	0	0	0	0	0	1	1	2						50%	50%	100%
- Emphasis an issue	1	3	1	3	0	3	2	13	8%	23%	8%	23%		23%	15%	100%
b) Limitations in scope:																
- Qualified opinion	8	14	17	8	6	7	3	63	13%	22%	27%	13%	10%	11%	5%	100%
- Disclaimer of Opinion	0	0	2	0	1	2	1	6			33%		17%	33%	17%	100%
c) Disagreement with management:																
- Qualified opinion	0	0	0	0	0	0	0	0								
- Adverse opinion	0	0	0	0	0	0	0	0								
TOTAL:	**12**	**24**	**29**	**27**	**25**	**37**	**34**	**188**	**6%**	**13%**	**15%**	**14%**	**13%**	**20%**	**18%**	**100%**

DESCRIPTION	QUANTITY							Total:	%							Total:
TYPE OF OPINION	Year -1	Year -2	Year -3	Year -4	Year -5	Year -6	Year -7		Year -1	Year -2	Year -3	Year -4	Year -5	Year -6	Year -7	
RECOMMENDATIONS:																
Absent IC	14	5	7	3	4	2	1	36	39%	14%	19%	8%	11%	6%	3%	100%
Absent but implement some procedures	7	16	18	21	16	4	4	86	8%	19%	21%	24%	19%	5%	5%	100%
Exist/do not apply procedures	0	1	0	1	1	1	1	5	0%	20%	0%	20%	20%	20%	20%	100%
Exist/inefficient IC	2	1	0	0	0	0	0	3	67%	33%	0%	0%	0%	0%	0%	100%
Total no. of recomendation	138	235	299	180	136	133	112	1233	11%	19%	24%	15%	11%	11%	9%	100%

Sources: Authors calculation

Test of hypotheses:

X-1 = The more regular audits of the financial statements that are done, the greater are the opportunities for obtaining an unqualified opinion for the financial statements

Graph 1: Type of Opinion

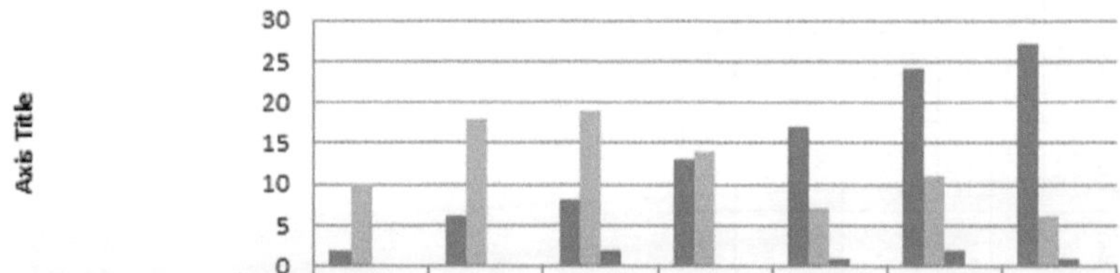

	2004	2005	2006	2007	2008	2009	2010
1) Unqualified opinion	2	6	8	13	17	24	27
2) Qualified opinion:	10	18	19	14	7	11	6
3)Disclaimer of Opinion	0	0	2	0	1	2	1
4)Adverese opinion							

X-2 = The more regular audits of the financial statements that are done, there will be less recommendations for adjustments

Graph 2: Recommendations

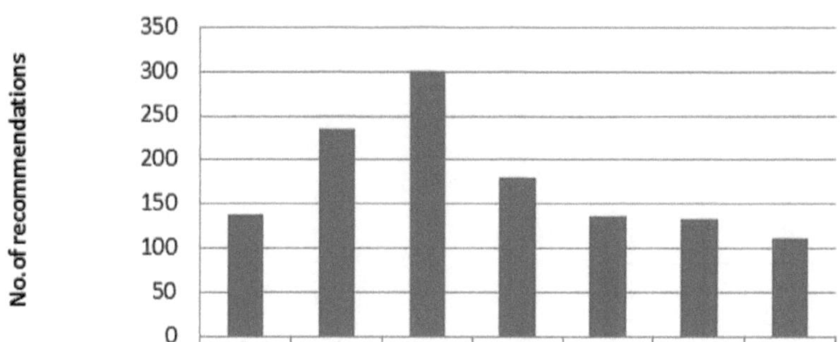

	1	2	3	4	5	6	7
Total no. Of recomendation	138	235	299	180	136	133	112

5. Conclusion

Results of survey indicate that the frequency of auditing of Financial Statements contribute to reducing the acceptable level of misstatements in financial statements, increasing the possibility of obtaining unqualified opinion and in accordance with that, increasing the reliability of the financial Statements of limited liability companies. Therefore, the "Quality" of the financial statements relies on external auditing.

Future Research:

Future research should focus on research of corporate governance perspective as the perspective of the agency.

The future research should be made to identify influence of corporate governance and other factors such as the Board of Directors, Audit Committee and the internal auditor, on the quality of financial statements LLC's in Kosovo.

Research in this area would contribute to a comprehensive analysis of impacts on the quality of financial reporting, in terms of the Kosovo's reality, and would contribute in increasing reliability in the quality of financial reporting in the future.

References

Abbott, L. J., Y. Park, and S. Parker. 2000. The effects of audit committee activity and independence on corporate fraud. *Managerial Finance* 26: 55–67.

Abbott, L. J. and S. Parker. 2000. Auditor selection and audit committee characteristics. Auditing: *A Journal of Practice & Theory* 19 (Fall): 47–66.

Abbott, L. J., S. Parker, G. F. Peters. 2001. The effectiveness of blue ribbon recommendations in mitigating financial misstatements: an empirical study. *Auditing Mid-year Conference*. Houston, Texas.

Abbot, L.J., S. Parker, G.F. Peters, and K. Raghunandan. 2003a. The association between audit committee characteristics and audit fees. Auditing: *A Journal of Practice and Theory* (September): 17–32.

Beasley, M., J. Carcello, D. Hermanson and P. D. Lapides. 2000. Fraudulent financial reporting: Consideration of industry traits and corporate governance mechanisms. *Accounting Horizons* (December): 441–454.

Beasley, M., and K. Petroni. 2001. Board independence and audit firm type. Auditing: *A Journal of Practice and Theory* (March): 97–114.

Blue Ribbon Committee. 1999. Report and Recommendations of the Blue Ribbon Committee on Improving the Effectiveness of Corporate Audit Committees.

New York: New York Stock Exchange and National Association of Securities Dealers.

Carcello, J., D. R. Hermanson, T.L. Neal and R. Riley, Jr. 2002. Board characteristics and audit fees. Contemporary Accounting Research (Fall): 365–384.

Carcello, J., and T.L. Neal. 2000. Audit committee composition and auditor reporting. The Accounting Review (October): 453–468.

Carcello, J., and T.L. Neal. 2003. Audit committee characteristics and auditor dismissals following "new" going concern reports. *The Accounting Review* (January): 453–468.

Clapman, P. 2000. Letter of Peter C. Clapman, Senior Vice President and Chief Counsel, Investments. TIAA-CREF. September 21, 2000. Available at http://www.sec.gov/rules/proposed/s71300/clapman1.htm.

Cohen, J., and D. Hanno. 2000. Auditors' consideration of corporate governance and management control philosophy in preplanning and planning judgments. Auditing: *A Journal of Practice and Theory* (Fall): 133–146.

Cohen, J., G. Krishnamoorthy, and A. Wright. 2002. Corporate governance and the audit process. Contemporary Accounting Research (Winter): 573–594.

Cohen, J., L. Pant, and D. Sharp. 1995. An exploratory examination of international differences in auditors' ethical perceptions. Behavioral Research in Accounting (7): 37–64.

DeAngelo, L. 1981. Auditor size and audit quality. *Journal of Accounting and Economics* (August): 183–99.

DeZoort, F. T. 1997. An investigation of audit committees' oversight responsibilities. Abacus (September): 208–227.

DeZoort, F. T. 1998. An analysis of experience effects on audit committee members' oversight judgments. Accounting, Organizations and Society 23(1): 1–21.

Jeffrey Cohen, Ganesh Krishnamoorthy, Arnie Wright. 2004. THE CORPORATE GOVERNANCE MOSAIC AND FINANCIAL REPORTING QUALITY Journal of Accounting Literature (2004, pp. 87–152).

Johnstone, K. and J. Bedard. 2003. Risk management in client acceptance decisions. The Accounting Review (October): 1003–1025.

Krishnamoorthy, G. 2002. A multistage approach to external auditors' evaluation of the internal audit function. Auditing: *A Journal of Practice and Theory* (March): 95–121.

Krishnamoorthy, G., A. Wright and J. Cohen. 2002a. Audit committee effectiveness and financial reporting quality: Implications for auditor independence. Australian Accounting Review (November): 3–13.

Krishnamoorthy, G., A. Wright and J. Cohen. 2002b. Auditors' views on audit committees and financial reporting quality. *The CPA Journal* (October): 56–57.

Krishnan, J. 2001. Corporate governance and internal control: An empirical analysis. American Accounting Association Annual Meeting. Atlanta, Georgia.

Krugman, P. 2002. The insider game. New York Times (July 12).

Raghundan, K., W. Read and D. Rama. 2001. Audit committee composition, "gray directors" and interaction with internal auditing. Accounting Horizons (June): 105–118.

Ramsay, I. 2001. Ramsay Report. Independence of Australian company auditors: Review of current Australian requirements and proposals for reform. http// www.treasury.gov.au.

Sarbanes, P., and M. Oxley. 2002. Sarbanes-Oxley Act of 2002. Washington, DC: U.S. Congress.

Wild, J. J. 1996. The audit committee and earnings quality. *Journal of Accounting, Auditing & Finance* 11: 247–276.

Wolnizer, P. W. 1995. Are audit committees red herrings? Abacus 31: 45–66.

Wright, A., G. Krishnamoorthy and J. Cohen. 2004. The impact of corporate board focus on auditors' program planning judgments. Working paper. Boston College.

Utku Altunöz[1]

Validation of Feldstein-Horioka Hypothesis for the Turkish Economy

Feldstein-Horioka Hipotezinin Türkiye'de Geçerliliğinin Sinanmasi

Abstract The presence of a relation between saving and investment is important for the determination of economic policies. According to the Feldstein-Horioka hypothesis, the presence of the relationship between savings and investments depend on the degree of international capital mobility. In case of high capital mobility, the relation between saving and investment is strong. However, in the form of restricted capital mobility, the relation falters. In this paper, the validity of the Feldstein - Horioka hypothesis is examined for Turkey by using the ARDL bound test covering the period between 1980 and 2013. According to empirical results, the F-H Theory is supported for Turkey.

Özet Yatırım ve tasarruf arasındaki ilişkinin varlığı, ekonomik politikaların belirlenmesinde oldukça önemlidir. Feldstein-Horioka hipotezine göre yatırım ve tasarruf ilişkisi, ulusşararası sermaye hareketliğinin derecesine bağlıdır. Yüksek sermaye hareketliliği durumunda değişkenler arası ilişki güçlü olmaktadır. Bununla birlikte sınırlı sermaye hareketliği durumunda, yatırım ve tasarruf arasındaki ilişkide problemler belirmektedir. Çalışmada Feldstein-Horioka Hipotezi, 1980–2013 yılları için Türkiye ekonomisinde sınır testi yaklaşımı ile test edilmektedir. Ekonometrik modelin sonucuna göre ilgili dönemler için Türkiye'de Feldstein-Horioka Hipotezi desteklenmektedir.

Introduction

Efficiency of saving depends on the perfect mobility of capital among economies. Feldstein and Horioka argued in their study that there was a relationship between saving and international capital.

In economic science, the investment-saving relationship was examined by a variety of ways. The study by Feldstein-Horioka is cornerstone for them. In later years, the relation among variables was tested by Feldstein (1983) and Feldstein

1 Utku Altunöz, Yrd.Doç.Dr.Sinop Üniversitesi, utkual@hotmail.com

and Bachetta (1991). Being higher of relation in the following studies, the phenomenon entered the literature as a Feldstein-Horioka paradox.

Theorical Framework of Feldstein-Horioka Theory

Feldstein and Horioka claim the relatively immobility of capital. According to the Feldstein-Horioka theory, the presence of the relationship between savings and investments depend on the degree of international capital mobility. In their study, the saving-investment relationship was examined by using cross-section regression over the period of 1960–1974 in a sample of 16 OECD countries.

Accroding to Feldstein-Horioka;

$$(I/Y)_i = a + b(\tfrac{S}{Y})_i \qquad (1)$$

Y: Gross Domestic Product
I: Investment
S: Saving

Feldstein-Horioka claim under the perfect mobility assumption that there should not be a relationship between domestic investment and domestic saving. If capital is a perfect mobility, an increase in saving for any country will increase the total investment all around the world. Mentioned increase in investment will distribute to countries in proportion to the startup capital stock and marginal efficiency of capital (Kibritçioğlu ve Ninjbat, 2006, 5).

Literature Survey

There are many studies on the subject of Feldstein and Horioka in the literature. A portion of the work is about the theoric research, however, the studies on the other part is about the examination of validity. As well, there is not an agreement of whether or not Feldstein-Horioka (F-H) theory is valid for every country. In the other words, several studies have researched the correlation between domestic investment and saving for various countries by means of different empirical methods. Among these, some recent studies find precise evidence supporting the F-H relationship while Ho rejects the validity of an interaction between saving and investment reflecting the high capital mobility.

Jansen (1996) points out if a significant number of countries are found to be linked with international capital markets, this may be significant evidence of international capital mobility (see Jansen 1994 and Gundlach and Sinn 1992 for a complete analysis).

Blanchard ve Giavazzi (2002) examined the relationship between saving and investment in OECD countries for the period of 1960–2004. In the result of the study, it was understood that the relationship decreased over time. In the same study, they reached the same result for euro zone countries for the period of 1991–2001.

Özmen and Parmaksız (2003) tested the F-H Theory for the United Kingdom covering the period of 1948–1998 by using an estimation of the F-H coefficient. As a result, the F-H relation does not exist for the countries in their study.

Bangake ve Eggoh (2009), tested 37 African countries for the period between 1970–2006. By using panel OLS, panel DOLS and panel FMOLS co integration analysis, they reached the coefficient between 0 and 1 in accordance with expectations.

Data and Methodology

In classical co integration tests, we expect the variable to be stationary at the same level. However, the ARDL approach, which was developed by Pesaran et al. (1996), enables for variables to be examined at different levels.

"The autoregressive distributed lag (ARDL) model deals with single cointegration and is introduced originally by Pesaran and Shin (1999) and further extended by Pesaran et al. (2001). The ARDL approach has the advantage that it does not require all variables to be I(1) as the Johansen framework and it is still applicable if we have I(0) and I(1) variables in our set."

The ARDL bounds testing consist of two parts. In the first part, relationships among variables will be tested for the long run by using the equation (1) below,

$$\Delta R_t = a_0 + \Sigma_{i=1}^{p} b_i \Delta R_{t-i} + \Sigma_{i=0}^{p} c_i \Delta \pi_{t-i} + \lambda_1 R_{t-1} + \lambda_2 \pi_{t-1} + \varepsilon_t \quad (1)$$

After obtaining the long term relationship by using equation (1), one needs to obtain the short run relationship among the variables. For this purpose, equation (2) listed below will be used.

$$\Delta R_t = a_0 + \Sigma_{i=1}^{p} b_i \Delta R_{t-i} + \Sigma_{i=0}^{p} c_i \Delta \pi_{t-i} + \lambda_1 R_{t-1} + \lambda_2 \pi_{t-1} + \mu ecm_{t-1} + \varepsilon_t \quad (2)$$

The error correction term was added to equation (1) and equation (2) was then obtained. The ERM term is a dynamic model in which "the movement of the variables in any periods is related to the previous period's gap from long-run equilibrium."

"An advantage of using ARDL bounds testing is that the ARDL does not need that all the variables under study must be integrated of the same order and it can be applied when the under-lying variables are integrated of order one, order zero or fractionally integrated" (Mouniri 2012, 12).

In this study, S/GDP ratio and I/GDP ratio were obtained from the Republic of Turkey's Ministry of Development for the years of 1980–2013. The E-view 5 software was preferred for econometric analysis. In order provide stationary, all variables were applied to the ADF, PP and KPSS unit root tests.

Table 1: I / GDP

	ADF unit Root		Philips Perron Unit Root		KPSS Unit Root	
	Constant	**Constant and with Trend**	**Constant**	**Constant and with Trend**	**Constant**	**Constant and with Trend**
At Level	-2.11	-2.90	-2.22	-2.44	0.21	0.11
	-2.88*	-3.23*	-2.90*	-3.33*	0.98*	0.17*
	-2.76**	-3.11**	-2.69**	-3.11**	0.24**	0.14**
First Difference	-4.12	-5.33	-4.88	-4.67	0.12	0.08
	-2.80*	-3.34*	-2.93*	-2.99*	0.66*	0.14*
	-2.34**	-2.90**	-2.59**	-2.86**	0.55**	0.10**

* Denotes critical values at 5% significant level and ** denotes critical values at 5% significant level.

In table 1, a null hypothesis which means "unit root exist" for ADF and PP was examined for I/GDP variable. According to the result of the unit root test, series are not stationary at each level except for the first level. Because, the computed ADF test-statistic is smaller than the critical values at 10%, 5%, 1% significant level, respectively, therefore we can reject the first level. However, According to the result of the KPSS test, which accepts "unit root not exist" for null hypothesis, variable is stationary not only at level but also at first level.

Table 2: S / GDP

	ADF unit Root		Philips Perron Unit Root		KPSS Unit Root	
	Constant	**Constant and with Trend**	**Constant**	**Constant and with Trend**	**Constant**	**Constant and with Trend**
At Level	-1.61	-1.87	-1.76	-1.88	0.19	0.18(x)
	-2.87*	-2.89*	-2.21*	-3.76*	0.44*	0.15*
	2.91**	-3.11**	2.82**	-3.22**	0.39**	0.10**
First Difference	-5.21	-6.22	-5.98	-6.66	0.10	0.06
	-3.23*	-3.21**	-2.99*	-3.36*	0.50*	0.19*
	1.32**	-3.34**	-2.96**	-3.34**	0.36**	0.10**

* Denotes critical values at 5% significant level and ** denotes critical values at 5% significant level.
(x) denotes the rejection of null Hypothesis at 10% significant level.

According to table 2, the test results of ADF and PP for the S/GDP shows that the variable has unit root at level but not at first level like the I/GDP variable. However, results in the KPSS test is different compared with the same test of the I/GDP variable. According to KPSS this result, the variable has unit root at 10% significant levels. So that stationary of variable could provide the first difference.

In this paper, the ARDL bounding test was preferred for co integration which was found by Pesaran and Pesaran (1997), Pesaran and Smith (1998), and Pesaran and Shin (1999). The basic advantage of the ARDL test lies in its flexibility that it can be applied when the variables are of a different order of integration (Pesaran and Pesaran 1997). The second important advantage of this approach is that the model takes sufficient numbers of Lags to capture the data generating process in a general-to-specific modeling framework (Laurenceson and Chai 2003). Another advantage is that the bounds test allows a mixture of I(1) and I(0) variables as regressors, that is, the order of integration of appropriate variables may not necessarily be the same. Therefore, the ARDL technique has the advantage of not requiring a specific identification of the order of the underlying data. Third, this technique is suitable for a small or finite sample size (Pesaran et al., 2001).

The first stage of ARDL test is to determine the appropriate Lag Length Criteria. In this study, according to Akaike Information Criterion, the ARDL (1,0) model was selected as an appropriate model.

Table 3: ARDL (1,0) Result

Variables		**Coefficent**	**t-values**
I/Y(-1)		0.4311*	3.2311
S/Y		0.3212*	4.3218
c		8.8117*	3.2118
Diagnostic Tests**			
R2	0.66		
Otocorelation	1.322(.399)		
Heteroscedasticity	0.3213(.668)		

Note: * values are significant at 1%, 5%, and 10%. The values in parentheses denotes P values. Akaike Information Criteria was used for Model. Dependent variable is (I/Y).

In order to estimate the model, the OLS method was used. According to the result of the diagnostic tests, there is no problem as deterministic and stochastic, which means there is no autocorrelation and heteroskedasticity problem in the model. Following the ARDL estimation, the existence of co integration was examined by the f statistic.

A null hypothesis which refers to whether there is a co integration relationship among variables or not is formed as indicated below:

Ho: λ1 = λ2 = 0

H1: λ1 ≠ 0, λ2 ≠ 0

Table 4: Calculation of F statistic for determining the Long run Relationships

the number of variables	10%	5%
1	I(0)–I(1)	I(0)–I(1)
	3.98–4.96	5.24–5.73
Calculated F Statistic	6,221*	

Note: * denotes the existence of co integration among the variables both 5% and 519 significant levels.

According to results which can be seen from table 4, variables are cointegrated. In case the F statistic is greater than the top limit of critical, the null hypothesis is rejected. That means there is a long run relationship among variables.

In this section, long run coefficients should be determined. Mentioned coefficients are presented in table 5.

Table 5: ARDL (1,0) Model Estimated Result for long run Relationship

Variables	Coefficent	t-values
S / Y	0.44120*	3.2119
c	12.0412*	5.212

Note: I/GDP are a dependent variable.

According to the result of ARDL (1,0) which is followed from table 5, there is a positive relationship between saving and investment in long run relationships. In a parallel of results, we can say that the Feldstein-Horioka Theory is valid in Turkey for the selected dates. In other words, in case of increasing the international capital movement in the long term, the relationships between saving and investment will be weakening.

An error correction model is not a model that corrects the error in another model. Error Correction Models (ECMs) are a category of multiple time series models that directly estimate the speed at which a dependent variable—*Y*—returns to equilibrium after a change in an independent variable—*X*. In order to provide the consistence of the error correction model, the coefficient should be negative.

Table 6: Error Correction Model

Variables	Coefficient	t-Values
S/Y	0.3411	2.7411
ERM	-0.3811	-2.9847
c	5.8041	3.0784

In accordance with the results of the ECM in table 6, the coefficients are significance. The ECM coefficient is negative as was expected. The meaning of it being -0.38 of the ERM coefficient is that the effect of shock will come to equilibrium at a speed of 38% within the first year.

Conclusion

The presence of a relation between saving and investment is important for the determination of economic policies. By the liberalisation of input and output, the importance of saving-investment relationship increased. In this study, the Feldstein-Horioka hypothesis is examined for Turkey by using the ARDL bound test covering the period between 1980 and 2013. According to the result of econometrical analysis, it is reached that there is a positive directional relationships between saving and investment. This result is suitable with our expectations. According to Feldstein-Horioka, increasing capital movements weakens the relationship between both variables. Using the ERM model tested short run relationships among variables. The meaning of being -0.38 of the ERM coefficient is that the effect of shock will come to equilibrium at a speed of 38% within the first year.

This study presents that the Feldstein-Horioka hypothesis is supported in Turkey for the period of 1980 and 2013.

References

Bangake, C. ve Eggoh, J.C. (2009), International Capital Mobility in African Countries: A Panel Cointegration Analysis, http://193.49.79.89/leo/images/espace_perso/bangake/WP_2178.pdf, (Erişim Tarihi: 15.06.2010).

Belloumii Mounir (2012), The relationship between Trade, FDI and Economic growth in Tunisia: An application of autoregressive distributed lag model, Presented at the 15th Annual Conference on Global Economic Analysis, Geneva, Switzerland.

Blanchard, O. ve Giavazzi, F. (2002), "Current account deficits in the Euro area: The end of the Feldstein_Horioka puzzle?", Brookings Papers on Economic Activity, 2, 147–209.

Feldstein, M. ve Horioka, C. (1980), "Domestic Saving and International Capital Flows", Economic Journal, 90, 314–329.

Feldstein, M. (1983) "Domestic Saving and International Capital Movements in the Long Run and the Short Run" European Economic Review, 21: 331–353.

Feldstein, M. ve Bachetta, P. (1991) "National Saving and Economic Performance" Shoven, et al (eds.) National Saving And International Investment, USA University of Chicago Press.

Jansen W.J. (1996), 'Estimating saving-investment correlations: evidence for OECD countries based on an error correction model', Journal of International Money and Finance, 5, 749–781.

Kibritçioğlu, A. ve Ninjbat, U. (2006), Uluslararası Sermeye Hareketliliğinin Derecesi ve Feldstein-Horioka Bilmecesi, Ankara Üniversitesi Sosyal Bilimler Enstitüsü İktisat Yüksek Lisans Programı Seminer Çalışması.

Laurenceson J. and Chai J. 2003. Financial Reform and Economic Development in China. Cheltenham, UK, Edward Elgar.

Pesaran, M. H., Shin Y., ve Smith R., (1996), "Testing for the Existence of a Long-Run Relationship," University of Cambridge, DAE Working Paper No. 9622.

Pesaran, M. H. ve Shin, Y. (1999), "An Autoregressive Distributed Lag Modelling Approach to Cointegration Analysis", http://www.econ.cam.ac.uk/faculty/pesaran/ardl.pdf, (Erişim: 29.09.2011).

Pesaran, M. H., Shin, Y. ve Smith, R. (2001), "Bounds Testing Approaches to the Analysis of Level Relationship", Journal of Applied Econometrics, 16(3), 289–326.

Pesaran MH, Pesaran B. 1997. Working with Microfit 4.0: Interactive Econometric Analysis. Oxford, Oxford University Press.

Pesaran MH, Smith RP. 1998. Structural Analysis of Co integrating VARs. Journal of Economic Survey 12: 471–505.

Pesaran MH, Shin Y. 1999. An Autoregressive Distributed Lag Modelling Approach to Co integration Analysis. In S. Strom, A. Holly and P. Diamond (Eds.), Econometrics and Economic Theory in the 20th Century: The Ragner Frisch Centennial Symposium. Cambridge, Cambridge University Press. Available at: www.econ.cam.ac.uk/faculty/pesaran/ADL.pdf.

Pesaran, M.H., Y. Shin., and Smith R. (2001) Bounds testing approaches to the analysis of level relationships, *Journal of Applied Econometrics,* 16, 289–326.

Arş. Gör. K. Burcu Öngen Bilir, Prof. Dr. Mustafa Aytaç &
Prof. Dr. Necmi Gürsakal

Analysing Turkey's Coal Mining Disaster Data (1983–2014) with Poisson Change-Point Models

Abstract Poisson with two change points had been studied by Carlin, Gelfand and Smith (Carlin, Gelfand and Smith, 1992) and multiple change-point models had been studied by Chib (Chib, 1998). Using time series data and Bayesian analysis with an R package MCMCpack, we may determine the change points of a time series. After a brief literature survey on change point models, Bayesian analysis, theoretical foundations of change point models and MCMC will be explained. Also the essentials of the R package MCMCpack will be given in this section.

We have the yearly coal mining disaster data within Turkey between 1983 and 2014. Studying this time series data and using the Bayesian MCMC approach, change points were determined. Our paper ends with a discussion section that takes into account the regulative and inspectional regime changes and tries to explain the meaning of these change-points according to these changes.

Keywords: Poisson change point models, Bayesian analysis, MCMCpack.

1. Introduction

Coal mining disaster forecasts are very important in human life in terms of estimating hazards and managing emergency systems. Defining of disaster characteristics plays an important role in these forecasts. Of these characteristics, one is the frequency distribution of disaster and the other is the magnitude distribution of the disasters. Each statistical distribution has many parameters describing the actual distribution.

In their studies, Gelfand and Smith (1990) and Green (1995) used the Poisson distribution of disaster at any magnitude level. The Poisson distribution is generally used for disasters of a large magnitude, and the disaster occurrences with time/space can be modeled with the Poisson process in which, as is known, the Poisson distribution is one that counts the events that have occurred over a certain period of time. Change-point problem estimating the posterior distribution of the change-points sequence. An MCMC method suitable for estimating the posterior distribution of the change-points sequence. Green (1995) used the reversible jump algoritm for estimating posterior distribution but this algorithm converges slowly, and many iterations are needed for estimating correctly the posterior distribution.

There is a significant amount of research on the change point as applied to coal mining disaster data. Jaudet (2009) used a nonparametric method for the detection of change points in the frequency magnitude distributions. Yigiter & İnal (2010) used earthquake data for their method developed for the estimator of the change point in the Poisson process. Aktaş et al. (2009) investigated a change point in Turkish earthquake data. Jaudet (2009) applied the hierarchical Bayesian method for the change point in data, taken from the Italian NT4.1.1 catalogue. Much research for changepoint models is based on MCMC. Stephens (1994) and Chib (1996) the use of MCMC. Green (1995) for different number of changepoints reversible jump, the MCMC is used to explore model and parameters. There are more studies of the Poisson change model: Raftery and Akman (1986) used a Bayesian approach for the estimation of a change point in homogenous Poisson process and Loader (1992) considered the change point in non-homogenous Poisson process.

Many studies have considered multiple change points in the literature. Henderson and Matthews (1993) examined the situation where there are multiple change points in the sequence of Poisson random variables. In their study, they used the binary segmentation process to search for multiple changes. Chen and Gupta (1997) considered testing and locating multiple variance change points in a sequence of independent Gaussian random variables, and Chen and Gupta (2007) studied two change points model, consisting of a smooth change followed by an abrupt change using the Bayesian approach. Hinkley (1970) studied the change point problem in a sequence of binomial variables. Worsley (1986), Haccou, Meelis and Geer (1988), Jandhyala and Fotopoulos (1999, 2001), Boudjelaba, MacGibbon and Sawyer (2001) and Fotopoulos and Jandhyala (2001) all investigated change-point Poisson variables.

In this paper, a single change point model in the homogeneous Poisson process is thoroughly examined.

2. Method

Change-point models change in the parameters of the underlying distribution. It interest point in time. Change-point analysis application is wide, but it is particularly relevant in finance, the environment, and medicine.

The use of the Markov chain Monte Carlo (MCMC) methods to evaulate integral quantities have exploded over the last two decades. Begining with the seminal review paper by Gelfand and Smith (1990), the rate of publication of MCMC works has grown exponentially. While this is relatively a recent development, the genesis dates back to two important works: the 1953 essay by Metropolis et al., and Geman and Geman's (1984) introduction of the Gibbs sampler as a method for obtaining difficult posterior quantitites in the process of image restoration (Gıll, 2008).

The analysis of Bayesian changepoint models, assuming an unknown number of changepoints, goes back to Yao (1984) who estimates a discrete-time changepoint model with Gaussian noise by a sequential algorithm. Barry and Hartigan (1993) propose a sequential algorithm for the estimation of a discrete-time changepoint model based on the product partition model. A continuous-time changepoint model was analysed by Green (1995) using the reversible-jump algorithm. Fearnhead (2006) extends the sequential algorithm of Barry and Hartigan (1993) to the case of prior that can be factorised to a prior on the number of changepoints and a prior on the location of the changepoints given the number of changepoints, as used in Green (1995).

We will use the Poisson model on the much analysed data set of yearly numbers of Turkish coal-mining disasters during the 32-year period of 1983–2014. Frequentist change-point investigations appear in Worsley (1986) and in Siegmund (1988), while Raftery and Akman (1986) apply their Bayesian model to investigate a continuous single change-point. Broemeling and Grequrich (1996) investigated a discrete single change-point, while Carlin, Gelfand and Smith (1992) used Gibbs sampling in examining for a single change-point. Green (1995) considered multiple change-points with the reversible jump algorithm.

Poisson Change-Point Model

Consider the much-used data set of annual counts of Turkish coal mining 'disasters' from 1983 to 2014. The data, covering the years 1983 to 2014, are in Table 1.

Table 1: Turkish coal mining disaster count between 1983–2014

1983	1984	1985	1986	1987	1988	1989	1990	1991	1992	1993	1994	1995	1996	1997	1998	1999	2000	2001	2002	2003	2004	2005	2006	2007	2008	2009	2010	2011	2012	2013	2014
3	0	0	0	1	0	0	2	0	2	0	0	1	0	0	0	0	0	0	0	2	2	1	1	8	0	1	4	1	3	2	2

Figure 1: Number of explosions per year in Turkish coal mines

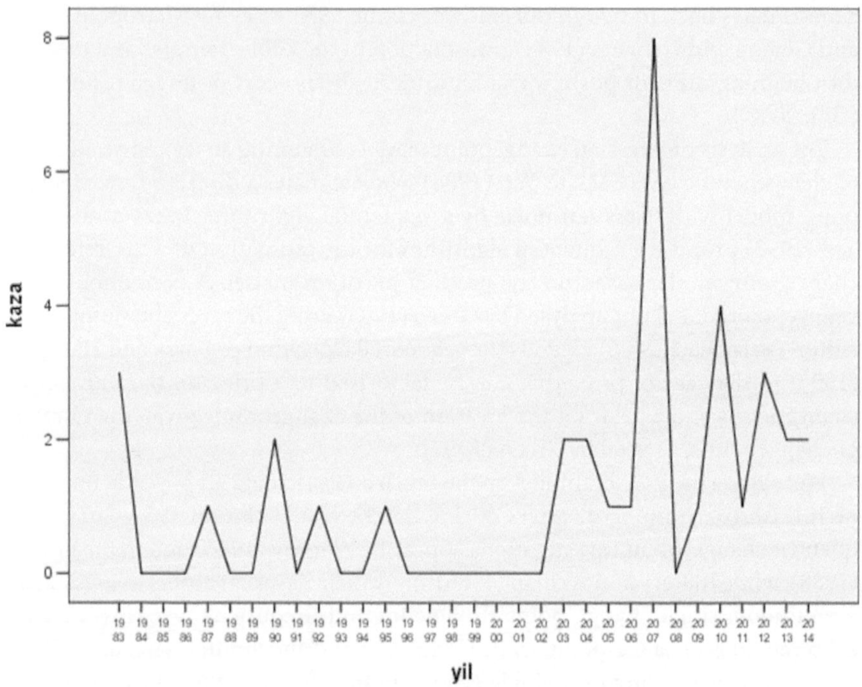

Looking at the data suggests that the rate of accidents decreased sometime around 1900, so a plausible first model is that the counts are independent Poisson with mean λ_1 before time Γ and mean λ_2 from time Γ onwards, where we expect $\lambda_2 < \lambda_1$. This is the simplest possible case, and we could consider more than one changepoint.

For a Bayesian analysis we need a prior distribution on the three parameters $(\Gamma; \lambda_1; \lambda_2)$. If we take them as independent and of conjugate form, the posterior can be found analytically (Gamerman & Lopes, 2006, pp. 143), but a realistic prior will have a dependent distribution of $(\lambda_1; \lambda_2)$. That is easy to do in the MCMC framework by re-weighting—for a more complex application to radiocarbon dating see Gilks et al. (1996).

We will consider computing posterior distributions via MCMC in two ways. R package MCMCpack has a function MCMCpoissonChange with an MCMC scheme coded in C++, implementing the method of Chib (1998). This has independent gamma priors for the rates and beta priors for the transition point(s). The R code is simple:

```
N=32
D=c(3, 0, 0, 0, 1, 0, 0, 2, 0, 1, 0, 0, 1, 0, 0, 0, 0, 0, 0, 0, 2, 2, 1, 1, 8, 0, 1, 4, 1, 3, 2, 2)
data=list
parameters<-c("changeyear", "b")
inits=function(){list(b=c(0,0),changeyear=16)}
coalmining.sim<-c(data, inits, parameters,
+ «kömür», n.chains=3, n.iter=1000)
print(coalmining.sim)
## D is an integer vector of N = 32 counts.
library(MCMCpack)
kömür<- MCMCpoissonChange(D ~ 1, m = 1, c0 = 1, d0 = 1,
burnin = 1000, mcmc = 1000)
plot(kömür); par(mfrow=c(1,1))
acfplot(kömür); effectiveSize(kömür)
summary(kömür)
plotState(kömür)
plotChangepoint(kömür, start = 1983)
summary(kömür.sim)
```

The arguments say that we are looking for m = 1 changepoints, and specify a gamma(1; 1) prior for the mean counts λ_i. In that approach, someone else has done all the work in designing and coding a suitable MCMC scheme—this is fast but not general.

Figure 2: Posterior distribution for the year of change in disaster rate. The red dashed line marks the median

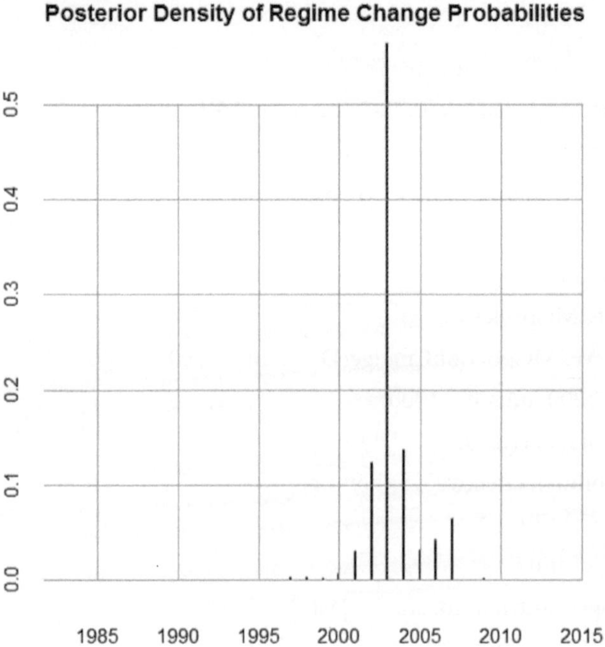

As MCMC is an iterative scheme we have to supply initial values of the parameters: it is possible to supply (as a list of lists as here) separate starting values for each run, or a function that will give a random list result.

The result object can be summarised and plotted. The printout looks like

1. Empirical mean and standard deviation for each variable,
   plus standard error of the mean:

	Mean	SD	Naive SE	Time-series SE
(Intercept)_regime1	0.4669	0.1623	0.005133	0.005804
(Intercept)_regime2	2.1423	0.4316	0.013648	0.013648

2. Quantiles for each variable:

	2.5%	25%	50%	75%	97.5%
(Intercept)_regime1	0.2044	0.3481	0.4452	0.5596	0.8525
(Intercept)_regime2	1.3952	1.8333	2.1143	2.4064	3.0682

3. Discussion

This suggests that there was an observed decrease in the rate of occurrence between 1983–2002 period, rather than a sustained gradual decrease. This may be associated with changes in the coal industry around that time, namely a severe decline in labour productivity at the end of the 2000s. A possible causal link is suggested by Dwyer who argues that industrial accident rates are closely tied to the state of functioning of social relations in the workplace. While factors associated with higher labour productivity, such as overtime, may cause an increase in accident rates. The Gibbs sampler appears to be a suitable method for estimating. The full posterior distribution since. The full conditionals can be found algebraically. The conditionals are easy to sample from. We found the changepoint between the two levels of disaster rates to be at about 2003.

References

Akman V. E. & Raftery A.E. (1986). Asymptotic Inference for a Changepoint Poisson Process, The Annals of Statistics, Vol. 14, No. 4, 1583–1590.

Aktaş, S.; Konşuk, H. & Yiğiter, A. (2009). Estimation of change point and compound Poisson process parameters for the earthquake data in Turkey, *Environmetrics*, Vol. 20, No. 4, 416–427.

Alan E. Gelfand; Adrian F. M. Smith (1990). Sampling-Based Approaches to Calculating Marginal Densities, *Journal of the American Statistical Association*, Vol. 85, No. 410. 398–409.

Barry D. & Hartigan J. (1993). A Bayesian analysis for change point problems, Journal of the American Statistical Association, 88 (1993), 309–319.

Boudjellaba, H., MacGibbon, B. and Sawyer, P. (2001). On exact inference for change in a Poisson sequence. Commun. in Statist. A: Theory and Methods, 30(3), 407–434.

Broemeling, L. D. and Gregurich, M. A. (1996). On a Bayesian approach for the shift point problem. Commun. Statist. Theory Methods. 25, 2267–2279.

Carlin, B.P., Gelfand, A. E., Smith, A.F.M. (1992). Hierarchical Bayesian Analysis of Changepoint Problem. Applied Statistics, 41, 389–405.

Chen, Jie and Gupta, A. K. (1997). Testing and locating variance change points with application to stock prices, J. Amer. Statist. Assoc., 92, 739–747.

Chib, S. (1996). Calculating posterior distributions and modal estimates in Markov mixture models, Journal of Econometrics, 75, 79–98.

Chib, S. (1998). Estimation and comparison of multiple change-point models. Journal of Econometrics, 86, 221–241.

Dwyer, T. (1983). A new concept of the production of industrial accidents: A social approach. N. Z. J. Ind. Rel. 8, 147–60.

Fearnhead, P. (2006). Exact and efficient Bayesian inference for multiple change-point problems. Stat. Comput. 16, 203–213.

Fotopoulos, S.B. and Jandhyala, V.K. (2001). Maximum likelihood estimation of a change-point for exponentially distributed random variables. Statist. and Prob. Letters, 51, 423–429.

Gelfand, A. E., Smith, A. F. M. (1990). Sampling-Based Approaches to Calculating Marginal Densities, Journal of the American Statistical Association, Vol. 85, No. 410.

Geman and Geman, (1984). Stochastic Relaxation, Gibbs Distributions, and the Bayesian Restoration of Images, IEEE Transactions on Pattern Analysis and Machine Intelligence, Vol. 6, 721–741.

Gill, J. (2008). Bayesian Methods A Social and Behavioral Sciences Approach, Chapman & Hall / CRC, U.S.A.

Green, P. T. (1995). Reversible jump Markov chain Monte Carlo computation and Bayesian model determination, Biometrika, 82 (4).

Haccou, P., Meelis, E. and Geer, S. (1988). The likelihood ratio test for the shift point problem for exponentially distributed random variables. Stochastic Process and Their Applications, 27, 121–139.

Henderson, R. and Matthews, J. N. S. (1993). An investigation of changepoints in the annual number of cases of haemolytic uraemic syndrome. *Applied Statistics*, Vol. 42, 461–471.

Hinkley, D. V. (1970). Inference about the change point in a sequence of random variables, Biometrika, 57, 1–7.

Jandhyala, V.K. and Fotopoulos, S.B. (1999). Capturing the distributional behaviour of the maximum likelihood estimator of a change point, Biometrika, 86(1), 129–140.

Jandhyala, V.K. and Fotopoulos, S.B. (2001). Rate of convergence of the maximum likelihood estimate of a change-point. Sankhya A, 63(2), 277–285.

Jaudet, M. (2009). Change-point analysis of coal mining disasters data in various time resolutions, Mehran University Research Journal of Engineering and Technology; v. 28(1); ISSN 0254-7821; Jan 2009; p. 31–40.

Loader C. R. (1992). A Log-Linear Model for a Poisson Process Change Point, The Annals of Statistics, Vol. 20, No. 3, pp. 1391–1411.

Siegmund D. (1988). Confidence Sets in Change-Point Problems, International Statistical Review / Revue Internationale de Statistique, Vol. 56, No. 1, 31–48.

Stephens D.A. (1994). Bayesian retrospective multiple-changepoint identification, Applied Statistics, 43, pp. 159–178.

Worsley, K. J. (1986). Confidence regions and tests for a change point in a sequence of exponential family random variables, Biometrika, 73, 91–104.

Yao Y.C. (1984). Estimation of a noisy discrete-time step function: Bayes and Empirical Bayes approaches, Annals of Statistics, 12 (1984), pp. 1434–1447.

Yigiter, A. & İnal, C. (2010). Estimation of change points in a homogeneous Poisson process with an application to earthquake data, Pakistan Journal of Statistics, Vol. 26, No. 3, pp. 525–538.

Asst. Prof. Ozgur Emre Koc* & Asst. Prof. Mustafa Taytak**

Regulatory Government Approach Application of Independent Administrative Authorities and Turkey, as Policy Implementers***

Abstract Today, the government has become an institution that establishes and monitors regulatory rules, in order to eliminate trouble in the market and to prevent any trouble from occuring. The public sector regulates and monitors the markets through independent administrative authorities with the aim of resolving market failures. Independent administrative authorities function in a wide range varying from the energy sector to the banking sector.

In this study, information on the changing role of the government and independent administrative authorities established according to the regulation theory will be presented. Additionally, a comparative analysis will be performed by country examples regarding the working areas of these authorities in Turkey.

Keywords: Regulatory Government, Independent Authorities, Regulation

1. Introduction

Globalisation tendencies to become more widespread today has caused the evolution of the activities, which the government realises as an economic element, from economic interventionism towards regulative interventionism. When considered from the perspective of two functions, Buchanan classified the government as the producer and protector. It is possible to state that the producer role of the government has remained in a limited area today. The protector role of the government on the other hand has acquired a new dimension. In the new economic approach, the government is expected to be smaller, take on the coordination role only, acquire a more functional quality, make legal regulations and to have a more flexible structure.

The topic about the necessity of what the role of the government needs to be in the economy has found a place within the main approach coming from the past to

---

* Hitit University, Faculty of Economics and Administrative Sciences, Corum, Turkey, oemrekoc@hitit.edu.tr

** Usak University, Faculty of Economics and Administrative Sciences, Usak, Turkey mustafa.taytak@usak.edu.tr

*** This study was supported by the Hitit University Scientific Research Projects Unit. Project No: BEDE 1908–04

the present. These thoughts have been listed in the subtitles of liberal, conservative, social democrat, and socialist thoughts. Differing from each other, these thoughts gave the government different tasks and roles within the economy. An analysis of the relationship of government with the economy caused different government types to emerge (Sarisoy, 2008).

2. Changing Role of Government

In the study named "Changing Role of the Government in the Economy," Tanzi stated that historical developments created differences in the role of the government and summarised the changing role of the government into five main headings. According to Tanzi, behaviours resulting from cultural or religious traditions, economic development level regarding the magnitude of the government intervention to the economy in addition to the effectiveness of market and private institutions, openness level of the economy, occurrence or removal of natural monopolies against financial markets and technological changes, quality of public administration determining the borders of government intervention to economy all enabled the role of government in the economy to change (Tanzi, 1997).

The two main characteristics of the regulative government are: (i) "institutional regulations" and (ii) "regulative applications." The neo-regulative government allowed the establishment of independent regulative institutions unique to sectors regarding institutional regulations. This situation especially stands out as the principal characteristic in England. In countries other than England, regulative government applications have a common characteristic in terms of institutional regulation (Bartle & Müller, 2002).

New Deal practices, which were developed in the United States of America (US) where regulative government is practiced as an open policy, and regulative government practices in the post-World War II period have been assessed as a success of the American leftists. Although regulative government practices started to be structured as a legal, political, and administrative tool of the administration in the US since the second half of 19th century; regulative government practice in Europe can be described as part of the efforts of catching up to the New Deal program (Jordan & Levi-Faur).

The regulative government in the US is based in the new public administration approach in terms of understanding. New public administration aims to re-define public services within the framework of a private sector understanding (Scott, 2003). In line with this aim, public and private sector can provide public service simultaneously. In this respect, public service regulations can exist within the context of the acts of institutions providing public service to be directed by regulative institutions (Cope & Goodship, 1999).

The regulation practice in Europe is different than the New Deal in terms of quality. However, the regulative government in Europe, where nationalisation developed instead of regulation as a response to the rise of large businesses and social concerns, the government has felt the need to intervene with the market through mechanisms that allow intervention before the damage occurs and to make corrections through mechanisms such as punishment after the practice is realised (Braitwaite, 2000).

The World Bank used the concept of "market friendly government" (Peker, 1996) and according to this new government understanding, the government acted supportively at a degree to minimal government understanding of neo-liberal economy approach, by stating that government should act not to replace the market but to eliminate its deficits (World Bank, 1991).

3. Regulation Concept

Although the word of regulation seems to be related to the science of law since it includes a regulative, monitoring and leading understanding; it is also related to other fields of science. In the financial literature, the term of regulation does not have a clear definition. Regulation can broadly be defined as regulating the financial activities of the private sector in a way that will increase the well-being of the society (Francis, 1993). In today's practice, the regulation concept constitutes regulation, monitoring and leading activities performed by autonomous institutions.

The regulation concept is defined in two different ways in the financial literature. The first of these definitions is regulation in a narrow meaning. According to this definition, regulation is a complete set of rules supported by sanctions, which individuals and governments and firms established to prevent economically and socially unwanted behaviours. The second regulation definition was made broadly, and is described as controlling and regulating all kinds of activity and processes through any authority or mechanism, which holds the opportunity to create sanctions (Guasch & Hahn, 1999).

Purposes regarding regulative policies can be listed as follows (OECD, 2002):

- Contributing to the realisation of social welfare by effectively directing and balancing social and financial policies,
- Assuring consumer welfare by encouraging market entry, competition and competitiveness and realising economic growth,
- Controlling in a way that will increase effectiveness in production by decreasing the costs of regulative process,

- Executing effectiveness, responsibility and efficiency in public sector through reform studies regarding public administration,
- Enabling the practice of laws in a convenient and effective way.

4. Independent Regulatory Institutions (Management Authorities) and their Characteristics

The concept of an independent management authority is public institutions with legal entities that performs the activities of regulation, monitoring, and leading in financial and social sectors with basic rights and freedoms (Ulusoy, 2003), owns administrative autonomy, uses its powers independently, and have accountability within the framework of principles determined in their laws (Karacan, 2001, Akıncı, 1999).

Independent regulatory agencies are the primary institutions becoming prominent within the governance structure the government will settle in order to fulfil its regulation, monitoring, and audit functions (Majone, 1994; Scott, 1999; Gilardi, 2002).

IROs, as one of the elements becoming prominent since the 1990s, reflect the new understanding the government focuses on to determine the rules that economic actors will be required to obey and to enable these rules to be implemented.

Various names are being made in the literature for independent regulatory commissions, which are not similar to any of the administrative structures that existed until today, such as supreme courts, regulatory boards, regulators, regulation institutions, and autonomous establishments.

Both organisations and functions of these agencies differ from country to country. For instance, in the US these agencies are defined as "Independent Regulatory Agencies," while in England the "Quangos" (quans Autonomous Non-Governmental) concept is used. On the other hand, French law states them as "Les Autorités Administratives Indépendantes." In Turkey this concept is explained in a way similar to France with the statement defined as "independent administrative authority" (Autorités Administratives indépendantes). In Turkey names such as autonomous institutions, supreme boards, regulatory boards, independent regulators, and supervisory boards are used (Özdağ, 2002).

IRCs, which were built within the framework of restructuring of the government after the 1980s, draws attention with its three characteristics taking place in its concept. The word independent represents the independency of the institution against execution in organic and functional terms; the word regulatory displays its executive organ quality; the word commission expresses these are not consulting organs but institutions that have regulatory and administrative decision making authority, that is, institutions that make and implement decisions influencing the legal status (Gözübüyük ve Tan, 2004).

One of the most important fields of activity of these institutions is to prevent the acts that depart the market from rules, that is, to play a regulative role in the market in economic activities in the areas from which the government withdrew. The essence of these interventions should be enabling the free market conditions not to fail. The government should act as a referee here. The interventions of politicians also take place within all kinds of threatening interventions that might occur against market conditions (Aslan, 2010).

Within the context of the regulation concept, these institutions realise monitoring and auditing activities. They control whether both laws and their own legislations are respected or not. Perhaps the most important activity of these institutions is their authority to implement sanctions. These institutions are awarded sanction authority with the aim of enabling conformity to current rules about their areas of activity. Indeed, the characteristic that transforms these institutions as management authorities is this. The sanction these institutions own are "penal sanctionings given by a transaction of the agency directly, without entering a judicatory verdict and with methods unique to administrative law, in cases that laws clearly permit or do not forbid" (Aslan, 2010).

5. Emergence of Independent Regulatory Agencies (Management Authorities)

The widespread government approach today is the minimal government approach, which leaves the operation of the economy to market forces and acts as a referee in the operability of the market economy with the institutions and rules it owns, instead of the producing-intervening wealth government approach that emerged after the Second World War.

This new understanding switched the function of the public sector as determining the rules regulating economic activities and auditing the adaptation all economic actors to these rules, instead of direct intervention to the economy.

The US is the first country, in which IRCs appeared. A commission was formed in the 19th century to solve the problems of regulating increasing traffic and transportation of produced goods, growing railway, truck and water transportation, which emerged in the process of industrialisation experienced in the US. The US President delegated the execution authority to the Interstate Commerce Commission (ICC) with a special statute introduced in 1887. Therefore, the ICC went down in history as the first IRC (Günay & Özen, 2004).

So-called regulation and auditing function of public sector is realised through Independent Regulatory Agencies (Management Authorities). Independent regulatory agencies are defined as the building Stones of the regulatory government. They have become a very important institution, which prevents market deficiencies from occuring and conducts regulations and audits protecting the market structure.

This development, which was experienced at the federal level, displayed its influence in the state level as well. This new understanding started much earlier in states such as New York, Wisconsin, and Massachusetts. For instance, the Massachusetts State Commission that was established in 1885 is responsible for telegram, transportation services, and regulation in the electricity sectors (Müftüoğlu, 2002).

As Continental Europe is analysed, Independent Regulatory Agencies are seen to have emerged widely in England with the influence of the Anglo-Saxon system in the years following the Second World War. Thatcher separated the independent regulatory agencies into two, in line with the basics of market theory, as agencies regulating the functioning of markets and institutions making regulations directed to protect public welfare. Institutions in the first group have the regulatory powers such as preventing unfair competition in the market, issuing licences, and performing price controls. The institutions that are included in the second group on the other hand, in order to maintain public service in areas other than competition, perform the practices such as determining standards in related areas, issuing licences, preventing supply more than the authorised amount, and enabling necessary information flow in topics of environment and health (Thatcher, 2002).

The aim of protecting a more organised operation of market mechanisms as secure authorities via basic rights and freedoms against political power and economic pressure groups and without their intervention, pressure or influences were under the establishment of these rules in Europe. Although inspired from the US as a sample, when the unitary structure of many European countries, especially France is considered, the organisation type in Europe displays different properties. While these rules are named as the Fourth Power, they were accepted as units included in executive power in many European countries.

6. Duties and Authorities of Independent Regulatory Commissions

One of the characteristics that differentiate independent regulatory commissions from classical administrative structure is the duties these institutions took over and the responsibilities they own. While these commissions conduct regulations in the areas they operate in, they can also use authorities such as auditing whether actions comply with the regulations and imposing sanctions if necessary. Other than these, independent regulatory commissions also have duties and authorities such as monitoring, research-investigation, expressing opinion, resolving conflict, and taking individual measures.

6.1 Regulation Authority

Regulation authority is the authority to impose general and abstract norms. Regulation authority independent regulatory commissions have results from the institution laws determining their areas of. Regulation authority mainly constitutes the existence reason of independent regulatory commissions and aims to regulate important sectors of life in line with public welfare and public order requirements.

An important reason of the establishment of independent regulatory commissions is to perform regulations for the audit of variables such as price, quantity, market entry and exit conditions, quality, and security in the name of increasing effectiveness in market operations in areas market failures exist. Independent regulatory commissions can use this authority by making legislations, since they are public corporate entities.

6.2 Supervision and Audit Authority

Independent regulatory commissions have to take necessary precautions by observing whether the rules they put in via laws and their own regulations are obeyed or not. Because of this reason, these institutions request the information and documents it considers necessary from the related parties, consults their knowledge and conducts physical site visits when needed (Akıncı, 1999).

Whether the enterprises willing to get permission for the entrance to the sector holds the required conditions or not and whether produced goods and services have predetermined quality or not enters into the scope of supervision and audit authority of the independent regulatory commissions.

6.3 Authority to Present Opinions

Independent regulatory commissions also perform a consulting function by presenting opinions to related ministries and other institutions a similar statuses about the topic that are placed under their own working area (Tan, 2003).

As expert institutions in their own fields, IRCs may perform the consulting function by presenting their opinions to private or public agencies and institutes intended for the field they operate in (Akıncı, 1999).

6.4 Authority to Apply Sanctions

IRCs have the authority to impose important sanctions in the areas they are related to. This is one of the characteristics distinguishing IRCs from other institutions. Even the fact that they have the authority to impose sanctions causes discussions of whether they can be qualified as judicial or quasi-judicial institutions (Parlak ve Sobacı, 2005).

Authority to impose sanctions is the authority of independent regulatory commissions that highlights their unique properties the most. These powers of the authorities play an effective role especially in removing the dense pressure of the market economy on individual freedoms.

In case independent regulatory commissions identify contradictions to law in areas they regulate and audit; methods like warning the related party before imposing sanction, allowing written and oral defense, maintaining a proportionality between the sanction and the act, and justifiably declaration of the verdict to be made (Dönmez, 2003).

7. Independent Regulatory Agencies (Management Authorities) in Turkey

Aims of regulating market economy in the financial area became prominent in the Turkish practice of supreme boards. Supreme boards were established in the first half of the 1980s with the effect of liberalisation policies, which started with the January 24 decisions, on government organisation. Dependency to international finance institutions within the process because of financial negativities directly affected the development of supreme boards. The relationships with the European Union (EU) adaptation process on the one hand and IMF and World Bank on the other hand, which foresee radical changes in public administration, caused a process of establishing an increasing number of supreme boards in Turkey.

7.1 Capital Market Board

The first IRC built in Turkey was the Capital Market Board. The Capital Market Board was settled in 1981. It is a public institution, which independently uses its authorities under its own responsibility and which has administrative and financial autonomy. The ministry it is related to is the Ministry of State assigned by the Prime Minister. The board consists of seven members in total with the assignment of the Council of Ministers. Two members are among the four candidates identified by the government house, and one person each from two candidates recommended by the Ministry of Finance, Ministry of Customs and Trade, BRSA,

Turkish Union of Chambers and Exchange Commodities and association of capital market intermediary institutions.

The board performs the duties of regulating, monitoring, researching and questioning market instruments, and the cancellation and punishment of this area. Audit and monitoring tasks that the commission undertook can be named as activities directed towards the aim of assuring the order again, in case the economic order in the capital markets break down.

The main duties and authorities of the commission include: (i) Regulating and auditing issuance, public offering and sale of capital market instruments, (ii) Tracking and auditing the activities of institutions, stock markets and other organised markets operating in capital market, (iii) Regulating options contracts and the institutions that will operate in the stock markets, in which these options will be traded, (iv) Regulating borrowing and leasing, short selling and repo transactions of stocks and bonds, (v) Identifying the principles regarding the independent audit practices in the capital market, including electronic media.

7.2 Radio and Television High Council

The government monopoly in this area was broken together with the start of multi-channel radio and television broadcast period, which was a result of the establishment of private radio and televisions especially since 1990s. Obstacles towards private radio and television broadcasts were removed with legal regulations. The High Council consists of nine members, who are selected by the Turkish Grand National Assembly and who have adequate professional knowledge and experience, and are over 30 years old.

Duties and authorities of the High Council are as follows: (i) Issuing release and license to applicant institutions, which fulfilled the pre-conditions, (ii) Issuing the permission of building and operating broadcasting transmitter facilities to radio and television institutions for their national, regional and local broadcasts, and to audit the adequacy of the conditions, (iii) Issuing the permission to build and operate telecommunication facilities to radio and television institutions, and auditing the operation of the facilities in accordance with the principle, (iv) Encouraging the institutions to broadcast in different parts of the country, (v) Determining necessary pre-conditions and standards, which public and private radio-television institutions should meet for broadcasting permission.

7.3 Competition Authority

The ministry it is related to is the Ministry of Customs and Trade. The Competition Authority is composed of seven members in total, of which one of them is the President and another is the Vice President.

The main duties and authorities of the institution is to prevent agreements, decisions and practices that prevent, spoil, or limit the competition in product and service markets, and to prevent misuse of the dominance of enterprises that rule over the market, to assure competition by making necessary regulations and audits for this.

7.4 Information and Communication Technologies Authority

The institution was settled with the purpose of building effective competition through regulation and audit in electronic communication sector, taking consumer rights in hand, wide spreading services throughout the country, using resources efficiently and productively, encouraging technological improvement and new investments in the area of communication infrastructure, network and service, and determining the procedures and principles related to these.

Duties and authorities of the institution are: (i) Making regulations devoted to building and sustaining competition in the electronic communication sector, and removing practices that prevent, spoil or limit competition, and taking necessary precautions, (ii) Auditing competition violations occurring in electronic communication sector, imposing necessary sanctions in case of a violation, (iii) Making necessary regulations and auditing regarding the processing personal information and protection of privacy, (iv) Controlling the proper establishment and operation of radio systems according to determined techniques and methods, (v) Determining the scope of commercial secrets and information of operators that can be publicised, protecting the privacy of commercial secrets and investment and business plans of operators, and preserving these other than the demands of legal authorities, (vi) Determining the principles about independent audit activity and the qualities of institutions that will perform audit activities in the electronic communication sector.

7.5 Energy Market Regulatory Board

The institution has been assigned to regulate electricity, natural gas, liquid petroleum gas (LPG) and oil markets, which are associated with the Ministry of Energy and Natural Resources.

The commission has the authority to make regulations and audits on the natural gas market, petrol market and LPG markets.

Table 1: Duties of the Energy Market Regulatory Board

Duties of the commission about natural gas market	**Duties of the commission regarding the petrol market**	**Duties of the commission about LPG**
Specifying opinions and recommendations about plan, policy and applications related to natural gas market.	Making all kinds of regulations related to market practices and assuring their execution.	Making all kinds of regulations corresponding to LPG market and assuring their execution.
Fulfilling obligations, which emerge as a result of international agreements that are directly adhered and are about natural gas market practices.	Presenting opinions and recommendations regarding the plans, policies, and applications about petrol activities.	Specifying Commission's opinions and recommendations related to plans, policies and applications about the LPG market practices.
Approving all kinds of regulations concerning natural gas practices and securing the execution of these.	Carrying out audit, research, and investigation transactions concerning petrol market activities.	Executing audit, preliminary survey and investigation transactions about LPG market activities.
Making and implementing all kinds of decisions corresponding to granting license and certificates, and their execution and cancellation.	Designating license and transaction prices about licenses in petrol market.	Determining fees for license and transactions about licenses in the LPG market.
Making decisions aimed at determining price and fixing limitations and obligations about the market in special cases.	Inspecting the audited financial statements of individuals operating in the petrol market, or having these inspected.	Analysing the financial statements of individuals operating in the LPG market, or having them analysed
Regulating principles and procedures pertaining to price and tariff in areas, in which competition is not formed or inadequately formed within the natural gas market.	In cases, in which tariffs and regulations, license decrees and conditions and Commission decisions are offended against, imposing a monetary fine and cancelling licenses	Making all kinds of regulations corresponding to LPG market and assuring their execution.
Approving tariffs or making decisions about tariff revisions.	Making all kinds of regulations related to market practices and assuring their execution.	Specifying Commission's opinions and recommendations related to LPG market practices.

7.6 Public Procurement Authority (PPA)

The PPA was established with the purpose of assuring transparency and a competition environment in public tenders, and building a fast and effective audit mechanism for illegal transactions and acts of administrations that makes a tender (Sezer, 2002).

Duties and authorities of the institution about tenders are: (i) Bringing complaints to a conclusion by examining them in transactions, which are done in a time period from the start of the tender to the signing of the contract, (ii) Preparing and developing standard tender documents and standard contracts, and guiding the application, (iii) Providing trainings for procurement legislation, assuring national and international coordination, (iv) Keeping records of individuals, who have been given proscriptive decision for entering tenders, (v) Having research and development activities.

7.7 Tobacco, Tobacco Products and Alcoholic Beverages Market Regulation Board (TABMR)

The TABMR's function of regulating and auditing the market includes activities devoted to preventing flaws of the markets defined as economic regulation and improving market effectiveness, activities that are stated as social regulation towards protecting the rights and increasing the wealth of the society, and activities named as administrative regulation regarding the body of rules about in what way the transaction in which government gets involved will be realised.

Duties and authorities of the commission are: (i) Making necessary sectoral regulations or making decisions and taking precautions and executing these, enabling their execution and monitoring and auditing market activities in order to assure the realisation of activities in its market in an orderly, transparent, and secure way, (ii) Implementing administrative sanctions in sectors or areas for which it is responsible of regulating and auditing, and having administrative measures, (iii) Making regulations devoted to determination competition and commercial conditions regarding sale and exhibition activities of tobacco products and alcoholic beverages, monitoring activities, guiding and auditing, (iv) Making regulations and studies that will prevent activities, which will encourage tobacco and alcohol consumption.

7.8 Banking Regulation and Supervision Agency (BRSA)

The main mission of the BRSA is to create the adequate environment, in which banks and private financial institutions will operate in market discipline in a healthy, effective and competitive structure, and thus to contribute to long term growth and stability of the country.

The basic goals of the agency can be listed as: (i) Protecting rights and interests of account owners, (ii) Sustaining the trust to the sector permanently, (iii) Minimising the harms the sector may create over the economy, (iv) Improving the sustainability of the sector, (v) Increasing the effectiveness and competition ability of the sector (BDDK, 2001).

Main duties, authorities and responsibilities of the agency are: (i) Regulating procedures and principles regarding owning and using bank cards and credit cards, and bartering and offsetting transactions, (ii) Regulating establishment and activities, mergers, separation, share barter and liquidation of financial leasing, factoring and finance companies, (iii) In case of demand, providing information to the Undersecretariat of Treasury, State Planning Organization and the Central Bank about the execution of money, credit and banking policies, (iv) Preventing all kinds of transactions and application that might jeopardise the rights of account owners and the operation of banks, and create serious damages, (v) Assuring the operation of credit system in an effective way.

8. Conclusion

Developments experienced in the global economy since the 1970s and the practices started in the UK and the US influenced the entire world with the help of international institutions. As a result of developments experienced in this period, the regulatory government concept entered the literature. This new government understanding brought together distribution, stability, and regulation (increasing productivity by removing market deficiencies) functions.

While the government in the regulatory government gains a strategic importance that re-regulates financial activities; it also took a shape that protects competition power, regulates competition and tries to prevent the formation of risks that will endanger the functioning of the market.

Together with this new understanding, the government started to be highlighted with its character that is regulative on behalf of the market in accordance with a Neoliberal understanding. The regulatory government takes its power from independent regulatory commissions.

Independent regulatory commissions have the property of combining three forces of government with the regulating, auditing, imposing sanctions and conflict resolution authorities it owns. With this status, independent regulatory commissions are in a position as the fourth force of the government. By purifying economy from political pressures via the independent regulatory commissions it has, regulatory government degrade economy management to a technical incident.

References

Akıncı, M. (1999). *Bağımsız İdari Otoriteler ve Ombudsman*. Ankara: Beta Yayıncılık.

Bartle, I., Müller, M. M., Sturm, R. & Wilks, S. (2002). The Regulatory State:Britain and Germany Compared. Retrieved September 9, 2015, from http://www.agf.org.uk/cms/upload/pdfs/R/2002_R1268_e_regulatory_state.pdf.

BDDK, (2001). Bankacılık Sektörü Yeniden Yapılandırma Programı. Ankara.

Braithwaıte, J. (2000). The New Regulatory State And Transformation of The Criminology. *Brit. J. Criminol.* Is. 40. 222–238.

Colin, S. (2003). Regulation in the Age of Governance: The Rise of the Post-Regulatory State. *National Europe Centre Paper*. No. 100, 6 Australian National University. Retrieved December 13, 2015, from http://dspace.anu.edu.au/bitstream/1885/41716/2/scott1.pdf.

Cope, S., & Goodship, J. (1999). Comparing Regulatory Regimes in the New Governance. *Regulating The New Governance Panel.* Retrieved December 11, 2015, from http://www.psa.ac/uk/cps/1999/cope.pdf.

Dönmez, E. (2003). Türkiye'de Bağımsız İdari Otoriteler. *Ankara Barosu Dergisi.* 2. 55–78.

Francis, J. G. (1993). *The Politics of Regulation: A Comparative Perspectives.* Blackwell Pub., Camridge.

Gözübüyük, Ş., & Tan, T. (2004). *İdari Hukuku.* Ankara: Turhan Kitabevi.

Guasch, L. & Hahn, R. (1997). The Cost and Benefits of Regulation: Implication for Developing Countries. *The World Bank Research Observer.* 14. 1. February.

Günay, A., & Özen. A. (2004). Bağımsız Düzenleyici Kurumlar ve Türkiye. *Vergi Sorunları Dergisi.* 184, 169–189.

Jordana, J. & Levi-Faur. D. The politics of regulation in the age of governance. Retrieved September 9, 2015, from http://ggpp.upf.edu/web/book/doc/chapter1.pdf.

Karacan, A. İ. (2001). Özerk Kurumların Özerkliği. *Rekabet Dergisi.* 8 (3–59).

Kovancılar, B., Miynat, M. &. Bursalıoğlu, S. (2007). *Kamu Maliyesinde Küresel Değişimler.* Gazi Kitapevi.

Müftüoğlu, M. T., & Karabudak, H. B. (2002). İktisadi Politikalar Bağlamında Hukuki Düzenleme (Regülasyon) Üzerine Düşünceler. *Rekabet Dergisi.* 11. 3–14.

OECD (2002). Regulatory Policies in OECD Countries: from Interventionism to Regulatory Governance. *OECD Reviews of Regulatory Reform*. OECD, Paris-France.

Özdağ, M. Savaş. (2002). Özerk Kurullar. *Avrasya Stratejik Araştırmalar Merkezi.* Ankara Çalışmaları Dizisi No: 13. Ankara.

Parlak, B., & Sobacı, Z. (2005). *Kuram ve Uygulamada Kamu Yönetimi Ulusal ve Global Perspektifler*. Alfa Aktüel, İstanbul.

Sarısoy, S. (2008). *Devletin Ekonomideki Düzenleyici Rolü: Türk Elektrik Piyasası Örneği*. Marmara Üniversitesi SBE Maliye Anabilim Dalı Maliye Teorisi Bilim Dalı Yayımlanmamış Doktora Tezi. İstanbul.

Sezer, Y. (2002). Kamu İhale Kanunu: Şeffaflık ve Rekabet. *Amme İdaresi Dergisi.*

Talat Aslan, N. (2010). Yönetimin Yeni Yapı Taşları Bağımsız İdari Otoriteler: "Yavru Leviathanlara Doğru". *Sosyal Siyaset Konferansları*. .59. 2010/2. 25–49.

TAN, T. (2003). Bağımsız İdari Otoriteler veya Düzenleyici Kurumlar. *Türkiye'de Kamu Yönetimi* (Ed. Aykaç, B., Durgun, Ş., & Yayman, H.). Ankara: Yargı Yayınevi.

Tanzi V. (1997). The Changing Role of the State in the Economy: A Historical Perspective. *IMF Working Paper.* September.

Thatcher, M. (2002). Delegation to Independent Regulatory Agencies, Pressures, Functions and Contextual Mediation. *West European Politics.* 25–1, 125–147.

Ulusoy, A. (2003). *Bağımsız İdari Otoriteler.* Ankara: Turhan Kitabevi Yayınları.

World Bank (1991). *World Development Report.* Oxford University Press for World Bank. Oxford.

Asst. Prof. Neslihan Koc*

Tax Expenditures in Turkey: Problems and Evaluations[1]

Abstract Tax expenditures express public revenues, which are dispensed through exemption, exclusion and discounts. Formation of tax expenditures statement was made obligatory by the law no. 5018. This is a positive development, in the sense of providing the connection of tax expenditures with the budget process. However, a set of problems, such as what will be taken into account as tax expenditures and the burden that tax expenditures will create in the budget or the tax burden created for the taxpayers, which are caused by the concept itself or the application, exist. Not being able to reach detailed information related to tax expenditures means these expenditures will be subject to neither parliament nor public control.

Keywords: Tax Concessions, Tax Expenditures, Fiscal Transparency

1. Introduction

The basic operation of public finance is related to providing public services devoted to societal needs. Therefore, public spending is made within the framework of the budget and its financing is largely provided through taxation or borrowing. Although they should be collected during the taxation process, revenues that are not collected due to fiscal, financial or social reasons are named as tax expenditures and assessed as public spending.

A set of deficiencies observed in our country about tax expenditures, which can be assessed as a finance policy tool, shadow positive goals that are desired to be achieved. In our study, identification of tax spending purposes, general problems about tax expenditures and practices in our country and problems in practices are reviewed.

2. The Concept of Tax Expenditures

In broad terms, tax expenditures include tax exemptions, allowances, credits, rate relief, and tax deferral (Biçer& Yılmaz, 2009: 72). Tax expenditures indicate public

* Hitit University, Faculty of Economics and Administrative Sciences, Çorum, Turkey neslihankoc@hitit.edu.tr

1 This study was supported by the Hitit University Scientific Research Projects Unit. Project No: IBF52.16.001.

revenues waived through exemption, exception and discounts, or tax losses caused by privileged conditions of tax laws.

On the other hand, when considered in terms of the budgeting process, tax expenditures are viewed as a kind of "concealed expenditure" (Saraç, 2010: 263). Tax expenditures are a tax incentive mechanism, just like keeping tax rates low, tax deferrals, and investment allowances practices. While some tax expenditures create continuous income loss for the government like public expenditures; some cause the income to be deferred to the future. These, in a sense, qualify as an interest-free loan given to the taxpayer (Giray, 2002: 33).

Some distinguishing features are used in the description of tax expenditures (OECD, 1996: 9):

- tax concession to benefit a specific industry, activity of taxpayer group,
- tax system to serve a purpose, which can be realised with other tools, other than its effectiveness,
- the related tax to have a wide enough scope, in order to be able to measure the value of a privilege against a benchmark (standard tax practice),
- change of the tax system to be possible in administrative terms, in order to remove tax expenditure,
- having no other provisions in the tax system that can remove the benefit tax expenditures provide.

Accordingly, the strictest practice is the acceptance of only the most basic elements in the tax system as a benchmark. This will enable many tax provisions to be accepted as a privilege and tax expenditure. Countries decide on their own in accordance with their own preferences, about which practices provide a deviation from the standard norm, that is, a tax privilege. According to the assumptions about standard tax system, an increase or decrease of amount of tax expenditures is in question. One of the points that need to be underlined here is the fact that the acceptance of all kinds of deviation from the norm as a tax expenditure might make calculations difficult.

One of the criteria mentioned about tax expenditures was stated as its ability to serve a purpose, which can be realised via other tools as well. For instance, making child relief or a direct transfer payment serves the same purpose. In order to analyse which one is more effective in terms of obtaining the specified purpose; in case tax allowance is applied, it would be more appropriate to include these allowances in the tax expenditure calculation.

According to Saraç, elements in the tax system to be able to cause tax expenditure depends on the condition that it creates a privilege to the standard tax system. For instance, depreciation does not create privilege to investment goods owners among themselves. Because of this reason, it is not considered as tax expenditure. However, accelerated depreciation, which creates distinction between investment goods owners, qualifies as tax expenditure (Saraç, 2010: 265).

In the classification of public expenses in terms of economic effects, the distinction of current, investment (reel), and transfer expenditures is used. Expenses that create a factor of production and are done in return for a good or service are defined as reel expenses. In this respect, tax expenditures can be accepted as an indirect transfer expense. However as seen in Table 1, there are differences between the two of them in terms of practice or the output obtained.

Table 1: Comparison of Tax Expenditures and Direct Expenses

	Tax Expenditures	**Direct Expenses**
Accessibility for Beneficiaries	Simple because of automatic application	Requires filtering More complicated
Administrative and accommodation costs	High if exemptions are followed completely	Medium depending on the necessity of filtering and allotment system
Possible violations	Evasion, evasion, and rent-seeking	Arbitrariness, inefficiency and taking hold of the society being allotted
Flexibility	Operates with constant laws that can produce also idleness, other than stability	Operates with budgets, assessments, and redistribution
Transparency and accountability	Not interested in control mechanisms or accountability	Approved by the house of legislature, just like in all public expenditures
Spending control	Uncertain, limitless and final expenses in a way that might cause financial imbalance	Programmed and controlled expenses, limited via budget law
Effectiveness	Added value aimed from the activity is not guaranteed.	Difficulty of guaranteeing added value and risk of replacing private sector.
Equality	Only the potential taxpayers–ones that usually have the most income-provide most benefit	Increasing targeted beneficiaries through discretionary power may enable more equitable access

Source: Luiz Villela et al., Tax Expenditure Budgets (Concepts and Challenges for Implementation), IBD Working Paper Series, April 2010, pp. 12.

If income tax is considered in line with the comparison in Table 1, while keeping the base wide causes low marginal rates to be applied; application of exemptions widely may help reaching equality goals and reducing administrative and accommodation costs (Tyson, 2014: 5).

Contrary to direct transfer expenditures, indirect transfer expenditures are expenditures that affect the incomes of consumers and producers in an indirect way (Mutluer et al., 2007: 138). Tax expenditures as indirect transfer expenditures are done through elements reducing the tax burden of taxpayers in the tax system, instead of government budget (Ferhatoğlu, 2005: 78). At this point, it is clear that privilege practices, such as collecting less tax from the ones with less income in the tax system through the practice of progressive tax table, cannot be assessed as tax expenditure.

3. Purposes of Tax Expenditures

Tax expenditures are against the principle of universality for some taxpayers because of the tax privileges it creates. These expenditures are applied with a specific social and/or economic purpose, and collection is waived at the cost of creating privilege, which enables the generation of effects they will exhibit. Providing a tax advantage with an economic or social purpose prevents tax evasion or tax avoidance (Saraç, 2010: 264).

Application of tax expenditures is an intervention of the government, which it realises with the purposes of assuring equality in income distribution, economic growth and employment, other than the aim of effectiveness in resource allotment. As seen, tax expenditures are a tool of fiscal policy. While tax expenditures with social purposes qualify as income transfer; tax expenditures with economic purposes qualify as incentives.

As soon as investment increases that tax incentive measures within the context of tax expenditures create are more than tax loss increases; bearing these costs can be accepted as adequate. On the other hand, in a contrary case increases in investments will be less than the tax loss government bears in order to create these increases. At this point, the government to abandon leaving the funds it will receive as tax to the private sector and to separate all these funds for investments concludes an increase in total investments (Ferhatoğlu, 2005: 85).

The unemployment problem that occurs in depression periods causes an already inadequate demand to reduce more and a cycle that feeds the problem to be entered in. For this reason, incentive measures intended to both booting the demand and preventing discharges need to be taken. Tax expenditure that will be done within the framework of the policy aiming to reduce employment costs will most probably be less than the tax expenditure that will be made afterwards (Karaca, 2014: 279; Erdoğdu, 2010: 338). As seen, it is possible to consult tax expenditures as a tool that prevents the crisis from intensifying.

Some tax expenditures can be applied with both social and economic purposes. For instance, tax regulations which are sensitive to gender, such as differentiating expenses that can be discounted from the tax assessment or providing exemption and privilege to taxpayers at different rates, can be realised. By encouraging the individual retirement system, both the life quality of taxpayers after retirement can be increased, and burdening the government treasury with greater loads in the future can be prevented. Many parts from disabled to amateur sports clubs can be included within the context of tax expenditures.

Tax expenditures provide an advantage that can be defined as tax income in a way similar to consumer income from the perspective of taxpayers. How consumers will use this extra income on the other hand, is related to their consumption and saving tendencies (Saraç, 2010: 272). Shortly, tax expenditures may mean capital accumulation for the ones with high saving tendency, and demand increase for the ones with high consumption tendencies. However, here market structure and price elasticity should be considered. For example, a tax discount done with a social purpose on a product produced in a monopoly market can conclude in an economic incentive by not being reflected in consumer prices because of the firm's excess profit policy.

As known, both transfer expenses and taxes affect national income depending on the consumption tendency through a multiplier mechanism. The fact that tax expenditures qualify as a transfer expense deuces tax multiplier mechanism and reduces the contractionary pressure of tax on national income. İf stated reversely, the booster effect of tax expenses on national income is in question.

4. Tax Expenditures Practice in Turkey

In the Eight Five-Year Development Plan, tax expenditures are accepted as off-budget indirect expenses. These can mainly be defined as properties of the public and its savings and expenses, which it realised in accordance with the responsibilities it holds. These activities have reached significant expense magnitudes today, especially because of treasury guarantees and duty losses. Indirect expenses, which have become one of the main problems of the budgets of developing countries, appear in the fiscal system of many countries as a tool that is used in hiding public quantity (Günay, 2007: 276).

The government abandoned the revenue of 2.7 Turkish Liras of Corporation tax in return of each 1 Lira of corporate tax it obtained in the period of 1997–2001. When Income Tax, Value Added Tax, other tax laws, and the costs of tax expenditures taking place in other laws except from tax laws are added to this amount, the magnitude of the forgone tax revenue comes to light (Ferhatoğlu, 2005: 91).

Tax expenditure is placed in our legislation as a definition, although not as a concept, via 5018 numbered Public Finance Management Control Law item 15. According to this, tax revenues, which were forgone because of practices such as tax exemption, allowance and discounts, should be predicted and take place in the Central Government Budget Laws. By this means, the possibility of seeing all kinds of expenses together in the central government budget has been raised (GEP, 2007: 2). This practice is accepted as one of the main requirements of fiscal transparency. Today, 75% of the OECD countries are regularly publishing annual reports regarding tax expenditures (Günay, 2007: 282). In our country, tax exemptions, privileges and allowances, which are evaluated as tax exemptions, are given place in related tax laws. However, it is also seen that many laws bring together various tax exemptions, privileges and allowances that are suitable to their own purposes, although they are not related to tax (GEP, 2007: 4).

In the prediction of tax expenditures, three methods are used (Akdoğan, 2011: 182; Tyson, 2014: 15):

i. Foregone revenue method is the prediction of decrease emerging in the tax collection because of giving place to tax privileges.
ii. Earned revenue method is the prediction of the revenue magnitude, which can be obtained by considering various influences that can be created if tax privileges are removed.
iii. Equivalent direct expenditure method on the other hand, is the prediction public spending amount before such a tax, in order to reach a benefit level that is created after a tax that includes tax expenditure.

In our country, forgone revenue method is applied. The ones for any data cannot be obtained are exempted from the calculation.

According to cash based accounting, transactions are recorded to accounts when they are collected as cash or paid. Together with the start of accrual based public account application in our country, identification of these expenses, which are formulised under the "expenses" account, has been possible. However, tax expenditures such as tradesmen exemption, which are not subject to accounting at any times, will not be reported with accounting knowledge again (Karaaslan, 2007: 53).

In the Tenth Progress Plan, the Act Plan for Program of Increasing Quality of Public Revenues, it is stated that considering not only fiscal concerns, but also economic and social purposes has become a must of modern public fiscal management. An act plan has been prepared in the charge of the Ministry of Finance in line with the aim of determining exemptions, allowances and exceptions within the context of the program, analysis of the effects and measuring effectiveness. Determined acts are as follows:

- By taking inventory of exemptions, exceptions and allowances, data regarding these will be gathered from the related agencies and institutes.
- Tax expenditures report will be prepared. The first tax expenditure report will be completed by September 2016 and the results will be released to public. Afterwards the report will be released regularly every year by the end of June.
- Reports regarding the effectiveness of exemptions, exceptions and allowances will be prepared; design drafts will be prepared by revising the ineffective ones.
- Information technology and analysis capacity about administrative capacity will be increased.

Tax revenue loss, which tax expenditures create in outcome taxes, are more than other types of taxes. Because tax-free buyers will buy more than the product or service in question, since there is no tax. When pre-tax price is pushed to increase with additional purchases of tax-free liables, buyers subject to tax decrease their purchases. So these tax-free buyers benefit from both the exemption and the relative fall in the pre-tax price (Giray, 2002: 44). Because of this reason, a tax expenditure that will be given more weight in income taxes would be more suitable. As seen in Table 2, the practice in our country is in this direction. Especially while collecting tax from minimum waged people, who earn as little as being able to barely survive their physiological existence, keeping certain products and services tax-free does not seem fair.

Table 2: Total Tax Expenditure Estimates According to Tax Types (2006–2015) Million TL

Law	2015	2014	2013	2012	2011	2010	2009	2008	2007	2006
Income Tax Act	18.097	16.314	14.017	12.714	10.818	9.158	9.729	7.779	5.318	5.392
Corporate Tax Law	4.130	4.313	4.776	2.156	3.968	2.850	2.439	2.857	2.798	2.533
Value Added Tax Law	1.805	1.246	1.242	896	947	803	857	426	482	436
Special Consumption Tax Law	462	410	375	339	289	244	260	213	254	230
Other Laws	1.616	1.603	2.004	1.810	1.542	1.306	1.396	1.166	-	-
Total	26.112	23.888	22.416	17.917	17.565	14.363	14.684	12.443	8.854	8.592

Source: BUMKO, http://www.bumko.gov.tr/TR,926/butce-kanunu-ve-ekleri.html (10.06.2015)

Tax expenditures, which were predicted as 8.5 billion TL in 2006, are seen to have risen three times in 2015. Table 2 presents tax expenditures in respect to tax types.

Tax expenditures were estimated as 26.1 billion TL in 2015 budget. Around 85% of these taxes, whose collection were waived, are as part of income or corporation tax.

Table 3: Annual Total Tax Revenue Forecasts (2006–2015) Billion TL

Years	2015	2014	2013	2012	2011	2010	2009	2008	2007	2006
Tax Revenues	427	378	347	300	250	212	220	187	173	137
Net Budget Revenue	442	394	362	322	292	231	244	200	184	173
Tax Expenditures Total	26	23	22	17	17	14	14	12	8	8
Tax Exp. /Tax Revenues	%6,1	%6,3	%6,4	%5,9	%7	%6,7	%6,6	%6,6	%5	%5,8

Source: BUMKO, http://www.bumko.gov.tr/TR,926/butce-kanunu-ve-ekleri.html (10.06.2015)

Table 3 displays sums of budget revenues and tax revenues and the share of tax expenditures in tax revenues. While creating the table, the rate between tax expenditures, which define the forgone tax revenues, and tax revenues should be considered. Tax revenues already constitute almost around whole of the budget revenues. For instance, share of tax revenues for 2015 in all revenues is 96.4%.

According to Table 3, the ratio of tax expenditures to the tax revenues predicted to be collected the same year is 6%. Therefore, taxes that have been forgone through tax expenditures have been understood to be a potential significant source of revenue. In the period of 2006–2015, tax expenditures in our country displayed a three times rise parallel to the increase in tax revenues and its ratio to tax revenues realised around 6%.

5. Problems and Evaluations Regarding Applications of Tax Expenditures in Turkey

Tax expenditures affect both the tax system and the fiscal system in general. Tax expenditures are accepted as ineffective because of the beneficiaries not to be identified clearly. Specific interest groups may lobby in this area, thinking that providing an open spending support for themselves will be harder than receiving tax expenditure (Tyson, 2014: 4).

Tax expenditures may spoil the justice. While a policy that reduces taxable income in a gradual tax system benefits a group, which takes place in the highest marginal tax bracket; it may not present a benefit to the ones outside this tax system except from creating a potential cause for using tax credit (Tyson, 2014: 3).

Villela et al. (2010: 10): approach tax expenditures as tax incentives in general. Problems they identified in this area can be summarised as follows

i. Tax incentives are inversely progressive and are for the benefit of taxpayers. Since tax incentives will not cover the poorest in an increasing proportional tax system, they will not provide benefits from tax expenditures. However applying exemptions in consumption taxes together with this may contribute to develop progressive commensurateness in the tax system and this judgement to be reversed.
ii. Tax incentives may create unexpected earnings. Tax incentives provide incentives for individuals to do something they will do in any case. In short, one person is encouraged; however the cost is compensated by everybody.
iii. Management and control of tax incentives are difficult: Tax administrations do not have adequate experience in the topic of managing and controlling public spending programs. Tax expenditures are of course applied, however controlling this system, which includes many exemptions, may cause larger and unintended failures.
iv. Tax incentives twist the decision making ability of the market: If tax incentives favour a specific sector in the economy; a production, in which resources are directed towards the favoured sector, is realised. Actually in case tax expenditures, which are put forward with investment and saving incentive measures, try to correct an irregularity that has been caused before by the tax itself, tax expenditures do not create a significant disadvantage.
v. Tax incentives require high tax rates to be applied: With the purpose of gaining the potential income, which is lost because of the application of tax expenditures, higher tax ratios will be required to be implemented.

With the law numbered 5018, creation of tax expenditures tables has become mandatory. This is a positive development, in terms of tax expenditures to have the possibility to be related to the budget process. However, existence of a set of problems, occurring because of the tax expenditures concept itself or the practice, is in question.

Determination of which decrees taking place in either tax laws or special laws will be counted as tax expenditures is a comprehensive and difficult process. This difficulty is also in question in terms of international comparisons. Because, a decree accepted as tax expenditure in one country may not be assessed within the same context in another country. It can also be seen that some tax expenditures, which corresponds to values that may be numbered as unimportant, are not taken into evaluation. From this perspective, practices in developed countries should be followed and adapted to the system as much as possible. Basically, an income required to be taxed not to be excised can be thought as a main benchmark in the determination of tax expenditures.

Furthermore, including tax expenditures in special laws other than tax laws is an element, which complicates the tracing of the practice. As the government abandons an amount that would enter its cash, it would be more appropriate for this practice to take place in tax laws. Otherwise, the legislation, which is already dispersed, to become completely complicated comes into question.

In case spending is done by waiving tax, instead of being done directly by the government; any change does not occur with regards to beneficiaries. In this case, analysis of only the direct spending does not reflect the real situation in terms of identifying the magnitude of public sector.

While analysing how much of the resources are used by the public, tax expenditures need to be calculated as much as GBE (Government Business Enterprises) expenses that are not reflected to the budget directly or indirectly, and funds.

The magnitude of tax spending is one of the factors causing budget deficits in Turkey (Günay, 2007: 260). Especially in the period of 1984–1995, serious tax losses were encountered because of exemption, exception, and incentives (Emil& Yılmaz, 2005: 12). Tax expenditures mean loss from the perspective of the treasury. Limiting these tax expenditures, which cause tax loss in the developed fiscal rules, is advised.

Inability in the identification of which institution failed to pay and what amount of tax was not paid because of tax spending; it is possible in some items to calculate total cost of service imperfectly. This situation may conclude in the calculation of the total cost of service deficiently in some items. The same situation is valid for the military tax expenditures too. In our country, tax exemptions with the defense and military aims are considered as structural elements of the tax system and are accepted as a benchmark. According to Yentürk (2011: 68) publishment of these expenditures by being calculated would be useful in terms of enlightening the public and the parliament.

It is important also with regards to the realisation of fiscal transparency that tax expenditures to be included in the budget in a correct and detailed way. It is known that amounts given place in the budget are not complete and calculated by prediction. Principle of universality means all income and expenses to take place in the budget. Thus, the related parts of the fiscal system to evaluate the data on the budget may be possible.

As seen, principle of universality is directly associated with transparency and the efficient use of budget right. Failure of knowing tax expenditures exactly may cause an effect such as removing some public resources from parliament audit or hiding them from the public. This situation, which is also caused by the inefficacies in obtaining data, may be overcome through improving technological and statistical infrastructure of public institutions.

While budgeting public spending, analytical budget classification is used. In this classification, it is possible to understand which institution did this payment with what purpose, how the spending will be financed, and its economical influences. Tax expenditures to be shown over a list over the total amounts leads to this classification to be used and not to include a proposition regarding how tax expenditures will be compensated.

As known the effects created in the economy by fiscal policy tools such as public spending, taxes and borrowing are different. In this respect, knowing tax expenditures is required also for being able to measure the effects it will create in the economy. These effects of tax expenditures to be known is important in terms of determining whether exemptions and exceptions given place obtain their goals and shaping future policies.

Expanding exceptions and exemptions will mean the increase of tax load for other parties, as long as tax expenditures are not reduced. On the one hand, the government excludes some taxpayers from tax via the exemptions and exceptions it identifies, and on the other hand it has to concentrate on indirect taxes for its missing financing need. Indirect taxes negatively affect income distribution fairness to the detriment of the poor; so as one of the purposes of tax expenditures is the improvement of social justice and reformation of income distribution. Excluding the parts of society, who are defined as disadvantaged, by considering their difficulties in paying taxes, is in a way applying a tax benefit. However, as seen the practice of tax expenditures has the risk of correcting on the one hand while damaging justice on the other hand.

Tax expenditures also have the risk of damaging vertical and horizontal justice in taxation. For instance, in the VAT law "on the condition of being related to searching, operating, enriching and refining activities about gold, silver and platinum; deliveries and services conducted to individuals executing these activities" have been exempted. This exemption of profit margin provides more advantage to an already high production area. However, VAT is collected from basic consumption items, education and health services, which concern low income groups.

The tax paid by 1761000 taxpayers, who are named as proclaimed taxpayers for 2011 and are mostly composed of financiers that gain investment income as profit share/dividend, interest and unearned income, constitute only 1% of the total tax, the tax paid by 705000 taxpayers, who are bound to single entry, form 0.1% of total tax, and the tax paid by nearly 660000 institutions and companies (including State Owned Enterprises) constitute 10% of the total tax, while workers' form 13%. That is to say, the ones earning labour income pay 13% points, that is 68% of the Income Tax, which has a 19% point share among total tax revenues. 91% of the Income Tax is collection at source and 5.6% is annual declaration. 67.8% points of this 91% on the other hand, is collected from workers (Durmuş, 2013). The importance of these numbers is the opportunity of investment income earners to be able to write many spending items as expenditures, and the workers not having any tax discount opportunities, other than the regulation such as subsistence discount, which provides a limited contribution. However, in the principle of assortment, which is used to enable justice in taxation, lighter taxation of workers compared to ones earning investment income is recommended.

Financial purpose of tax expenditures is supporting production, exportation or sectors that are newly formed but can create competitive strength in the future through tax. In short, the purposes are economic growth and development. However, it is almost impossible within the current structure to determine how much of these purposes are truly met by the tax expenditures list, which is put forward numerically in the budget.

For instance, the positive effect of a tax expenditure applied for investment on employment is uncertain. From this perspective, first just like giving place to the performance evaluation of public services provided while preparing annual reports; same practice need to be done for tax expenditures as well. At this point, it is true that service outcomes that pay regard to public welfare are not always measurable, however the main purpose of the performance based budgeting system is the evaluation of conclusion beyond outcomes. The necessity of making such an evaluation with regards to tax expenditures for such a regulation the government applies with a special purpose is obvious.

Secondly, incentives given through tax expenditure to depend on certain conditions should come to the fore. For example, it might be benefiting from tax privileges in return of providing certain employment of conducting a certain amount of export. Such a practice is seen to take place in the ad-hoc 2. Paragraph of Free Trade Areas Law numbered 3218. Salaries paid to the personnel employed by taxpayers, who export at least 85% of the FOB amount of the products produced in these regions, are exempted from income tax.

Providing a general incentive with tax expenditures causes sectors or individuals, who do not need the incentive, to benefit from tax advantage. However, as mentioned before incentives may create competitive distortions in the economy when directed to specific firms, sectors or regions, and the intervention done to the market to spoil market functioning comes into question.

It is also probable that tax expenditures will increase borrowing because of decreased sources of financing as a result of eroding tax base. Borrowing is known to produce different effects depending on the resources it was obtained. However, in any case it has the risk to excessively increase the tax loads of future generations, unless directed to productive areas.

6. Conclusions

It is a known fact that the government does not leave social and economic developments to their own devices and there are interventions. Necessity of these interventions is a different matter of discussion. However, if the aim is to create an economic or social benefit, it is obvious that tax expenditures will support this purpose. Encouraging private investments via tax will of course positively influence employment, national income, and growth. Tax discounts with social purposes contribute to social peace and development. However, maintaining a large tax base unnecessarily and excluding individuals although they have the ability to pay causes certain problems resulting in tax erosion.

The balance between aimed and obtained benefit and endured cost should be taken into consideration in terms of keeping, changing or removing tax expenditures. However, this is only possible with a transparency that will allow assessment of the causes, amounts and effects of expenditures. Tables showing tax expenditure predictions are published in the budget appendix. However, a report displaying how much additional income is transferred to which parts through tax expenditures is not published. If these numbers could be obtained, which tax expenditures were for realising a social cause could be determined and they could be compared with a social expense in the same area. As can be seen, the biggest problem about tax expenditures is the fact that often it leaves questions related to what is being aimed and what is bring gained unanswered.

References

Akdoğan, A. (2011). *Kamu Maliyesi*. Ankara: Gazi Kitabevi.

Biçer, M. & Yılmaz, H. H. (2009). Parlamentonun Kamu Politikası Oluşturma ve Planlama Sürecindeki Konumunun Yeni Kamu Mali Yönetim Sistemi Çerçevesinde Değerlendirilmesi. *Yasama Dergisi*, 13, 45–84.

Durmuş, M. (2013). *Vergilemede Adalet-Nasıl?* Retrieved April 17, 2015, from http://www.sendika.org/2013/02/vergilemede-adalet-nasil-mustafa-durmus/.

Emil, M. F. & Yılmaz, H. H. (2005). *Kamu Borcu Nasıl Oluştu? Bu Noktaya Nasıl Gelindi?* İstanbul: Tesev Yayınları.

Ferhatoğlu, E. (2005). Bir Kamu Harcaması Türü Olarak Vergi Harcaması ve Türk Kurumlar Vergisi Açısından Değerlendirilmesi. *Eskişehir Osmangazi Üniversitesi Sosyal Bilimler Dergisi*, 6 (2), 77–93.

Gelir Politikaları Genel Müdürlüğü-GEP (2007). *Vergi Harcamaları Raporu*. Ankara.

Giray, F. (2002). Vergi Harcamaları: Harcama Vergileri Açısından Analizi, *Uludağ Üniversitesi İktisadi ve İdari Bilimler Fakültesi Dergisi*, XXI (1), 27–52.

Günay, A. (2007). *Mali Disiplinin Sağlanmasında Anayasal Denk Bütçe Yaklaşımı ve Türkiye'de Uygulanabilirliği*. Ankara.

Karaarslan, E. (2007). *Genel Yönetim Kapsamındaki Kamu İdareleri İçin Soru ve Cevaplarıyla Devlet Muhasebesi*. Ankara: Mitaged Yayınları.

Karaca, C. (2014). Uygulanan Para ve Maliye Politikaları Açısından Geçmiş Krizler ve 2008 Küresel Ekonomik Krizinin Karşılaştırmalı Analizi. *Çankırı Karatekin Üniversitesi Sosyal Bilimler Enstitüsü Dergisi*, 5(1), 263–286.

Mutluer, K., Öner, E. & Kesik, A (2007). *Teoride ve Uygulamada Kamu Maliyesi*, 1. Edition. İstanbul: İstanbul Bilgi Üniversitesi Yayınları.

OECD (1996). *Tax Expenditures: Recent Experiences*, OECD Yayınları.

Onuncu Kalkınma Planı (2014–2018). *Kamu Gelirlerinin Kalitesinin Artırılması Programı Eylem Planı*. Retrieved April 16, 2015, from http://dap.gov.tr/yeni-Dosyalar/Kaynaklar/odop/5.pdf.

Saraç, Ö. (2010). Vergi Harcamaları ve İktisadi Etkileri. *Maliye Dergisi*, 159, Temmuz-Aralık, 262–277.

Tyson, J. (2014). *Reforming Tax Expenditures in Italy: What, Why, and How?* IMF Working Paper.

Villela L. et al. (2010). *Tax Expenditure Budgets (Concepts and Challenges for Implementation)*, IBD Working Paper Series.

Yentürk, N. (2011). *STK'lar İçin Askeri ve İç Güvenlik Harcamalarını İzleme Kılavuzu*, İstanbul: İstanbul Bilgi Üniversitesi Yayınları.

Asst. Prof. Ersin Karaman, Mahmut Ensar Göktaş,
Murat Can Aktaş, Hilal Çalişir, Ayşegül İşci &
Sümeyra Demir*

City Usability Evaluation: A Case from the Erzurum Municipality

Abstract In recent years, we have come across the term "usability" frequently at different points in our life; such as, the objects we use in daily life and the systems and interfaces. Recent researches have started out from a given object or a system and reviewed from there onwards. In this research, we have considered the concept of usability from a different point of view, and we have examined the usability of cities. Basically usability includes efficiency, effectiveness, and satisfaction concepts based on the four main dimensions i.e. task, context, interface and user. Moreover, in the literature usability of interfaces is evaluated via different tests such as experimental, guideline based, experts based and model based test approaches. The aim of this study is to provide a city usability evaluation methodology. To do so, the usability concept is discussed and criticised for it application to cities. In addition, experimental usability tests have been conducted to evaluate the Erzurum Municipality in Turkey.

In the experiments, randomly selected 17 first-time visitors of Erzurum, who are of ages between 19–50 years, have participated in the study. Each participant was given a task to complete in the city. Their behaviours were recorded via a video recorder if it was permitted. Participants help attempts and hesitancies were evaluated. At the end of the experiment, a short interview was conducted and they were given a memory card as a small gift. According to the frequency analysis and content analysis, participants had some problems in some points such as direction signs, cross walking lines, traffic lights harmony for pedestrians and vehicles. In the problematic places, participants had been waiting and confusing more than well designed places. This case increases their mental load which decreases the city usability.

Keywords: Usability, City of Erzurum, City usability, Experimental city evaluation

---

* Ataturk University Faculty of Economic and Administrative Sciences Department of Management Information Systems. karamanersin@gmail.com; mensargoktas@gmail.com; iletisim@e-murat.com; hilal_calisir_65@outlook.com; aysegulisci@e-mail.com.tr; sumeyracoskun0@gmail.com

1. Introduction

Changes in human being's satisfaction levels and understanding of service provided to change their expectations towards the objects they interact. Similarly they started to evaluate their satisfaction within the framework of effectiveness and efficiency. From this emerges the usability concept. In this literature upon this movement various studies have been made regarding the concept of usability.

The concept of usability has been the subject of several studies in relation to objects, interfaces, and systems. For example, Gurses (2006) evaluated library web sites; Dog (2012) investigated remote training systems usability; and Terzi (2010) highlighted the customer-based systems usability. Yilmaz, Karaman and Karaman (2013) proposed the applicability of city usability concept in relation with city branding. In Celikte and Sakıcı (2013), focused on usability of the recreation area of the city of Kastamonu in Turkey. Akbulut and Eyiçıtakta (2006) worked on the usability of the rail transport system within the Current Innere City Transportation Plan in Afyonkarahisar.

In this study it is aimed to propose an experimental city usability evaluation methodology. This is inspired from the human-computer interaction study, and a city is thought as an interface for visitors and people.

1.1 The Concept of Usability

The concept of usability was coined in the 1980s and is widely used in software and PC design. There are also overlapping areas between applications of ergonomics, human interactions, and design. The concepts of usability and ergonomics are used interchangeably. This concept in general was defined in the 1980s, as easy-to-use objects. In addition to this, in literature there are a number of definitions of usability. For example, Çağıltay (2011) defined usability as "completion of a task efficiently by users, who are the targeted audience, within the suitable environment and with the necessary training and technical support." According to the ISO 9241–11 standard, issued by the International Standards Organization (ISO), usability is the level of efficiency, effectiveness, and satisfaction of a product obtained by users in a specified context of use. In other words, it is the user's efficiency, effectiveness, and satisfaction while performing operations on a product, service, or interface. Efficiency is defined as the level of completeness of task, while effectiveness is related with the consumed or used resources such as time and effort during the task performed.

In addition, according to Nielsen (1993), usability is examined under five subtitles namely; learnability, which means that the system can be learnt easily, efficiency, memorability, errors, and satisfaction. Error refers to the ratio of mistakes made by the users while satisfaction refers to the level of users' pleasures. In short, usability is related with ease of use level. In this context, cities and their components are considered as man-made objects interacted by residents and visitors of a city. In this respect we can consider the usability of a city. Karaman (2013).

1.2 Usability Evaluation

Usability tests can be divided into two groups as user-based and products-based Bevan (1991). On the other hand, Cagiltay (2011) summarised the usability testing method into four groups, i.e. experimental testing, guideline (standards) based, expert opinion, and model based. Moreover, this test can be applied on a service or product during the production process or at the end of this process. In-process (formative) tests are carried out during the development process of a product. Post-process tests (summative) are applied after the product is produced.

1.2.1 Guidelines

Guidelines ensures consistency of the interface elements, however, do not guarantee the usability. That is this method is used to ensure compatibility and consistency within designs. In terms of the city usability, any guidelines developed for this aim is encountered (Karaman 2013).

1.2.2 Expert-Based Approach

An expert-based approach is the assessment of a product by an expert in accordance with a certain criteria. This approach uses "heuristics." The expert-based approach mostly uses Nielsen's ten heuristics which are: visibility of system status, match between system and the real world, user control and freedom, consistency and standards, error prevention, recognition rather than recall, flexibility and efficiency of use, aesthetic and minimalist design, help users recognise, diagnose, and recover from errors, help and documentation:

1.2.3 Model-Based Approach

The physical and cognitive behaviours are assessed with the help of a model. This method can be considered in terms of the usability of the city. The data obtained through this method can be used in city models and new regulations and improvements can be made by this way.

1.2.4 Experimental Approach (User-based approach)

This method is employed through allocating real tasks to real users in the real context and interface. Real users can use different methods for usability tests. In this type of method, data is captured via observation and technological devices such as eye tracking glasses. Users may be asked to think aloud and video/audio recording may be used (Sahin 2014). Experimental usability tests aim to analyse efficiency, effectiveness and satisfaction by analysing the data. This approach can be used in the work of the usability of the city (Yılmaz, et al. 2013).

Analysis can be made regarding the most commonly used and needed fields and the services in the cities. Problems can be spotted more accurately and fixed more quickly in cities by experimental usability tests. Since the participants of the test will give instant responses, the observation of the problem can be made more easily.

With this method it is possible to make assessments in relation to the city and to solve current problems:

- Transportation (road routes, bus times, prevents traffic on nearby roads and the mark on the plate located on stalk lifter point inaccurate or incomplete conditions)
- Tourism (steering gaps)
- Hospital, police, police stations were all given transportation (steering and information gaps)
- The terminal to the bus terminal, etc. transportation venues, places of worship, transportation (steering gaps and accessibility issues).
- Environmental layout and the urban aesthetics (accessibility issues and landscape problems)

With this method, a first-visitor of a city can be allocated a task about finding a place or completing an issue to evaluate city usability.

1.3 The Usability of the City

The most common meaning of the usability of the city is the application of similar tests mentioned above. In this study, the experimental usability test method is adopted for city usability. This term is proposed to rank cities in terms of mental and physical load level of people. The term is used for the self-evaluation of cities.

2. Methodolgy

The purpose of this study is to validate experimental usability test in terms of the applicability on cities. To do so, an experimental usability test design has been made and six different tasks were determined. 17 volunteer new visitors to Erzurum, Turkey were asked to complete one task. This research consists of further steps stated below.

2.1 Participation form

In terms of ethical issues, all participants were asked to fill out the participation form including their personal information (age, name, profession, education level, visiting history, visiting reason) and permission level (video recording, audio recording, taking photo, noting think aloud process and sharing obtained data). They could permit one or more of them.

2.2 Participants

The participants were selected via the simple random sampling method and based on voluntariness. The detail information about the participants is shown in Table 2.1.

Table 1: Participants demographic information

Gender		Marital Status		Educational Level		Total
Female	: 1	Single	: 14	Primary School	: 1	17
Male	: 16	Married	: 3	High School	: 3	
				Vocational School	: 4	
				Undergraduate	: 8	
				Post-Graduate	: 1	

2.3 Data Collection Tool

Initially the project was briefly introduced to the participants and objectives of the study were explained. They were also showed the permission card of the University. They were asked about participation in the study. If a participant accepted to participate in the study, more detailed information was provided and the personal and permission form were signed. Each participant also was informed about the small gift (memory stick) given by the project supporter, Atatürk University. The participants were then assigned a task. The task was selected randomly from the six tasks prepared beforehand and they included finding: the president's office of Ataturk University, the Anatolia Religious Vocational High School, the Center for Life-long Education, the Erzurum land registry office, the Erzurum courthouse, and the Erzurum Metropolitan Municipality buildings. The starting point was the meeting point of Erzurum called University Junction.

Until the participant reached his destination, s/he was accompanied by two researchers. During the experiment, the head movements of the participant, facial expressions, grimaces, and focused points were noted. At the same time this process was recorded. At the end of the task the participant also were asked to fill out a post-experiment form including the role of the technological devices, need for navigation, and misunderstanding of any signs, need for help, and other comments.

2.4 Data Analysis

In this study, new results have been acquired through analysing the content collected throughout the data collection phase.

Behaviours of participants and our notes, voice recordings and shootings were examined in accordance with our task distribution in the team. Upon examination, a map has been prepared for each participant. In this map the starting point of the task, finishing point, and problem areas were located. Also voice and visual recordings were analysed digitally for each participant and a project report is prepared in relation to participant's suggestions, problem areas, etc.

All participants completed the task of finding the desired destination points from participants, the participants followed the routes, traffic, and environment-induced problems had been prepared taking into account the field reports. According to the report, suggestions made for solutions in relation to all points in consideration with including common problems mentioned by the participants.

3. Findings

According to the observation and participants' comments, it is found participants tried to ask somebody for help in general. Although participants had the opportunity to use technology, only three people tried to use a mobile phone and map. The remaining 14 participants asked other people walking around. In addition, eleven participants also tried to find their destination with the help of signs and relevant estimations. When we look at the experiment time, the three participants using the mobile devices were assigned the task at the evening hours. During the evening hours, since there were less people on the street, they tried to guess the destination.

Half of participants (eight participants) complained of the lack of signs or signs insufficiency. It is important to note that one participant coming from another country pointed out that official buildings lacked visibility. Six of the participant also mentioned about the lack of signs stated the touristic place signs. It is important to note that any task does not include reaching a touristic place. Another problematic point is the lack of signs for pedestrians rather than vehicles. That is, some traffic signs and direction signs are out of the pedestrians' point of view. Five of the participants stated that most of the signs placed on the road and on the sidewalk were not-well designed and may cause injury because of their height. The lines representing a crosswalk, side walk, and roads are not suitable for handicapped people in addition to the lack of wheelchair ramps.

According to the frequency analysis, it also extracted the problematic points of the task route. You can see the sample representation of miss-routing. Red lines represent miss routes or longer ones.

Mold 1: Courthouse

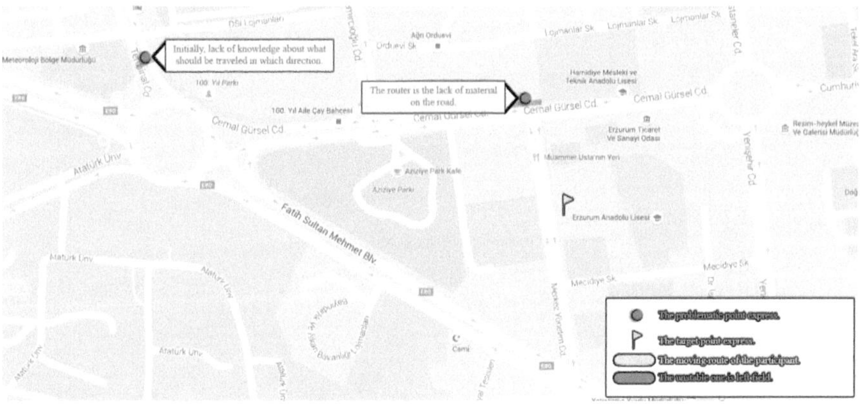

Mold 2: Anatolian Imam Hatip High School

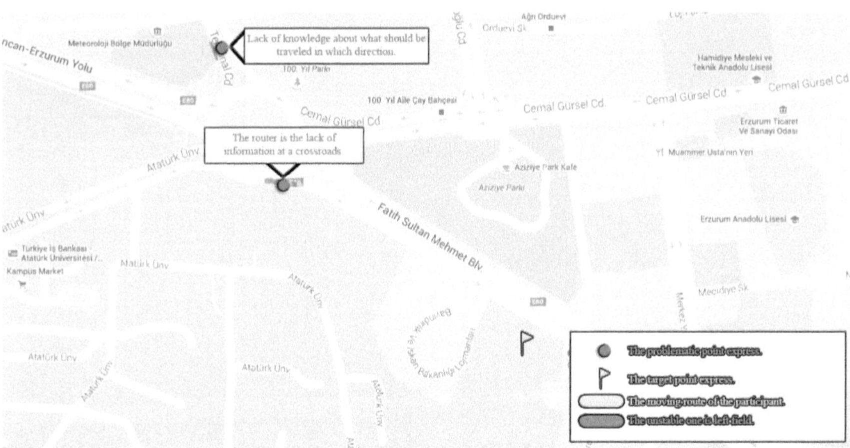

Mold 3: Erzurum Metropolitan Municipality

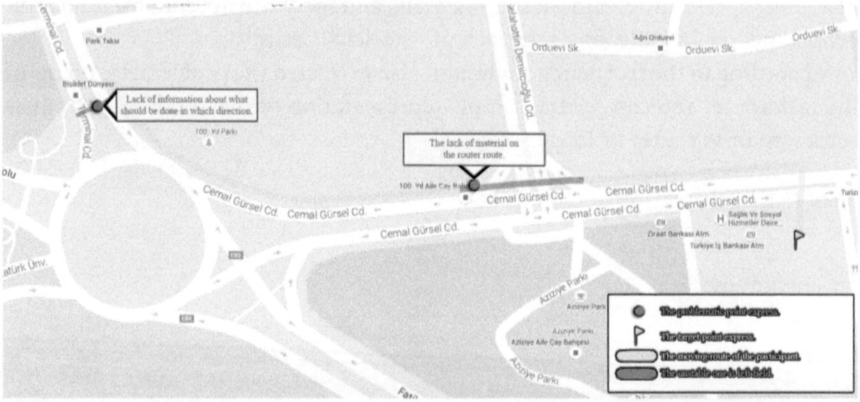

Mold 4: Public Education Center

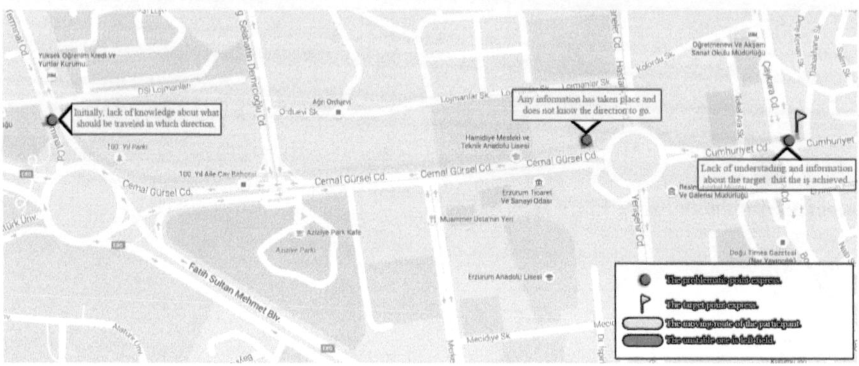

Mold 5: Rectorship (Erzurum Ataturk University)

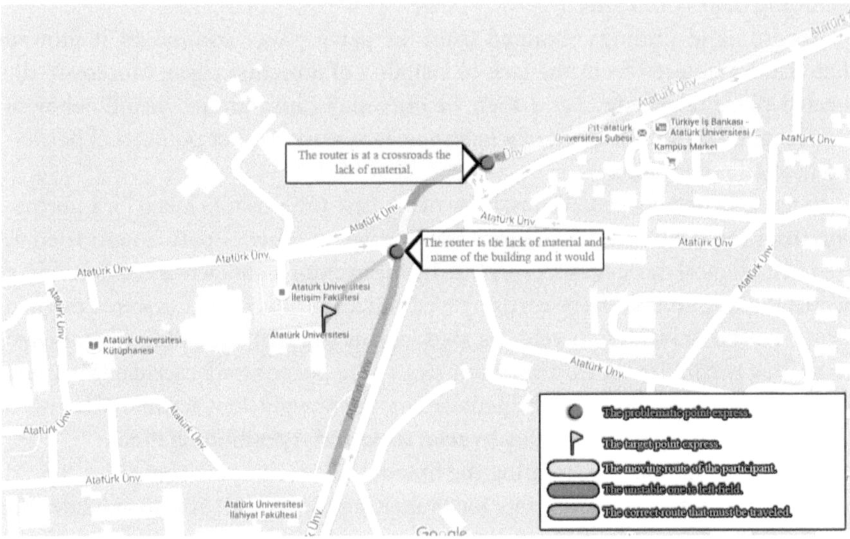

Mold 6: Land Registry and Cadastre

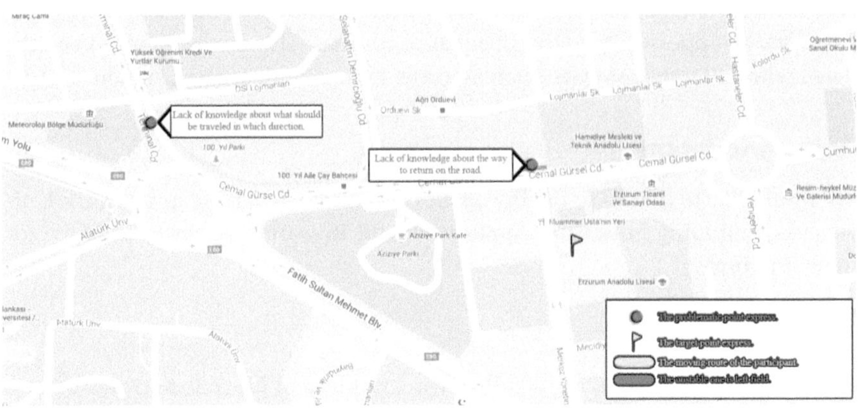

4. Results

In this study, the term usability forms the city usability perspective and adapts the experimental usability test to measure city usability. The experimental steps were designed and six tasks were defined. In Erzurum, Turkey, first-visitors were assigned tasks and their behaviours was recorded for analysis. In addition to personal and permission form, they were asked to fill out a post-experiment form including their comments.

According to findings obtained from the participants' comments, it showed that visitors suffered from the lack of visibility of direction signs. Moreover, the located place of the signs and their heights may cause injury. Insufficiency of handicapped signs and a lack of wheelchair ramps were other points that participants often mentioned.

In terms of helping procedures, most of the first-time visitors asked for information from someone to complete the task. A small number of participants tried to use technological devices especially during the evening hours when the number of people walking around the street decreased. Since the direction lines were designed for the people travelling in vehicles, pedestrians suffered in finding the targeted place. That is, some of the existing traffic signs were causing traffic accidents because of their limited view point for the pedestrians, their height, location, etc. They need to be replaced by the municipality by relocating and repositioning them.

The visual analysis representing the misrouting also implies that cities should be tested via this method not only for evaluating the city but also to validate this city usability evaluation method. Respective arrangements based on the findings of this method may provide gains in terms of time and reduce travelling cost. This also reduces both pedestrians and vehicle traffics. Moreover, handicapped people may have an opportunity to live in equal conditions. This method should be validated with different contexts; such as, time, season, and targeted audience, etc.

Acknowledment

We would like to thanks to the President of Ataturk University and Atatürk University Continuing Education Application and Research Center (ATASEM) for their support.

References

Akbulut, H., & Eyiçıtak, Z. (2006) Afyonkarahisar İli Mevcut Kent İçi Ulaşım Planı İçerisinde Raylı Sistem Kullanılabilirliğinin Araştırılması. Yapı Teknolojileri Elektronik Dergisi 2006 (1) 13–19. Afyonkarahisar: Afyon Kocatepe Üniversitesi, Teknik Eğitim Fakültesi.

Bevana, N., Kirakowskib, J., and Maissela, J. (1991, September). What is Usability? Stuttgart.

Çağıltay, K. (2011). İnsan Bilgisayar Etkileşimi ve Kullanılabilirlik Mühendisliği: Teoriden Pratiğe. Ankara: ODTÜ.

Doğ, M. R. (2012) Usability Metrics on E-Learning Systems. İstanbul: Bahçeşehir University.

Gürses, A. E. (2006) Kütüphane Web Sistemlerinde Kullanılabilirlik ve Kullanılabilirlik İlkerine Dayalı Tasarım. Ankara.

Nielsen, J. (1993). Usability Engineering. Boston: Academic Press.

Sakıcı, Ç., & Ayan, E., & Ayan, Ö., & Çelik, S. (2013, March). Kastamonu Kentindeki Açık Yeşil Alanların Farklı Kullanıcılar Tarafından Kulllanılabilirliğinin İrdelenmesi ve Sistem Kullanılabilirliğinin Araştırılması. *Kastamonu Uni. Journal of Forestry Faculty*, 2013, 13 (1), 129–143.

Terzi, M. E. (2010) Müşteri Odaklı Tasarımda Kullanılabilirlik Faktörleri ve Bir Uygulama. Ankara: Gazi University.

Yılmaz, K.G., & Karaman, E., & Karaman, G. (2013). A New Dimension of City Brand: Usibility. *Journal of Tourism and Gastronomy Studies* 1/4 (2013) 69–76. USA.

Cansu Tayaksi* & Birce Dobrucalı**

Eliminating Muda and Increasing Level of Service in Airports: A New Model Using iBeacon Technology

Abstract The contemporary goal of today's service providing firms is to increase both their efficiency and customer satisfaction. It is crucial to reduce waste and increase the level of service (LOS) in order to reach that goal and survive in a highly competitive environment, such as airport operating industry. Existing LOS measurement standards and methods have been widely criticised by airport professionals due to the lack of extensive and objective passenger input (Correia et al., 2008). Major problems arise while measuring LOS in consequence of poor data. In 2013, Apple introduced iBeacons which are small computers that emit Bluetooth signals to communicate with smart devices nearby and are mainly used for indoor positioning. The indoor positioning and tracking capability leads to the emergence of numerous applications, such as wayfinding and location based information sharing. The underlying principle that makes the whole concept so usable is the ability to bind both the physical and digital world together.

In this study, the conceptual infrastructure of iBeacon is investigated, advantages for the airline industry are listed and a new model is built for improving business processes. With the usage of this model, airports can reduce waste, increase level of service by enhancing wayfinding, which is the second important airport LOS determinant (Correia et al., 2008), and obtain customer data simultaneously. Lastly, recommendations are made for improving this model.

Keywords: *iBeacon technology; Level of service; Muda reduction; Airport management*

1. Introduction

Increased mobility of individuals strengthened the role of air transport due to its advantage of being the most timesaving medium of transportation. In 2014, the economic magnitude of the global airline industry reached USD 751 billion (ATIG, 2015) with 33.4 million flights, and 3.31 billion passengers (IATA, 2015). Since airports are an inseparable part of air transport, depending upon the current affairs, airports undertook noteworthy structural changes to create a more responsive and dynamic environment in accordance with market changes and passenger preferences (IATA, 2013).

* Izmir University of Economics, cansu.tayaksi@ieu.edu.tr

** Izmir University of Economics, birce.dobrucali@ieu.edu.tr

Until the deregulation of the air transport industry, airports were frequently viewed either as free public services, or a service provided by governmental or quasi-governmental entities, hence marketing was not playing a significant role for airport management (Fodness and Murray, 2005). After the deregulation, airports began competing for airline routing, realised the significance of pull marketing strategy for attracting passengers, and started offering improved services with exceptional level of service (LOS) and satisfaction promise (Fodness and Murray, 2005).

Wander (1998) stated that travelers need safety, time, elimination of unknowns, comfort, and facilities for feeling at ease, and Caves and Pickard (2000) highlighted the fact that travelers can only pay attention to the LOS only when these necessities are provided. It can be noted that wayfinding is the most significant element of this balance. Flawless wayfinding decreases the necessary journey time to its minimum, whereas the exact opposite situation increases both the uncertainty in predicting the needed time and average time taken, which is not preferable since individual's prime psychological concern is to eliminate the unknowns (Caves and Pickard, 2000).

In addition to departing and arriving passengers, airports host retailers and concessionaires, such as cafes, restaurants, bookstores, and beauty shops. These retailers and concessionaires hold an important place for airports for two reasons; (1) travelers are expected to spend the remaining time before their flights by utilising these retailers and enhance satisfaction (2) continuity of airport's commercial agreements with those retailers is required for increasing profits of airports. Hence, once the muda is eliminated and wayfinding is successfully achieved, an increase in the perceived LOS is expected.

2. Literature Review

2.1 Level of Service

Level of service (LOS) refers to perceived experience quality encountered in an airport (Müller and Gosling, 1991). LOS evaluation is based on the psychometric scaling technique established by Bock and Jones (1968) and further applied by Müller (1987) and Ndoh and Ashford (1993).

At airports, passengers come across both tangible and intangible services in a physical setting; such as, corridors, queues, signs and complex interactions (Fodness and Murray, 2005). The passenger's perception of the airport terminal's level of service is dependent on these factors (Brink and Madison, 1975). According to Airports Council International (2000) and Seneviratne and Martel (1991), the most important determinants include; waiting time, processing time, walking time, walking distance, level changes, orientation, space availability for passengers, space availability for cars, and number of seats. If an airport cannot attend to these activities and measures used in determining LOS efficiently, airport service quality, airport facilities, and LOS will be perceived as low by travelers (Martin-Cejas, 2006).

The LOS measures for airports has been of growing interest in the last decades due to strengthened competition in the industry (i.e. Frunin, 1972; Brink and Maddison, 1975; Novak, 1978; and Ashford, 1988). However standards and measurement methods have extensively been criticised by professionals, due to the lack of passenger input, and taking the passenger's subjective perception into account rather than an objective input (Correia et al., 2008). Even though collecting data regarding the characteristics of individual facilities (i.e. individual waiting time at check in encounter) is relatively easier than collecting data regarding overall measures (i.e. individual walking distance), since collecting detailed data is challenging, a wide measure reflecting the LOS is considered as almost impossible (Correia et al., 2008). Furthermore, entire researches obtain data through passenger surveys, which can be stated as a primitive technique when existing technology is considered.

2.2 Indoor Positioning

When someone tries to find his way in an indoor or outdoor environment, the action is called as "wayfinding." Wayfinding refers to the process of finding one's way in a geographical or constructed environment, in other words, being capable of recognising current location and knowing how to get to a target destination (Fewings, 2001).

Today there are so many settings for outdoor localisation like the signs by the roads, GPS tracking, signage, and some other applications for wayfinding. When it comes to indoor positioning, the market could be considered as empty when compared to outdoor positioning. Indoor positioning would have the advantages of altering human reactions and experiences in a building or in a venue (Martin et al., 2014). That kind of experience and reaction change could add value to the process of an organisation. Some organisations have already started to establish these indoor settings with the help of the newest technology. For example, retail firms are getting benefits from indoor positioning applications as increasing their customer retention rate and gaining more profit. One outstanding opportunity is "Airport usage" of indoor positioning.

Some of the existing airports are large constructions so that for an infrequent traveler, wayfinding may be a distressing experience either for reaching a destination or knowing exactly where they are at any point in time (Fewings, 2001). The perceived LOS and satisfaction are influenced by the extent to which passengers can easily find their way through the terminal building.

Due to financial grounds, only basic layouts of directional and facility signs have usually been installed in airports. However, with the sharp increase in passenger numbers, financial considerations are changing because improving passenger flow indirectly increases airport capacity.

2.3 Conceptual Infrastructure of iBeacons

In today's age of Big Data, with regard to the latest technology, there exist various instruments to obtain data. One of the most useful tools for data collecting is BLE (Bluetooth Low Energy) beacons, which seem more promising when compared with NFC (Near Field Communication) technology in terms of data collecting (compatibility and security issues in NFC).

In the year 2013, Apple Inc. introduced a device called iBeacon, which can be used for indoor positioning and collecting data. The term iBeacon is used by Apple to describe their own BLE beacon technology implementation by using iOS 7. iBeacons are small, complex computers with integrated Bluetooth radios and they originated from BLE beacon technology. Nowadays, the iBeacon term is started to be used synonymously with the general term BLE beacons. Although the introduction of the device to the market was made by Apple Inc., today, the technology is also started to be supported by Android and Blackberry operated devices. In other words, devices like smartphones and tablets can also be used as BLE Beacons (Newman, 2014).

Even though the iBeacon technology is not extensively studied in the literature, some innovative companies have started to use these devices for various purposes. iBeacons can be considered as small computers, which have their own Central Processing Unit (CPU), accelerometer, temperature sensor, and Bluetooth 4.0 radio. They use the Bluetooth Low Energy network technology and send signals to every compatible device within a 70 metre radius. The communication line is one way (from beacon devices to smart devices), which enables them to send notifications to the smart devices of the users. The main usage area of these devices is "indoor wayfinding."

3. A new model for wayfinding in Airports by using iBeacons

As shown in the below flow-diagram, the system consists of two modules; navigation module and flight information module.

If a user enters the system with the intention of obtaining flight information, he should decide to be navigated to that module by choosing it on the upcoming screen and the system would be directed to the first module, where the necessary information could be reached. Following action after the entrance to the information module is entering the "Passenger Name Record (PNR)" Number. In the sequel, all the necessary information related to the PNR number will be taken from the "Airport Database" and transferred to the passenger's screen. Once the flight information is obtained, three choices are offered to the passenger. The passengers would be able to have access to their "Gate Number Information," "Flight Status/Delay Information," or they would be able to get "Remaining Time Information." If the passenger chooses the first option, he will get the information related to the gate number. If there is a change about the gate number status, or if there are more than one flight combined to one gate, the passenger would be informed. If the second option is selected, the passenger would get the updates about his flight status. Delay information is one of the most important situations in an airport and the passengers should be informed properly about the reasons and the current situation about the delay. Lastly, if the passenger would choose to check how much time is left to the flight, the system would give advices according to the remaining time before flight. If the passenger has more than 30 minutes, a list of attractions in the airport is planned to be shown in the screen. However if the remaining time before the flight is calculated as less than 30 minutes, the passenger will be directed to the navigation module, which will navigate the passenger to the gate. All the information flow in this module is realised through "one-way information sending with notifications" capability of iBeacon devices.

The navigation module contains a more innovative process. The aim of this module is locating the users in the facility with the help of the radio signals emitted from iBeacon devices and helping to take them to the desired location with the shortest route possible by using the optimisation algorithm installed in the system. Navigation depends upon the communication between the user and the iBeacons. This module can be selected when the passengers enter to the system for the first time or they could be navigated to the module after taking advantage of the fight information. For the users who do not have a PNR number, the system is planned to automatically navigate them to the "Ticket Sale or Information Desk," where they could be informed about the buying process. On the other hand, if the user has a PNR number, the system will navigate the user to the desired location with the help of the airport database and iBeacons. Passengers using this module will be able to take advantage of the navigation module for obtaining route description to the "Gate," to the "Counter," and/or to "Attractions." The attraction list is envisaged to be a combination of café, lounge, restaurant, or duty free options according to the remaining time to the flight of the passenger.

4. Outputs and Benefits of the Model

As mentioned before, the main aim of the model is Muda elimination and LOS increase. The term, "Muda," comes from the Japanese translation of the word "waste." For making a service/manufacturing organisation leaner and more productive, muda should be eliminated from all perspectives. As Taiichi Ohno defined in its work in 1988, Muda is *"any human activity that uses resources but creates no value in return."* Muda holds an important place for organisations, since no organisation wants to spend its resources for creating waste. Ohno (1988) stated the well-known seven wastes as: overproduction, waiting inventories, unnecessary transport, waiting times, unnecessary motion, over-process and defective products. Unnecessary motion is the emphasised muda type in this study, which can be viewed as redundant movement of passengers in airports. With the usage of the proposed model in airports, unnecessary motion is aimed to be decreased. Thus, consequently, the decrease in the unnecessary motion is planned to increase perceived LOS by passengers.

In order to explain the factors of the muda decrease more effectively, it is crucial to understand the importance of data collection. With the system entrance of a passenger, the program will automatically start to collect data regarding actions taken by the user like walking pace, mostly used paths and the preferred venues. With the extensive usage of the program by passengers for a sufficient amount of time, airports would have collected detailed and objective data. However, it should be noted that solely data collection is not sufficient for making improvements. In order to make it useful, the data should be transformed into its meaningful form, which is called information. The bigger data sets the airport collects, the more useful information could be created, which could be used for decreasing muda and determining and improving LOS.

One of the most important and hard to create things in a facility is layout and after an airport had the information regarding to the preferred venues and walking patterns of the passengers, it would be so much easier to create a new layout design. By taking the information driven from the system it would be substantial to improve the facility according to the needs of the customers. If a facility would understand customers' needs and redesign itself according to that, the ability to compete will increase.

As also mentioned previously, one of the basic drawbacks of the LOS measurement is the lack of objective passenger input. With the data obtaining ability which comes with the usage of the system, this drawback is planned to be eliminated. Moreover, obtained information will lead to a better understanding of customers' needs. In conjunction with better understanding of the passengers needs, airports could improve their ability to compete. Furthermore, the retailers and concessionaires in the airport will be supported in the new layout of the airport, by locating these stores into places where passengers spend more time or pass through.

5. Limitations and Future Research

One of the basic limitations of the system is the neccessity of keeping the smartphone's Bluetooth open for the users during the system usage. Although the new Bluetooth 4.0 technology would consume very little energy of the passengers' smartphones, there is a possibility that people will not be aware of the fact and close their smartphone's Bluetooth like the old times. Awareness about the new Bluetooth Low Energy technology and its low battery consumption rate should be increased. System promotion should be made and instructive actions should be taken for the recognisation of the system.

The other limitation is the time to adjust to the process on customer side. Since the technology is rather new, people need time for learning and getting used to the system. With the instructive actions mentioned above the adjustment time could be decreased.

The indoor positioning market with the usage of iBeacons could be still considered as empty. By thinking the other usage areas of these devices in airports there are so many opportunities like indoor navigation for disabled people or positioning of the workers in the airports. Also the positioning technique could be improved and used for detection of missing personal items.

References

ATIG. (2015). *Havayolu Sektör Raporu*. ATIG. Retrieved from http://www.atig.com.tr/arastirma/raporlar/tr/havayolu-sektor-raporu-17-02-2015-09-33-17.pdf.

Bock, R. D., & Jones, J. V. (1968). The measurement and prediction of judgment and choice.

Caves, R., & Pickard, C. (2000). The satisfaction of human needs in airport passenger terminals. *Transport, 147*(1).

Correia, A., Wirasinghe, S., & de Barros, A. (2008). Overall level of service measures for airport passenger terminals. *Transportation Research Part A: Policy And Practice*, *42*(2), 330–346. http://dx.doi.org/10.1016/j.tra.2007.10.009

Evaluation of Airport Access Level of Service. (1993). *Airport Planning, Operation, and Management*, (1423), 34–39.

Fewings, R. (2001). Wayfinding and airport terminal design. *Journal Of Navigation, 2*, 177–184.

Fodness, D., & Murray, B. (2007). Passengers' expectations of airport service quality. *Journal Of Services Marketing, 21*(7), 492–506. http://dx.doi.org/10.1108/08876040710824852.

Fodness, D., & Murray, B. (2007). Passengers' expectations of airport service quality. *Journal Of Services Marketing, 21*(7), 492–506. http://dx.doi.org/10.1108/08876040710824852.

IATA. (2013). *IATA Annual Review*. IATA. Retrieved from https://www.iata.org/about/Documents/iata-annual-review-2013-en.pdf.

IATA. (2015). *IATA Annual Review*. IATA. Retrieved from https://www.iata.org/about/Documents/iata-annual-review-2015.pdf.

Kaplan, E. (1987). *Air transportation issues*. Washington, D.C.: Transportation Research Board.

Martin, Paul et al. "An Ibeacon Primer For Indoor Localization". Proceedings of the 1st ACM Conference on Embedded Systems for Energy-Efficient Buildings - BuildSys '14 (2014): n. pag. Web. 27 Feb. 2016.

Müller, C., & Gosling, G. (1991). A framework for evaluating level of service for airport terminals.

Newman, Nic. "Apple Ibeacon Technology Briefing". J Direct Data Digit Mark Pract 15.3 (2014): 222–225. Web. 23 Feb. 2016.

Ohno, T. "Toyota Production System: Beyond Large-Scale Production". Productivity Press, Portland, OR. (1988)

Transportation Planning and Technology, 16(1), 45–61. http://dx.doi.org/10.1080/03081069108717470.

Rendeiro Martin-Cejas, R. (2006). Tourism service quality begins at the airport. *Tourism Management, 27*(5), 874–877. http://dx.doi.org/10.1016/j.tourman.2005.05.005.

Transportation Research Board. (1975). *Identification and Measurement of Capacity and Levels of Service of Landside Elements of the Airport* (pp. 92–111). Retrieved from http://trid.trb.org/view.aspx?id=37014.

Prof. Dr. Bekim Berisha* & MSc. Bernard Berisha**

Value Relevance of Accounting Information in Kosovo

Abstract This paper examines the value relevance of accounting information in pre and post-periods of the International Financial Reporting Standards (IFRS) implementation using the regression and portfolio approaches for sample of the Kosovo companies. A comparison of the results for the periods before and after adoption, based on both regression and portfolio approaches, shows a decline in value relevance of accounting information after the reform in accounting standards. It could be interpreted to mean that following to IFRS in Kosovo did not improve value relevancy of accounting information. However, results based on and portfolio approach shows that cash flows' incremental information content increased for the post-IFRS period.

Keywords: Value Relevance, IFRS, Accounting Information, Kosovo.

1. Introduction

Our paper investigates the value relevance and reliability of accounting information in Kosovo. Kosovo has obliged companies based on certain criteria to use the IFRS since 2011 in order to unify the financial reporting system for easier integration into international markets through the use of international accounting standards and auditing. Reporting of financial information based on the International Standards of Financial Reporting, without doubt it is a good opportunity for Kosovo companies, to enable all stakeholders international access easy and identifiable for the position and performance of companies to be able to make decisions for eventual investment in those companies.

Even though Kosovo has no capital market, and Kosovar companies mainly operate with own capital, but this does not mean that we should not apply IFRS for SMEs.

Accounting information contained in financial statements is expected to be useful for decision makers. In order to provide this, financial statements should meet some basic characteristics. "*If financial information is to be useful, it must be relevant and faithfully represent what it purports to represent. The usefulness of*

---

* University of Prizren, bekim_@hotmail.com
** College AAB Prishtina, bernard@qendra.org

financial information is enhanced if it is comparable, verifiable, timely and understandable" (Conceptual Framework 2010: A33).

As it has previously noted, Sibel. K (2013), basic qualitative characteristics of financial statements are relevance and faithful presentation. "*Relevant financial information is capable of making a difference in the decisions made by users. Information may be capable of making a difference in a decision even if some users choose not to take advantage of it or are already aware of it from other sources*" (Conceptual Framework, 2010: A33). Besides relevance, financial information is needed to be presented faithfully. "*To be useful, financial information must not only represent relevant phenomena, but it must also faithfully represent the phenomena that it purports to represent. To be a perfectly faithful representation, a depiction would have three characteristics. It would be complete, neutral and free from error. Of course, perfection is seldom, if ever, achievable*" (Conceptual Framework, 2010: A34).

Pervan and Bartulovic (2013) state that accounting information is considered value relevant if it is correlated with the market value of a company. If there is no statistically significant relation between accounting information and market value of a company it can be concluded that accounting information is not value relevant which implies that financial statements do not meet one of the fundamental objectives of financial reporting.

Recent studies (e.g., Healy and Palepu, 2001; Bushman and Smith, 2001; Lambert, Leuze, and Verrecchia, 2005) suggest that enhanced financial reporting may have important economic implications in increasing the efficiency of investment.

The Kosovo Financial Reporting Council (KCFR) as a regulatory body, from 2011 issued in use IFRS for Commercial companies which they are obligated to prepare the financial statements for general purposes in accordance with IFRS.

Before 2011, in Kosovo were the applicable KAS and IAS.

The purpose of this paper is to provide a clearer picture on the financial reporting environment in Kosovo, and the importance of accounting information value in Kosovo.

1.1 Kosovo Accounting System and IFRS

In 2001, the UNMIK approved Regulation 2001/30 ON THE ESTABLISHMENT OF THE BOARD FOR FINANCIAL REPORTING OF KOSOVO AND THE REGIME OF FINANCIAL REPORTING OF BUSINESS ORGANIZATIONS, under which commercial enterprises anticipated obligations for maintaining accounting records and forms financial statements based on principles.

During 2001, the Central Fiscal Authority (CFA) issued the Kosovo Accounting Standards (KAS). From October 29 2001 with the entry into force of Regulation

2001/30 UNMIK, KAS are applicable in Kosovo for all business organisations whose turnover annually is about DM 200,000 (100,000 EUR) or the value of assets which is about DM 100,000 (50,000 EUR) starting with their application from January 1 2002.

The Board shall issue accounting standards in accordance with International Accounting Standards (IAS). The Board decides which of the IAS standards are to be applied, taking into account the business environment in Kosovo. The Board shall issue auditing standards in accordance with ISAs.

According to Article 5 of the Regulation Paragraph 5.1 business organisations that have an annual turnover or total assets worth over DM 500,000 (or € 250,000 from the time when such currency is introduced in Kosovo), their statements of financial position for purposes general will be checked by licensed auditors in accordance with applicable auditing standards.

The Kosovo Assembly adopted the Law on Accounting, Financial Reporting and Auditing number LAW NO. 04 / L-014 on 29 July 2011.

According to Article 3 p. 1 commercial companies prepare financial statements for general purposes in accordance with this law.

Commercial companies-rated according to the criteria of this law in Kosovo must apply IAS / IFRS and interpretations, recommendations and necessary guidance issued by the Board for International Accounting Standards approved by KCFR.

Based on this law, the implementation of IFRS started in 2011.

2. Literature Review

According to (Rodrigo S. Verdi, 2006) assumed that the highest quality of financial reporting can improve this efficiency investment by reducing asymmetric information in two ways: (1) it reduces the asymmetry of information between the company and the investor, and it reduces the cost of the firm in fundraising, and (2) it reduces the information asymmetry between investors and managers and thus reduces the cost of monitoring of managers by shareholders.

Value relevance is being defined as the ability of information that is presented by financial statements to capture and summarise firm value. Value relevance can be measured by the statistical relations between information that financial statements present and stock market values or returns (Suadiye, 2012). Even though the concept is not new, the term "value relevance" was used by Amir et al. for the first time in 1993 in the related literature (Carnevale et al., 2009; Suadiye, 2012).

The value relevance of accounting information has been studied in many perspectives. Miller and Modigliani's (1966) study was one of the first studies investigating relations among accounting figures and other financial parameters.

Karampinis and Hevas (2011) investigated IFRS implementation and value relevance of accounting data. They explored potential effects of IFRS implementation on two salient properties of accounting income: value relevance and conditional conservatism. Their results show that only minor improvements have been observed related with selected properties of income. Karampinis and Hevas (2009) found similar results for value relevance of mandatory application of IFRS in Greece.

In Turkey value relevance of accounting information has also been analysed in several perspectives. Kirkulak and Balsari (2009) analysed the effect of inflation-adjusted data on explaining the market value of equity and stock returns in Turkey. They reported that both historical cost-based book value and earnings information and inflation-adjusted information are value relevant and they complement each other. Using them together results to more value relevance. However, they also stated that comparing value relevance of inflation-adjusted information is a unique opportunity since firms reported their financial statements in both historical cost numbers and inflation-adjusted numbers only for the year 2003. Because of lower inflation rates and the implementation of international accounting standards since 2005, applying inflation accounting would not be needed (Gücenme & Poroy Arsoy, 2006).

Also in Kosovo importance of accounting information is analysed from different aspects. Maloku and al (2014) analysed the Importance of the Application of International Accounting Standards in Kosovo businesses. They concluded that each company is significantly influenced by certain standards and these effects should be taken into consideration. Business organisations in Kosovo should advance in the preparation of financial statements in accordance with IAS. Over financial reporting, business organisations must disclose all elements of financial statements, in order to be complete, accurate, and reliable.

3. Data and Research Methodology

The analysis of the value relevance of accounting information was conducted on the company that have audited financial statements and have submitted the KCFR which they are obliged by the Law of Accounting and Auditing. Companies were selected for the study according to a random sample. The criterion for selection was the annual turnover over four million or the value of assets over two million and those companies who have worked before 2011 and after 2011.

Although none of the selected companies are listed on the stock exchange, they have a legal obligation to apply IFRSs for their compilation of financial statements. Selected for study are 28 companies divided by activities. The number of companies selected according to the activities are shown in Table 1.

Table 1: The research sample by the activities

	Production	**Trading**	**Construction**	**Services**	**Others**
Number of Observations	6	10	8	4	

Source: Authors calculation

The financial statements of the companies selected for the study are for the period of 2007–2014, and data are collected from web pages and directly from companies.

By activities, we have presented the value of assets and turnover for the relevant period, as well as growth rates after the period of implementation of IFRS shown in Table 2.

Table 2: Numbers of firms 2007–2014

Company		2008–2010		2011–2013		%	
		Assets	Revenua	Assets	Revenua	Assets	Revenua
PRODUCTION	1	2,700	4,200	2,600	4,300	0.96	1.02
	2	2,600	4,600	2,900	4,700	1.12	1.02
	3	3,200	5,400	3,200	5,800	1.00	1.07
	4	4,100	5,200	4,000	6,000	0.98	1.15
	5	4,500	6,000	4,700	6,500	1.04	1.08
	6	4,900	5,800	5,200	6,800	1.06	1.17
	Total:	**88,000**	**124,800**	**90,400**	**136,400**	**1.03**	**1.09**
TRADING	1	12,000	23,000	12,300	24,000	1.03	1.04
	2	14,500	32,000	14,000	33,000	0.97	1.03
	3	18,000	28,000	17,500	26,500	0.97	0.95
	4	15,000	34,000	16,000	36,000	1.07	1.06
	5	24,000	45,000	25,000	42,000	1.04	0.93
	6	27,500	51,000	26,000	54,000	0.95	1.06
	7	23,000	44,000	22,000	48,000	0.96	1.09
	8	13,500	24,000	16,700	29,000	1.24	1.21
	9	16,700	29,600	20,800	33,000	1.25	1.11
	10	29,000	56,000	32,000	62,000	1.10	1.11
	Total:	**772,800**	**1,466,400**	**809,200**	**1,550,000**	**1.05**	**1.06**
CONSTRUCTION	1	1,600	4,100	1,600	4,200	1.00	1.02
	2	1,500	4,200	1,500	4,650	1.00	1.11
	3	1,900	4,700	1,800	5,350	0.95	1.14
	4	2,200	4,600	24,000	5,600	10.91	1.22
	5	3,150	5,300	3,600	6,100	1.14	1.15
	6	2,250	5,600	2,850	4,800	1.27	0.86
	7	3,400	6,200	4,200	6,600	1.24	1.06
	8	4,100	11,000	4,400	13,500	1.07	1.23
	Total:	**80,400**	**182,800**	**175,800**	**203,200**	**2.19**	**1.11**
	TOTAL:	**941,200**	**1,774,000**	**1,075,400**	**1,889,600**	**1.14**	**1.07**

Source: Authors calculation

3.1 Research Methodology

Comparison was made of the value of assets and the annual turnover between before 2011 and after 2011 to identifying the importance of accounting information for decision makers.

Comparison was made of the value of assets and the annual turnover bbefore 2011 and after 2011 to identify the importance of accounting information for decision makers, as well as to the contribution that will increase the market value of assets and the annual turnover.

Based on recent theoretical insights in the area of the value relevance of accounting information, unable to evaluate whether there is a correlation between accounting information and share process, because in Kosovo there are no companies listed in the stock markets, we explored the importance of the implementation of IFRS and their impact on the presentation of the real market value of assets, annual turnover, and the use of accounting information for decision makers.

4. Results and Suggestions

The results of the data analysis prove that the companies before the implementation of IFRS have not published financial statements, or very few of them, only 24,4%. While after the application of IFRS, 92% of them have published financial statements.

The real value of the companies in the period after the implementation of IFRS is about 1,07% greater compared to the prior year to the implementation of IFRS and as a result of the publication and submission of financial statements in KCFR as required by law. Also, the annual turnover increase in the financial statements following the implementation of IFRS is about 1,14% greater in comparison with the annual turnover of the company before the implementation of IFRS.

By activities, manufacturing companies have increased the value of assets to 1.03% and 1.09% annual turnover in comparison with the years prior to the implementation of IFRS. Trading Companies have increased the value of assets of 1.05% and to 1.06% in turnover compared with the years before the implementation of IFRS. Construction companies with years prior to the implementation of IFRS have increased the value of assets to 2.19% and 1.11% in turnover compared with the years before the implementation of IFRS.

Due to limitations of the source of information by companies, we have not been able to prove how decision makers use accounting information for their economic decisions. Future studies will prove this.

Figure 1: Assets ratio and turnover for production enterprises

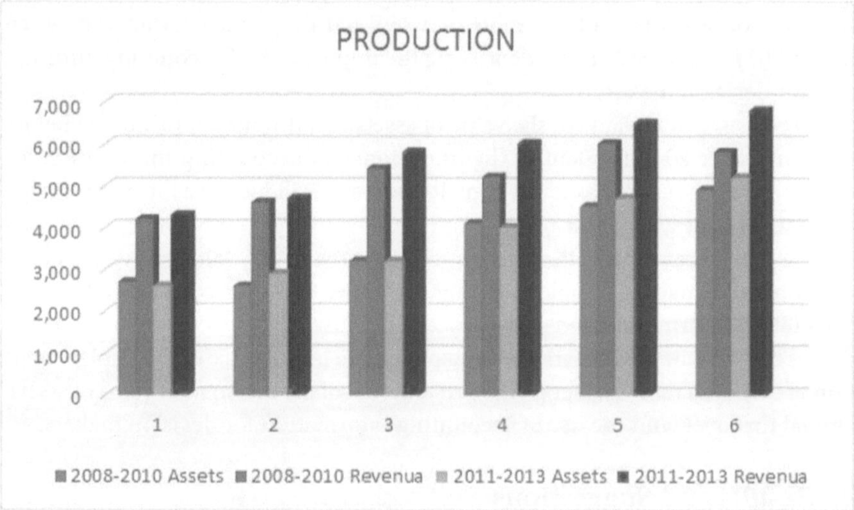

Figure 2: Assets ratio and turnover for trading enterprises

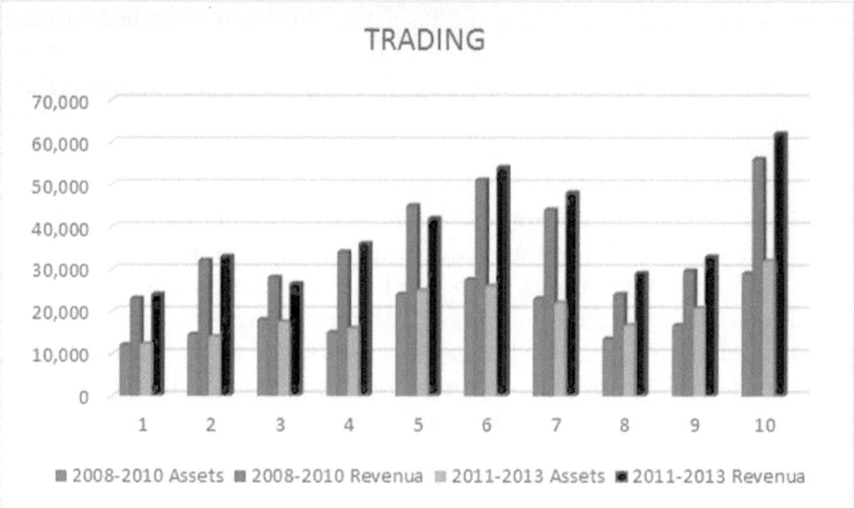

Figure 3: Assets ratio and turnover for construction enterprises

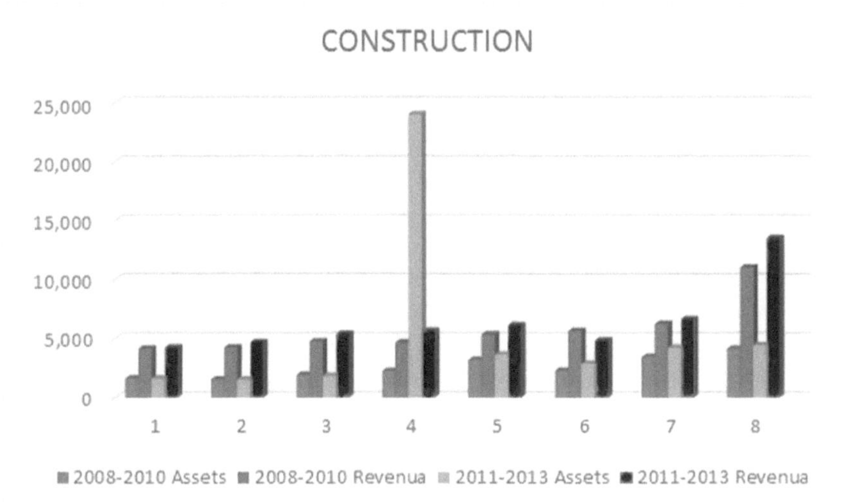

5. Conclusion

Based on research results, and declarations of the respondents, it appears that the Kosovo companies in the period after the implementation of IFRS for the preparation of financial statements in the first year of reporting have had problems of a technical nature, even in terms of conversion carrying, presenting the value of assets at their fair values, but also in terms of their preparation by accounting experts. This has affected the commitment of Chartered Accountants as well as increased spending accounting services.

Despite this, the implementation of IFRS, Kosovo companies have raised the level of financial reporting in standardised, continuously they have published their financial statements as well as through external audit of the added value of accounting information.

Although Kosovo companies are not listed on stock exchanges, raising the value of the accounting information as a result of the implementation of IFRS should be understood as an opportunity, through standardisation of financial reporting system, to compete in global markets, and to be able attract investments from abroad as necessary for their further development and economic development.

References

Aktaş, H. (2009). *Hisse Senetleri Piyasasında Muhasebe Bilgilerinin Önemi: IMKB'de Değer İlişkisi Analizi*. Ankara: Gazi Kitabevi. (Magnitude of Accounting Information in Stock Markets: Value Relevance Analysis. Ankara: Gazi Press).

Alali, F. A., & Foote, P. S. (2012). The Value Relevance of International Financial Reporting Standards: Empirical Evidence in an Emerging Market. *The International Journal of Accounting, 47*, 85–108. http://dx.doi.org/10.1016/j.intacc.2011.12.005.

Ali, A., & Hwang, L. S. (2000). Country-Specific Factors Related to Financial Reporting and the Value Relevance of Accounting Data. *Journal of Accounting Research, 38*(1), 1–21. http://dx.doi.org/10.2307/2672920.

Carnevale, C., Giunta, F., & Cardamone, P. (2009). The Value Relevance of Social Report. *The European Financial Management Association*. Retrieved from http://www.efmaefm.org/0EFMAMEETINGS/EFMA%20ANNUAL%20MEETINGS/2009-milan/EFMA2009_0722_FullPaper.pdf.

Core, J. E., Guay, W. R., & Van Buskirk, A. (2001). Market Valuations in the New Economy: An Investigation of What has Changed. *JAE Boston Conference*, June 2001. http://dx.doi.org/10.2139/ssrn.262619.

(e.g., Healy & Palepu, 2001; Bushman & Smith, 2001; Lambert, Leuze, & Verrecchia, 2005). Financial Reporting Quality and Investment Efficiency. University of Pennsylvania 1303 Steinberg Hall-Dietrich Hall Philadelphia, PA 19104. http://areas.kenan-flagler.unc.edu/Accounting/Documents/Verdi%20Paper.pdf.

Gücenme, Ü., & Poroy Arsoy, A. (2006). Changes in Financial Reporting in Turkey: Historical Development of Inflation Accounting from 1960 to 2005. *Eleventh World Congress of Accounting Historians*, Nantes, (France), July 19–22, Papers of Turkish Delegation. Retrieved from http://journal.mufad.org/attachments/article/204/a5-changes_in_financial_reporting_in_turkey.pdf.

Iatridis, G., & Rouvolis, S. (2010). The Post-Adoption Effects of the Implementation of International Financial Reporting Standards in Greece. *Journal of International Accounting, Auditing and Taxation, 19*, 55–65. http://dx.doi.org/10.1016/j.intaccaudtax.2009.12.004.

Karampinis, N. I., & Hevas, D. L. (2009). The Effect of the Mandatory Application of IFRS on the Value Relevance of Accounting Data: Some Evidence from Greece. *European Research Studies, 12*(1), 73–100.

Karampinis, N. I., & Hevas, D. L. (2011). Mandating IFRS in an Unfavorable Environment: The Greek Experience. *The International Journal of Accounting, 46*, 304–332. http://dx.doi.org/10.1016/j.intacc.2011.07.001.

Khanagha, J. B. (2011). Value Relevance of Accounting Information in the United Arab Emirates. *International Journal of Economics and Financial Issues, 1*(2), 33–45.

Kirkulak, B., & Balsari, C. K. (2009). Value Relevance of Inflation-Adjusted Equity and Income. *The International Journal of Accounting, 44*, 363–377. http://dx.doi.org/10.1016/j.intacc.2009.09.007.

Maloku, E., & al (2014). Importance of the Application of International Accounting Standards in Kosovo Businesses. *Journal of Knowledge Management, Economics and Information Technology, Vol. IV, Issue 2, April 2014.* Httpp://www.scientificpapers.org.

Marquardt, C. A., & Wiedman, C. I. (2004). The Effect of Earnings Management on the Value Relevance of Accounting Information. *Journal of Business Finance & Accounting, 31*(3&4), 297–332. http://dx.doi.org/10.1111/j.0306-686X.2004.00541.x.

Papadatos, K., & Bellas, A. (2011). The Value Relevance of Accounting Information under Greek and International Financial Reporting Standards: The Influence of Firm-Specific Characteristics. *International Research Journal of Finance and Economics, 76*, 6–23.

Perera, R. A. A. S., & Thrikawala, S. S. (2010). An Empirical Study of the Relevance of Accounting Information on Investor's Decisions. University of Kelaniya, Kelaniya, Sri Lanka. Retrieved from http://repository.kln.ac.lk/91/1/FIN002.pdf.

Rodrigo S. Verdi, (2006). Financial Reporting Quality and Investment Efficiency. Massachusetts Institute of Technology 50 Memorial Drive E52–403A Cambridge, MA 02142 http://ssrn.com/abstract=930922.

Sibel. K. (2013). The Impact of IFRS on the Value Relevance of Accounting Information: Evidence from Turkish Firms. *International Journal of Economics and Finance; Vol. 5, No. 4; 2013 ISSN 1916-971X E-ISSN 1916–9728* http://dx.doi.org/10.5539/ijef.v5n4p71.

Suadiye, G. (2012). Value Relevance of Book Value & Earnings under the Local GAAP and IFRS: Evidence from Turkey. *Ege Akademik Review, 12*(3), 301–310.

Hasan Türedi* & Duygu Celayir**

Evaluation of Corporate Sustainability Reports in Terms of Assurance Services

Abstract Sustainability is a concept that has gained more attention especially amongst the business world, and social and economic actors in recent years. Also, it has led to changes in the concept of reporting. The reporting types which were known as "environmental reporting" or "social reporting" so far, now relinquished its place to the type called "sustainability reporting" or "corporate social responsibility" reporting. Apart from financial information, it is issued that non-financial information must be reported too, as it is issued that there has to be triple reporting in economic, social, and environmental terms. The change was not only in reporting format; there also emerged a new concept named "sustainability expectaion" for stakeholders. Surely this situation has made apparent the requirements in assurance activities about the sustainability expectations and needs that have to be refined in these terms. Primarily, the study clarifies the concepts of sustainability, sustainability reporting and assurance, and gives importance the reliability of the information that were given in the reports and the importance and necessity of the sustainability reports in this context through an independent assurance/auditing process as well. In addition to this, the developments in Turkey concerning the reliability of sustainability reports have been reviewed.

Keywords: Sustainability, Assurance, Assurance Services

1. Introduction

Nowadays, the expectations of society have changed against the past, changing these expectations have led corporations to new searches. One of these concepts that led to the new searches is "sustainability."

Sustainability in corporations predicates that economic expectations should be appreciated in a balanced manner along with environmental and social awareness. Leading the international economies by the corporations has brought the social and environmental responsibilities as well as the economic responsibilities. On the other hand, the corporations have become responsible to all stakeholders, not only to their shareholders or potential investors. Many reasons that are arised from these responsibilities have revealed the need of taking into account the sustainability concept by corporations during their management policies.

* Prof. Dr., Istanbul Commerce University
** Res. Assist., Istanbul Commerce University

Corporate sustainability emphasizes the necessity of focusing on social and environmental issues that arise while they operate, and are a new management mentality within the dynamic and variable business world. The company's ability to profit is crucial in order to reach corporate sustainability. However, the company has to follow social purposes regarding the sustainable development that constitutes from economic welfare, environmental integrity, and social equity concepts too (Wilson, 2003). In this context, the corporations that are aiming to survive had to consider the triple dimension of the corporate sustainability as a whole and this relevant necessity have revealed the reporting of the sustainability. By the reporting of sustainability, triple reporting has been made concerning to the environmental, social and economicially then, reporting of the non-financial informations have been ensured except financial information as well.

Sustainability reports have created a positive impact for the stakeholders of the corporation, then the demand for independent assurance has come to the surface in the related reports. Cohen has stated in his report that was made through a search in the United States of America (USA) in 2014 and determined that professional investors demand sustainability information more and prefer secure information as well (Brown-Liburd, H., and Zamora, 2014). The assurance of sustainability reports is a complex process as they are being based on either a voluntary basis (Adams and Evans, 2004) or on qualitative data (O'Dwyer et al., 2011). Nevertheless, it has become crucial from the point of many company stakeholders today (Adams & Evans, 2004).

In this study, sustainability, reporting on sustainability, and assurance concepts become intense. It has been attempted to concentrate on the reliability of these statements that were given in this report and the importance, necessity and difficulties of the independent assurance/auditing process of the information that was given in this context. Finally, the approaches of the corporations that are taking part in Istanbul Stock Exchange (BIST) Sustainability Index towards the assurance of the sustainability reports, within the scope of their completing from assurance/verification, have been reviewed.

2. Corporate Sustainability and Sustainability Reporting

Corporate sustainability is specified as a combination of environmental and social sustainability. In this context, the corporations should go towards long termed profit goal instead of short term (Dyllick and Hockerts, 2002). From this aspect, being the corporation in a way that creates the economic value and being a manufacturer will not be sufficient; it needs to minimise the negative effects while these corporations are operating as well (Kuşat, 2012).

Sustainability at the corporate level can be acquired by taking consideration to create long termed value in the operations of environmental and social factors of the corporations and decision mechanisms and through the efficient management of the risks related with these factors. A corporation should acquire corporate sustainability by adopting transparency, equity, accountability and social responsibility; conducting production through environmentally-conscious technologies; ensuring the consciousness of environment protection in all areas of the corporation; creating healthy products; ensuring healthy working conditions for employees and keeping their rights; and improving energy efficiency in the corporation (Once et al, 2015).

Whether or not having a profit motive, the declarations about the financial, environmental, social and management performances of any corporation that are shared with its stakeholders clearly are specified as sustainability reports (Clausen et al., 2005). The corporations are asserting their social, conversion, work ethic, security, health and environmental management policies within the context of their sustainability reports. Reporting sustainability has risen in the business world of the 21st century. Even though, it comes to the surface in very few environmentalist and community-oriented corporations, it is carried out by many corporations all around the world today (EY, 2010) The reports about sustainability comprise the social and environmental strategies of business management for the future. The corporations turn towards increasing their abilities to achieve the specified goals, facilitate the environmental, financial and social strategy applications, create awareness regarding the environmental issues throughout the corporation by transmitting the corporation's message to the stakeeholders clearly for reasons such as increasing transparency and accountability.

Some regulations concerning the reporting of sustainability have been made and guidelines are followed. The standards that are globally used have become standards under the title Global Reporting Inititiative (GRI). (Ballou et al. 2006), The GRI has developed a comprehensive framework regarding the reporting of sustainability that is used worldwide to encourage this sustainability report to be done by corporations (GRI, 2015). With this framework, increasing the number of the corporations that carry out the reporting has been ensured.

The growing trend in the reporting of sustainability and publishing these reports brought the question of the accuracy and reliability of the relevant reports. Performance data of sustainability is a powerful tool from the point of view of the current situation and future image of the corporation. By increasingly trust-seeking concerning to the performance data quality, independent assurance services ensure the reliability of this data and ensure they are used in the resolution process. The report that is carried out by Global Reporting Institute proposes the independent assurance for the corporations that are made the sustainability reports.

3. Assurance of Sustainability Reports

The information within sustainability reports are used in the decisions taken by the stakeholders. Due to this, the transparency and accuracy of the relevant information are important for the parties who will utilise these reports (CorporateRegister, 2008: Manetti and Toccafondi, 2012). The need for the reliability of this non-financial information brings independent assurance to the forefront.

Within this context, assurance is defined as independent professional services that increase the quality of the information in order to increase the quality of any information that will be utilised by decision makers (ACCA, 2012). Assurance is given by independent auditors or other members of a profession. Assurance services are aim at increasing the quality and reliability of financial or non-financial information.

Corporations use a variety of approaches to increase the reliability of the reports. The corporations, being a part of the management and reporting processes of the knowledge, including the internal audit functions, may have internal control systems. These internal systems are crucial from the point of general integrity and plausibility of the report. However, giving an independent external assurance is incentive to increase corporate transparency.

Recently, studies are made in order to ensure the effectiveness of the information that are in existing sustainability reports and to provide assurance to the knowledge.

Although there are increasing number of regulations concerning to the assurance of sustainability reports, it remains an unsolved issue in the sense of the corporations. Some of the reasons for this are having different standards in practice, diversity of the assurance providers and hinging on a voluntary basis have made the problem more apparent. Corporations adopt a variety of approaches for the sake of intensifying the reports. Like sustainability assurance that is given internally, stakeholder panel or assurance is given by specialists. However, the recommended and contributory one is independent assurance.

As well as being the independent, the (external) assurance of sustainability reports are important in order to ensure applicable, comparable, and transparent reports that are requested by stakeholders, it is one of the key elements of good reporting. Although, there are a lack of internatioanally accepted assurance standards concerning sustainability reporting, studies are being performed in order to create standards accordingly. The studies in point reflect the development tendency of international sustainability assurance standards.

Most know are two standard sets regarding the assurance of sustainability reporting. They are the Accountability 1000 (AA1000) principles that are published by The Institute of Social and Ethical Accountability and assurance standard

(ISAE 3000) numbered 3000 that is published by the International Federation of Accountants (IFAC) (Kolk and Perego, 2010). Although, criticism has been expressed for the standards, as most of the standards are based on the financial assurance model and it may be incapable of the evaluation of social, ethical, and environmental performance data (Dando and Swift, 2003).

The Accountability Principle (AA1000): The Accountability Principle 1000 (AA 1000) published in 1999 by The Institute of Social and Ethical Accountability is influenced from financial accounting principles. A key element is that it gives a place for the "inclusivity" principle. This principle means to consider the request and needs of all interest groups related with the corporation at all stages of the reporting and auditing process. Said principles were developed in 2003 and Exactitude/integrity, materiality and responsiveness factors come into prominence. In general, the AA1000 featured the basic principles to consider from the point of the assurance of the reports. The main standard that should be considered during the assurance process is the standard numbered 3000 that was published by the IFAC.

The International Standard on Assurance Engagements (ISAE) 3000: Another major regulation of assurance services in the world is standard 3000 (ISAE 3000) with regards to assurance agreements that are made by the International Federation of Accountants-IFAC. Today, many countries take the international regulations of IFAC as reference concerning to assurance services.

Standard is valid for all assurance services; in order to meet increasing demands, for the assurance reports such as environment, social and sustainability reports, information systems, internal auditing, corporate governance with regard to rapport, have been carried into effect by IFAC. At present, members of the profession take the ISAE 3000 standards in consideration in the assurance services except audit and review.

This standard defines two types of assurance level as "reasonable assurance" and "limited assurance" that can be carried out by the assurance provider in order to determine the limits of assurance applications. *"Reasonable assurance"* is a preeminently assurance. The auditor attains reasonable assurance by obtaining sufficient and appropriate audit evidence to reduce the assurance risk to an acceptable low level. The goal of reasonable assurance applications is reducing the risks that are belonging to the assurance application till the acceptable level in a way to allow the auditor's opinion in a positive manner.

In the limited assurance, collecting evidence, the structure, timing and content of the processes are more limited in comparision with reasonable assurance agreements. The purpose of limited assurance, as well as reducing the risk of assurance agreement to the acceptable level in terms of agreement, the risk for this kind of member of a profession is higher than reasonable assurance agreement with regards to being a basis for a negative result that is reached by the member of a profession. In the limited assurance agreement, the opinion is stated with inverted sentence indirectly.

Standard is based on tripartite relation. Tripartite relation is one of the elements of assurance agreements. The assurance agreements contain three different parties as implementer, responsible party, and intended users. "Implementer" concept means the member of profession of accountants who are working free. Responsible party (Generally can be stated as management or boad of management also) is a party that responsible for the determination of the subject, criteria selection and making an agreement with the member of a profession (Altıntaş, 2010).

Also, intended users are the person or persons who are subject to the report that is prepared by the member of a profession (for instance, banks or regulatory bodies).

Criteria that will be used in the assurance study is constituting the important element of the standard. While the criteria reaching the member of the profession's opinion are important due to the giving information to the users according to the service matter that is reviewed or measured on which basis. Due to this reason, the criteria should be open to access for information users in order to comprehend the subject on how to be measured and evaluated. As the member of profession can carry out assurance services, experts from outside may carry out as well.

In practice, there are audit firms (generally big four), consultancy firms, certification firms, experts (sustainability experts/ consultants) within the assurance providers (Anttila, M, 2013).

3.1 The Challenges on the Assurance of Sustainability

There are some challenges about the assurance process. The first is accuracy of the information. There are challenges concerning the accuracy of the information, transparency, comparability and assurance declaration of the information in the sustainability reports. Appropriate reporting criteria, being the reported information as qualitative but reporting in a digital information form is a difficult period. Congruity and prediction of materiality of the information can create difficulties also.

Figure 1: Challenges on Assurance Period

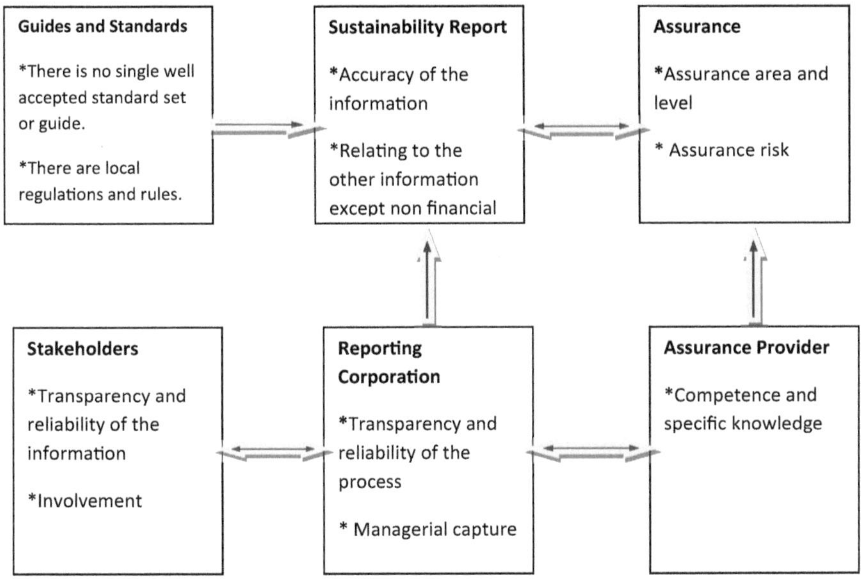

Source: Anttila, Mattilda (2013), "Exploring the Challenges of Assuring CSR Information, Aalto University Schhol of Business.

Another area that creates the difficulty is the level of the assurance. Reasonable assurance contains positive declaration concerning the accuracy of the reported information. On the other hand, limited assurance contains a negative statement. As a matter of course, high assurance relating to the accuracy is not possible.

Even though, the sustainability reports include the complex issues to examine, forming this relevant process harmonising two varied types of information is difficult. Due to the nature of the information, generally limited assurence is mostly preferred (Anttila, 2013).

Sustainability reports may require the opinions of experts from different areas due to the complex and differential nature. Assurance providers may apply different assurance methodologies for disparate issues in different areas (Smith et al. 2011). Inability of assurance provider may restrict the process. At this point, it needs to utilise the experts who provide assurance services. Due to the wide and complex service issues, difficulties are encountered in the development of assurance services relating to the sustainability reports and determination of the appropriate criterion as well. For instance, the determination of appropriate criterion in the more narrow-scoped service issues such as Carbon emission reporting is easier. The assurance services about the greenhouse gas statements of the corporations may be provided as well (Altıntaş, 2010).

4. Reviewing the Assurance of Sustainability Reports from the View Point of Turkey

Today, assurance services for sustainability reports can be provided by a variety of firms notably audit firms. In developed countries, sustainability reports and its assurance and the numbers of corporations that publish this reports are considerably less than in the developing countries including our country. From Turkey's perspective, "Corporate Governance Principles" that are declared by the Capital Markets Board (CMB), reporting the stakeholder policies and thereby corporate social responsibility applications have constituted an awareness and comprehension regarding the sustainability reports.

The Carbon Disclosure Project (CDP) carried out since 2010 provides an environment to submit the strategies of the corporations regarding climate change to the international corporate investor's knowledge and are deemed as the most common environment attempt of the world.

The CDP has requested information in 2014 from the corporations that are taking part in the BIST-100 index and 41 corporations have replied. Only 29% of 41 corporations have assured their data through the third parties (CDP Report Turkey, 2014).

There were 46 corporations that replied in 2015 and the quantity of the corporations that are utilising assurance services have increased compared to the previous year. There have been 39% of the total 46 corporations have utilised the assurance services (CDP Report Turkey, 2015). In the upcoming years, increasing stakeholders and verification demands of investors are expected to encourage the verification of the reports by third parties. Public Oversight, Accounting, and Auditing Standards Authority (KGK), SAE 3000 Assurance Engagements Other Than Audits or Reviews of Historical Financial Information was published in November 2015.

By creating the Istanbul Stock Exchange (BIST) Sustainability Index, along with giving importance on sustainability by internal and external stakeholders, the numbers of corporations that publish sustainability reports or share the information regarding the social and environmental concept with their stakeholders has begun to increase (www.borsaistanbul.com).

The necessity of transparency in the information has increased the need for assurance services. However, the number of corporations that publish sustainability reports and the ratio about assuring this report from an independent assurance service remained too low.

In the study, in the new period (November 2015- October 2016), the latest published sustainability reports of 29 corporations that are taking a place in Istanbul Stock Exchange (BIST) have been discussed and it has been examined whether these reports have been assured through independent assurance. Besides this, due to the greenhouse gas emission declarations of some corporations within the scope of the Carbon disclosure project, the corporations may benefit from assurance services for emission reports. In this context, within the scope of carbon disclosure project, whether they have taken the assurance for their greenhouse gas emissions have been examined also.

The Corporations in Index During November 2015

	Last Reporting Date	GRI Practice Statement	Independent Assurance of Sustainability Reports	Declaration within the scope of Carbon Disclosure Project/ Assurance
Akbank	2014	+	-	+ / -
Aksa	2014	+	-	-
Anadolu Efes	2014	+	+ (limited assurance / assurance provider: one of the Big 4 (audit firms)	+/
Arçelik	2014	+	+ (reasonable assurance-certification body for greenhouse gas emission data)	+ (Verified emission data for carbon disclosure project)
Aselsan	2014	+	-	+ / -
Brisa	2014	+	+ limited assurance / assurance provider: one of the Big Four (audit firms)	+ / +
Coca Cola	2013	+	+ limited assurance / assurance provider: one of the Big Four (audit firms)	+/ +
Doğuş Oto.	2013	+	-	-
TSKB	2013	+	+ reasonable assurance / certification body	+
TAV	2013	+	-	-

	Last Reporting Date	GRI Practice Statement	Independent Assurance of Sustainability Reports	Declaration within the scope of Carbon Disclosure Project/ Assurance
Tofaş Oto.	2014	+	+ reasonable assurance for greenhouse gas emission data/ assurance provider: Foreign partnered audit firm	+/+
Turkcell	2014	+	-	+/-
Tüpraş	2013	+	-	-
THY	2014	+	-	+/-
Türk Telekom	This corporation doesn't declare the sustainability data through report.		-	-/-
Ülker	This corporation doesn't declare the sustainability data through report.		-	-/-
Vakıf Bank	2014	+	-	+/+limited assurance/assurance provide: one of the Big Four (audit firms) in order to verify the greenhouse gas emission
Vestel	Sustainability data is being reported in Zorlu group. There is no separate report accordingly.			+/-
Yapı Kredi	2014	+	-	-
Erdemir	2014	-	-	-
Ford Otosan	A common corporate social responsibility (csr) has been started to publish as from the year 2014 for Koç society. It has not been benefited from independent assurance services.			+/+
Garanti Bank.	2014	+	+ / limited assurance / assurance provider: one of the Big Four audit firms	+ Limited assurance report concerning to the greenhouse gas emission / water report in 2015
İş Bank.	2014	+	-	-

	Last Reporting Date	GRI Practice Statement	Independent Assurance of Sustainability Reports	Declaration within the scope of Carbon Disclosure Project/ Assurance
Koç Holding	A common corporate social responsibility report (csr) has been started to publish as from the year 2014 for Koç society. It has not benefited from independent assurance services.			The calculations of Arçelik, Ford Otosan, Tofaş, and Opet corporations were confirmed.
Migros	2014	+	-	+/-
Otokar	2014	+	OHSAS 18001 verification process	+/+
Petkim	This corporation doesn't declare the sustainability data through report			+/-
Sabancı Holding	2014	-	-	+
Saf GMYO.	This corporation reports in AKKÖK.	-	-	

Within this scope, only eight of 29 corporations have utilised independent assurance services for theirsustainability reports. Four of eight corporations have preferred one of the Big Four (audit firms) astheir assurance provider and limited assurance was brought into the reports. Also, one corporation has utilised the assurance service for greenhouse gas emission data only within the context of reporting of the sustainability. Foreign partnered audit firm has taken the assurance providing task for this report that was given reasonable assurance. Also, two corporations have utilised the certification bodies in order to receive assurance, one of these reports that has sufficient/reasonable assurance has been examined from the point of emission data only. Also, one corporation has been verified within the technical standard framework relating to labour safety.

Conclusion

Reporting of sustainability is a crucial tool in order to ensure risk management, development of management systems in environmental, social and economic areas, increasing the awareness and motivation of the employee, creating the financial value by improving the stakeholder's value including continuity of the corporation.

Within the framework for all these reasons, sustainability reports should contain accurate and reliable information. Obtaining and submitting to the stakeholders accurate and reliable information and increasing the quality of the reports can only be possible with independent auditing/assurance services. In opposition to the independent auditing that is essential for publicly held corporations, it is not possible to say that assurance services are used widely. In order to increase the quality of sustainability reports and making it serviceable to stakeholders, the reporting and auditing/assurance standards need to be developed. Due to the lack of internationally well accepted legal or organisational framework concerning the reporting of sustainability, there are difficulties in obtaining data relating to the three dimensions implicated into information flow processes. Due to this reason, the financial and non-financial information needs to be measured accurately and should be included in the reports by assuring. In order to do this, it needs to create a common framework by developing assurance services in the direction of a quality increase. The sustainability issue in developed countries is important in order to show new opportunities and that the accounting and auditing profession struggles with modern issues. The creation of assurance services in our country even though not common like in developed countries is inevitable if requested by corporations, the public body, investors, and other interest groups.

References

Adams, C. A. and Evans, Richard. (2004). Accountability, completeness, credibility and the audit expectations gap. Journal of Corporate Citizenship.

Altıntaş, Nergis N, "Bağımsız Denetim ve Vergi Denetimi Dışındaki Güvence Hizmetleri: Türkiye'de ki Uygulamalar Hakkında Bir Araştırma", İstanbul Üniversitesi, S.B.E., Yayınlanmış Doktora Tezi, 2010.

Anttila, Matilda., "Exploring the Challenges of Assuring CSR Information", Aalto University School of Business, Master Thesis, Calgary/Alberta, 2013.

Ballou, B., D. Heitger, and C. Landes. 2006. "The Rise of Corporate Sustainability Reporting: A Rapidly Growing Assurance Opportunity". Journal of Accountancy (December): 65–74.

Brown-Liburd, Helen, and Valentina L. Zamora. "The role of corporate social responsibility (CSR) assurance in investors' judgments when managerial pay is explicitly tied to CSR performance." Auditing: A Journal of Practice & Theory 34.1 (2014): 75–96.

CDP Report Turkey, 2014 https://www.cdp.net/CDPResults/CDP-turkey-climate-change-report-2014.pdf.

CDP Report, Turkey, 2015 https://www.cdp.net/CDPResults/CDP-Turkey-Climate-Change-Report-2015.pdf.

Clausen, J., Loew, T., & Westermann, U. (2005). Sustainability Reporting in Germany. Summary of the Results and Trends of the 2005 Ranking.

Çalışkan, A.Ö. (2012). İşletmelerde Sürdürülebilirlik ve Muhasebe Mesleği İlişkisi, Mali Çözüm Dergisi, Temmuz-Ağustos.

Dando, N. and Switft, T. (2003). Transparency and Assurance: Minding the credibility Gap. Journal of Business Ethics.

Dyllick T, Hockerts K (2002). Beyond the business case for corporate sustainability, Business Strategy and the Environment, John Wiley & Sons, Ltd. and ERP Environment. 11(2): 130–141.

EY (2010). www.ey.com.

Global Report Initiative (GRI). 2015. Sustainability Reporting Guidelines.

IFAC, www.ifac.org.

Borsa İstanbul, www.borsaistanbul.com.

Janković, S, and Dubravka K. (2014). Environmental accounting as perspective for hotel sustainability: literature review. Tourism and Hospitality Management 20.1, 103–120.

Kolk, A. and Perego, P. (2010). Determinants of the Adoption of Sustainability Assurance Statements: An International Investigation. Business Strategy and the Environment.

Kuşat, Nurdan. "'Sürdürülebilir İşletmeler İçin Kurumsal Sürdürülebilirlik ve İçsel Unsurları." *Afyon Kocatepe Üniversitesi İİBF Dergisi* 14.2 (2012): 227–242.

Manetti, G. and Toccafondi, S. (2012). The Role of Stakeholders in Sustainability Reporting Assurance. Journal of Business Ethics 107: 363–377.

O'Dwyer, B., Owen, D. and Unerman, J. (2011). Seeking Legitimacy for New Assurance Forms: The Case of Assurance on Sustainability Reporting. Accounting, Organizations and Society. 36: 31–52.

Once, S., Onay, A., & Yesilcelebi, G. (2015). Corporate Sustainability Reporting and Situation in Turkey. Journal of Economics Finance and Accounting, 2(2).

Pflugrath, G., Roebuck, P. and Simnett, R. (2011). Impact of Assurance and Assurer's Professional Affiliation on Financial Analysts' Assessment of Credibility of Corporate Social Responsibility Information. Auditing: A Journal of Practice & Theory. Vol. 30.

Smith, J., Haniffa, R. and Fairbrass, J. (2011) A Conceptual Framework for Investigating 'Capture' in Corporate Sustainability Reporting Assurance. Journal of Business Ethics.

Wilson, M. (2003). Corporate sustainability: What is it and where does it come from? Ivey Bus. J. Jul/Aug 2003. 67(6).

Ersin Yavuz

The Implications of Governance Ratios Over Five Fragile Countries

Abstract The motive of this study is to analyse the fragile five countries in terms of both economic and governance dimensions. Current account deficit in terms of economic ways, gross domestic product, inflation rates and goverment debt ratios are taken into account, on the other hand in terms of governance ratios political stability, terrorism, efficiency of government, accountability, corruption ratios are evaluated. Moreover political rights in the fragile five countries, civil rights, internet and press freedom are examined. According to the study it has been established that the fragile five countries have important conundrums in both economical and governance ways. Governance factors such as transparency in the country, perception of trust to law, freedom level, political stability, terrorism has been affected by growth and development of the country. In developed countries having sufficient ratios in fragile five countries having problems in terms of both domains reveals that these two concepts aren't independent on the contrary they are complementary parts of each other. Therefore it has been figure out that the fragile five countries are fragile in governance and freedom domains too.

Keywords: Fragile five, Governance, Political Stability

Introduction

Emerging market economy has become popular within the last years. This concept was first introduced by Antoine W. Van Agtmael from the International Finance Corporation, a foundation conjoined to the World Bank. Emerging market economy encompasses developing economies alogside with having low and middle income per capita economies, which Turkey takes parts in. Countries participating in emerging market economy compromise roughly 80% percent of the world's population. They represent 20% of global economy (Atik, 2005, p. 5 & Kaya et al., 2009, p. 316).

BRIC countries taking part in emerging market economy are not only among rapidly developing economies but also it is predicted that they will be among the richest countries through the mid-century. This concept was first introduced by Jim O'Neill in 2003. Over time Mexico, South Africa, East Europe, Turkey extended being added to these countries. Common features of BRIC countries are being primary industry countries (China, India), primary industry input importer (Brazil, Russia) and low wage. Turkey, India, Brazil, Indonesia, South Africa are categorised as fragile five countries being excluded from China and Russia (Eğilmez, 2013).

1. Fragile Five Concept

Fragility concept is evaluated in micro and macro ways economically. Fragility in micro economic way phrases the effects over household shoke. Fragility in macro economic way phrases the effects over economic growth shoke (Seth & Ragap, 2012). Acording to another description fragility means undergoing highly overseas economic powers' policies (Briguglio & Galea, 2003, p. 3).

The fragile five concept was first introduced by James Lord on August 1 2013 in the report prepared by the United States (US) investment bank, Morgan Stanley. Turkey, India, Brazil, Indonesia, South Africa are categorised as the fragile five countries (Stanley, 2013).

There has been severe decreases since the FED stated that they would diminish bond purchase on May 22 2013. After the FED statement, the value for currency in Brazil, India, Indonesia, Turkey and South Africa mostly depreciated in emerging market economics. Due to this reason, these countries are entitled as the Fragile Five Countries (Eğilmez, 2013).

Common features of the BRIC countries are as follows: High current account deficit, low growth performance, high inflation rates, outsourcing neccesity about upcoming terms and non economic potential risks in corresponding countries (Çeviş & Ceylan, 2015; Eğilmez, 2013).

1.1 Current Account Deficit in Fragile Five Countries

Current account deficit can be explained as the deficit a country undergoes due to economic relation or not getting sufficient foreign currency out of products sold (Çak, 2013: 15). For Current account deficit to be sustainable, to which extent should current account deficit to national product ratio threshold is 4–5%. According to Freund, sustainability threshod is 5% and after this ratio should be perceived as crisis signal for economy (Freund, 2000).

When the fragile five's current account deficit/GDP ratios through 2000–2014 are reviewed, Turkey and South Africa's current account deficit problem poses more of a threat compared with other countries. The current account deficit average through corresponding years is as follows: Brazil -1.17, India -1.34, Indonesia 1.02, South Africa -2.87, Turkey -4.50. When the last years are examined, all fragile five countries suffer from current account deficit. As of 2014, the best situation belongs to India, the worst situation belongs to Turkey. As of 2014 in terms of sustainability of current account deficit Turkey and South Africa are over the critical threshold (Graph 1).

Graph 1: Current Account Deficit / GDP (2000–2014)

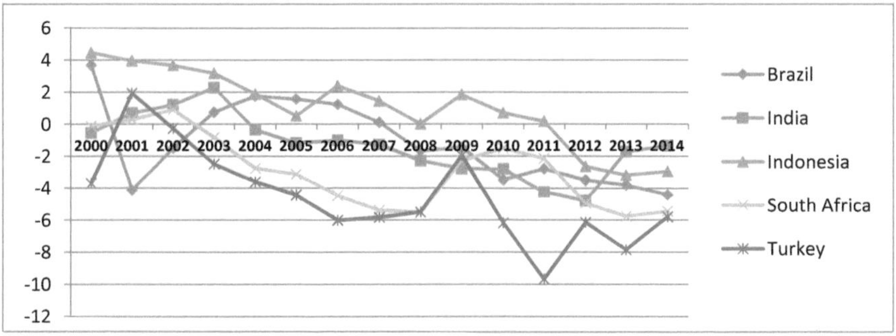

Source: IMF, World Economic Outlook Database, October 2015

1.2 Growth Performance in Fragile Five Countries

When the fragile five's GDP ratios through 2000–2014 are reviewed, India and Indonesia show a better performance. The growth ratios average through corresponding years is as follows: Brazil 3.30, India 7.02, Indonesia 5.44, South Africa 3.20, Turkey 4.31. When the last years are examined, just India's performance has increased, the other countries' performance decreased (Graph 2).

Graph 2: GDP Percent Change (2000–2014)

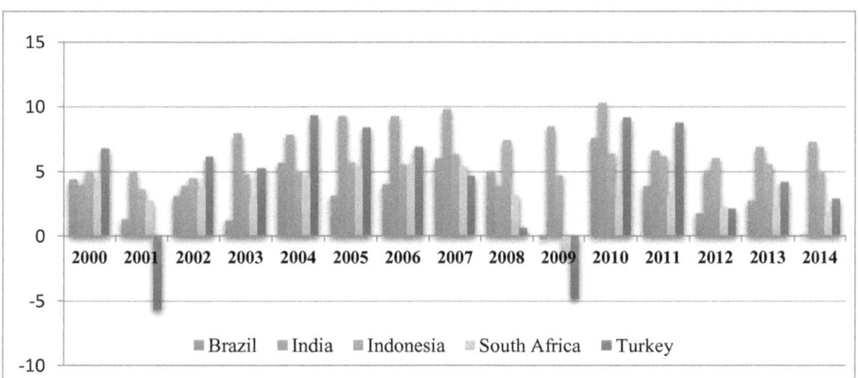

Source: IMF, World Economic Outlook Database, October 2015

Another important indicator of growth is the GDP ratio per capita. As of 2014, Brazil, South Africa, and Turkey are in the high-middle income countries' category. India, Indonesia are in the low-middle income countries' category. According to the GDP indicators, Brazil and Turkey are on a close course to the high income countries (Table 1).

Table 1: GDP Per capita ($) (2010–2014)

Yıl	Brazil	India	Indonesia	South Africa	Turkey
2010	11.300.70	1.429.599	3.178.133	7.389.04	10.001.63
2011	13.237.592	1.513.85	3.688.531	8.089.874	10.437.717
2012	12.106.002	1.476.928	3.744.53	7.592.197	10.490.121
2013	11.893.714	1.488.985	3.667.345	6.889.698	10.821.44
2014	11.572.700	1.607.646	3.524.075	6.482.753	10.381.025

Source: IMF, World Economic Outlook Database, October 2015

1.3 Inflation Rates in Fragile Five Countries

When the fragile five's inflation rates ratios through 2000–2014 are reviewed, although Turkey's inflation rates experiences decrease within last years, it is seen that it is generally high. Inflation rates average through corresponding years is as follows: Brazil 6.56, India 6.79, Indonesia 7.47, South Africa 5.86, Turkey 18.11. When the last years are examined, the fragile five countries' inflation rates have fluctuated between 5% and 10% (Graph 3).

Graph 3: Inflation Percent Change (2000–2014)

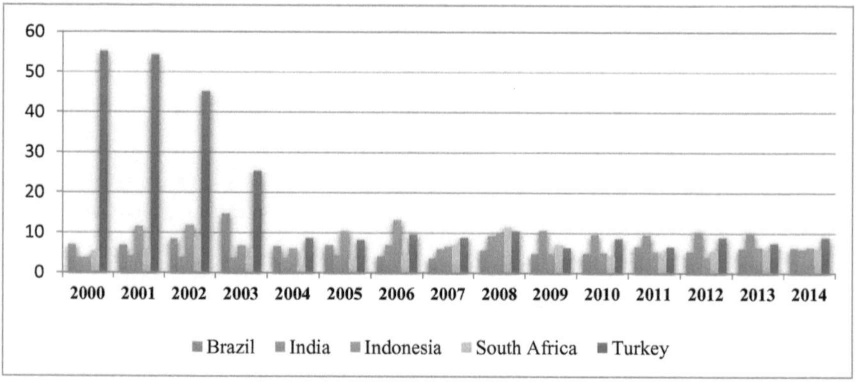

Source: IMF, World Economic Outlook Database, October 2015

1.4 General Government Net Debt in Fragile Five Countries

When the fragile five's general government net debt in fragile five countries through 2000–2014 are reviewed, India and Turkey's ratios are comparitively higher than other countries. The general government net debt average through corresponding years is as follows: Brazil -3.36, India -8.09, Indonesia -0.98, South Africa -2.05, Turkey -4.64. When the last years are examined, among the fragile five countries it is observed that Turkey's performance has evolved and Brazil and India's performance has aggrevated (Graph 4).

Graph 4: General Government Gross Dept / GDP (2000–2014)

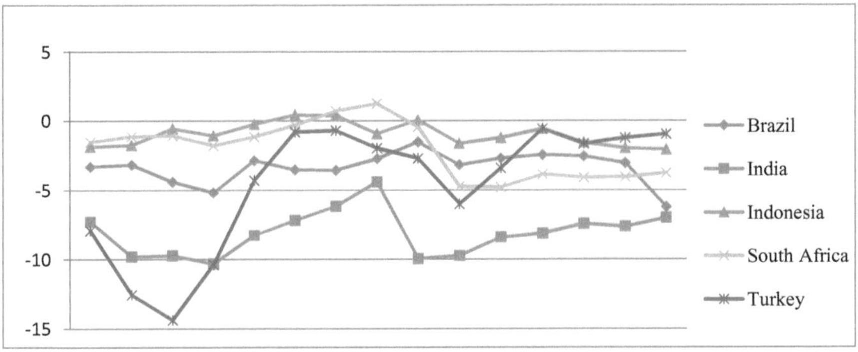

Source: IMF, World Economic Outlook Database, October 2015

1.5 Governance Ratios in Fragile Five Countries

While evaluating the development of a country both economic and political governance ratios have an important part. Economic and political stability are directly affecting each other and are complementary concepts. Political stability in a country and a terrorism situation, to what extent the law has been enforced, corruption, accountability of government, indexes to what extent government is efficient affects the economic situation in the country directly. Data are compiled from the Worldwide Governance Indicators database. Indexes are placed between 0 and 100. As the index approaches 0, it states a negative situation. As the index approaches 100, it states a positive situation. In the following graphs, in addition to the fragile five, developed countries such as Norway, US, and Japan are represented.

When the fragile five's political stability and terrorism index through 2002–2014 are reviewed, India, Indonesia and Turkey's situations are feeble. Average through corresponding years is as follows: Norway 93.11, US 57.69, Japan 81.34, Brazil 41.71, India 13.4, Indonesia 16.37, South Africa 43.28, Turkey 18.97. When the last years are examined, the index in Indonesia ameolirates, Turkey aggravates. Brazil, India, South Africa have a close course to their own line. There is a substantial differance between fragile five and developed countries (Graph 5).

Graph 5: Political Stability and Terrorism (2002–2014)

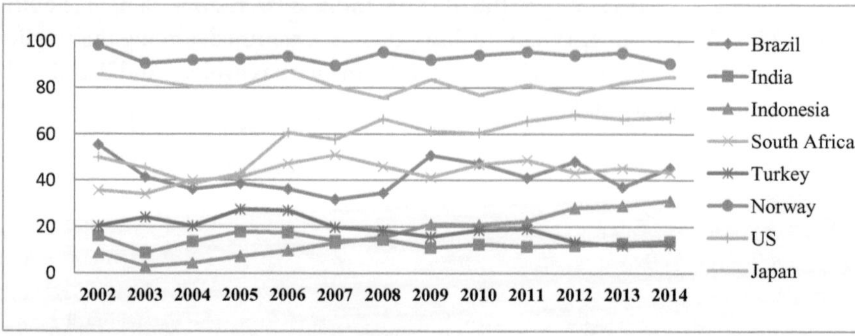

Source: Worldwide Governance Indicators

When the fragile five's law enforcement index through 2002–2014 are reviewed, Indonesia and Brazil are comparitevely worse. Average through corresponding years it is as follows: Norway 98.89, US 91.53, Japan 87.76, Brazil 47.02, India 13.4, Indonesia 30.17, South Africa 56.93, Turkey 56.38. When the last years are examined, India has a close course to their own line, other fragile five contries are on their half way (Graph 6).

Graph 6: Rule of Law (2002–2014)

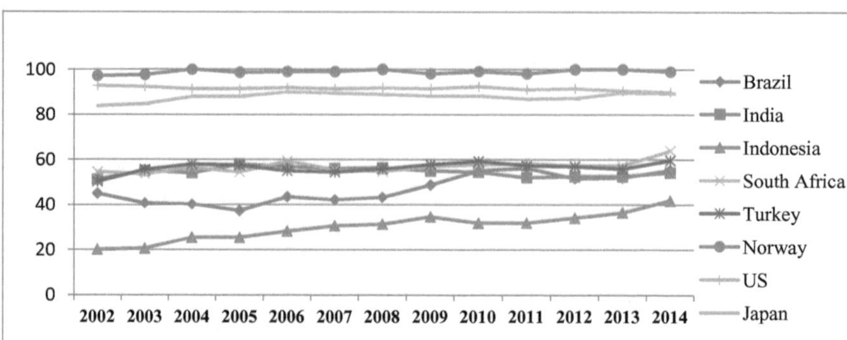

Source: Worldwide Governance Indicators

When the fragile five's corruption index through 2002–2014 are reviewed, India and Indonesia's bad situations stand out. Average through corresponding years is as follows: Norway: 89.63, US, 96.72, Japan: 88.56, Brazil 55.86, India 39.65, Indonesia 24.46, South Africa 62.79, Turkey 55.87. When the last years are examined, corruption in South Africa, Brazil and India increasingly goes up, Indonesia and Turkey (excluding 2014) have plummeted. In developed countries, there is nearly little to no corruption (Graph 7).

Graph 7: Control of Corruption (2002–2014)

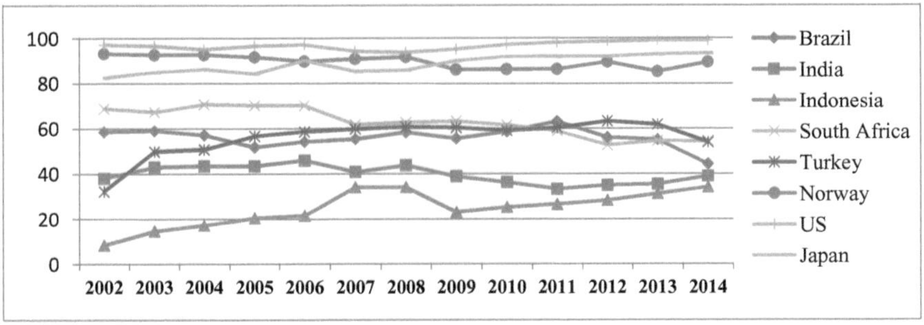

Source: Worldwide Governance Indicators

When the fragile five's accountability index through 2002–2014 are reviewed, Indonesia and Turkey have a lower accountability level. Average through corresponding years is as follows: Norway 99.14, US 86.44, Japan 79.77, Brazil 61.40, India 59.94, Indonesia 45.72, South Africa 67.25, Turkey 43.85. When the last years are examined, the situation in Turkey has aggrevated, while Indonesia performs a remarkable amelioration. In developed countries Norway's performance is most trustworthy (Graph 8).

Graph 8: Voice and Accountability (2002–2014)

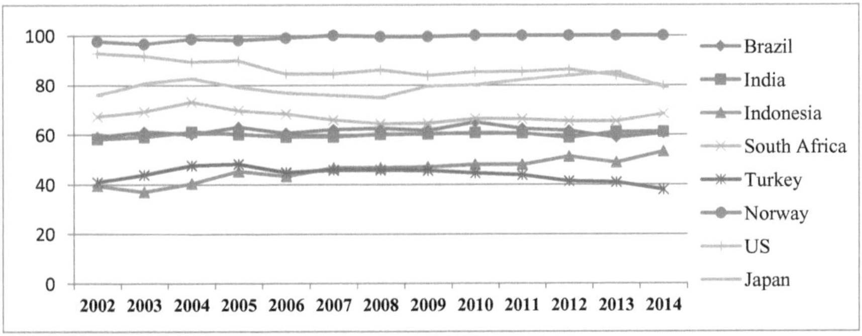

Source: Worldwide Governance Indicators

When the fragile five's government efficiency index through 2002–2014 is reviewed, Indonesia and Brazil have a worse level. The average through corresponding years is as follows: Norway 97.05, US 91.26, Japan 89.46, Brazil 52.57, India 53.06, Indonesia 44.65, South Africa 69, Turkey 62.83. When the last years are examined, Indonesia and Turkey illustrates a positive outlook, Brazil, India, South Africa have performed in a negative view (Graph 9).

Graph 9: Government Effectiveness (2002–2014)

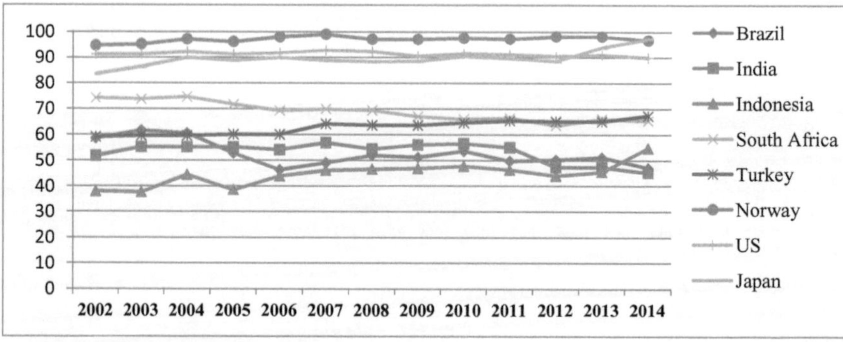

Source: Worldwide Governance Indicators

One of the concepts of governance ratios have affected is the freedom level in the country. Freedom House is an international foundation preparing reports and determining the freedom levels of countries. Countries in the report are categorised as free between 1–2.5, partially free between 3–5, and non free between 5.5–7. The freedom level is obtained by the average of civil freedom and freedom degree of political rights.

As of November 2015, Turkey and Indonesia are partially free, Brazil, India, South Africa are labeled as free. Brazil passed from partially free to free in 2003. It increased its level twofold in 2006. India has stayed at 2.5 level between 2001–2015. South Africa has maintained a free country level. Indonesia was partially free until 2006; in 2006 it increased its level to 2.5 and became free. Yet this case changed in 2014 and fell to the level of partially free. Turkey has not rescued itself from the partially free situation. The Freedom level was 4.5 as of 2015. It has gone up to 3 over time but as of 2015 it was at 3.5. The Freedom level of developed countries range between 1 and 1.5 (Graph 10).

Graph 10: Freedom Rates (2001–2015)

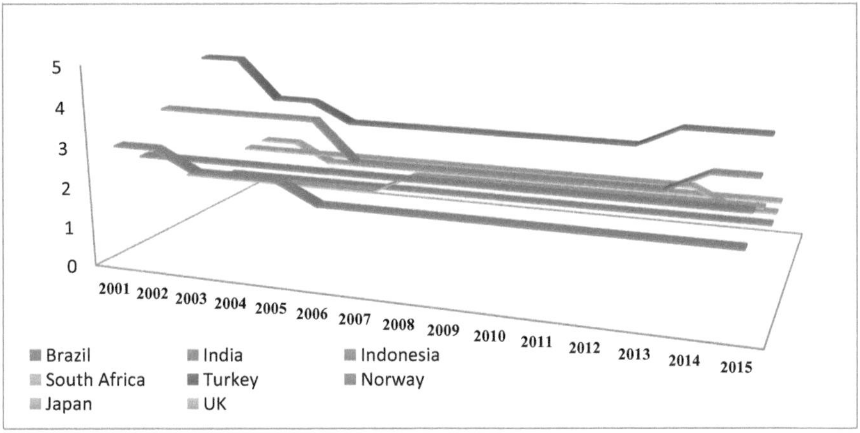

Source: Freedom House, 2015

The 2015 world internet freedom ranking is as follows. Brazil is ranked as 29th on the rise, India 40th on the rise, Indonesia 42nd, South Africa on the decline, Turkey 58th on the decline.[1] Press freedom ranking is as follows. Brazil 45 points (partially free), India (partially free) 39 points, Indonesia (partially free) 49 points, South Africa (partially free) 37 points, Turkey (non free) 65 points.[2]

Conclusion

The inside global economoy that has a high capital inflow development of countries has become dependent not only on economic stability but also the freedom atmosphere. The countries' hold to become plausible to attract short and long run capital foreign investment. Therefore factors such as political stability, terrorism, trust of law, accountability, and government efficiency has effected reasonably economic development. In developed and high income countries having both sufficient economic and governance ratios shows that these two concepts have a strong correlation.

Common features of BRIC countries are slow growth ratios, high current account deficit, and high inflations. According to the result obtained by this paper,

1 https://freedomhouse.org/report/freedom-net/freedom-net-2015 (02.11.2015).

2 https://freedomhouse.org/report/freedom-press/freedom-press-2015#.Vjfa77fhBD8 (02.11.2015).

the fragile five countries' governance ratios range between 30 and 60, while developed countries range between 70 and 100. This case reveals that these countries are not only fragile in terms of the economic domain but also in terms of the political stabilty and governance domains.

Another striking result is the high level of freedom data recorded by the fragile five. Turkey and Indonesia should immediately transit from partially free to free. There are lots of steps that these five should take, because in low freedom levels, high level of innovation and creativity can not be expected. It is a self evident fact that developed countries, having high freedom, getting brain drain have evolved their economies. Therefore, the freedom level in the country is integrated with both the economy and governance ratios.

One popular concept of the new era is the middle income trap. All of the fragile five countries take part at the middle income level. These countries should realise both economic and governance reforms are not to be caught in fragility and the middle income trap. The steps that can be taken to this extent are as follows: Democracy culture should be ameoliorated in the society, trust of law should be reinforced by enforcing new legislations, elections should be held on time, political stability should be performed, terrorism should be minimised by solving on a constitutional basis, transparency in public management should come true by performing accountability atmosphere, and all freedom fields in the country should be extended continually.

References

Atik, A. H. (2005), Finansal Krizlerin Gölgesinde Yükselen Piyasa Ekonomileri, *Türkiye Kalkınma Bankası A.Ş. Araştırma Müdürlüğü*, GA-05-01-02, Ankara.

Briguglio, L. & Galea, W. (2003). *Updating and Augmenting the Economic Vulnerability Index,* Retrieved, October 29, 2015, from https://www.um.edu.mt/__data/assets/pdf_file/0012/44130/eviar_briguglio_galea_ver4.pdf.

Ceviş, İ. & Ceylan R. (2015), Kırılgan Beşlide Satın Alma Gücü Paritesi (SAGP) Hipotezinin Test Edilmesi, *Journal of Yaşar University,* Vol: 10(37), pp. 6381–6477.

Çak, M. (2013), *Türkiye'de Cari Açık,* Beşir Kitabevi, İstanbul.

Eğilmez, M. (2009), *Makro Ekonomi Türkiye'den Örneklerle*, Remzi Kitabevi, 6. Edition, İstanbul.

Eğilmez, M. (2013), *Kırılgan Beşli,* Retrieved, October 29, 2015, from http://www.mahfiegilmez.com/2013/11/krlgan-besli.html.

Freedom House, *Freedom Database,* Retrieved November 2, 2015, from https://freedomhouse.org/report/freedom-world/freedom-world 2015#.VjfFd7fhBD9.

Freund, C. L. (2000), Current Account Adjustment in Industrialized Countries, *Board of Governers of the FED International Finance,* Discussion.

IMF, *World Economic Outlook Database*, October 2015, Retrieved November 12, 2015, from http://www.imf.org/external/pubs/ft/weo/2015/02/weodata/index.aspx.

Kaya, V., Yılmaz, Ö. & Talaş, E. (2009). "Yükselen Piyasa Ekonomileri ve Türkiye, 1990 2006: Neredeyiz?", *Atatürk Üniversitesi Sosyal Bilimler Enstitüsü Dergisi*, Vol: 13(1), pp. 315–342.

Seth, A. & Ragab, A. (2012). Macroeconomic Vulnerability in Developing Countries: Approachs and Issues, *International Policy Centre for Inclusive Growth Working Paper*, Vol: 94, pp. 1–20.

Stanley, M. (2013). FX Pulse, Morgan Stanley Research, *Global Currency Research Team*, pp. 1–37.

Worldwide Govarnance Indicators, Retrieved, October 30, 2015, from http://info.worldbank.org/ governance/wgi/index.aspx#countryReports.

Phd. Elif Yılmaz*, Phd. Selin Ertürk Atabey** &
Phd. Işıl Fulya Orkunoğlu Şahin***

Effectiveness of a Tax Audit: An Evaluation and the Case of Turkey

Abstract A tax audit is the investigation of administration and taxpayers on if they fulfill their legal liabilities or not, in order to ensure that payable tax collection is on time and done correctly.

The satisfaction of public needs at the highest level by providing effectiveness at taxation and so achieving financial, economical, social and legal aims can be possible by an effective tax auditing. Essentially, the existence of the declaration system as a modern taxation method, necessitates checking the accuracy of declarations of taxpayers and therefore it makes essential that there is an effective tax auditing system. A tax audit, iss a vital importance for the horizontal and vertical equity between people in the society and for the prevention of unfair competition.

The quality of a tax audit is as important as the quantity of a tax audit in terms of its effectiveness in preventing tax loss and evasion. One of the factors that reduces this effectiveness is the reconciliation as a solution method of tax disputes at the administrative phase. Also the problems related with tax legislation and the number of tax auditors, the problems related with the document layout, tax awareness level and the lack of security measures are determinative on this topic.

In this study, application as compared to selected countries, the current legal and factual obstacles to the effective tax auditing will be discussed, and solutions will be focused on.

Keywords: Tax audit, declaration system, equity in taxation, control mechanisms, effective auditing, Turkey.

Introduction

To achieve the principal and main financial or fiscal purpose of taxes constituting the most important finance source of public services, optimal tax revenue must be ensured. Accordingly, tax loss will be prevented and optimal tax revenue will be

* Gazi University Faculty of Law, Financial Law, elifyilmaz@gazi.edu.tr
** Gazi University Faculty of Economics and Administrative Sciences Department of Public Finance, selinerturk@gazi.edu.tr
*** Gazi University Faculty of Economics and Administrative Sciences Department of Public Finance, iforkunoglu@gazi.edu.tr

obtained only if taxpayers fulfill their taxes and other liabilities arising from tax laws in line with legislation, completely and accurately by applying tax laws effectively.

The principle of modern taxation is based on the fact that the tax base is returned by the taxpayer that is adopted by the Turkish tax system as well since it serves for ensuring the principle of justice in taxation by providing that tax is received according to ability to pay. An audit is the most effective way to ensure security in taxation in modern tax systems based on the principle of tax return. Because, the success of applying the principle of return obliges an audit of taxpayer returns whether they reflect the truth or not.

A tax audit appears as the most effective method in preventing tax loss and tax evasion as well as achieving purposes expected from the taxation. For the success of a tax audit, its quality is as important as its quantity and certain problems occurring in application decreases the effectiveness of a tax audit.

In the first section of the study, the concept of a tax audit, the reason of why a tax audit exists, purposes and features of a tax audit will be examined. In the second section, practices of various countries will be mentioned. In the third section, the current situation and flaws in tax audits in Turkey will be examined and suggested solutions will be offered.

1. Conceptual Framework of a Tax Audit

In this section of the study, the concept of a tax audit will be defined, the reasons for the existence of a tax audit will be expressed and purposes and features of a tax audit will be mentioned.

1.1 The Concept of a Tax Audit

Audit is a romance word and means hearing, listening carefully (Özdemir, 2000: 48). According to the definition of the Turkish Language Association, an audit is the process of evaluation and collecting evidence executed by a specialist unit for determining and reporting the suitability of the information regarding public or private institutions to criteria specified before (İktisadi Terimler Sözlüğü). In the legal sense, an audit is inspecting whether public institutions as well as institutions founded according to private law provisions work pursuant to the provisions of law and regulations (Tekin & Çelikkaya, 2005: 32).

A tax audit as a type of public audit on the other hand, is investigating whether the administration and taxpayers fulfill their liabilities arising from the legislation or not by the authorities of tax administration to ensure that the tax debt required to be paid is paid on time completely (Pehlivan, 1986: 3). In other words, a tax audit covers activities confirming that the business records and financial affairs of taxpayers have been notified correctly by the taxpayers and the tax is calculated and paid pursuant to the tax laws (Hasil, 2015: 2). To sum up, a tax audit is inspecting taxpayers regarding their fulfillment level of legal liabilities of tax administration.

1.2 Purposes and Features of a Tax Audit

In the taxation relationship between the State with the title of creditor and the taxpayer with the title of borrower, there is a conflict of interest between parties. Thus, the tax audit has arisen from the need of ensuring balance of interest in question controlling the taxation process by an objective structure or persons for preventing tax loss or evasion and fair taxation. Also, meeting public needs in highest level by ensuring effectiveness in taxation and reaching financial, economic, social and legal purposes expected from the taxation are possible with an effective tax audit.

Within this context, the most important purpose of a tax audit is to investigate the accuracy of taxpayer returns. Another purpose is ensuring increasing tax revenues and volunteer compliance of taxpayers to the tax by preventing tax loss and evasion for the full collection of tax on time (Tecim 2008: 56). A tax audit also aims at training and increasing awareness of taxpayers and reaching targeted financial and economic policies more quickly and easily (Tecim, 2008: 56). The main features that a tax audit has to have are accuracy, effectiveness, objectivity, transparency, justifiability, completeness, and consistency (OECD, 2006: 33).

2. Tax Audit in Terms of Practices in Various Countries

2.1 Tax Audit in France

The units in charge of a tax audit in France are categorised according to their mission and scope of authority. Local units are responsible for the audit of all taxpayers who are not in the scope of authority of a special unit expert on tax audit. In the preliminary audit made on taxpayer returns in France, the person conducting the inspection makes an audit on the return without reviewing books and documents by going to the work place of the taxpayer. On the other hand, an audit in a work place is an inspection conducted by going to the work place of the taxpayer and reviewing from its return, books and documents to other external sources (Kılıçdaroğlu, 1982: 4).

In France, county audit units conduct tax audits or interregional tax audit directorates depending upon the size of business, tax audits for the large businesses are conducted by national and international audit directorate (Tax4BusinnesFR,

2015: 1). Institutions responsible for the tax audit in the country are DVNI (Direction des Vérifications Nationales et Internationales), DICOFT (Directions Spécialisées de Contrôle Fiscal) and DSF (Direction des Services Fiscaux) (Doğan & Kapusuzoğlu, 2005: 27). The DVNI is responsible for the audit of large companies, the DIRCOFI is responsible for the audit of medium sized companies and the DSF is responsible for the audit of small sized companies (Thierry, 1998: 13). However, with taxational regulations made in 2013 in France, large companies has been able to use electronic invoices since January 1 2014 (PWC, 2014: 1). Therefore, today it is thought that tax audits will be conducted through information technologies predominantly in France as in many developed countries.

2.2 Tax Audit in England

In a tax audit in England, taxpayers are grouped according to their business volume and units to conduct inspection are determined according to this. Tax audits are conducted by tax offices affiliated with Inland Revenue and tax audits for large businesses are conducted by the Special Compliance Office. However, in cases where local tax offices do not make an audit or there is serious potential of tax loss, when having a doubt for transactions of certified public accountants, in cases that may result as tax evasion and having a doubt for accounts of businesses, tax audits can be made ex officio by the Special Compliance Office. In England, HM Customs and Excise carries out the audit of indirect taxes and the Department of Social Security carries out the audit of insurance premium. However, there is information sharing between these institutions (Doğan & Kapusuzoğlu, 2005: 27–33).

2.3 Tax Audit in United States of America

Methods followed in the selection of returns to be subject to a tax audit in America consist of the system trying to determine participants of potential tax evasion transactions, computer point scoring system, annual inspections of returns of large companies, information matching, inspections regarding business partnerships and investors and other inspections. The numeric scoring is made for each return in the computer point scoring system. While The Discriminant Function System (DIF) scores change potential in past IRS (Internal Revenue Service) returns having similar yields, The Unreported Income (DIF) scores unreported income potential of returns. In information matching, methods such as matching data of interests received from banks and taxpayer accounts are used (IRS, 2006: 1). Tax inspection can be carried out via mail or on the records of taxpayer or face to face. The inspection can be carried out in the IRS office (office audit) or in the taxpayer's home, workplace or in an accountant's office (field audit). The IRS has four types of tax audits. These are the correspondence audit, office audit, field audit, and incidental audit. The correspondence audit is conducted for correspondences like information request regarding receipts sent to prove charitable cuts the taxpayer made. In an office audit, if revenue administration has more questions to ask about their tax return, invitation for calling the IRS office is made via mail for the audit. Since a tax audit is carried out more seriously in the office audit, taxpayers may participate in these audits with their accountants or tax lawyers. The field audit is the most serious type of audit; therefore, Revenue Administration conducts audit by visiting taxpayers in their homes or work places (IRS, 2013: 1).

3. Tax Audit in Turkey

Information about organisation and process of tax audit in Turkey will be given under this title at first, then certain reasons decreasing effectiveness of a tax audit will be discussed.

3.1 Organisation and Process

In 2005, central and provincial organisation of Revenue Administration were founded and in 2011, the Tax Inspection Board was founded in Turkey. The Tax Inspection Board is affiliated with the Minister directly and it consists of a President, Vice-Presidents, Group Presidents, and Tax Inspectors (Tax Chief Inspector, Tax Inspector and Tax Deputy Inspector). The headquarter's of the board is in Ankara. Working principles of Tax Inspectors have been regulated in accordance with their permanent and temporary places of duty. Tax Inspectors work as a team or on their own in permanent and temporary inspection places (VDK, 2016: 1).

The different types of tax audits are inquiry, tax inspection, searching and data collection in Turkey. In accordance with article 127 of the Tax Procedure Law (VUK), it is aimed to investigate and identify taxpayers and financial incidents, records and issues related to the taxation with the inquiry. However, as stated in article 134 of the VUK, tax inspection is a more detailed investigation operation conducted on books, records and inventories of taxpayers compared with the inquiry and with tax inspection, it is aimed to investigate, determine and ensure the accuracy of taxes that must be paid. Searching is regulated between articles 142–147 of the VUK is referred to as inspection with searching (Ünsal, 2013: 96). According to article 148 of the VUK, public administrations and institutions, taxpayers or other natural and legal persons dealing with taxpayers are obliged to give information that the Ministry of Finance or the authorities entitled to conduct tax inspection will request. Hence, data collection is the tax audit method including the tax administration's right to request information from taxpayers and persons affiliated with taxpayers.

3.2 Certain Reasons Decreasing Effectiveness of Tax Audits in Turkey

According to the 2014 activity report of the Tax Inspection Board monitoring performance indicators of conducting tax audits in Turkey, number of current year inspection and investigation assignments, number of tax inspection reports, number of tax inspection bases, number of cross examines in electronic (e-inspection), rate of inspected tax base increase, rate of increase in the number of inspected taxpayers can be regarded as indicators of tax audit performance taken into consideration in our country. According to this, the targeted number of assignments regarding inspections and investigations conducted in the current year was 550 in 2014, however, 381 was actualised at the end of the year. Reason of deviation from this target stated in the report is that investigation assignments are not systematic and programmable. Targeted number of assignments made for the struggle with underground economy and tax inspection in the current year was 90,000 in 2014, however, 85,000 was actualised. Although the rate of increase in the number of inspected taxpayers was targeted as 10%, -13.00% was actualised in 2014. As the reason of not being able to reach these two targets stated in the report, it was indicated that it was focused on basic trainings and in-service trainings provided to 4500 tax deputy inspectors caused insufficient tax inspection. Increase rate in the inspected tax base, although 2014 target was 10%, actualised rate was 37% at the end of the year. However, even if inspected number of taxpayers decreased proportionally, increase in the stated target was actualised due to the increase in transaction volume of taxpayers. The number of tax inspection reports issued as a result of inspections was 100,000 for 2014; however, the number of reports actualised was 131,587. The number of cross examinations conducted within the scope of e-inspection was 90,000,000, however, the actualised number of examinations was 307,727,819 at the end of the year (VDK, 2014: 1). The data shows that even though revision carried out for the organisation of tax audit units and proceeding of audit operations was successful to a large extent, an increase of tax audit performance remained in the limited level.

One of the reasons for the decreasing effectiveness in tax audits in Turkey is low awareness of tax in the society and that this awareness cannot be established as it should be. The main reason of this condition is existence of widespread belief in individuals and the society in general that "the taxes they pay do not return as services to them due to corruptions" (Karyağdı, 2001: 146). Therefore, it is obligatory to take measures that will ensure creation of tax awareness in society and taxpayers' compliance with the tax voluntarily (Tecim, 2008: 133).

An organisation problem of which its importance is unquestionable in all corporations is also significant in terms of the tax audit (Tecim, 2008: 58). In addition, establishment of document order, auto-control mechanisms to be placed in the tax system will be measures to increase effectiveness in tax audits.

The ability to re-conciliate, being one of the solutions of tax disputes in administrative stage, is considered as another reason that decreases effectiveness of tax audits in Turkey. Because existence of reconciliation causes people to consider like "I will pay my unpaid tax in installments after discounts are made with their penalties" and it decreases prevention or deterrent effect of penalties to a large extent (Tecim, 2008: 135). Also, uncertainties and emptinesses in the tax legislation is another factor decreasing effectiveness in tax audits since it causes different interpretations due to frequent change of laws and application ways because of complicated structure of the system.

To sum up, it is possible to state reasons for decreasing effectiveness of tax audits in Turkey as, factors arising from organisation, the number of audit personnel and their working conditions, not establishing document order sufficiently, insufficient auto-control mechanisms, not being able to create tax awareness, existence reconciliation and factors arising from the structure of tax legislation.

Conclusion

In modern tax systems based on return principle, determination of the accuracy of the tax that must be paid obliges conducting a tax audit. Although a tax audit is not the only way to increase tax revenues, it is the most effective method to decrease tax losses.

A tax audit is also important for ensuring justice of taxation and equality between taxpayers (Üstün, 2013: 11), removing unfair competition, expanding tax base, and struggling with an underground economy. As long as an effective tax audit is not conducted, it is impossible to mention the success of tax administration. The main factors affecting the success of tax administration are effectiveness of tax control and audit, compliance with developments and that tax laws are clear simple and understandable, taxpayers have tax awareness and ethics (Akdoğan, 2009: 535).

Since the success of a tax audit is in parallel with the success of auditor, auditor must have knowledge and experience in high level to collect data sufficiently and in adequate quality. However, the most important qualification that the auditor must have is acting independently (Bozkurt, 1998: 24).

If we make a general evaluation for Turkey, the performances of tax audit personnel must be regarded among the important factors determining the success of the tax audit system. For example, it is considered that tax audit performance measurements brought with "*Regulation of Tax Inspection Board Performance Evaluation System*" published in the Official Gazette numbered 29590 and dated January 11 2016 in Turkey on this issue will contribute directly to the increase of tax audit effectiveness. With this regulation, principles regarding constituting performance evaluation system for the evaluation of professional competencies of Tax Inspectors and Tax Deputy Inspectors within one calendar year comparatively and objectively (based on criteria such as success levels in various in-service and other trainings, tests, etc.) are regulated. Pursuant to article 26 of the aforesaid regulation, Tax Inspectors and Tax Deputy Inspectors are regarded as successful only if their general performance evaluation score is at least 70 points over 100 points according to the performance evaluation results. Therefore, the increase in the performance quality of tax inspection personnel, will positively affect performance quality of tax inspections. Also, unless the number of tax audits is increased in the level of securing the justice, it is impossible to mention effectiveness of tax penalties. In this respect, effectiveness of tax penalties is closely related to tax audits and effectiveness in tax audits will ensure effectiveness in tax penalties.

In Turkey, in terms of tax security, tax audits based on labour in general are accepted as tax security measures, however, since all the taxpayers cannot be inspected, this method is both sufficient and costly to prevent tax loss and evasions. Hence, for monitoring total tax base, effective tax security measures are required by also utilising technical opportunities in the Turkish tax system (Şanver & Oktar, 2013: 2)

Making taxpayers comply with the tax is also important; taxpayers must be made to comply with the tax through inspection (Üstün, 2013: 7). The accuracy of taxpayers' returns can be audited with tax inspections to be made later, also, economic and legislation based measures can be taken that will make taxpayers provide accurate returns (Şanver & Oktar, 2013: 3). For taxpayers to return their actual incomes, there must not be expensive, time-consuming, labour based methods that can be subjective and mostly insufficient but more effective general and private tax security measures that will be included in the tax system (Şanver & Oktar, 2013: 3).

Consequently, integration of states in the globalising world obliges also integration in taxation area as a result of the increase of electronic commerce, speed of socio-economic events, globalisation of goods and services. This condition shows that not the delegation of taxation authority but full objectivity in the tax audit must be ensured. At this point, we suggest to constitute the *International Tax Inspection Board* that controls/solves disputes in the tax audits of countries in order to prevent injustices arising from the tax audit of taxpayers and reach international standards, as in the examples of International Court of Justice and European Court of Human Rights in the judicial system.

The constituting International Tax Inspection Board is important in terms of taxpayers and the tax administration. That is, ***in terms of taxpayers***: big steps will have been taken regarding principles of equality, justice and state of law in the taxation that will serve for expanding right to legal remedies for taxpayers who claim that they have exhausted domestic remedies but the relief has not been provided. ***In terms of the tax administration:*** it will decrease the possibility of arbitrary use of state's tax audit functions that tax audit personnel may do. One of the most important indicators of this condition is the fact that most of the tax cases submitted to the court are resulted against the administration in Turkey.

References

Akdoğan, A. (2009). *Kamu Maliyesi*. Ankara: Gazi Kitabevi.

Bozkurt, N. (1998). *Muhasebe Denetimi*. İstanbul: Alfa Basım Yayın Dağıtım Ltd. Şti.

Doğan C. & Kapusuzoğlu, T. (2005). Çeşitli Ülkelerde Vergi Denetiminin Organizasyonu Ve Çıkarılabilecek Bazı Dersler. *Vergi Dünyası Dergisi*. Mart 2005, 283, pp. 22–31.

Hasil (2015). *Tax Audit Framework of Malaysia*. February 2015, from http://www.hasil.gov.my/pdf/pdfam/tax_audit_framework_2015.pdf (23.02.2016).

IRS (2013). *Understanding Income Tax Audits*, from https://www.irs.com/articles/income-tax-audits (23.02.2016).

IRS (2006). *The Examination (Audit) Process,* 10. January 2006, form https://www.irs.gov/uac/The-Examination-(Audit)-Process) (22.02.2016).

İktisat Terimleri Sözlüğü, from www.tdk.gov.tr, (23.02.2016).

Karyağdı, N. (2001). *Toplam Kalite Yönetimi ve Türk Vergi İdaresi*. Ankara: Ankara Sanayi Odası, No: 51.

Kılıçdaroğlu, K. (1982). *Fransa' da Vergi Denetimi ve Vergi Kaçakçılığı*, Vergi Dünyası Dergisi CD'si, Ağustos, 12.

OECD (2006). *Strengthening Tax Audit Capabilities: General Principles and Approaches,* from http://www.oecd.org/tax/administration/37589900.pdf, October.

Pehlivan, O. (1986). *Vergi Denetimi ve Vergi Denetiminde Etkinlik*. Vergi Dünyası Dergisi CD'si, Ekim 1986, 62, pp. 35–42.

Özdemir, H. S. (2000). *Türleri ve Fonksiyonları Bakımından Denetim Kavramı*. Vergi Raporu Dergisi. Ankara.

PWC (2014). *French Tax Audit New Obligations for French Law Practices.* March 2014, from https://www.pwc.com/us/en/law-firms/assets/pwc-lfs-news-alert-march-2014-french-tax-audit.pdf (22.02.2016).

Şanver, C. & Oktar S. A. (2013). *Gelir Üzerinden Alınan Vergilerde Vergi Güvenlik Önlemleri ve Mükelleflerin Ba-Bs Bildirimlerine Bakışı Araştırması.* Siyaset, Ekonomi ve Yönetim Araştırmaları Dergisi, 1:1:3, pp. 1–23.

Tecim, B. A. H. (2008). *Kayıtdışı Ekonomide Vergi ve Vergi Denetiminin Önemi,* İzmir: Dokuz Eylül Üniversitesi Sosyal Bilimler Enstitüsü İktisat Anabilim Dalı Yüksek Lisans Tezi.

Tekin, F. & Çelikkaya, A. (2005). *Vergi Denetimi.* Ankara: Seçkin Yayıncılık.

Tax4BusinnesFR (2015). *The French Tax Administration How Does It Work?* from http://www.impots.gouv.fr/portal/deploiement/p1/fichedescriptive_6960/fichedescriptive_6960.pdf, 22.02.2016.

Thierry L. (1998). Contröle Fiscal – Droit et Pratique, Paris: Pres Universitaires de France.

Ünsal, H. (2013). *Vergi Hukuku ve Türk Vergi Sistemi.* Ankara: Gazi Kitabevi.

Üstün, Ü. S. (2013). Nasıl Bir Vergi Denetimi ve Vergi Yargısı. İstanbul: Beta Yayıncılık.

VDK (2014). *2014 Yılı Faaliyet Raporu.* from http://www.vdk.gov.tr/File/?path=ROOT%2FDocuments%2FDosya%2FVDK+2014+Y%C4%B1l%C4%B1+Faaliyet+Raporu_1102.pdf (23.02.2016).

VDK (2016). *İdari Yapı.* from http://www.vdk.gov.tr/default.aspx?nsw=Y/dkfWCgR0OAeV0QSKUxiQ==-H7deC+LxBI8=&nm=1004, (22.02.2016).

Nesrin Ada* & Aslı Ercan**

The Management Paradigm in Family Business in Turkey

Abstract Family businesses have been integrated with one's own business culture and are transmitted from generation to generation. The aim of this article is to examine the paradigm in family business management and the different management paradigms to uncover. Primarily, family business and properties have been defined. After that family business management paradigms were discussed. In the research section, the research report of the "Family Business Congress" which is held every two years in Turkey is presented. They were examined by qualitative research which is a kind of document analysis. The findings are discussed in the conclusion section.

Keywords: family businesses, management paradigms

1. Introduction

In this article, a new management paradigm for the problems of family businesses in Turkey is aimed to be developed. The importance of the article is to analyse the detection of management problems and solutions with a holistic perspective. In the first part of the article, the family business is described and then its problems, advantages and features are examined. Old and new management paradigms are discussed further in the article. In the research section, using qualitative content analysis and the document scanning method, themes of management issues related to family businesses in Turkey are identified and analysed. In the conclusion, a new paradigm for the management issues of the family business is recommended.

2. Family Businesses, Features, and Management Problems in Turkey

As indicated in the literature family businesses have an unique characteristic, and they are separated from other types of businesses. Also (Klein, Astrachan, & Smyrnios, 2005, p. 322) the *"literature suggests three principal ways in which definitions can be considered: content, purpose, and form. Most definitions focus on content. Many early definitions concerned ownership, management involvement*

* Ege University, nesrin.ada@ege.edu.tr
** Ege University, ercan.ercanasli@gmail.com

of an owning family, or generational transfer. In contrast, more recent definitions concentrate on family business culture."

Management based family business definition is defined by specific characteristics. Family business is defined as the scope of these features (Collins et al., 2012). A family business is,

- ✓ If "Family," with more than 50 percent share of the business management,
- ✓ Involved in several generations of family business,
- ✓ Business functional and operational processes are controlled by senior management member of the same family,
- ✓ Family members describe the workplace as a family business.

Families and businesses, reveals the differences in the coexistence of these two concepts. The coexistence of family and business system also reveals their differences. Characteristics of the family system include unconditional acceptance of family members due to the birth right, in terms of capital accumulation "*collectivism, collaboration, equality* between family members and it is an emotional decision. Conversely, business systems include, *"conditional acceptance, capitalistic, competitiveness,"* competence and efficiency are values (Schuman, Stutz & Ward, 2010, p. 26). In this scope, family businesses have interconnectedness-trust, mutual appreciation, open communication, communication among the family members, and can overcome a common crisis. Moreover, family business of "being a family" feature is involved in a commercial activity of family values and the involvement of family characteristics are the result of business management. According to Lumpkin et al, the specific features of family business include (Lumpkin, Martin & Vaughn, 2008, p. 131) "*Tradition*" (certain roles, rituals, common history), "*Stability*" (resistance to change, to be certain rules, limits, predictable behaviour), *"Loyalty"* (duties and responsibilities, sense of gratitude, sense of allegiance, togetherness*)* "*Trust*" (safety, security, reciprocity, reliability), and *"Interdependency"* (emotional bonds, their family members to support each other). However, the business system values are related to the reason for existence of the business. So this value is the business' establishment purpose. As a result there are certain areas of family business advantages and disadvantages. The advantages and disadvantages of family business are stated in Table 1.

Table 1: The advantages and disadvantages of family businesses (adapted from Collins et al.)

Advantages	Disadvantages
- preparing a long-term strategic plan provides a competitive advantage, - independent and flexible of action, - using the reputation of the family name as a family culture - resist the economic crisis within the family financial resources to create, - knowing the business-training to next generations who are family members	- less reach to capital markets - complex organisational structure - family conflict - nepotism - financial strain - succession issues

Source: Collins et al., 2012, p. 11,21.

40 percent of the world's largest 500 companies are family businesses. 90 percent of businesses in Turkey have been operating as a family business. In 2012, as a consultancy company, PricewaterhouseCoopers (PwC, 2012) conducted a global survey of family businesses. According to this survey, the family businesses in Turkey are resistant to the major global economic recession, and they have "confidence, they prepare growth plans for the next period, and take quick decisions." In addition to these features, there are also general issues of family businesses in Turkey. In particular, the source of this problem is based on management. Soyuer pointed out in 2004 that the elements present as these administrative issues are considered. (Soyuer, 2004):

- ✓ Lack of institutionalisation and uncertainty of strategic goals,
- ✓ As a result of traditional decision-making system, difficulties in developing new products and new business models,
- ✓ Intuitive behaviour patterns in the management process,
- ✓ Authoritarian management style,
- ✓ As a result of centralisation of the management and decision-making process, inability to establish an effective reporting and information management systems within the organisation,
- ✓ Nepotism,
- ✓ Conflict; such as conflict of between family and firm purposes,
- ✓ Issues of succession management.

In PwC's 2012 survey, in addition to these determinations, in the coming period "talented human resources, integration into the global economy, the management of innovation and successor-predecessor process" would be important for family businesses (PwC, 2012). Also, due to incorrect and incomplete management, the life cycle of most of the family businesses in Turkey is shortened. This is an important management problem. If sustainability is unobtainable, the company is accelerating the process of entering its death.

3. Paradigm and Management

The current literature and existing research results has emphasised the majority of problems for family businesses. These problems have been connected to the paradigm of management. Because of this reason, the paradigm of management is a crucial fact of the business system. According to Chevallier, "*management has multidimensional and scientific intersection*" (Çiner, 2008, p. 158, so it advocates the need to open new paradigms. Therefore, new management paradigms for family of business management issues need to be developed.

In "The Structure of Scientific Revolutions" which the concept of paradigm was introduced in 1970 by Thomas Kuhn, he explained the concept of paradigm "*perspective, scientific methods, theoretical draft*" (Çüçen, 2012, p. 174) has been used in more than one sense. Scientific paradigms according to Kuhn, anomalies vary depending on revolutionary period. Hence, management paradigms are emerging in the period anomaly. Management paradigms change was realised at the end of each anomaly period process (Kuhn, 2008). Knowledge has become a management value since 1970s, so the value of knowledge in the global new world inspired very different business models, forms of production, management styles, to the emergence of forms of organisation also caused reshaping of the management process. In this context, displaying transition to a new world management paradigm shift from the old world management paradigm structure has been shown in Table 2.

Table 2: The paradigm shift

ORGANISATIONS	OLD WORLD	NEW WORLD
Context	Stable	Turbulent
Temporal Focus	Mid-term (planning)	Now and for ever (long-term)
Risks	Low or medium	High
Competitive advantage	Excellent production	Superior thinking
Priority	Operational productivity	Innovation and thought productivity
Relation with external world	Secluding, secretive	Inclusive, open, transparent (but sometimes opaque)
Productivity focus	Worker productivity	Knowledge/thought productivity
Work	Pay	Fun and personal development
Employee commitment	Loyalty	Challenges and goal-oriented team work
Business is	Company-centric	Customer-centric
Focus	Ends	Processes

Source: Lindgren, 2012, p. 51

According to Clarke and Clegg (2000, p. 62), *"Paradigm shifts as strategic responses to changing competitive circles, Information technology as the technical core of current paradigm shifts, Learning and innovation as the central rational of new paradigms, the importance of wider conceptions of stakeholders to new paradigms, the overwhelming need for new business paradigms to be based on sustainability."* Table 2 has shown this paradigm shift in the management field, resolver of family businesses management problems in Turkey reveal the need for a new management paradigm. Furthermore, the old management paradigm affects negatively the process of existence of the company in the new global world.

4. Method and Research

In this study a qualitative analysis process is used. Qualitative content analysis and document analysis methods were used in the research. The purpose of this research is to identify the existing management problems of family businesses in Turkey and to propose a new management paradigm for future research. The universe of this study is 213 research papers in books of family businesses congresses (FBC) held every two years by the University of Culture in Turkey since 2004. The research sample has examined 123 research papers according to the themes of institutionalisation, entrepreneurship, succession management, sustainability and culture. When the 2004–2014 decade in the research papers are analysed, classified by year has been determined on the basis of changes related to the management of the family business. The first step in this analysis was to determine the factors influencing the management processes in the family business and to separate themes. After that, these factors are grouped in themes and sub-themes and then the research sample was investigated during the time period (2004–2014). Thus, a management paradigm affecting management habits of the family business in Turkey has been developed. Classified by year, research papers of family business congresses are shown in table 3. Institutionalisation is defined as the first theme because it is the biggest problem of institutionalisation element of family business. The ranking of the theme except the theme of institutionalisation was not any priority. Numbers of research papers in the congress were grouped according to themes identified in Table 3. The numbers of papers have been grouped according to themes in Table 4.

Table 3: Family Businesses Congresses

	YEAR	
1.FBC	2004	65
2.FBC	2006	53
3.FBC	2008	35
4.FBC	2010	26
5.FBC	2012	22
6.FBC	2014	12
Total		213

Table 4: According to congress and themes the numbers of research papers

THEMES	1.FBC 2004	2.FBC 2006	3.FBC 2008	4.FBC 2010	5.FBC 2012	6.FBC 2014	Total
Institutionalisation	20	15	10	6	4	3	58
Entrepreneurship	5	0	2	2	1	2	12
Succession management	4	16	4	1	2	2	29
Culture	4	4	5	4	1	0	18
Sustainability	4	1	2	5	0	0	12
Total							129

A limitation of this study is that, after the first congress of the family business, reduction in the number of papers is the cause of the downsizing of the sample.

In addition, the Congress in some years, the absence of a report containing relevant themes, has blocked the exposure of more information which will be used for future research.

5. Results

Using qualitative content analysis and document analysis methods, inquiries were performed according to the number of papers and themes in Table 4. The sample is examined within the management issues which have been identified where the various sub-themes within the main themes. The main theme and sub-themes are described in detail in the section.

Institutionalisation theme:
In Institutionalisation, 58 papers were examined related to the main theme. Sub-themes in 2004, the problems of family businesses, corporate governance, institutionalisation processes, family constitution, management functions, strategic planning and strategic management, professional management, attitudes towards professional managers have been determined. In 2006, it is seen that the administration's decision-making sub-themes are highlighted. In 2008, the importance of strategic planning, family constitution, decision-making problems, institutionalisation-conflict dilemma and according to the Turkish trade law institutionalising the sub-themes have been identified. 2010 sub-themes, strategic management, quality management, organisational culture, the influence of individual problems within the family business management and organisational culture differences have been identified. Themes determined in 2012 are leadership, the importance of the board of directors according to the Turkish commercial law, family market introduction of the company, and the brand value of the family business. In 2014, sub-theme of institutionalisation, strategic management, professional management and family business issues in information technology were identified. Considering the 10-year period for this theme, the theme of institutionalisation was comprised of several sub-themes. General sub-themes which are institutionalisation issues, corporate governance, strategic management, professional management, management functions (planning, organisation, coordination, execution, control) family constitution, the organisation's culture and conflict.

Entrepreneurship theme:
Twelve papers have been examined on the Entrepreneurship theme. Sub-themes in the 2004 intrapreneurship, entrepreneurial leadership, entrepreneurship and technological sense, corporate identity, perception is the next generation of entrepreneurship. In 2006, there is no paper about this theme. In 2008, the family's

perception of women entrepreneurs in the family business and innovation in business has been the sub-theme. 2010 sub-themes, types of entrepreneurship, entrepreneurship perspective of future generations, have been identified. In 2012, intrapreneurship, and in 2014 the perception of entrepreneurship and innovation sub-themes have been identified. General sub-themes, intrapreneurship, innovation, entrepreneurship perception of future generations, leadership, and institutional entrepreneurship types have emerged. However, it is noteworthy that there are few papers about entrepreneurship. In future research examining this issue is recommended.

Succession management theme:
In this study, the successor-predecessor system and its elements are discussed in the management cycle theme. 29 papers have been examined. Common sub-themes have combined more than one sub-theme. In the 2004–2014 ten-year period, the transfer of management to the next generation, the next generation of education, conflict, power and nepotism sub-themes have been identified. Conflict sub-theme, attitudes towards women with conflict between relatives-generation (gender discrimination), have been diversified.

Culture theme:
18 papers were examined regarding the culture theme. Regarding the cultural theme in 2004, the corporate culture, the determinants of organisational culture, institutionalisation and culture impact the sub-themes have been identified. In 2006, the family culture, intrapreneurship, the effect of family culture on business culture, organisational image, cultural differences between family businesses and sub-themes were determined. In 2008, work values, ethics and corporate governance has emerged as sub-themes. In 2010, the element of trust, management of emotions, and in 2012, the family relationship between the founding values of the company and the value of the firm has been identified as sub-themes. All this under the theme of culture, family culture, business culture, organisational culture, organisational image, entrepreneurial culture, governance, ethics, trust, were decisive sub-themes. Culture theme of family in the business of Congresses have been studied in a wide range of sub-themes.

Sustainability theme:
Sustainability, in other words, the continuity of the family life cycle of business contact was examined in twelve papers. While there were reports on this theme in the first four congresses, there were no reports in the last two congresses. Overall, the family constitution to ensure the continuity of the family business, the importance of family culture, organisational backup, family business continuity features

that create a strategic plan for the life cycle efforts were mentioned as sub-themes. Under this theme, sub-themes were family constitution, culture (business-family), organisational backup, strategic management; factors that maintain for continuity have been grouped. Sub-themes within **family constitution, culture (business-family), organisational backup, strategic management and continuity of the protective elements** have been grouped.

Taken together, these results suggest that there is an association between, Institutionalisation, entrepreneurship, succession management, culture and sustainability. These themes are interacting and they consist of relational network with one another. Taking into consideration of this situation, in discussion and conclusion part of this article, the proposal for a new management paradigm has been developed.

6. Discussion and Conclusion

In this article, the management problems of family businesses in Turkey have been identified then a new management paradigm that brings solutions to problems is proposed.

The most intensely existing management problems encountered by family businesses in Turkey are institutionalisation problems which are caused by traditional management and management complexity. Accordingly, in this research, five management themes are determined by qualitative content analysis method of research, the main problems, and the common problems are mentioned and this has revealed interrelated themes. Primarily, the results of the study indicate that the family business in Turkey emerges institutionalisation and management turnover issues. The causes of these problems can be arranged as follows:

- ✓ Founder of the family business that manages the company, wants to retain the decision-making power and refrained from transferring this power to someone else,
- ✓ The interests of the family is more important than the interests of the organisation (material and spiritual),
- ✓ The founder of the family business distrusts corporate management, mistrusts professional managers and is insecure about management transferee to other generations,
- ✓ Next generations of the family, they are not ready to take over management of the company,
- ✓ Because of traditional management system the next generations are concerned about taking responsibility of family business management,

✓ Entrepreneurial behaviour only exists in the establishment of the company, then it does not continue,
✓ Continuation of the closed system approach,
✓ Resistance to change.

As a result, the failure to complete the institutionalisation, before and after the succession process on management, it is emerging as major administrative problems. As a consequence, Institutionalisation and succession management directly affects the sustainability of family businesses. Sustainability theme is directly related to the theme in the same way with institutionalisation and succession management. Sustainability theme is associated with the well management of succession management process. People who will ensure the continuity of the family business are the new generations who took over the management. This research results has supported this situation. Other themes that affect the sustainability theme are entrepreneurship and culture. Entrepreneurship is a factor that caused the establishment of family business. However, after the process of establishment it seems to lose its effectiveness over traditional management process. In fact, contrarily, entrepreneurship should always be developed for sustainability. Moreover, family businesses can access the global market through using competitive advantage of various kinds of entrepreneurship. Family Businesses, unlike their competitors, can provide the company's competitive advantages and sustainability by their products, service and system applications. The future of family businesses, are being protected by the sustainability theme. Culture theme, institutionalisation, management turnover is linked directly or indirectly with entrepreneurship and sustainability themes. This research has also shown that, the culture is the unifying feature of the family business management. The family business culture that exists in Turkey plays a decisive role on business management. Culture of the founding family directly affects the organisational culture and business culture. For family businesses in Turkey, it is necessary to move away from existing management paradigms. Because of the unresolved issue of the management which is created by the existing management paradigm, family businesses status will affect the future existence of the company negatively. Thus, in order to achieve the competitive advantages brought about by globalisation, family businesses must pass to new management paradigm. This paradigm, institutionalisation, succession management, culture, sustainability-oriented entrepreneurship factor is the angle of a new management perspective.

New Family business management paradigm is,

✓ organisational structure, age, according to the scope of family businesses, offering a strategic management model supporting the institutionalisation,

- ✓ Family culture values and company culture values combining an atmosphere that will allow the creation of a new shared organisational culture,
- ✓ Within the company, eliminating the management of uncertainty, the determination of the family constitution in the process of institutionalisation and help define management processes to ensure the application,
- ✓ Supporting Organisational backup,
- ✓ Family and conflicts within the company, supporting the preventive model of communication,
- ✓ adapting to an open system that meets the information needs of the business change process,
- ✓ supporting a model of entrepreneurial behaviour within the organisation,
- ✓ Sustainability focus.

As a result, in this study a new paradigm of management of family businesses in Turkey is identified in which important elements are included. In future research, other factors affecting the new management paradigm should be investigated and solutions to the problems of family businesses in Turkey should be studied in the field of management. The researches which resolve the problems of family business in Turkey and more studies which are related to the management of family businesses should be done.

References

Clarke, T. & Clegg, S. (2000). Management Paradigms for the New Millennium. *International Journal of Management Reviews*. 2(1), 45–64. doi: 10.1111/1468-2370.00030.

Collins, L., & Grisoni, L., & Tucker, J., & Seaman, C., & Graham, S., & Fakoussa, R., & Otten, D., (2012). The Family Business. *The modern family business: relationships, succession and transition*, pp. 3–44, UK: Palgrave Macmillan. doi: 10.1057/9781137001337.

Çiner, C. U. (2008). Güncel Fransız Yönetim Yazını. (Current French Literature Management). *Memleket Siyaset Yönetim (Journal of Crucial Political Management)*, 8, 149–165. http://www.acarindex.com/memleket-siyaset-yonetim/guncel-fransiz-yonetim-yazini-20031#.VtyD__mLTcc.

Çüçen, K. A. (2012). *Bilim Felsefesine Giriş. (Introduction to the Philosophy of Science)* Ankara: Sentez Yayıncılık. ISBN:978-605-5790-37-0.

Klein, S. B., & Astrachan, J. H., & Smyrnios, K. X., (2005). The F-PEC Scale of Family Influence: Construction, Validation, and Further Implication for Theory. *Entrepreneurship Theory and Practice*. 29(3), 321–339. doi: 10.1111/j.1540-6520.2005.00086.x.

Kuhn, T. (2008). *Bilimsel Devrimlerin Yapısı. (The Structure of Scientific Revolutions)* (Turkish translation version-Turkish in Kuyaş, N.),İstanbul: Kırmızı Yayınları. ISBN:975-9169-08-8.

Lindgren, M. (2012). *21st Century Management: Making People Dance in the Thought Economy.* UK: Palgrave Macmillan. doi:10.1057/9780230343290.

Lumpkin, G. T., & Martin, W., & Vaughn, M., (2008). Family Orientation: Individual-Level Influences on Family Firm Outcomes. *Family Business Review,* XXI(2), 127–138. Family Firm Institute, Inc. http://fbr.sagepub.com/content/21/2/127.full.pdf+html.

PwC, Turkey (2012). *Global Family Business Survey Turkey Results Report 2012.* PricewaterhouseCoopers International Ltd. www.pwc.com/tr/ailesirketi.

Schuman, A., & Stutz, S., & Ward, J. L., (2010). *Family Business as Paradox.* UK: Palgrave Macmillan. doi:10.1057/9780230291768.

Soyuer, H. (2004). *Aile işletmelerinde Bilgiye Dayalı Stratejik Kaynak Planlaması. (Knowledge-based Strategic Resource Planning in Family Business).* Paper presented at the 1st Family Business congress, İstanbul.

Bünyamin Bacak, Ebru Kanyılmaz Polat* & Ali Şahin Örnek**

A Study about Job Search Behaviour of Unemployed Individuals with Higher Education Degree: The Case of Canakkale Province[1]

Introduction

Job search is one of the most elementary behaviours that eliminates unemployment. Job search behaviour constitutes one of the basic elements of getting a job. The duration of unemployment is reduced when job search is shaped by the influence of effective environmental and individual factors. It is mentioned in recent studies that effective and qualified job search process provided re-employment successfully (Vinokur and Schuller 2002: 80). As a result of an uneffective job search, individuals can find job which will not comply with their qualifications and expectations. Today, it is known that many people work in jobs that are below their qualifications and they do not like their jobs and have the intention to find new jobs while they are actively working. One of the most likely reasons of this situation which could be referred to as underemployment is the employment resulted after an uneffective job search.

On the other hand ineffective job search behaviour can lead to a longer duration of unemployment. The extended duration of unemployment negatively affects the individual psychologically and reduces the prospects for finding work. Job search behaviour of an individual whose hopes for finding a job decreases, and finally dissappears after a while and unemployment is the state of a vicious circle. In this situation that called the offended worker effect, individuals are pushed out of the labour market by giving up the job search behaviour although they are still unemployed (Biçerli 2011: 56).

Today, unemployment is among the most basic problems of many developed or developing countries. The unemployment rate of OECD countries are

---

* Corresponding Author-Dr. Ebru Kanyılmaz Polat, ekanyilmaz@comu.edu.tr
** Çanakkale Onsekiz Mart University

1 This study is partly produced from the PhD thesis "Investigation of Psychological Effects of Unemployment Experience over Individuals in the Scope of Job-Seeking Activities: The Case of Çanakkale Province."

7.3%; the average of the European Union member countries are 10.1% for 2014 (OECD). The August 2015 unemployment rate in Turkey was 10.1% (Turkish Statiscal Institute (TUIK)). On the other hand, the increase of unemployment rates of higher education graduates and increase of long-term unemployment rates in addition to the increase of unemployment, becomes the lead of current unemployment problems of many countries. The second highest unemployment rate after high school education graduates is the higher education graduates with the rate of 8.8% among OECD member countries (OECD). The highest unemployment rate among education groups in Turkey are among the unemployed of higher education graduates with 12.8%, according to the TUIK data (TUIK).

Individuals that left "job search behaviour" and moved away from labour market are one of the often mentioned issues in the ILO and the OECD report beside the increase of unemployment rates among higher education graduates. The ILO estimated that the amount of those people who reported in ILO and OECD sources as "offended" were 23 million all over the world. It is estimated that this amount would reach 30 million people in 2018 if the unemployment process continues in the same way. In other words, there is a population of 30 million individuals who were not in the labour force. This target group is not in the labour force because they have the "psychological" belief of inability to find jobs; even they have the potential and desire to work outside the labour market (ILO, 2014: 17). The ILO is talking about the risk of losing their skills and abilities of these people, because they are outside the labour market for a long time.

The examination of job search behaviours of unemployment in the countries of which higher education graduate unemployment and long term unemployment rates were tend to increase as Turkey, is important in terms of increasing of employability and not to exclude the skilled labour from the labor market. The lack of open jobs for higher education graduates confront higher education graduate unemployed with the risk of long term unemployment and "offended" unemployment in Çanakkale labour market analysis. In this matter, the determination of job search behaviours of higher education graduates in Çanakkale is important.

Job Search Behaviour

The simplest definition of the job search is to investigate employment opportunities. Time and effort must be paid to determine the alternatives on the labour market which had a dynamic structure and it was difficult to access complete information. Job search behaviour can be defined as the activities of individuals for determining the most suitable alternatives in the labour market (Güler

2012: 11). It can be expressed as a process of gathering information about selected job alternatives (Van Hoye 2015: 4).

The intensity and character of job search behaviour is an important tool in the re-employment of individuals. The higher qualifications of an individual, the more chance to find opportunities of learning the most appropriate employment possibilities according to intensive job search behaviour (Fort and Leroy 2011: 470–471). Job search is a dynamic process involving the phases of collecting information in the labour market, finding, evaluating, and selecting alternatives (Başbuğ 2008: 9).

Job search behaviour may be examined in two sub-groups as the preparation and active job search. The preparation phase begins from preliminary research for finding a job. To read job opportunities from newspapers, magazines and the internet, to revise their CV, to talk about job opportunities with friends and familiar are examples of the preparatory behaviour. To fill out job application forms, to contact employment agencies and to do job interviews are examples of active behaviour (Blau 1993: 315).

To determine the job search behaviour of those unemployed with associate degrees in the Çanakkale province is the goal of this study. The description which was announced and reflected to official unemployment figures by TUIK was used as the description of unemployed in this study. Accordingly, all individuals in the non-institutional working age, who used at least one of the job search channels in last three months for job search and who would be suitable for employment in 15 days among the individuals who were not in employment in the reference period (had no contact with any business such business as for profit, casual, paid or free) were included in unemployed (TUIK). To determine of density of high school graduates unemployed is important in terms of increasing the efficiency of job search. On the other hand the investigation of job search behaviour becomes important in terms of gaining individuals on the labour force whose job search behaviour were diminished or extinguished.

Materials and Methods

Survey meyhod is selected as one of the quantitative research methods, to determine the job search behaviours of higher education graduate unemployed in this study. The study population includes "unemployed individuals having education of associate, bachelor and master graduates; being registered in the Türkiye İş Kurumu (İŞKUR) in Çanakkale." During the study the target population included 1260 higher education graduates being registered as unemployed by the İŞKUR in the past year from the day this study was conducted (August 2013–2014). The survey was applied to 360 unemployed individuals with the face to face method and e-mail as well. 315 questionnaires were subjected to analysis after missing and invalid surveys from the collected entries were eliminated.

The Job Search Behavior Scale developed by Blau (1993) is used for collecting data. This scale was developed in 1993 by Blau to measure preparation and active job search behaviours (Blau 1993: 315–316). The scale questions the last four months of job search preparations and active behaviours of individuals. Both sizes consist of six questions asking how many times the specific job search behaviour is done. Some of the questions were taken from Blau and some of the questions were updated by several authors in addition of actual job search methods (such as job search via internet) (Vansteenkiste 2005: 276; Başbuğ, 2008: 55). Cronbach's alpha number of the scale was found as 0.921, General average of it was found as 1,764 and Standard Deviation was found as 40356.

Findings

The study included 315 people. 62% of participants were women (196) and 37% were men (118). Approximately 60% of participants were in the age group of 25–34 years old; while 38.1% is observed in the 19–24 age range. 75.5% of participants whose majority is in "young age" are single and 84.4% of them have no child. Information of the demographic data of the participants is shown in Table 1.

Table 1:

Sex	**N**	**%**	**Marital Status**	**N**	**%**
Female	197	62,5	Single	238	75,5
Male	118	37,5	Married	77	24,4
Total	315	100	Total	315	100
Age	**N**	**%**	**Education**	**N**	**%**
19–24	120	38,1	Associate	83	26,3
25–34	178	56,5	Bachelor	191	60,6
35–54	17	5,4	Master	41	13
Total	**315**	**100**	Total	315	100

Eleven questions were asked to unemployed individuals questioning their preperations of last four months and active job search behaviours (JSB). The expressions on the scale are as follows:

JSB 1: I read job advertisements on a newspaper, magazine or the internet
JSB 2: I applied employee seekers on a newspaper, magazine or the internet
JSB 3: I prepared or reviewed my CV
JSB 4: I sent my CV to an employer
JSB 5: I filled a job application form
JSB 6: I read a book about finding or changing a job
JSB 7: I did a job interview with an employer
JSB 8: I talked to friends or relatives about job opportunities
JSB 9: I made connection with some job search agencies
JSB 10: I did informative interviews and attended to meetings to learn about occupations or jobs that I was interested in
JSB 11: I contacted an employer via phone, e-mail or personally

Questions were answered with a Quintet Likert-type grouping. Frequency range is determined for each response (0 = 0 time, 1 = 1–2 times, 2 = 3–5 times, 4 = 6–9 times, 5 = 10 or more times) (Blau 1993: 319). No significant difference determined according to the variables such as sex, marital status, education, age, unemployment duration in terms of job search behaviour in the independent dual sampling t tests and ANOVA tests related whether the scale varies or not according to categorical variables. The frequency of each item being marked is defined for determining the frequence of the use of substances in the scale.

The most frequent job search method of high school graduate unemployed is the examination of job advertisements via a newspaper, magazine or internet and applying to them. The frequent use of the internet rather than others is understandable today because the internet is used widely in all areas. The other most frequent job search method is to prepare or review CV and send it to employers and that method is used frequently in today's environment. On the other hand individuals applied to read books on finding a job and to attend informative meetings. To choose active job search behaviour such as job interview with an employer and contacting with a job search channel is relatively low.

The significant difference on which subject between education and job search with ANOVA were investigated and a significant difference was found in only one subject; "I read a book about finding and changing a job." The associate graduates that are unemployed were significantly more in this behaviour rather than bachelor and master graduate unemployed statistically. Further percentages for job search behaviours are given in Table 2.

Table 2: Percentage of Respondents Related to Job Search Behaviour They Use

	JSB 1 (%)	JSB 2 (%)	JSB 3 (%)	JSB 4 (%)	JSB 5 (%)	JSB 6 (%)	JSB 7 (%)	JSB 8 (%)	JSB 9 (%)	JSB 10 (%)	JSB 11 (%)
0	9,5	21,3	13,0	22,2	23,5	**64,8**	**38,7**	8,6	24,8	**48,9**	**37,8**
1–2	9,8	17,8	27,3	21,6	21,6	19,0	29,5	21,9	**35,6**	21,9	29,8
3–5	12,7	14,6	22,5	16,2	18,4	5,4	17,1	25,7	17,5	11,7	13,7
6–9	12,1	11,1	7,9	11,1	8,3	2,2	5,4	11,1	6,0	6,3	7,0
10	**54,9**	**35,2**	**29,2**	**28,9**	**28,3**	8,6	9,2	**32,7**	16,2	11,1	11,7
Total	100	100	100	100	100	100	100	100	100	100	100

The average of the responses to the subjects according to the education is given in Table 3. Bachelor graduates unemployed used job search methods rather than others, when the average of the responses was examined. The job search activities of Master Graduate's unemployed were less than associate and bachelor graduates unemployed. The most frequent job search behaviours in terms of all levels of education are "Read job advertisements" and "talked to friends or relatives about job opportunities." The less frequent job search behaviours are "to read a book about finding a job or change jobs" and "to attend the informative meetings."

Bachelor graduates used the unilateral pre-application methods as preparation and sending of CV and filling application forms more often. The Associate Degree graduates used face to face job search methods as "running a business meeting and connecting with job search channels" more often.

Associate graduates have the advantage on the subject of the conclusion of their application with meeting because of their "professions" and experience gained from training. Especially in the local labour market, qualified associate degree graduates are suited to the expectations of employers rather than bachelor and master degree graduates.

Table 3: The Using Frequency of Job Search Methods According to Education Levels

Education		JSB 1	JSB 2	JSB 3	JSB 4	JSB 5	JSB 6	JSB 7	JSB 8	JSB 9	JSB 10	JSB 11
Associate	Av.	2,94	2,24	2,12	1,90	1,94	1,06	1,40	2,43	1,78	1,23	1,23
	N	82	82	82	82	82	82	82	82	82	82	82
	S.D.	1,400	1,599	1,494	1,607	1,542	1,485	1,481	1,379	1,449	1,460	1,345
Bachelor	Av.	3,06	2,26	2,19	2,12	2,03	,64	1,11	2,38	1,51	1,07	1,28
	N	190	190	190	190	190	190	190	190	190	190	190
	S.D.	1,363	1,571	1,424	1,539	1,545	1,140	1,195	1,374	1,352	1,347	1,343
Master	Av.	2,58	1,87	1,82	1,85	1,70	,30	,98	2,25	1,20	,82	1,10
	N	40	40	40	40	40	40	40	40	40	40	40
	S.D.	1,517	1,652	1,299	1,442	1,539	,758	1,000	1,296	1,159	1,238	1,297
Total	Av.	2,96	2,20	2,12	2,03	1,96	,71	1,17	2,38	1,54	1,08	1,24
	N	313	313	313	313	313	313	313	313	313	313	313
	S.D.	1,406	1,586	1,426	1,542	1,541	1,221	1,258	1,361	1,361	1,363	1,334

(coded as 0 = 0; 1–2 = 1; 3–5 = 2; 6–9 = 3; 10 = 4)

Another point of view, a possible cause of the lower applications and job interviews of individual with higher education degree is the increase of qualification and expectation of them. In addition, bachelor and master degree graduates do more applications in the national market, while associate degrees are finding more opportunities for application in the local labour market. The local labour market applications could be ended with more frequent job interviews; while applications in the national market ended with lower frequency according to the great number of applications with the announcement. Indeed, 7.2% of employers are looking for their employees among the higher education degree graduates, while 31.4% of employers are looking for their employees among the equivalent of high school and 15.8% of employers are looking for their employees among the secondary education according to "Labor Market Demand Study" of İŞKUR in 2014. The most employee job searches are waitresses, garment worker, canner, furniture craftsman, machinists, and sales consultant. Associated education opportunities of these profesions are another possible cause of lower job interviews of bachelor degree graduates.

The frequency of engaging in activities for job search of the master degree graduates is lower. The most widely used methods are "read job advertisements on a newspaper, magazine or internet" and "talk to friends and relatives about job opportunities." The average of the job search behaviours such as to contact with an employer via phone, e-mail or making job interview in the past four months, become lower rather than others. In other words master degree graduates have the lowest number of job interviews.

Discussion

The job search of those unemployed were active and all job search channels were used by them, were seen in the study related to the job search behaviours of higher graduates that are unemployed in Çanakkale. However, the lack of suitable vacancies for higher education graduates is drawing attention, when the labour and employment-related structure of Canakkale province is examined. The results of Labour Market Analysis conducted in 2014, gives an idea about the opportunities in the Çanakkale province. According to this report the rates of vacant jobs suitable for associate degree is 7.5% for women and 2.6% for men. While there were no jobs for women with a bachelor degree, the rate of vacant jobs suitable for men is 2.3%. The firms which need bachelor's degree graduates most are the ones working with foreign partnership (24.5%) and exporting firms (4.9%) (İş-Kur 2015: 50–51).

This case left the unemployed in the province with the risk of being unable to find jobs in the long-term and to be offended. One of the frequently mentioned issues in the ILO and OECD reports are individuals left "job search behaviour" and moved away from the labour market. The number of these people who are named as "offended" in ILO and OECD sources are 23 million people all over the world. If unemployment process continues in the same way, the number of them is estimated to reach 30 million in 2018. In other words, 30 million individuals who were not in labour force because of their belief of not being able to find a job, although they have the potential and desire outside the labour force market, are in question (ILO, 2014: 17). The ILO is talking about the risk of losing the skills and abilities of these people because they are outside the labour market for a long time.

Encouraging of entrepreneurship in order to increase employment opportunities for higher education graduates in the province is crucial. Individuals, who have yet to enter the process of leaving the job search behaviour, are faced with the risk of offense to the labour market, in case of extension of the duration of unemployment.

References

Başbuğ, Gökçe (2008), *"Üniversiteden Yeni Mezun Olan Gençlerin İş Arama Davranışlarının Planlı Davranış Teorisi Bağlamında Araştırılması"*, Yayınlanmamış Yüksek Lisans Tezi, İstanbul Üniversitesi, Sosyal Bilimler Enstitüsü, Psikoloji Anabilim Dalı, İstanbul, 2008.

Blau, G. (1993), "Further Exploring the Relationship Between Job Search and Voluntary Individual Turnover", *Personnel Psychology*, 46, pp. 313–330.

Biçerli, Mustafa Kemal (2011), *Çalışma Ekonomisi*, Beta Yayınları, İstanbul.

Fort, Isabelle; Flora JAcquet, Nais Leroy (2011), "Self-efficacy, Goals, and Job Search Behaviors", Career Development International, Vol: 16, Issue: 5, pp. 469–481.

Kümbül-Güler, Burcu (*2012*), "İş Arama Davranışı: Bütüncül Psiko-Sosyal Bir. Yaklaşım" "İşGüç" Endüstri İlişkileri ve İnsan Kaynakları Dergisi, 14(2), pp. 7–32.

International Labour Office (2014), "*Global Employment Trends 2014 Risk of a Jobless Recovery?*", International Labour Office, Genova.

İş-Kur (2015), "İşgücü Piyasası Analizi Raporu", Türkiye İş Kurumu Genel Müdürlüğü, Çanakkale.

Van Hoye, Greet (2015) "Job Search Behviour as a Multidimensional Construct: A Review of Different Job Search Behaviours and Sources", (edt: Khele, Christine and Hooft, Edwin A. J.), *The Oxford Handbook of Job Loss and Job Search*, New York: Oxford University Press.

Vansteenkiste, Maarten, Willy Lens, Hans De Witte, N.T. Feather (2005), "Understanding Unemployed People's Job Search Behaviour, Unemployment Experience and Well-Being: A Comparison of Expectancy-Value Theory and Self-Determination Theory", *British Journal of Social Psychology*, 44, pp. 269–287.

Vinokur, Amiram D.; Yaacov Schul (2002), "The Web of Coping Resources and Pathways to Reemployment Following a Job Loss", *Journal of Occupational Health Psychology*, Vol: 7, No: 1, pp. 68–83.

Katarzyna Wierzbicka*

High-risk Capital as a Form of Financing Innovative Activity – Poland in Central and Eastern Europe

Introduction

Venture capital funds are an important part of the process of creating innovation. On the other side, the basis for the development of enterprises, and thus the whole world economy is innovation and advanced technologies. In the modern economy, an increasingly important role in their creating and disseminating is played by small and medium-sized enterprises. In addition to flexibility and involvement in innovative projects, the implementation of the company modern technology requires not only technical knowledge but also knowledge of the issues economic, legal, market, and managerial competencies. Companies want to be competitive on the market that is why usually the implementation of innovative solutions is associated with considerable expenditure. In relation with the creation and maintenance of innovative potential requires companies to acquire the appropriate resources, including financial means.

The aim of the present study is the presentation of the subject of venture capital that is high-risk capital and analysis of financing directions of enterprises in Poland. The research deductive method has been used on the basis of quantity data from the European Venture Capital Association (EVCA) and publications about innovations and venture capital. Data analysis has been conducted in terms of results comparison, achieved by Polish sector of vc compared to other countries from the region of Central and Eastern Europe.

1. Innovative Activity and Financing

Financing innovating activity is an extremely important aspect of their development. Increased competition, globalisation, and the emergence of the knowledge society make the contemporary world characterised by – to much greater extent than before – deep social, economic and technological changes. Changes occur

* PhD, Faculty of Economics and Management, University of Bialystok; kwierzbicka@o2.pl

everywhere, and facilitate for the process of innovation adapting to these changes. Innovations play a special role in market activities of enterprises. They are seen as an effective tool for building a profitable position in competitive companies. Companies developing innovations in this respect have a number of benefits, which are not available to its competitors not making innovations. The impact of innovation for the enterprise was analysed, for example, in the scientific publications of R. Deshpande, A.U. Farley, F. E. Jr. Webster (Desphande, Farley, Webster 1993, p. 23, 27), A. Subramanian'a and S. Nilakanta (Subramanian, Nilikanta 1996, p. 631) and S. Yamin'a (Yamin, Mavondo, Gunasekaran, Sarros, 1997, p. 161). Some scientists also claim that there is a relationship between innovation and the ability of the company to survive in the market. Growth and the capacity for innovation is more likely to survive for companies from different industries and sectors of the economy.

Figure 1: Innovative activity-conditions

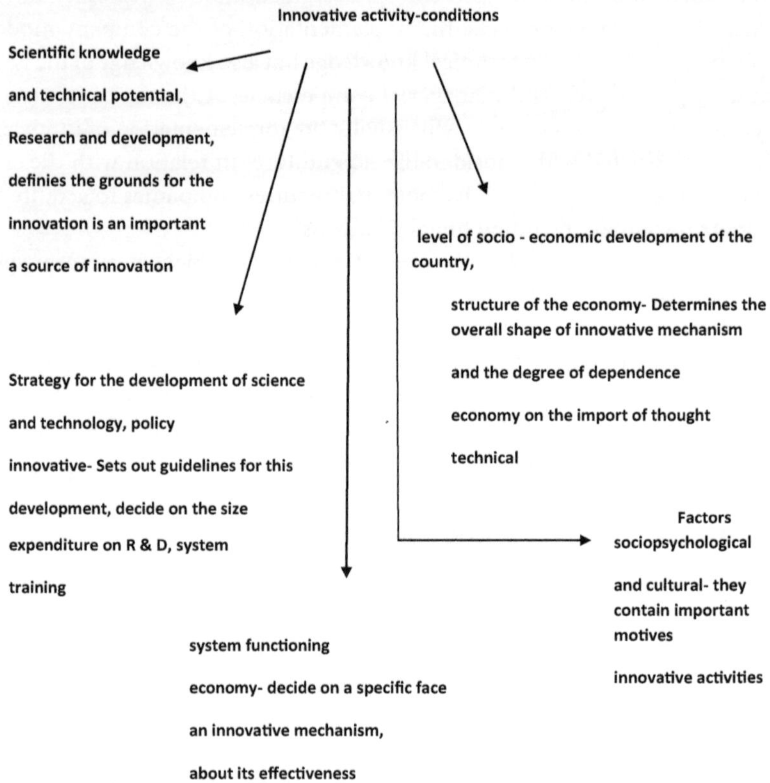

Source: own elaborations on Mesthene 1970, Pomykalski 2001

Innovativeness is forced by competition and competitiveness induces pro-innovative behaviours. These feedbacks cause the economy to face greater market demands and achieve at a higher level. Creation of such an economy occurs because of the creation and development of enterprises based on knowledge, that means innovative enterprises. Their influence on the development of the world economy through globalisation will intensify activities and sources for the creation of innovative companies of a start-up and spin-off types. It is in accordance with the "new economy" of the OECD. The condition of sine qua non is the creation of innovative companies of a considerable development potential and competitiveness is the use of knowledge transfer and newest technological generations. It is closely correlated with acquirement and use of various forms of their financing (Lewandowska 2011, p. 93).

Financing of innovative activity is at the moment a very important issue by analysing them in Poland and other developing countries. In Poland, the expenditure on R&D activities are insufficient. The GERD (Gross Domestic Expenditure on Research and Development) in Poland oscillates among 0,90% of the GDP in 2013; it is higher than the percentage in Slovakia, Mexico, Latvia, Cyprus and Romania, but lower than the percentage in the remaining countries of the OECD and the European Union (EU), where the average is approximately 4,74% of GDP (highest score is in Luxembourg, Germany, Finland). Budget expenditure in Poland on R&D is approximately 0,32% of GDP (constitutes 1,5% of budget) and they are relatively low in comparison with the level of expenditure of other EU countries. Moreover, also off-budget sources are indicated for financing science and significantly lower than in other EU countries. The participation of business in financing R&D in Poland is slightly more than 33% when the average in Union is approximately 55%. Negative for Poland is also highest in EU indicator of research non-directed for the indicated socio-economic aim.

Table 1: Gross domsetic expenditure on R&D, 2003–2013, %

	2003	2004	2005	2006	2007	2008	2009	2010	2011	2012	2013
EU-28	**1.8**	**1.76**	**1.76**	**1.78**	**1.78**	**1.85**	**1.94**	**1.93**	**1.97**	**2.01**	**2.03**
Euro area (EA-19)	1.81	1.78	1.78	1.8	1.81	1.89	1.99	1.99	2.04	2.1	2.11
Belgium	1.83	1.81	1.78	1.81	1.84	1.92	1.98	2.05	2.15	2.36	2.42
Bulgaria	0.47	0.48	0.45	0.45	0.44	0.46	0.51	0.59	0.55	0.62	0.65
Czech Republic	1.15	1.15	1.17	1.23	1.31	1.24	1.3	1.34	1.56	1.79	1.91
Denmark	2.51	2.42	2.39	2.4	2.51	2.78	3.07	2.94	2.97	3.03	3.08
Germany	2.46	2.42	2.42	2.46	2.45	2.6	2.72	2.71	2.79	2.87	2.83
Estonia	0.77	0.85	0.92	1.12	1.07	1.26	1.4	1.58	2.34	2.16	1.74
Ireland	1.13	1.18	1.2	1.21	1.24	1.39	1.63	1.6	1.56	1.5	1.58
Greece	0.55	0.53	0.58	0.56	0.58	0.66	0.6	0.	0.67	0.69	0.8
Spain	1.02	1.04	1.1	1.17	1.23	1.32	1.35	1.35	1.32	1.27	1.24
France	2.11	2.09	2.04	2.05	2.02	2.06	2.21	2.18	2.19	2.23	2.24
Croatia	0.95	1.03	0.86	0.74	0.79	0.88	0.84	0.74	0.75	0.75	0.81
Italy	1.06	1.05	1.05	1.09	1.13	1.16	1.22	1.22	1.21	1.27	1.3
Cyprus	0.32	0.34	0.37	0.39	0.4	0.39	0.45	0.45	0.46	0.43	0.46
Latvia	0.36	0.4	0.53	0.65	0.56	0.58	0.45	0.6	0.7	0.66	0.6
Lithuania	-	0.75	0.75	0.79	0.8	0.79	0.83	0.78	0.9	0.9	0.95
Luxembourg	1.65	1.62	1.59	1.69	1.61	1.64	1.71	1.53	1.5	1.29	1.31
Hungary	0.92	0.8	0.93	0.99	0.97	0.99	1.14	1.15	1.2	1.27	1.41
Malta	0.24	0.49	0.53	0.58	0.55	0.53	0.52	0.64	0.69	0.86	0.85
Netherlands	1.81	1.81	1.79	1.76	1.69	1.64	1.69	1.72	1.9	1.94	1.96
Austria	2.18	2.17	2.38	2.37	2.43	2.59	2.61	2.74	2.68	2.89	2.96
Poland	**0.54**	**0.56**	**0.57**	**0.55**	**0.56**	**0.6**	**0.67**	**0.72**	**0.75**	**0.89**	**0.87**
Portugal	0.7	0.73	0.76	0.95	1.12	1.45	1.58	1.53	1.46	1.38	1.33
Romania	0.38	0.38	0.41	0.45	0.52	0.57	0.46	0.45	0.49	0.48	0.39
Slovenia	1.25	1.37	1.41	1.53	1.42	1.63	1.82	2.06	2.42	2.58	2.6
Slovakia	0.56	0.5	0.49	0.48	0.45	0.46	0.47	0.62	0.67	0.81	0.83
Finland	3.3	3.31	3.33	3.34	3.35	3.55	3.75	3.73	3.64	3.42	3.3
Sweden	3.61	3.3	3.39	3.5(e)	3.26	3.5	3.45	3.22	3.25	3.28	3.3
United Kingdom	1.67	1.61	1.63	1.65	1.69	1.69	1.75	1.69	1.69	1.63	1.69
Iceland	2.73	-	2.69	2.91	2.56	2.53	2.66	-	2.49	-	1.87
Norway	1.68	1.55	1.48	1.46	1.56	1.56	1.72	1.65	1.63	1.62	1.65
Switzerland	-	2.68	-	-	-	2.73	-	-	-	2.96	-
Montenegro	-	-	-	-	-	-	-		0.32	-	0.38
Serbia	-	-	-	-	-	-	0.87	0.74	0.72	0.91	0.73
Turkey	0.48	0.52	0.59	0.58	0.72	0.73	0.85	0.84	0.86	0.92	0.95
Russia	1.29	1.15	1.07	1.07	1.12	1.04	1.25	1.13	1.09	1.13	1.13
United States	2.55	2.49	2.51	2.5	2.63	2.77	2.82	2.74	2.77	2.81	-
Japan	3.14	3.13	3.31	3.41	3.46	3.47	3.36	3.25	3.38	3.34	3.47

Source: Science and technology, Eurostat, Statistics, http://ec.europa.eu/eurostat/statistics-explained/images/5/53/Gross_domestic_expenditure_on_R&D,_2003%E2%80%9313_(%25_of_GDP)_YB15.png, 28.02.2016

A lot of publications about finance and innovation sought to document the particular challenges associated with financing R&D and to quantify the degree to which innovative firms faced financing constraints. Brown, Martinsson and Petersen (Brown, Martinsson, Petersen 2012, p. 1521–29), provide evidence that young, high-tech, publicly-traded firms finance their R&D investment almost entirely through internal cash flow and external equity markets. They argue that "information problems, skewed and highly uncertain returns, and lack of collateral value likely make debt a poor substitute for equity finance." Therefore, to the extent that these firms face financing constraints, exogenous changes in the supply of external equity should have significant effects on R&D. Authors argue that the US experienced a finance-driven cycle in R&D from 1994 to 2004, when privately financed R&D to GDP rose from 1.4% in 1994 to 1.9 % in 2004 and was driven by the young, publicly-traded firms in seven high-tech industries that benefited from the stock market boom in that period. They argue that their estimates can explain 75% of the aggregate R&D boom and subsequent decline.

The key-role of the technological and innovative progress for the economic successfulness finds its support in the economy theory. Also economic empirical research (embracing well-developed countries) indicates that the outlays for the researches, development and innovations accelerate economic growth through the raise of productivity dynamics. Moreover, limited human resources of work and environment as well as decreasing income from the investment into real and human capital have an effect in an increased effectiveness of use of those production factors which are able to ensure economic growth in a long period of time. In the case of well-developed countries which in terms of own technological and organisational development have reduced possibilities to pattern one selves on others, means necessity to invest part of the incomes on research and development works. It does not mean that the pro-innovative politics is the problem of the richest countries.

There are various means of financing innovative ventures. Sources may come from internal enterprise funds, as well as external sources. One of them is high risk capital, that is venture capital.

The Market of high risk investments-Venture Capital (VC) in Poland remains in the phase of early development whereas the supply of the capital designed for creation of new innovative enterprises is rather small in comparison with its accessibility in Europe and the United States (EVCA Central, 2013). The value of the Polish market PE/VC constituted in 2014 is 0,098% GDP, while in countries of Eastern Europe it is 0,063% GDP and across all of Europe is 0,253% GDP (EVCA Annual 2014, p. 2).

Poland departs from the world standards in terms of participation of VC investments in the GDP. Additionally, the Polish VC market is characterised by quantity and quality equity gap and lack of convergence with the financing needs (Zelek 2013, p. 3). It results from the shortages of high risk capital as well as the specifics of the investment structure of those investments. The portfolio of the most functioning on Polish market funds VC are dominated by investments in mature businesses or being in phase of intensive growth. The Polish market of VC is relatively small, especially in comparison with the West-European countries. Even though Poland is placed in 28th place in the rank of the most attractive world markets for VC funds, which constitutes a promising perspective for Polish funds (The Venture Capital, 2015).

2. Venture Capital – Definition and Issue

While no standard definition of venture capital exists, there is wide consensus that it corresponds to the professional financing of young, unlisted dynamic ventures through equity or equity-like instruments like convertible securities. Unlike wealthy individuals who occasionally invest in start-ups ("business angels"), venture capitalists are professional investors, organised in small limited partnerships, who raise funds from wealthy individuals and institutional investors and invest on their behalf. They specialise in financing young firms which typically have not yet produced any sales, but which have high growth and earnings potential–many investees are "start-ups" which come into life through venture financing. Venture capital is considered to be the most appropriate form of financing for innovative firms in high–tech sectors. Venture capital has greatly developed over the last three decades in the United States, but much less so in Europe, where policy–makers are striving to help channel more funds into this form of financial intermediation.

Venture capital is a form of intermediation particularly well suited to support the creation and growth of innovative, entrepreneurial companies (Hellmann, Puri, 2002, p. 172; Kortum, Lerner 2000, p. 676). It specialises in financing and nurturing companies at an early stage of development ("start-ups") that operate in high-tech industries. For these companies the expertise of the venture capitalist, its knowledge of markets and of the entrepreneurial process, and its network of contacts are most useful to help unfold their growth potential (Da Rin, Nicodano, Sembenelli 2004, p. 1). Author also said, that by contrast, when venture capital is applied to companies at a later stage of their growth, or in companies which operate in technologically mature industries, it has less of an opportunity to "make a difference." Economics thus points to the relevance of providing an adequate share of venture investments in high-tech and early stage companies.

The preferred solution, which is increasing in businesses in recent years is the offer of private quity/venture capital. In Europe financing venture capital concerns enterprises of a broad activity spectrum. The European Association Private Equity/Venture Capital (EVCA) provide medium and long terms investments based on purchasing enterprises shares unquoted on the stock exchange and used for gaining benefits in effect of growth of the enterprises value is defined as private equity. In this understanding they can concern various types of enterprise development, commencing with its establishment and starting activity through all types of development, and ending with introduction on the stock exchange.

In the classic embrace of financing by means of PE/VC, it is frequently identified with small, medium, and innovative enterprises. It underlines that high-risk is closely correlated with investment but most of all the major aim of the investor is the achievement of a high return rate. Venture capital is defined as "own capital paid for limited period of time by external investors to small and medium enterprises possessing innovative product, production method or service which were not verified by the market yet, and create high risk of investment failure, but simultaneously in case of investment success, supported in the management by investors, ensure significant increase value of the invested capital which is realized by the sale of shares" (Węcławski, 2004). VC is the element of PE which refers to financing of commenced activity of the enterprise, early phase of its development or further expansion (Mikołajczyk i Krawczyk, 2007). According to the definition of EVCA (EVCA Annual, 2013), private equity is "the share capital, supplied to enterprises unquoted on the stock market relating mainly to management buy-out or purchase of shares in enterprise from other institution offering VC or its shareholders or the purchase of companies shares noted on the stock market in order to withdraw its shares from the public turnover" (EVCA, 2013). However, the Polish Association of Capital Investors defines PE/VC as "investments on the non-public capital market, in order to achieve medium and long term benefits from the increase of the capital value" (EVCA Annual, 2013).

It should be emphasised that Venture capital is a particular type of sharing capital private equity, invested in the enterprise on the early phases of development and further expansion where the reward is the above average rate of return. In the EVCA statistics there are three investment segments distinguished: private equity/venture capital, buyout, and diversified projects (generalist).

There are four stages and roles of venture capital financing (Bottazzi, Da Rin 2001, p. 10):

- Seed finance: Small investment, in the order of a few hundred thousand euros at most, which allows an entrepreneur to verify whether his project is feasible and economically attractive. At this stage the venture capitalist helps explore the viability of a project.

- Start-up finance: Investment aimed at making a firm operational by attracting the necessary employees and executives, developing a prototype and/or implementing marketing tests. At this stage the venture capitalist may become involved in the organisation of the company. His contribution to shaping corporate strategy is felt most heavily at this stage.
- Expansion finance: Investment aimed at reaching the scale of industrial production, upgrading the production facilities and attracting further employees. At this stage the venture capitalist may help find additional financing and help the company contact clients and suppliers. As the company grows and needs revenue, he may also help recruit marketing and other non-technical executives.
- Later stage finance: Investment aimed at helping the firm grow fast enough to become a market leader and unleash its earning potential and to make it ready for a trade sale or for listing on a stock exchange. At this stage the venture capitalist may help set the stage for either a trade sale or an Initial Public Offering.

Significant features of venture capital are: (Lewandowska 2011)

- investing in enterprises highly innovative, and simultaneously of a high risk,
- expecting relatively high return rates from the engaged capital, active participation in the management of the invested enterprise, influencing positive chances of successful development of enterprise through introduction of know-how,
- selection of investment projects according to credibility of a good idea criterion, documented by the market analysis, high qualification of Contractors and Entrepreneurs, and finally expected return rate,
- financing investments in the interval of 5–10 years, and then disinvestment,
- drawing attention on the level of enterprises investments of potential purchasers of the capital (VC interested in the early phases of development),
- transformation of the sharing structure for the period of financing enterprise and creation of co-ownership with potential relations consequences donor-recipient of the capital,
- creation of economic environment around enterprises supported financially by VC in terms of management and in form of business contacts,
- circle of capital donors of VC funds consisting of non-formal (family, friends, so called business angels) and formal donors (private, prosperous investors, huge enterprises investing own capital reserves, pension funds, insurance companies, banks and country),

- creation of foundation for cooperation among various types of institutions and enterprises as well as corporation networks among economic organisations,
- support of private equity/venture capital markets by various organisations caring about development of entrepreneurial activity, innovative and high-tech transfer to newly-created and functioning on the market enterprises

Research results indicate that VC investments in technological companies positively influence innovative activity (Allen, Hall 2011, p. 115–124; Bertoni, Croce, D'Adda 2010, p. 317–320). The literature confirms that VC investments stimulate growth of new technological companies (Bertoni, Colomboand Grilli 2011, p. 1028–1043). The VC investment effect is reflected in the growth of economic quantities, especially in the growth of employment. When technological companies encounter problem with access to financing sources, it results in reduction of growth and threats surviving on the market. Even though, VC financing contributes to overcoming those barriers, it possesses some demand limitations. The cost of participation of VC funds can be considerably high for young technological companies. The role of politics in supporting innovativeness conducted on the country level can be of significant importance. In the literature there is a voice raised that there is a need to create systems of incentives and levelling financial barriers of those companies through the system of direct grants (Colombo, Grilli, Verga 2007, p. 381). Colombo enumerates human capital and VC as two basic factors of technological companies successfulness. Human capital in the form of a qualified management team of technological enterprises is the factor encouraging VC companies to undertake investments. The European market of increased risk develops rapidly, mainly because of public politics directed on entrepreneurial and technological support. Innovations are developed and created by VC investments and innovativeness and entrepreneurship is the initial condition of access to financing VC. Modern economies are dependent on innovations which improve their competitiveness and contribute to their growth. Therefore, the European challenge seems to be improvement of capital financing accessibility on the early phase of activity in order to improve innovativeness. On the PE/VC market high risk funds appear as agents between investors who shared own capital and portfolio companies where the high risk investments are conducted. The presence of the funds in the role of an agent has its justification in the investment specifics of a type PE/VC. It is characterised by higher than the average risk level and higher complication level from the investment in to share or bonds conducted directly by investors.

Venture Capital – Place of Poland in CENTRAL AND EASTERN EUROPE

Poland is still a very small market venture capital on the European stage and the world. The history of the funds existence in Poland is very short, therefore, market participants do not know the rules of operation listed institutions. Venture capital investments grew significantly in 2014 in countries included in the study. Those countries share of European venture investment value was 2.7% in 2014 compared with 2.1% in 2013. Meanwhile, the region accounted for 6.5% of total European companies receiving venture capital financing in 2014 versus 5% the previous year. Across the Central and Eastern Europe (CEE) region only, the venture capital sector accounted for 7% of total private equity investments by value and 72% by number of companies.

Poland was the first country on the VC market in Central and Eastern European Countries (CEE)[1] in 2013, but in 2014 the situation was changed. Hungary remained the leading CEE destination for venture capital investments in 2014 with 32 milion euro accounting for 33% of the region's total venture investment value. Poland again followed with 23% of the total or 22 milion euro. Both of these markets grew substantially in 2014– by 92% in the case of Hungary and by 41% in Poland. Together they accounted for over half of the venture capital investment by value across the CEE region in 2014.

Investment activity remained highly concentrated in the most populous EU markets in the region. Poland, the Czech Republic, Romania, and Hungary accounted for 82% of all Central and Eastern Europe investments in 2013, compared with 71% of all investments in 2012.

Poland was the largest and most active market for private equity in the CEE region, accounting for almost half the capital invested. However, it too reflected the region-wide fall in activity, with a 20% decline in investment to 380 milion euro in 2013, driven by a fall in buyout transactions. Nonetheless, Poland remained the largest buyout market in CEE in 2013, with 206 milion euro of buyout investments completed, or 48% of the region's total. Poland also took the lion's share of growth capital investments in 2013, with 150 million euro, or 58% of the region's total. Looking at the data in terms of companies, 89 businesses in Poland received investment in 2013, compared with 74 the previous year, driven by a near doubling

1 Central and European Countries: Bosnia and Herzegovina, Bulgaria, Croatia, the Czech Republic, Estonia, Hungary, Latvia, Lithuania, Macedonia, Moldova, Montenegro, Poland, Romania, Serbia, Slovakia, Slovenia and Ukraine.

of the number of venture financed companies to 59. At the same time, the number of buyout & growth financed companies declined by 32% to 30 (EVCA CEE 2013).

Lithuania and the Czech Republic were the next largest CEE venture capital markets in 2014, drawing ten milion euro and nine milion euro of investment respectively. While venture investment in Lithuania remained relatively stable compared to 2013, the venture investment value in the Czech Republic grew three-fold. The foregoing four leading countries accounted for 75% of all venture capital investments by value in the CEE region in 2014.

Figure 2: The value of investments VC funds in Poland in the years 2008–2014 (in thousand euro)

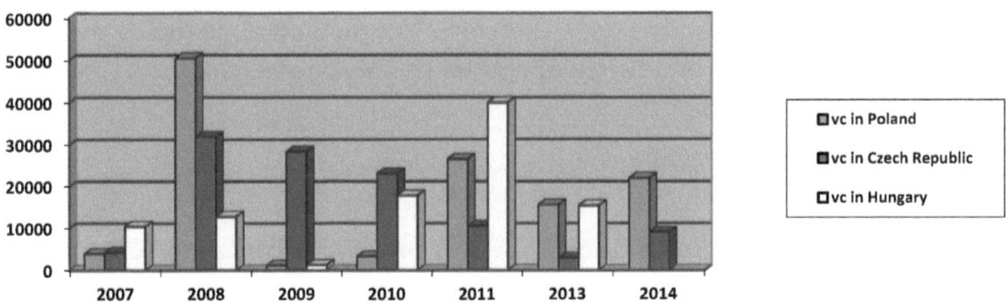

Source: own study based on EVCA CEE 2014, http://www.investeurope.eu/media/403969/EVCA-CEE-Statistics-2014.pdf, 23.02.2016

In the years 2008–2014 the prevailing interest in VC funds in Poland related to mature companies that allocate most of the invested amounts on buyouts (a buyout), refinancing (replacement capital) or restructuring (rescue / turnaround) companies. At relatively high levels during the analysis remained investments in companies at growth (growth), due to the interest funding companies with high growth potential. The growing popularity of investing PE/VC funds in the young company at the stage of start-up or seed since 2007 due to the creation of specialised investment funds, which at this stage are characterised by a relatively high risk.

Venture capital is located in the highly innovative branches, that is: biotechnologies, IT, pharmacy, medicine, fuel and energy industry, media and multimedia, services for the business, etc.

Conclusions

High-risk capital constitutes a significant alternative for available methods of financing investments, in particular of an innovative character. Financing modern technologies through PE/VC can be a great chance for their development. High-risk funds can stimulate innovativeness of enterprises. The reflection of such a situation can be seen in an improvement of effectiveness of investment outlays which cause improvement of management processes and innovation systems. Investors help portfolio companies to focus their own activities on innovations through introduction of criteria such as success probability and economic value of the innovation potential.

Despite the perspectives which stand before the sector of advanced technologies, Polish companies and scientific teams still have some difficulties in acquiring finances on development and commercialisation of the projects. However, it is to be expected, that the market VC will grow with the development of the financial market in Poland and will provide an important source of funding for innovative activities. The increasing competitiveness and the good condition of the Polish economy could bring new investors, therefore, this method of financing may become popular in Poland, and the prospects for the development of the VC market Poland may be promising.

Bibliography

Allen, W. D. i Hall, T. W., *Entrepreneurs investors, and Equity Financing*: A Resource-Economic Analysis. Review of Business, 2011, 31(2).

Bottazzi L., Da Rin M, *Venture Capital in Europe and the Financing of Innovative Companies*, Economic Policy, University of Munich, 2002.

Bertoni, F., Croce, A. i D'Adda, D., *Venture capital investments and patenting activity of high-tech start-ups: a micro-econometric firm-level analysis.* Venture Capital, 2010, 12(4).

Bertoni, F., Colombo, M. G. i Grilli, L., *Venture capital financing and the growth of high-tech start-ups: Disentangling treatment from selection effects.* Research Policy, 2011, 40(7), 1.

Brown James R., Martinsson G., Petersen B. C., *Do Financing Constraints Matter for R&D?* European Economic Review 56 (November) 2012.

Colombo, M. G., Grilli, L., Verga, C., *High-tech Start-up Access to Public Funds and Venture Capital: Evidence from Italy*, International Review of Applied Economics, (2007). 21(3).

Da Rin M., Nicodano G., Sembenelli A., *Public Policy and the Creation of Active Venture Capital Markets*, Working Paper n. 270, IGIER – Università Bocconi, October 2004.

Deshpande, R., Farley, J.U., Webster, F.E. Jr., *Corporate Culture, Customer Orientation and Innovativeness in Japanese Firms: A Quadrad Analysis*, Journal of Marketing, vol. 57, 1993, no. 1.

EVCA Annual Activity Statistics, http://www.evca.eu/research/activity-data/annual-activity-statistics/, 28.02.2016.

EVCA CEE 2014, http://www.investeurope.eu/media/403969/EVCA-CEE-Statistics-2014.pdf, 23.02.2016.

Hellman T., Pur M., *Venture Capital and the Professionalization of Start-Up Firms: Empirical Evidence*, The journal of finance, Vol. LVII, No. 1, Feb. 2002.

Lewandowska L., *Wybrane koncepcje finnasowania innowacyjności*, Zeszyty Naukowe Polskiego Towarzystwa Ekonomicznego nr 9, Kraków 2011.

Mikołajczyk, B. i Krawczyk. M., Aniołowie biznesu w sektorze MSP. Difin, Warszawa, 2007.

Węcławski, J., *Venture capital. Nowy instrument finansowania przedsiębiorstw.* PWN, Warszawa, 1997.

Subramania A., Nilakanta, S., *Organizational Innovativeness: Exploring the Relationship Between Organizational Determinants of Innovation, Types of Innovations, and Measures of Organizational Performance*, Omega, vol. 24, 1996, no. 6.

Yamin, S., Mavondo, F., Gunasekaran, A., Sarros, J., *A Study of Competitive Strategy, Organizational Innovation and Organizational Performance Among Australian Manufacturing Companies,* International Journal of Production Economics, vol. 52, 1997, no. 1.

Mesthene E.G., *Technological Change. Its Impact on Man and Society*, New York, 1970.

Zelek, A., *Nowoczesna inżynieria finansowa dla firm start-up w Polsce w latach 2009–2012. Raport z badań screeningowych,* Wydawnictwo Naukowe Zachodniopomorskiej Szkoły Biznesu w Szczecinie, Szczecin, 2013.

Chapter II
Law

Adil Korkmaz*

On the Measure of Quickness of Judging in Turkish Courts

Abstract In this study, the average periods of trials in Turkish courts are estimated by a formula proposed by this author in his earlier study. Those periods obviously give ideas about the quickness of judging in all the courts of Turkey because the shorter period of a trial implies the quicker judging. Based on the results of the estimated periods of trials, it is claimed that the average periods of trials in Turkish courts are highly long and they have no up or down trends except within the administrative cases.

Keywords: Judging, Quickness, Trial, Turkey, Justice, Estimation.

1. Introduction

In this study, the speed of trials is measured by the inverse of the average period of a trial. According to the formula derived previously by the author (Korkmaz, 2002), the average period of a trial can be estimated by three macro variables. The first one is denoted by X_t, which represents the number of cases postponed from the year $t - 1$ to the year t; the second one is denoted by Y_t, which represents the number of new cases in the year t; and the third one is denoted by Z_t, which represents the number of cases judged in the year t. Hence, the referred formula is as follows:

$$T = \frac{A(X_t + Y_t, X_t - Z_t)}{H(Y_t, Z_t)} \cdot 365 \text{ (in terms of days)}$$

where $A(X_t + Y_t, X_t - Z_t)$ is the arithmetic mean of $X_t + Y_t$ and $X_t - Z_t$ while $H(Y_t, Z_t)$ is the harmonic mean of Y_t and Z_t. The above variables can be obtained from the data given by Turkish Statistical Institution. The referred institution has been preparing the number of cases brought, the number of cases judged, and the number of cases postponed until next year. Note that the number of new cases equals "the number of cases brought" minus "the number of cases postponed from the previous year." The other variables are the same. Using the above formula and the data given by the referred institution, the average periods of trials in Turkish courts are given in the next section.

* Akdeniz University Department of Econometrics Faculty of Economics and Social Sciences

2. Estimations

Table 1: The Periods of Trial in According to Courts

Type of court	2005	2006	2007	2008	2009	2010	2011	2012	2013
Criminal Cases at First Order Courts	237	247	250	262	257	271	295	233	235
Civil Cases at First Order Courts	187	194	204	212	206	212	217	236	216
Administrative Courts	186	172	173	162	153	162	167	141	123
Criminal Cases at the Supreme Court	349	345	404	364	407	518	341	311	333
Civil Cases at the Supreme Court	76	83	94	117	141	161	162	133	119
Cases at the Council of State departments	397	407	394	434	501	575	508	536	464

Graphic 1: Change in the periods of criminal cases in first order courts

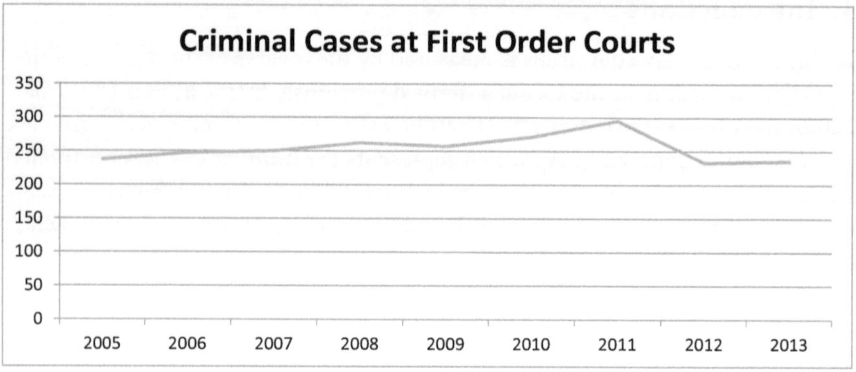

Graphic 2: Change in the periods of civil cases in first order courts

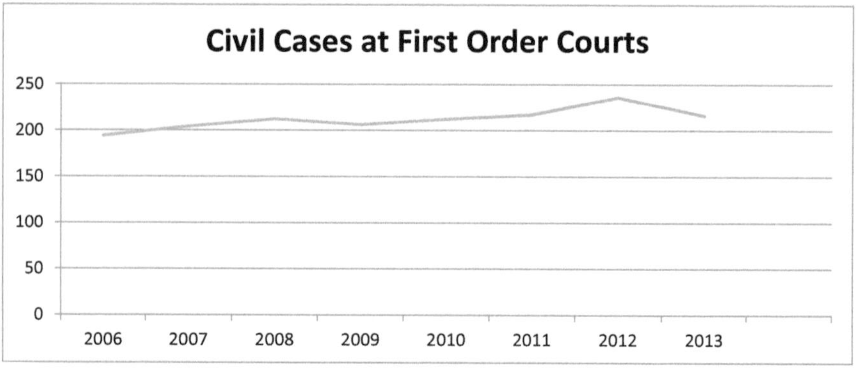

Graphic 3: Change in the periods of administrative cases in first order courts

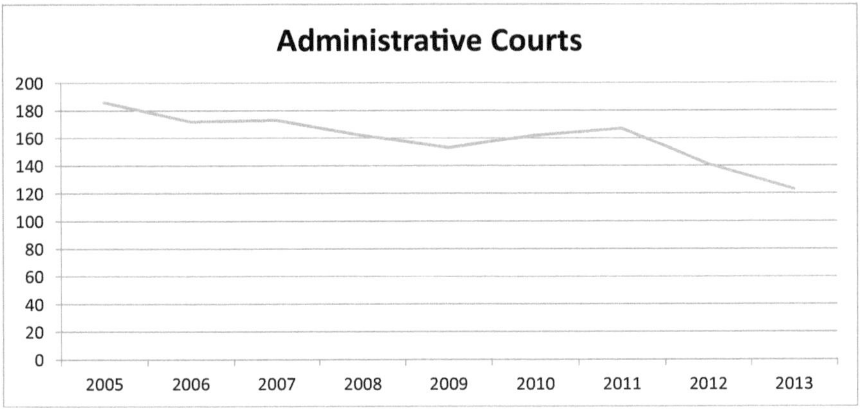

Graphic 4: Change in the periods of criminal cases in the Supreme Court

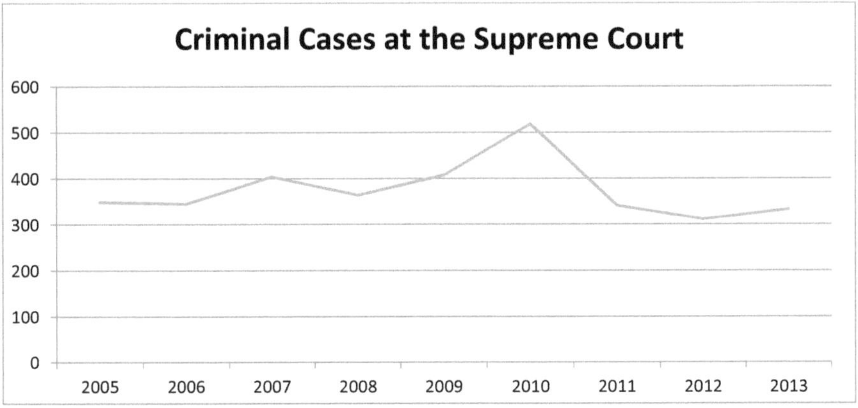

Graphic 5: Change in the periods of civil cases in the Supreme Court

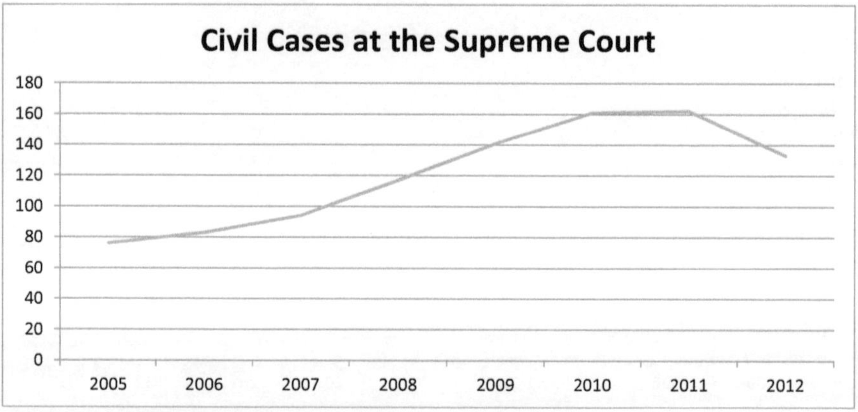

Graphic 6: Change in the periods of cases in the State Department

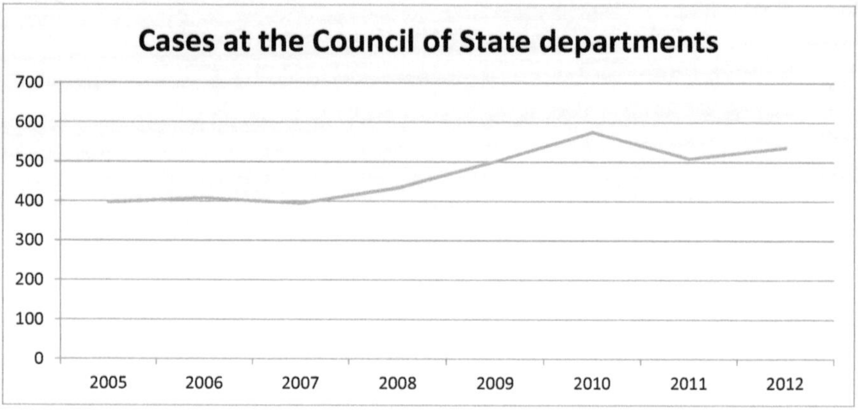

3. Conclusion

The first notable point is that, according to the above results, there is no up or down trend in the periods of trials in all the cases except the administrative cases in the first order courts. The second notable point is derived from this point. The existence of a down trend in administrative cases is the only point in favour of the increasing quickness in judging since the other cases are not hopeful. Another notable point is that the most dangerous point is related to the cases of the State department because the periods of trials exceed one year. Similar to this point, the period of the criminal cases in the Supreme Court reach to one year or exceed it. The other periods of trials unfortunately have a fluctuation of a long time period.

References

Korkmaz, A. (2002), Yargılama Sürelerinin Ölçümünde Kullanılabilir Bir Yöntemin Olasılıksal Temeli, İstatistik Araştırma Dergisi, C. 1, No 2: 75–83.

TÜİK Adalet İstatistikleri.

Appendix: Data

Cases by Type of Court

Criminal Courts

	2004	2005	2006	2007	2008	2009	2010	2011	2012	2013
Cases Brought	2888958	2673374	2709769	3058701	3060639	2949079	3129326	3096903	3180194	2785796
Cases Judged	1832204	1622748	1571930	1714883	1848906	1722284	1696635	1760476	2042675	1743048
Postponed Until Next Year	1056754	1050626	1137839	1343818	1211733	1226795	1432691	1336427	1137519	1042748

Civil Courts

	2004	2005	2006	2007	2008	2009	2010	2011	2012	2013
Cases Brought	2116746	2180305	2276843	2397875	2521418	2746968	2904853	2964061	2797566	3028375
Cases Judged	1398786	1422745	1456265	1497250	1568170	1719228	1799427	1858979	1707410	1868090
Postponed Until Next Year	717960	757560	820578	900625	953248	1027740	1105426	1105082	1090156	1160285

Administrative Courts

	2004	2005	2006	2007	2008	2009	2010	2011	2012	2013
Cases Brought	334684	390312	469308	478339	482251	515918	585233	584963	533426	579036
Cases Judged	215994	246046	313474	326826	337528	355473	386884	415672	405791	414644
Postponed Until Next Year	118690	144266	155834	151513	144723	160445	198349	169291	127635	164392

Cases at The Supreme Court

Criminal Cases

	2004	2005	2006	2007	2008	2009	2010	2011	2012	2013
Cases Brought	327873	336371	285209	323738	439922	522272	573576	758135	770815	730385
Cases Judged	139272	200236	144204	129420	197375	218201	209076	390806	429279	375250
Postponed Until Next Year	188601	136135	141005	194318	242547	304071	364500	367329	341536	355135

Civil Cases

	2004	2005	2006	2007	2008	2009	2010	2011	2012	2013
Cases Brought	361836	388106	395062	422081	446266	484751	524909	582559	659742	672061
Cases Judged	298259	318645	318355	326128	326109	334967	353095	395662	494228	507525
Postponed Until Next Year	63577	69461	76707	95953	120157	149784	171814	186897	165514	164536

Cases at The Council of State Departments

	2004	2005	2006	2007	2008	2009	2010	2011	2012	2013
Cases Brought	141339	157163	169924	206701	248678	275598	297841	345187	350142	357495
Cases Judged	59560	69484	73123	88278	99284	106959	103880	137921	140815	167446
Postponed Until Next Year	75649	81728	94629	118423	149394	168639	193961	207266	209327	190049

Source: Judicial Statistics 2013.

Volkan Özçelik*

Peremptory Term in the Civil Procedure Law

Introduction

One of the purposes of civil procedure law is to provide the provision of a subjective right violated regarding private law via courts. The conflict arising between parties is desired to be eliminated via the courts. For this purpose, procedural due process is implemented during the period from the opening of the case and until the finalisation of the judgment (Turkish Supreme Court, Decision of joint chambers, 1964).

Procedural due processes, as is known, are divided into two according to the person making the process (Üstündağ, p. 239; Karslı, p. 415; Pekcanıtez & Atalay & Özekes, p. 253). Court procedural due processes are carried out by the court and party procedural due processes are carried out by the parties involved in the proceedings. The classification for procedural due processes shows its importance about the sanction of the peremptory term. That is: both court procedural due processes and party procedural due processes are generally required to be performed within a certain term. However, periods anticipated for party procedural actions are of the nature of forfeiting the right. If the party fails to perform the procedural due process envisaged within the term prescribed by law, as a rule, he is not allowed to do it again (Kuru, p. 644; Pekcanıtez & Atalay & Özekes, p. 263.). But the failure of the court to perform the court procedural due process within the prescribed term does not lead to the same result. Then, the determination whether the term provided for parties is a peremptory term is of utmost importance. Therefore, we have selected "Peremptory Term in the Civil Procedure Law" as the subject of the paper.

I. The Concept of Peremptory Term

Peremptory term can be defined in the following way by the form of its appearance: it is the term prescribed by law or in the decision of the judge in accordance with the procedure without being prescribed by the law for the party to perform the procedural due process.

* Ondokuz Mayıs University, Faculty of Law volkan.ozcelik@omu.edu.tr

The nature of forfeiting the right of the peremptory term is a rule applicable for the parties. Although the procedural due process in a proceeding is performed by the parties and the court, it does not affect the validity of the process even if the court makes the transaction after the time specified in the law. The term indicated for the court by the law, is of a regulatory quality rather than a nature of forfeiting the right (Kuru, p. 644; Karslı, p. 449; Pekcanıtez&Atalay&Özekes, p. 263).

II. Reasons for Binding Party Procedural Due Process to Peremptory Term

There are various reasons for binding party procedural due process to peremptory term. It can be summarised as ensuring justice as soon as possible; preventing arbitrariness, the court from being engaged in the same job for a long time, in other words, from the position of not allocating enough time for other litigations or jobs; ensuring the finalisation of the case in accordance with the mandatory norms of supranational and national character in a reasonable period of time, in other words, fairness of the proceeding (Turkish Supreme Court, 2013).

To ensure the right to a fair trial, the state must do a number of positive regulations. In order for this right to be considered as not violated, the states are obliged to establish the necessary systems and check if the established system is functioning effectively or not for the establishment of the right (Pekcanıtez, p. 51). Of course, binding procedural due process to a certain period of time serves as an effective operation of the system (Turkish Constitutional Court, 2014). Especially, binding procedural due process to peremptory term and the presence of the threat of not being able to perform a process that is not performed during the (peremptory) term serves to complete the trial within a reasonable time (Turkish Supreme Court, 2013).

An important reason for binding procedural due process to peremptory term is to prevent the unnecessary prolongation of the proceeding. The person who has been given peremptory term and who does not want to lose the right side must make the process in that period. Since failure to perform the process in the peremptory term would lead to a loss of right, it must be used in accordance with the purpose. In other words, the peremptory term should not be transformed into a tool for dismissing the case.

On the other hand, the proceedings' not being prolonged and being completed in a reasonable time with the help of peremptory term, are for the benefit of the public as well the parties. Since the courts will not have to deal with a case for a very long time, the workload of the courts does not increase. This in turn, eventually serves as a more efficient and effective functioning of the judicial activity of the country as a whole. In addition, the completion of the trial within a reasonable time, increases trust in the judicial community. The individual, when his right is violated, believes to gain his right within a reasonable period of time. In contrast, violations of human rights can be avoided. Because in a society where no one's right is violated or in case of violation where justice is secured as soon as possible, decrease of conflicts is a likely result (Turkish Supreme Court, 2013).

III. Types of Peremptory Term by the Form of its Appearance

According to the Civil Procedure Code Article 94, which regulates the peremptory term, peremptory term can occur in two ways.

A. Peremptory Term Determined by Law

The term set by code is peremptory (CPC, Art. 94/1). When we look at the wording of the provision, both for the court and parties, it is understood that the terms set are peremptory. However, the sanction and the nature of the term set in the law are different. While the term set for the court is of regulatory characteristics, the term set for the parties is of a nature of forfeiting the right (Kuru, p. 644; Pekcanıtez&Atalay&Özekes, p. 263).

Besides, the court must perform the procedural due process within the term prescribed for the court. In civil procedure law, for the proceeding to be completed within a reasonable length of time, each procedural due process must be made in due time. If the Code has bound the court procedural due process to a certain term, it must be done in this term; if it has not, it must be done in a reasonable term. However, as mentioned above, failure to make the process within the prescribed term does not invalidate the process. Persons, whose rights have been violated due to these reasons, can sue the state for damages (CPC, Art. 46).

The "Code" clause in the provision does not only refer to the Civil Procedure Code. The legislation regulating all the procedural terms for the parties is included in the wording of "the code" (Turkish Supreme Court, 2013).

B. Peremptory Term Determined by the Judge

The judge, in an interim decision gives time to the party, two different situations arise with regard to stating whether the term is peremptory or not.

1. *Non-statement of the Judge on the Peremptory Nature of the Term in the Interim Decision*

If the judge does not state that the term is peremptory and the party fails to perform the procedural due process during this term, he gives extra an term on request. The second term given in this manner is peremptory in accordance with the code even if the judge has not specified in the interim decision (CPC, Art. 94/2).

In order for the judge to be able to set an extra term, he cannot have decided on the peremptory term. Indeed, when we look at the wording of the provision, it is understood that the judge can decide that the term is peremptory, if he has not, the party can ask for an extra term. If the party does not perform the process despite the decision of the judge on the peremptory term, the court does not give extra term. Because, in this case, procedural acquired right arises in favour of the opposite party. For example, if the plaintiff does not deposit exploration expenses although the judge has given the plaintiff peremptory term for it, the judge decides that the plaintiff has given up depending on evidence of exploration. The peremptory term of the Court is bound by the interim decision (Kuru, p. 644).

2. *Statement of the Judge on the Peremptory Nature of the Term in the Interim Decision*

If the judge has requested the interested party to perform the procedural due process in a peremptory term in an interim decision duly given, the term given is clearly a peremptory term. For example, the term in the decision for the party wishing to apply for evidence of exploration to deposit expenses of litigation required for exploration to the court's cashier in the time specified in the decision of the court duly given, is a peremptory term (Üstündağ, p. 255; Kuru, p. 644; Karslı, p. 450; Pekcanıtez&Atalay&Özekes, p. 265).

In the interim decision of the judge regarding giving a term, the judge may have some reasons for specification of the term as a peremptory term. The judge may act upon the general attitude of the party requesting the term. The judge may want to prevent the party from requesting an extra term because of not carrying out the procedure during the time given. Or, he may be convinced that the term is sufficient to perform the given procedure. In the interim decision that the judge has stated the peremptory term, he must also write the reasons for his decision. For whatever the reason is, he must decide with satisfactory reasons. Because the term set for the first time is not essentially peremptory. The judge has to write the reasons for it since he is going beyond the original (Yavuz, p. 135).

The following requirements must be met for the term to be peremptory term given by the judge (Turkish Supreme Court, 2013):

1. The decision which decides on peremptory term must be written clearly.
2. Tasks to be carried out must be specified in the decision.
3. The term given must be long enough to carry out the tasks.
4. Tasks requested to be performed must be necessary for the proceeding.
5. Tasks requested to be performed must be a realisable type for the party.
6. The results of failure to comply with the term should be described in the decision and the party should be warned.

IV. Results of Peremptory Term

The right to process given to the party who fails to perform the process in the peremptory term is eliminated (CPC, Art. 94/3).

The sanction of a peremptory term has a nature of forfeiting the right as can be understood from the expression of code. The right of the party to perform the process and obtain the expected benefit from this process is eliminated limited to the terms and results no matter what the process is (Yılmaz, p. 3185). If the judge decides on a peremptory term for the party to present evidence and deposit advance of evidence and the party fails to deposit the advance required during that term, he shall be considered as if has given up depending on that evidence (Kuru, p. 644).

The judge depends on a peremptory term. Because when a peremptory term is set, procedural acquired right arises in favour of the opposite party. The judge cannot make a decision that will eliminate the procedural acquired right. Also, the judge takes a peremptory term and effects of it into account ex officio.

During the peremptory term, if the party is unable to perform the process because of a reason not caused by his fault and if the conditions are appropriate, the method of reinstatement can be employed (Kuru, p. 647; Üstündağ, p. 255; Tercan, s. 1 etc.; Karslı, p. 451; Pekcanıtez & Atalay & Özekes, p. 274).

Conclusion

1. Peremptory term can occur in two ways. Firstly, the term set by law is peremptory. Second, peremptory term may be in question as a result of the decision of the judge.
2. At the first time, the judge may set peremptory term in his decision duly given.
3. Or he does not set peremptory term in the first decision. When the party exceeding the term asks for extra term, he sets a second term. The second term given by the judge is peremptory even if he has not specified it in the decision.
4. The main sanction of peremptory term is for parties. The right of the party who fails to perform the process during the peremptory term is eliminated.

5. The judge must take the presence and effects of peremptory term into account ex officio.
6. In case the judge gives a party peremptory term, a procedural acquired right arises in favour of the opposite party. Therefore, it is not possible for the judge to act in a way to eliminate this right or make a procedural due process.

Bibliography

Books and Articles

Karslı, A. (2012). *Medeni Muhakeme Hukuku*. 3. Baskı. İstanbul: Alternatif.

Kuru, B. (2015). *Medeni Usul Hukuku Ders Kitabı*. İstanbul: Legal.

Üstündağ, S. (1973). *Medeni Yargılama Hukuku*. İstanbul.

Pekcanıtez, H. (1997). Medeni Yargıda Adil Yargılanma Hakkı. *İzmir Barosu Dergisi*. S. 2. pp. 35–55.

Pekcanıtez. H.&Atalay. O. & Özekes. M. (2013). *Medeni Usul Hukuku*. 14. Baskı, Ankara: Yetkin.

Tercan, E. (2006). *Medeni Usul Hukukunda (Kesin Sürelerin Kaçırılması Halinde-Hali Sabıka İcra) Eski Hale Getirme*. Ankara: Yetkin.

Yavuz, N. (1975). Hukuk Usulünde Müddetler. *Ankara Barosu Dergisi*. C. 32. S. 2. pp. 133–140.

Yılmaz, E. Hukuk Muhakemeleri Kanununda Süreler. *Yaşar Üniversitesi Hukuk Fakültesi Dergisi*. C. 8, Özel Sayı, Prof. Dr. Aydın Zevkliler'e Armağan. pp. 3167–3190.

Case Law of Courts

Turkish Supreme Court. Decision of Joint Chambers. Date of Decisions 07.12.1964. Numbered 3/5.

Turkish Supreme Court. Assembly of Civil Chambers. Date of Decision 30.01.2013. Numbered 19-671/151.

Turkish Constitutional Court. Date of Decision 03.04.2014. Application Number 2013/5881.

Turkish Supreme Court. Assembly of Civil Chambers. Date of Decision 30.01.2013. Numbered 19671/151.

Ibid.

Turkish Supreme Court. 18 th Civil Chamber. Date of Decision 14.05.2013. Numbered 6409/8296.

Turkish Supreme Court. Assembly of Civil Chambers. Date of Decision 30.01.2013. Numbered 19-671/151.

Fatmagül Kale Özçelik*

The Right to Free Elections in Terms of the European Court of Human Rights and Turkish Constitutional Law

Introduction

The 1950 European Convention on Human Rights (ECHR) has a unique importance in international human rights law with its effective protection mechanism that it envisaged. Undoubtedly, this importance stems from the dynamic interpretation of the rights which were covered by the Convention and the respect shown to the necessary rights through case law by the European Court of Human Rights (ECtHR) which operates under the Convention. However this respect shown to the rights with case law has not yet been realised for the right to free elections regulated in the Additional Protocol to the Convention. One reason is the inability of the convention-makers to have a common conclusion on the right from the very beginning in preparatory studies. Therefore, the right to free elections is regulated in Article 3 of the Additional Protocol No. 1 to the European Convention on Human Rights. Another reason and perhaps as a result of the first reason, is due to the formation of the regulation of Article 3. Since the wording style of the article brings the obligation of the state to the forefront, rather than an emphasis on individual rights, the Court emphasises in its decisions that the states have broad discretion concerning the scope of this right. Nevertheless, the right to free elections is one of the most important rights in the realisation of effective political democracy regarded as the common heritage by The European Court of Human Rights. In fact, it remains important as a single political right regulated by the Convention.

In our study, it is aimed to specify the scope of the right to free elections within the framework of European Convention on Human Rights and case law of Court. While trying to do this, the right to free elections will primarily be put forward as a human right. Subsequently, the right to vote and stand for elections determined by the ECtHR case law as elements of the right to free elections will be discussed. While doing so, the regulations of the 1982 Constitution on the right to free elections will be discussed.

* Ondokuz Mayıs University, Faculty of Law, fatmagul.kale@omu.edu.tr

I. The Scope of the Right to Free Elections

According to the third article of the Additional Protocol No. 1 titled "the right to free elections," "the High Contracting Parties undertake to hold free elections at reasonable intervals by secret ballot, under conditions which will ensure the free expression of the opinion of the people in the choice of the legislature."

In the 1982 Constitution, the right to free elections is not regulated as a single norm. Regulations concerning election are included in a separate article. In this context, Article 67 of the Constitution may be considered as basic norms governing the elements of the right to free elections which will be discussed below. According to the first paragraph of this article held under the title "right to vote, right to stand for elections and right to engage in political activity," citizens have the right to vote, to be elected, to engage in political activities independently or in a political party, and to take part in a referendum. The second paragraph of the article regulates the principles of elections. According to this, elections and referenda shall be held under the direction and supervision of the judiciary, in accordance with the principles of free, equal, secret, direct, universal suffrage, and public counting of the votes. In the third paragraph, 18 was determined as the age to vote in elections and to take part in referenda. In the continuing paragraphs of the article, it is mentioned that the exercise of these rights shall be regulated by law, privates and corporals at arms, cadets, and convicts in penal execution institutions excluding those convicted of negligent offences shall not vote, the necessary measures to be taken to ensure the safety of voting and the counting of the votes in penal execution institutions and prisons shall be determined by the Supreme Board of Election and such voting is held under the on-site direction and supervision of the authorised judge, the electoral laws shall be drawn up so as to reconcile the principles of fair representation and stability of government and amendments to the electoral laws shall not apply to the elections to be held within one year from the entry into force date of the amendments.

There are other regulations that may be associated with the right to free elections in the Constitution. Article 76 under the right to be elected regulates the eligibility to the deputy. Article 77, which regulates the rule that elections shall be held every four years, is also a regulation located in the subject of the right to free elections. As it will be understood, regulations on the right to free elections in the Constitution are broader than the norm held in Article 3 of the Additional Protocol. However, the ECtHR preserves the guarantees in the Constitution through case law.

A. Is Free Election a Right That can Directly be Requested?

The rights held in the ECHR and its Protocols commonly have the form of a formulation as "Everyone has the right to ..." However, in Article 3, the expression "The High Contracting Parties undertake..." is used. As a result of this regulation, it creates an impression that Article 3 does not recognise rights to individuals directly but poses obligations to contracting states. However, the form of expression of the right to free elections does not show that it is different from other rights.

The reason for this form of expression is the importance of the obligation to fulfil the requirement as well as the will to make a more significant emphasis on conventional obligation and respect and protection obligations of states within the scope of this right. The scope of Article 3 has not been limited to the wording by the Court. It is expressed clearly in the case laws that the article does not only envisage obligations to contracting states but also contains individual rights. Accordingly, Article 3 is a right directly applicable and can be made the subject of litigation by nature (ECtHR, Matheiu-Mohin Clerfayt v. Belgium, 1978, para. 48–52).

B. Application Area of the Right to Free Elections

According to the wording of Article 3 of the Additional Protocol, the right to free elections envisaged in the article is a right only valid in elections of the legislature (Metin, 2007, p. 127). Only national parliaments should not be understood from the concept of "The legislature." Elections of organs with legislative powers operating in the international arena also fall within the scope of the legislature. An example of it is the implementation of the right to free elections in European Parliament elections (Çavuşoğlu, 1999–2000, p. 14).

The contracting state does not have an obligation to determine a unicameral or bicameral legislature in its constitutional order. In this regard, the constitutional orders of the contracting states are respected. However the ECtHR, if the bicameral system is in question, requires the implementation of the terms of the right to free elections in at least one of the parliaments (ECtHR, Mathieu-Mohin and Clerfayt v. Belgium, 1987, para. 53). In this regard, the responsibility of establishing a legislature created with the direct election by the people arises for the contracting state (Koçak, 2006, p. 129–130).

In addition to this, the right to free elections is not included in the application areas in the election of local government organs which do not display a legislative activity or carry out administrative tasks (ECtHR, Xuereb v. Malta, 2000). Referenda, plebiscites, and elections of heads of state are also excluded from the scope of the right to free elections (Koçak, 2006, p. 130).

The fact that the right to free elections only finds an application area in the elections of the legislature and it is invalid in the elections except this where individuals use the right to vote undoubtedly narrows the scope of Article 3 of the Convention. Here, the Court selects the idiomatic interpretation method strictly. However, considering the teleological interpretation, the application area of the right should be interpreted broadly to accomplish the purpose of preparation of the Convention. Only with such an interpretation can the ideal of a democratic state of law effectual in a common European public order be realised (Anayurt, 2004, p. 142). It should be noted that, while the ECtHR limits the application area of the right to free elections to parliaments with legislative activities; the Constitutional Court, has also implemented the regulations regarding the right to vote and to stand for elections in the upcoming elections of the administration, discipline, and control committees of professional organisations qualifying as public institutions (Turkish Constitutional Court, 2011). Thus, the Constitutional Court has found a more expansionary review (Akbulut, 2013, p. 544).

C. Elements of the Right to Free Elections

1. The First Element of the Right to Free Elections: The Right to Vote/ Suffrage

The right to vote is characterised by the active dimension of the right to free elections arranged in Article 3 of the Protocol by the ECtHR. Voting in free and single-level elections in which the principles of general, equal, secret ballot are accepted and carried out at regular intervals constitutes the basis of a democratic society. However, the right to vote is valid only for the candidates and parties written on the ballot. Therefore, this right does not include the freedom in the form of voting for a banned candidate or party (Altınkök, 2015, p. 47).

Today, widespread application of the states, is taking away the use of the right to elect certain people deprived of their liberty. Status of prisoners regarding this right is not regulated explicitly in the provision of the ECHR, which regulates the right to vote. However, the ECtHR accepts that restrictions on electoral rights can be imposed on an individual who has, for example, seriously abused a public position or whose conduct threatened to undermine the rule of law or democratic foundations (ECtHR, Hirst v. United Kingdom (Grand Chamber), 2005, para. 71). Therefore, while assessing the prisoners' right to vote, the ECtHR considers modern penal policies and understanding of the protection of human rights primarily in possible restrictions to the right. According to the Court, automatic and indiscriminate restrictions concerning prisoners' right to vote result in violation of the right because they do not fit for purpose of existence of the right. In this regard, the contracting states must set the border of the right taking the gravity of the crime, the term of imprisonment and the individual situation of the prisoner into account. According to the ECHR, as long as it is based on a decision given in accordance with the law, the only rights that the prisoners will automatically be deprived of are the right to liberty and security of person. Legitimate reasons for the deprivation of other rights must be the target and application of it proportional to the target.

In this context, in the doctrine, the rule located in paragraph 5 of Article 67 of the Constitution "convicts in prisons excluding those convicted of negligent offences cannot vote "is expressed to bring a ban which has a very high conflict potential with the ECtHR case law." Accordingly, the relevant regulation of the Constitution is a regulation including a holistic ban that ignores the gravity of the crime, the term of imprisonment, and the convicted person's individual situation (Akbulut, 2013, p. 546).

The Court does not find the issue of the necessity of residence requirement to be entitled to vote against the Convention (ECtHR, Melnychenko v. Ukraine, 2004, para. 56). In doing so, it lists the legitimising criteria. First, citizens living abroad may not be the direct addressees of the political development of the country. Yet, these people may have little impact in the determination of the candidates to be elected and the formation of the programs. It cannot be mentioned that they are directly affected by the election of legislators and the regulations made by the parliament. Finally, the legislator may also have a reasonable idea of reducing the voice of citizens residing abroad on issues mainly concerning the citizens living in the country. Given these conditions, limitation of the voting rights of citizens living abroad is not considered as a violation of their right to vote (ECtHR, Sitaropoulos and Giakoupoulos v. Grece, 2012).

In the exercise of the right to vote, the common practice of states is that they require a certain age limit. Voting age varies from state to state among European countries. The ECtHR does not consider the necessity of voting age as a violation of right stating that it might be in order to ensure that those participating in the election process have reached a certain maturity. However, it is also stated that higher age limit regulations which are not based on any legitimate reasons would violate the right to vote (ECtHR, Hirst v. United Kingdom (Grand Chamber), 2005, para. 62).

2. *The Second Element of the Right to Free Elections: The Right to Stand for Election*

According to the ECtHR, the right to stand for elections is the passive dimension of the right to free elections. Unlike the right to vote, contracting states may provide more stringent requirements to be elected to the National Parliament.

The Court explains this from this point of view that states may have a unique institutional structure and in a democratic state the Parliament, which has the primary role and legislative authority, may have some legitimate interests to safeguard functioning normally (ECtHR, Melnychenko v. Ukraine, 2004, para. 57).

The right to stand for elections is not a right of absolute character. This right can be subject to certain restrictions as the right to vote. Contracting States have discretionary powers in the determination of the constitutional provisions relating to the status of parliamentarians including the criteria governing the qualifications for candidacy in elections. The ECtHR gives a wide discretionary power to states in respect of who will the right to stand for elections be used by; however, finds restrictions imposed on the right which are meaningless, unexplained why needed and incompatible with the essence of the right contrary to the right to stand for elections (ECtHR, Ahmet and Others v. United Kingdom, 1998, para. 72–76). Also the Court rules that, in the exercise of the right to stand for elections which is one of the main fundamental rights, excessively formalistic interpretation of the legislation is a violation of the right to stand for elections (ECtHR, Namat Aliyev v. Azerbaijan, 2010). In reaching this conclusion, the Court relies on a document called "Code of Good Practice in Electoral Matters" adopted by the Venice Commission. Despite the strict control of the conditions laid down by states for the right to stand for elections by the ECtHR, it is observed that in our domestic law, applications in this respect are rejected by the Constitutional Court without being subject to control (Turkish Constitutional Court, 2015).

We see that the ECtHR investigates issues such as depositing a certain amount of money on consignment to be a candidate in the scope of the right to stand for elections, candidates being banned from the candidacy due to misleading information, requirement of knowing a specific language to be a candidate, the minimum residence condition, ethnicity of the candidates and behaviours or some political activities of the candidate posing an obstacle to be elected. For example, the ECtHR did not find banning the candidacy of persons who have worked in certain public offices for a period of more than three months within three years preceding the election in any electoral district contrary to the Convention. According to the Court, such a restriction safeguards candidates with different political opinions to have the opportunity to reach the public equally. It is also expressed in the decision that public officials are sometimes in a more advantageous position compared to other candidates. It should be stated that the regulations regarding the local government officials' leaving the job before the election would not create a breach of Article 3 of the Protocol.

Fees that have to be paid in advance for a candidacy have also been brought before the ECtHR within the scope of the right to free elections. In the application against Ukraine, the Court concluded that The Constitutional Court found the fees constitutional, the right to stand for elections was not violated taking into account that low-paid employees could be candidates in the region where the applicant was a candidate.

The inability to use the right to stand for elections which constitutes the passive dimension of the right to free elections effectively by the people who have been elected also brings the violation of the right to the agenda. Accordingly, for example, if the person is elected but it is decided to annul the election results by the state for a reason, the right to stand for elections is violated in favour of the person. The Court reaches this conclusion from the viewpoint of justified expectations of the voters to be represented in the national parliament by a person elected.

D. Election Systems

Article 3 of the Additional Protocol regulating the right to free elections, has not essentially determined the basic principles of the method of election of the legislature. According to this regulation, the legislature must be determined in conditions that the people are safeguarded to freely express their thoughts and as a result of free elections which are made at reasonable intervals and respect the principle of secret ballot. Apart from these conditions, the aforementioned regulation does not specify which method will be valid for the formation of the legislature in the contracting states. As a result of this, states are not under obligation to put one of the single-stage elections, proportional representation systems, or majority systems into effect in their domestic law.

The applications of electoral threshold accepted by the contracting states were brought before the ECtHR claiming that they violate the right to free elections (ECtHR, Yumak and Sadak v. Turkey, 2007). The Court concluded that this Article is not violated considering the application of electoral threshold in the context of the broad discretion of the government. However, the Court stated that the common practice in Europe was not at such a high rate and the rate determined by Turkey was excessively high. The decision on whether or not this rate undermines the essence of the right to free elections is open to criticism.

Conclusion

The right to free elections, which is the only political right guaranteed by the ECHR and which finds provision in the 1982 Constitution, is a fundamental right in a real democratic regime. Also Article 3, which regulates the most basic element of democracy, has a special importance in the Convention system. Democracy constitutes the essential element of the European common public order and the rights guaranteed by the right to free elections are of great importance in the establishment and protection of the foundation of an effective democracy governed by the rule of law. Therefore, this right must have an individual-based, review through case law by the European Court of Human Rights as well as the Constitutional Court. Thus, the protection area of the right will be expanded further in favour of individuals.

Bibliography

Books and Articles

Akbulut, O. (2013). İnsan Hakları Avrupa Sözleşmesi ve Anayasa-Anayasa Mahkemesine Bireysel Başvuru Kapsamında Bir İnceleme. Sibel İnceoğlu. (Eds). *Serbest Seçim Hakkı* (pp. 543–556), İstanbul: Beta Yayıncılık.

Altınkök, S. (2015). Avrupa İnsan Hakları İçtihadları Açısından Serbest Seçim Hakkı. *Uyuşmazlık Mahkemesi Dergisi*. Sayı: 5, 37–81.

Anayurt, Ö. (2004). *Avrupa İnsan Hakları Hukukunda Kişisel Başvuru Yolu*. Ankara: Seçkin Yayıncılık.

Çavuşoğlu, N. (1999–2000). Masstricht Antlaşması ve İnsan Hakları Avrupa Sözleşmesi Hukuku: D. Matthews/ Birleşik Krallık'a Karşı Davası (II). *İstanbul Üniversitesi Siyasal Bilgiler Fakültesi Dergisi*, Yayın No: 21–22, 13–18.

Koçak, M. (2006). Seçim Sistemleri ve Demokrasi Karşılaştırmalı Analiz: İHAM ve AB Ölçütleri. *Anayasa Yargısı Dergisi*, 23, 115–132.

Metin, Y. (2007). AİHS Çerçevesinde ve AİHM Kararları Işığında Serbest Seçim Hakkı. *Liberal Düşünce*, Yıl: 12, S. 47–48, 109–141.

Case Law of Courts

ECtHR, Matheiu-Mohin Clerfayt v. Belgium, Application No. 9267/81, 02.03.1978

ECtHR, Yumak and Sadak v. Turkey, Application No. 10226/03, 30.01.2007.

ECtHR, Ahmet and Others v. United Kingdom, Application No. 65/1997, 02.09.1998.

ECtHR, Namat Aliyev v. Azerbaijan, Application No. 18705/06, 08.04.2010.

ECtHR, Sitaropoulos and Giakoupoulos v. Grece, Application No. 42202/07, 12.03.2012.

ECtHR, Hirst v. United Kingdom (Grand Chamber), Application No. 74025/01, 06.10.2005.

ECtHR, Melnychenko v. Ukraine, Application No. 17707/02, 19.10.2004.

ECtHR, Russian Conservative Party of Entrepreneurs v. Russia, Application No. 55066/00-55638/00, 11.01.2007.

ECtHR, Hirst v. Birleşik Krallık (Grand Chamber), Application No: 74025/01, 06.10.2005.

ECtHR, Hirst v. Birleşik Krallık (Grand Chamber), Application No: 74025/01, 06.10.2005.

ECtHR, Melnychenko v. Ukraine, Application No: 17707/02, 19.10.2004.

ECtHR, Sitaropoulos and Giakoupoulos v. Grece, Application No: 42202/07, 12.03.2012.

ECtHR, Mathieu-Mohin ve Clerfayt v. Belgium, Application No. 9267/81.

ECtHR, Xuereb v. Malta, Application No. 52492/99, 15.06.2000.

ECtHR, Matheiu-Mohin Clerfayt v. Belgium, Application No. 9267/81, 02.03.1978.

ECtHR, Matthews v. United Kingdom, Application No. 24833/94, 18.02.1999.

Turkish Constitutional Court, Atilla Sertel, Application No. 6723/2015, 14.07.2015.

Turkish Constitutional Court, 2008/80, 2011/81, 18.05.2011.

Hakan Karakehya*

Information, Power, and Law

1. Introduction

In today's society, the importance of information increases constantly, as it is often stated. Knowing about the universe, society, people, nature, and the rules that control the nature brings ease of life to individuals or groups as well as provides them with an area of power to the extent of their knowledge. In this regard, getting to know things is usually achieved by examination and surveillance. Therefore, it can be stated that one needs to know to get power, and surveillance to get to know. In order to be in power and ensure its continuity, those who are in power who need information and thus surveillance often use law as a means in this respect.

By revealing the relationship between information and power, this study examines the surveillance activities conducted by those in power and the use of law as a means in these activities. In our opinion, analysing the relationship between information, power, and law would be influential for us to determine our stance in life as well as differentiate our views on some legal norms. In this context, the study is expected to make a contribution to the literature. On the other hand, the primary method employed in the study consists of putting forward our views within a cause-effect relationship by making use of different views in the doctrine.

2. Information-Power Relationship

There is a close relationship between power and information. As it is often stated, all individuals who are in power need information. Information legitimises power and makes it effective. Possessing information means having power (Bauman, 1996: p. 62). If you aim to control an object, an individual or a society, you first need to know them well, and this is possible by surveillance into their lives. In this sense, there is a close relationship between power and information.

Although this aspect of the power-information relationship is frequently emphasised, another aspect, which is the information production of those in power, is observed to be relatively neglected. In fact, as information serves power, power serves information. For example, even if the official language of a state were to be French or a geographical location were to be called differently, the information in

* Anadolu University, Faculty of Law, hkarakehya@anadolu.edu.tr

the social domain would change after those in power say that the official language is English, or change the name of that location; in other words, the new information has been produced by the power. In addition, those in power are observed to develop a new discourse that overlaps with their ideology in areas of social sciences such as history and sociology, and are inclined to disseminate this to a wide audience through the education system they control. Therefore, there is a bidirectional connection between the two concepts (Hunt and Wickham, 1994: p. 12).

Foucault emphasises this bidirectional relationship between the concepts of power and information. According to him, while information or knowing about something is required for the existence and continuity of power, those in power also produce information. Even the development of mere scientific knowledge is evolved depending on power relationships (Foucault, 2003: p. 248).

3. Surveillance as a Method of Power for Acquiring Information and Its Types

Surveillance can be described as monitoring individuals, groups or society in general for the purpose of acquiring information or disciplining people, or both. Contrary to what is believed, this monitoring does not usually come out in the form of directly observing the movements of individuals or groups, or social preferences and events. It can also be done by storing information and private data about individuals. For this reason, the concept of surveillance comprises a much broader meaning than its daily usage.

The concept of surveillance can be considered from two different perspectives. The first meaning refers to storing information about individuals, groups or the society which can be used to control their behaviours, whereas the second meaning includes directly observing the behaviours of individuals or groups, or the social behaviours in general (Giddens, 2008: p. 24). The first meaning can be named as storage surveillance, and the second one as observance surveillance.

Some authors argue that technically, for surveillance, there should be an authority relationship between the one who is surveilling and the one who is surveilled, which we agree with in principle. However, even though there is no authority relationship, we think that observance to form an authority relationship in the future should be evaluated within the concept of surveillance. In particular, such an authoritative connection can be established in observance relationships that emerge in the form of boss-worker or state-citizen; on the other hand, no such relationship exists in observing and storing activities of business firms related to customer behaviours which we evaluate in the scope of surveillance. However, these firms conduct such activities to direct individuals by observing their buying behaviours. Therefore, since there is an authority relationship with the person being surveilled however indirect and weak as a result of the observance, these activities should be considered within the scope of the concept of surveillance. At the same time, because there is no authority relationship within this scope in individuals' observance activities on other people merely because of curiosity and to make an evaluation about them (e.g. peeping into a neighbour's house, following what friends buy and sell online), these activities should not be considered within the scope of surveillance.

4. Surveillance to Acquire Information

4.1 Surveillance to Maintain Power By Acquiring Information

Being in power is a difficult task and requires foreseeing oppositional social movements and taking precautions against them beforehand. For this reason, individuals in power often use surveillance to determine the hazards that can come out with regard to their future, and take precautions against these issues. In this context, intelligence agencies of states meet this need of those in power by making use of technological facilities that are becoming increasingly technological. Besides, law enforcement officers such as gendarme and police are frequently used for intelligence purposes.

Surveillance to remain in power shows itself not only in the macro level as in the state-society relationship, but also in the micro level as in power relationships. Therefore, those in power would like to have information resources among foremen/workers, directors/officers, rectors/deans and faculty members to deliver complaints about it to the superior authorities or organise others to take a stand towards it. As a matter of fact, maintaining power and ensuring its continuity is one of the instinctive behaviours of human beings (Hobbes, 1995: p. 76, p. 127).

It is very common among people to carry information to the power, be its information resource and thus be inclined to be close to it. Similar to a magnet attracting metals, the power attracts the individuals around it. For individuals, it is difficult to resist "the unbearable lightness of being close to the power." However, like the metals that can hold on against the attraction of the magnet, only strong-willed individuals can resist to the attraction of power.

4.2 Surveillance to Direct by Acquiring Information

Surveillance is one of the tools that are used to direct target individuals, groups or societies into a certain direction. As a matter of fact, if you conduct surveillance on the life of an individual, a group or a society, you get to know and recognise them well. Consequently, you can control someone whom you know and recognise well more easily. In this regard, there is a need to know things to control people, and a need for surveillance to get to know these things. Individuals in power who want to direct society into a certain direction have always felt the need to recognise and conduct surveillance on the society that they rule. During the part of human history that comes across modernism, the states have taken as a mission to turn the people they rule into a society consisting of individuals who abide the laws they make. Such a society formed reasonably and rationally is seen as the ultimate goal of modern states (Bauman, 2003: p. 24).

This situation is not only valid at the macro level. In interpersonal relationships, there is a need to first recognise and know the other person to direct them into a certain direction. This can be possible by surveillance into various areas of that person's life. For instance, if you want to make a friend do something, you need to recognise him/her well. If your friend is a person who does not like being ordered, but prefer kindness, and react positively to kind behaviours, it will be enough to utter a few questions starting with "Could you …" and end with "please?" On the other hand, if you have an authoritarian friend who perceives kindness as a weakness, but do things when he/she is ordered to, you will need to utter sentences in the imperative mood when talking to him/her (see Batmaz, 2006: p. 48 for authoritarian personality). Or, if he/she is a person who act based on his/her own ideas and have difficulty accepting others' ideas, you can make him/her accept your ideas by saying "Is this what you mean?" and presenting them as his/her ideas. It is possible to find more examples. However, the common point in all examples is that to direct a person in the desired way, you first need to recognise him/her well. As for recognising someone well, it is possible through surveillance.

In today's society, some business firms are observed to conduct surveillance on people's lives to direct them especially by storing and classifying information. For example, as a result of the information shared among the banks, any bank can learn how much money and debt that a person has in other banks. This practice is a kind of a control over the part of individuals' economic activities and the active-passive balance. It is in this way that individuals can apply for a loan right through a text message including their identity number. Besides, hypermarkets have the opportunity to follow the buying habits of their customers by means of the discount cards they give them. These cards are read by a barcode reader before each purchase to get discount and earn points, and in this way, it can be recorded what each customer buys. After it is known what they spend their money for and what they need, it gets easier to direct individuals to buy a certain product.

5. Surveillance to Discipline

5.1 Discovery of the Disciplining Effect of Surveillance by the Western World

Surveillance can be done not only for acquiring information, but also for disciplining together with or independently from the first purpose. The wide discovery of the disciplining effect of surveillance by the western world was with the plague epidemic in Medieval Europe (Bauman, 1996: p. 51). In this period, some rules were set to be applied in the case of a plague epidemic in a city, and not obeying these rules was bound to heavy sanctions. This city would be immediately surrounded and closed for entrance, and the opposite behaviours would be punished with death. While stray animals would be killed, the city would be divided into smaller parts assigned with an inspector. Every family must have stored food beforehand. Small wooden channels were built between the streets and houses for bread and wine only. These enabled meeting everyone's need without any communication between the providers and the society. Whether the rules were obeyed or not was strictly inspected by the officials. In this system, inspections were continuous and glances were over everywhere (Foucault, 2006: p. 289).

In this way, thanks to these practices implemented for cities with the plague, it was noticed that locking individuals into a place made possible a disciplinary model in which all actions were inspected, the power worked hierarchically and constantly, and every individual was observed in almost all points in a closed area (Merquior, 1986: p. 27). Initially thought for cities with the plague, this model started to be also used for keeping tramps, insane people, and dangerous patients under surveillance, and thus, the historical process called "the great confinement" arose (Foucault, 2006: p. 292). In this regard, prisons, poorhouses, hospices, hospitals, and mental hospital played an important role as the places where this confinement happened (Özkazanç, 2002: p. 381). That these new institutions which came out in the early modernism period were not random inventions can be understood from their appearances that were surprisingly simultaneous in distant and functionally unrelated areas. As a matter of fact, the purpose was not to look after poor people, punish the criminals, or treat insane individuals. What was more important was organising the social control mechanism in a new format towards the great distress of the social power areas and re-ensuring them (Bauman, 1996: p. 59).

5.2 A Good Metaphor For Understanding the Disciplining Effect of Surveillance Panapticon

With regard to conducting observance in a closed area and doing this with the lowest cost effectively, Bentham's "Panapticon" project gives important clues (Foucault, 2006: p. 295). This is because in this project, Bentham aimed to both get informed and rehabilitate the prisoners by observing them. Besides, he would do this with fewer staff and less cost. For this reason, thinking this project would be operated with low cost would attract the interest of rulers, he hoped to gain a good profit from it. However, he was not able to actualise this project during his lifetime and it stayed as a great waste of time and money for him. On the other hand, almost all prisons built after Bentham, especially in the first half of the 19th century, were built by taking some of his practices as an example (Foucault, 2003: p. 86). Therefore, this project of Bentham's can be accepted as a project that never took place, but also applied repeatedly in a way. It should be noted that the Panopticon has not reached to us directly by Bentham. Although many scientists worked on punishment theory and penal systems were familiar with the importance of Panopticon long before, the recognition of Panapticon and its use in almost every writing on observance increased when Foucault got interested in it and gave it wide coverage in his work titled Birth of Prison (Lyon, 1997: 92).

Generally, in Panopticon, there is a building in the form of a ring, and a tower in the centre of this ring. This watchtower in the centre has large windows looking to the interior front of the ring-shaped building surrounding it which is divided into cells. Each cell has two large windows, one looking to the interior and the other looking outside. The window facing the interior comes right across the windows of the tower. Because of the light coming from the window facing outside, the silhouettes of the prisoners in the cells of the ring-shaped building can be easily followed from the tower. Since the interior of the tower does not reflect outside, it is not possible for the prisoner to know how many people there are in the tower. This arrangement that enables observation without being seen forms spatial units enabling constant view and quick recognition (Foucault, 2006: p. 295). Control is based on surveillance on the prisoners by individuals that cannot be seen. There is no place for the prisoner to hide and that can be described as a private area. The only reasonable option for the prisoner who does not know if he is being watched since he cannot see inside the tower, but assumes that there is someone inside to watch is obedience. Therefore, Bentham derived a word meaning "fully visible place" in Greek for his prison: "*Panopticon*" (Lyon, 1997: p. 93). Due to the ease of watching it provides and the feeling of "I'm being watched" that it creates in the prisoner, this prison does not need many guardians, which significantly reduces the operating costs.

Even though Panopticon was designed in the form of a prison, the logic behind it is the kind that can be implemented anywhere from mental hospitals to military barracks, or from schools to factories. For this reason, Panopticon is not only a prison, but a power technology, and a surveillance project (Foucault, 2003: p. 87).

Finally, it should be stated that one of the most important changes observed in social life with the modernist period is the professionalism of surveillance. It has now started to be done by people who acquire it as a profession in this new period. In this way, an occupational group that consists of individuals who are specialised in surveillance and will do it for those in power has emerged. This task in question is not an ordinary one, and requires from individuals more than using brute force; having skills of surveillance, specialisation and being an engineer of human behaviour (Bauman, 1996: p. 59).

5.3 Surveillance to Discipline at the Present Time

When surveillance to discipline first started to be systematically used in the historical process (early modernist period), there was a need for closed areas. As a matter of fact, in that period, individuals could only be observed in closed areas. No technological facilities were available to directly watch their activities outside and store information. However, it is possible to discipline individuals by making them feel that they are being pried without being in a closed area by means of technology.

By means of drones and satellite systems, certain regions and even the entire planet can indeed be monitored in the macro level by the states having such technological means (Lacoste, 2007: p. 48). On the other hand, through the use of facilities that organisations such as the Turkish Telecommunications Communication Presidency (TİB) have, we live with the concern that our phones can be tapped and our emails can be read any time. This concern disciplines us, and prevents us from making phone calls that can cause the power to impose sanctions, writing e-mails with illegal contents, or performing illegal actions where we can be seen by surveillance cameras. Therefore, surveillance disciplines us.

To approach the issue at a micro level, children do not misbehave as long as they think their fathers are watching them, or workers stop neglecting their job when they notice the head worker is watching them. Similarly, when a camera is placed at a junction where people violate the red light, the violations would probably decrease considerably, even if the camera does not work. Or, the model of a police vehicle that is placed on a road where people drive at a speed exceeding the legal limit would generate the reflex of breaking and slowing down in drivers.

6. Is the Surveillance by the Power Unnecessary?

Based on the explanations on the concept of surveillance, it can be thought that we support the unnecessariness of public surveillance in particular. For this reason, in the final section of this paper, we wanted to make some statements related to the necessity of public surveillance that is conducted by the state. In modern society, the simultaneous rise of democracy and surveillance attracts attention. This situation should be considered reasonable. The reason is that in democratic societies, the desire to live in safe and easy circumstances, and the demand to receive quality public services conveniently are the primary priorities of individuals. The modern state can provide this only by giving every citizen a number (e.g. identity number, social security number), keeping record of individuals, and conducting various activities of indirect and direct surveillance to ensure security. In many democratic societies, for the majority of individuals constituting the society, the only guarantee for safely walking at night in the streets of cities surrounded by buildings similar to the walls of a fortress is the police officers and security cameras surveilling the streets (Lyon, 1997: p. 45).

In terms of organising the social life and fighting against crime effectively, surveillance is indispensable in today's societies. In this context, it is apparent that surveillance has indispensable benefits although it has many aspects that can be criticised (Lyon, 1997: p. 10). Moreover, it is not only the states that make use of advanced technology for surveillance purposes. Criminals can develop new methods of committing crimes by using the advantages of the modern world. Particularly by means of information technologies and the Internet, communication and cooperation in organised crime, training of gang members (i.e. making bombs etc.) and new techniques for committing crimes have reached unbelievable dimensions. Besides, the damages caused in some crimes are not greater than it was in the past. Technology has not only provided ease in communication, transportation and production, but also enables stealing more easily and in greater quantities. In the face of the huge damages caused due to crimes, it has been more important to prevent crime compared to the past. In this sense, the state's increasing surveillance to an extent and developing it by using new techniques can be regarded as reasonable.

On the other hand, surveillance activities, which are closely related to the concepts of basic rights and especially the privacy of private life, should have certain limits. Otherwise, it would be indispensable to turn into a society of individuals who pass every moment of life with the psychology of being pried. In addition, giving those in power the authority of surveillance redundantly would lead to informing them excessively which would result in giving them excessive power.

7. Instrumentalisation of Law in Public Surveillance Sample of not Reporting a Crime

For public surveillance, the state is observed to often use the law as a means. In this regard, the state legitimises its activities such as tapping phones, following individuals' actions in the public space, and gathering personal information through legal regulations. In this way, surveillance activities becomes legal and are legitimised by being absolved by law. Besides, the state imposes on individuals the obligation of being its means of surveillance with some rules that it prescribes in many criminal laws. The state's forcing individuals to become its means of surveillance through the "crimes of not reporting crime" regulated under Article 278 and its subsequent articles of the Turkish Penal Code are examined in this section.

In the 2004 Turkish Penal Code (no. 5237), there are three articles that attract attention with respect to individuals' being used as a means of the surveillance conducted by the state. These are the crimes of not reporting crime in Article 278, public servants' not reporting crime in Article 279, and health professionals' not reporting crime in Article 280. While the first of these crimes can be committed by any citizen, the second one can be committed only by public servants, and the third one only by health professionals.

Each of these three types of crimes imposes the authorised bodies of the state the duty to report a crime. Therefore, with these crime types, the lawmaker puts the individuals who are the addressees in these articles in the position of a surveillance body of the state. These crime types are relatively more reasonable in terms of Articles 279 and 280. In this sense, the state brings such an obligation to those who will perform certain public duties, and it is acceptable that individuals have a right to choose and these regulations are sensible by claiming that they may not work in performing these public duties. However, putting such an obligation on health professionals in particular would result in perpetrators, who are in need of emergency medical aid, and victims, who do not want the crime to revert to the courthouse, abstaining from receiving medical services (Forensic Science Experts' Declaration, 2004: p. 241). Besides, it is open to discussion that how negatively a health professionals' being under the obligation of reporting a crime related to a patient who has the possibility of a victim or perpetrator would affect the patient-doctor relationship particularly in an important area of public service like healthcare. However, as we said, in these areas, individuals at least have the choice not to work in these occupations.

On the other hand, it is not possible to say the same for the crime of not reporting crime, which has been accepted in Article 278 as a crime as of the new Turkish Penal Code. With this regulation, individuals are not given the chance of not falling into the position of an informer in terms of the crimes that they witness being committed. This article is one of the most important reflections of the understanding that "if you are an individual living in this country, you have to be the eyes of the power" (Yarsuvat et al., 2004: p. 316). Consequently, for individuals who do not want to commit a crime or be in the position of an informer, there is no other chance in terms of the crimes that are being committed or those whose outcomes cannot be restricted. In this regard, in any case where they do not inform the authorities about a crime of which they have knowledge, they will have committed a crime. With this regulation, as Bentham states in his work Panopticon, "every citizen becomes an observer" (Foucault, 2003: p. 92).

At first glance, with Article 278 on not informing authorities about crimes, it can be thought that individuals are imposed such an obligation in order to call for help to those who are in need due to the crime (e.g. a person who is the victim of reckless injury as a result of a traffic accident). However, to impose criminal sanctions to not fulfilling one's humanitarian obligations, the crime of *not fulfilling the obligation of help and informing* was regulated under Article 98 of the Turkish Penal Code. Therefore, it is clear that the regulation related to crime in Article 278 do not have such a purpose. In our opinion, this type of crime is of great importance in terms of showing the extent of surveillance in today's Turkey.

8. Results

There is a close relationship between power and information. As it is often stated, all individuals who are in power need information. Information legitimises power and makes it effective. Possessing information means having power. If you aim to control an object, an individual or society, you first need to know them well, which is possible by surveillance into their lives. In this sense, there is a close relationship between power and information. Although this aspect of the power-information relationship is often emphasised, the other aspect, which is the information production of the power, is relatively neglected. In fact, as information serves power, power serves information. Therefore, there is a bidirectional connection between the two concepts.

Surveillance can be described as monitoring individuals, groups or society in general for the purpose of acquiring information or disciplining people, or both. Contrary to what is believed, this monitoring does not usually come out in the form of directly observing the movements of individuals or groups, or social preferences and events. It can also be done by storing information and private data about individuals. For this reason, the concept of surveillance comprises a much broader meaning than its daily usage.

Both in the macro level and in the micro level, it is observed that surveillance has two primary purposes as "acquiring information" and "disciplining." The surveillance for acquiring information is mostly due to the information-power relationship. As a matter of fact, all individuals in power need information. Information legitimises power and makes it effective. Possessing information means having power. In this regard, if you aim to control an object, an individual or society, you first need to know them well. It should also be noted that surveillance can be done not only for acquiring information, but also for disciplining together with or independently from the first purpose.

Although surveillance has many aspects that can be criticised, it should be stated that especially public surveillance conducted by the state appears as a need for society. In terms of organising the social life and fighting against crime effectively, surveillance is indispensable in today's societies. Moreover, it is not only states that make use of advanced technology for surveillance purposes. Criminals can develop new methods of committing crimes by using the advantages of the modern world. Technology has not only provided ease in communication, transportation and production, but also enables stealing more easily and in greater quantities, breaking down and killing. In this sense, the state's increasing surveillance to an extent and developing it by using new techniques can be regarded as reasonable. On the other hand, surveillance activities, which are closely related to the concepts of basic rights and especially the privacy of private life, should have certain limits. Otherwise, it would be indispensable to turn into a society of individuals who pass every moment of life with the psychology of being pried. In addition, giving those in power the authority of surveillance redundantly would lead to informing them excessively which would result in giving them excessive power.

For public surveillance, the state is observed to often use the law as a means. In this sense, on the one hand, the state completely legitimises its activities such as tapping phones, following individuals' actions in the public space and gathering personal data through legal regulations; on the other hand, it imposes individuals the obligation of being an observer for the state by means of some rules prescribed in criminal laws.

9. References

Adli Tıp Uzmanları Derneği Bildirisi (2004) TCK'nın 530. Maddesi Ortadan Kaldırılıyor, *Türk Ceza Kanunu Reformu İkinci Kitap: Makaleler, Görüşler, Raporlar,* Ankara: Türkiye Barolar Birliği Yayını.

Batmaz, V. (2006) Giriş, *Otoriteryen Kişilik*, İstanbul: Salyangoz Yayınları.

Bauman, Z. (1996) *Yasa Koyucular İle Yorumcular,* (Translated by Kemal Atakay), İstanbul: Metis Yayınevi.

Bauman, Z. (2003) *Modernlik ve Müphemlik,* (Translated by İsmail Türkmen) İstanbul: Ayrıntı Yayınları.

Foucault, M. (2006) *Hapishanenin Doğuşu*, (Translated by Mehmet Ali Kılıçbay), Ankara: İmge Kitabevi.

Foucault, M. (2003) *İktidarın Gözü*, (Translated by Işık Ergüden), İstanbul: Ayrıntı Yayınevi.

Giddens, A. (2008) *Ulus Devlet ve Şiddet*, (Translated by Cumhur Atay), -: Kalkedon Yayınları.

Hobbes, T. (1995) *Leviathan,* (Translated by Semih Lim) İstanbul: Yapı Kredi Yayınları.

Hunt, A. And Wickham, G. (1994) *Foucault and Law,* London-Sterling, Virginia: Pluto Press.

Lacoste, Y. (2007) *Büyük Oyunu Anlamak-Jeopolitik: Bugünün Uzun Tarihi,* (Translated by İsmet Akça), İstanbul: NTV Yayınları.

Lyon, D. (1997) *Elektronik Göz-Gözetim Toplumunun Yükselişi,* (Translated by Dilek Hattatoğlu), -: Sarmal Yayınevi.

Merquior, J. G. (1986), *Foucault*, (Translated by Nurettin Elhüseyni), İstanbul: Afa Yayınları.

Özkazanç, A. (2002) Örgütlü Modernliğin Çözülmesi Sürecinde Suçun Yeniden Siyasallaşması, *Yoksulluk, Şiddet ve İnsan Hakları*, Ankara: TODAİE İnsan Hakları Araştırma Merkezi Yayını.

Yarsuvat, D. et al., (2004) Türk Ceza Kanunu Tasarısı Hakkında Galatasaray Üniversitesi'nin Görüşü, *Türk Ceza Kanunu Reformu İkinci Kitap: Makaleler, Görüşler, Raporlar,* Ankara: Türkiye Barolar Birliği Yayını.

Ass. Prof. Dr. Nurdan Orbay Ortaç* &
Res. Asst. Belin Köroğlu Ölmez**

The Reflection of the Directive 2011/7 of EU on Turkish Commercial Code

Introduction

The consequences of late payment in agreements of supply of goods and services are issued in Article 1530 of the Turkish Commercial Code No. 6102 that came into force on July 1, 2012. The mentioned Article is stated on base of the Directive 2011/7 of the European Union (EU) (DIRECTIVE 2011/7/EU OF THE EUROPEAN PARLIAMENT AND OF THE COUNCIL of 16 February 2011 on combating late payment in commercial transactions)

In the preamble of Article 1530 of The Turkish Commercial Code, it is stated that paragraphs 2 and 7 of the Article which issue the consequences of late payment in the supply of goods and services agreements aims to protect the producers, small and medium sized enterprises and the people or commercial undertakings that serve in exchange of bill or equivalent payment demands against powerful commercial undertakings which insist their conditions especially against shopping malls like markets, supermarkets, hypermarkets. While this Article is being stated the protection of the weak one is preferred on the basis of the principle that freedom of contract will not be valid between the people and enterprises which are not equivalent in negotiation power and position.

The need to make this regulation arises from the usage of late payment as a finance instrument by most big and powerful commercial undertakings. As mentioned in the preamble this instrument puts the ones who supplies goods and services to markets, supermarkets, hypermarkets and such powerful commercial undertakings in a tight spot, dissolute the financial situation and even involved in a failure. A detailed regulation of late payment in agreements of supply of goods and services is provided to avoid the bad practice of these big and powerful commercial undertakings.

* Kırıkkale University Faculty of Law
** Çankaya University Faculty of Law

I. The Conditions of Default of Debtor According to Article 1530 of the Turkish Commercial Code

Paragraphs 2–7 of Article 1530 of the Turkish Commercial Code involve special regulations about the agreements of supply of goods and services. Therefore it is not possible to apply this provision for other cases that arises a debt between parties.

A. The Agreement of Supply of Goods and Services Shall be Concluded Between Commercial Undertakings

In the mentioned provision it is stated that the agreements of supply of goods and services shall be concluded between commercial undertakings in order to apply Article 1530 of the Turkish Commercial Code (TCC, Art. 1530/2). In the referred Directive of EU the regulations involves the agreements of supply of goods and services which both parties are commercial undertakings or the creditor is a commercial undertaking and the debtor is a public authority (Art. 2).

However in the Turkish Commercial Code the public authorities are not involved in the scope of the provision. Even the public authorities are not involved in scope of Article 1530 in the Turkish Commercial Code, the commercial undertakings which are run by a public authority in frame of private law provisions will be included in scope of Article 1530 of TCC as they are regarded as a merchant according to Article 16 of the mentioned Code (Ayhan & Özdamar & Çağlar, 2015, s. 43).

B. The Commercial Undertaking as a Creditor Shall Fulfill its Supply Obligation

In order to apply Article 1530 of the Turkish Commercial Code, the creditor commercial undertaking shall fulfil its supply obligation arise from the Code or the agreement (par. 2). Otherwise the conditions of default of pecuniary debtor will not occur as the creditor may face a non-payment defense (Ayhan & Özdamar & Çağlar, 2015, s. 43).

C. The Commercial Undertaking as a Pecuniary Debtor Shall not Fulfil its Obligation in Time

In accordance with the paragraph 2 of Article 1530 of the Turkish Commercial Code, the commercial undertaking as a pecuniary debtor of the agreement of supply of goods and services shall not fulfil its obligation in time which was set in agreement or mentioned Code. In such a case, differing from the general provisions of default, even the payment date is not fixed the pecuniary debtor in the agreement of supply of goods and services goes into default without the need to the warning.

D. The Pecuniary Debtor Party Shall be Faulted in Going Into Default

In Article 1530 of the Turkish Commercial Code, differing from the general provisions, the condition that debtor shall be faulted in going into default for being held responsible of default interest is required (TCC, Art. 1530/2). In other words the debtor may avoid the execution of this provision by proving that he is not faulted in going into default. However, in such a case the creditor may refer to the general provisions on the default of debtor of the Turkish Code of Obligations.

II. The Consequences of the Default of Debtor According to Article 1530 of the Turkish Commercial Code

The payment of default interest is one of the consequences of the default of pecuniary debtor. In frame of Article 1530 of the Turkish Commercial Code a different provision about default interest rate is stated other than the general provisions.

Unless otherwise agreed by the parties, the default interest rate in commercial transactions is 9% according to Article 2 of the Code of Legal Interest and Default Interest Code No. 3095. According to paragraph 2 of the mentioned Article, if the interest rate for short term advances in December 31 of the previous year applied by the Central Bank of the Republic of Turkey is higher than 9%, the default interest rate in commercial transactions may be demanded over this rate even if there is no agreement between. In addition to this, according to Article 1530/7 of the Turkish Commercial Code in the agreements of supply of goods and services which is in scope of the mentioned Article, if the default interest rate for the late payment is not provided in the agreement or related provisions are invalid, the interest rate that will be announced in January of each year by the Central Bank of the Republic of Turkey shall be at least plus 8% of the default interest rate in commercial transactions which was regulated by the Code of Legal Interest and Default Interest Code No. 3095. This provision is regulated differently from referred Directive of EU in terms of the calculation of default interest rate. This rate in the Directive of EU is mentioned as *"plus 8 points"* instead of *"plus 8%"* (Art. 3/1 (d); *"The level of interest for late payment which the debtor is obliged to pay, shall be the sum of the interest rate applied by the European Central Bank to its most recent main refinancing operation carried out before the first calendar date of the half year in question,* ***plus at least seven percentage points,*** *unless otherwise specified in the contract. (...)"*). In Article 288/1 of the German Civil Code which the Directive forms the basis, this rate is stated as *"plus 5 points of basic interest rate"* (Bürgerliches Gesetzbuch (BGB) § 288).

Some of the writers in doctrine submit that *"at least 8%"* expression shall be understood as *"at least 8 points"* (Ayan, 2012, s. 285; Kendigelen, 2011, s. 535; Yatağan, 2011, s. 86; Aydoğdu & Ayan, 2013, s. 267; Atamer & Nilsson, 2013, s. 56–57; Helvacı M. & Kaya A. & Ülgen H. & Kendigelen A. & Nomer Ertan F. (2014). *Ticari İşletme Hukuku,* İstanbul, 12 Levha Yayıncılık, s. 96). The source of this opinion is the mentioned provisions of the Directives 2000/35 and 2011/7 of the EU which forms a basis to Article 1530 of the Turkish Commercial Code. This rate is determined as *"at least plus seven points"* in the Article 3 paragraph 1 sub clause (d) of the Directive 2000/35 (Art. 3/1 (d); *"the level of interest for late payment which the debtor is obliged to pay, shall be the sum of the interest rate applied by the European Central Bank to its most recent main refinancing operation carried out before the first calendar dat of the half year in question, plus at least seven percentage points, unless otherwise specified in the contract. (...)"*) and as *"at least plus eight points"* in the Directive 2011/7 (Art. 2/6; *"statutory interest for late payment' means simple interest for late payment at a rate which is equal to the sum of the reference rate and at least eight percentage points"*). In grammatical interpretation of the paragraph 7 of the Article 1530 of Turkish Commercial Code, this rate may be recognised as *"at least 8%."*

The Central Bank of the Republic of Turkey determined the interest rate as *"11.50 percentage* in scope of the related Article according to paragraph 7 of Article 1530 of the Turkish Commercial Code on January 1, 2014 in such cases where the default interest rate for the late payment to creditor is not provided in the agreement or related provisions are invalid (http://www.tcmb.gov.tr/yeni/evds/pgm/temerrut.html (18.01.2015). The Central Bank of the Republic of Turkey determined the interest rate as 12.75% which is at least plus 8% of the advance interest rate that was provided for default interest in commercial transactions in the Code No. 3095. Therefore the determined rate is identified on the basis of *"eight percentage"* which is in compliance with the grammatical interpretation of paragraph 7 of Article 1530 of the Turkish commercial Code. It has to be stated that it is important to modify Article 1530/7 of Turkish Commercial Code in compliance with the referred Directive by mean of the deterrence of the provision. Yet the interpretation of the provision as plus 8% of legal default interest rate does not overlap the regulation aim of the provision. Since the rate difference of 1% will not avoid the big enterprises to use late payment as a finance instrument, this rate does not fit the regulation aim of the provision.

III. The Regulations About the Supply of Goods and Services that Take a Part in Referred Directive of EU which does not Take a Part in Turkish Commercial Code

Besides in the referred Directive of EU, the regulations involves the agreements of supply of goods and services which the creditor is a commercial undertaking and the debtor is a public authority, the mentioned regulation does not take place in Article 1530 of the Turkish Commercial Code. Although it is clearly mentioned that this provision aims to protect especially the weak ones who are not equivalent in negotiation power and position in the proposal made to the Grand National Assembly of Turkey about the preamble of mentioned Article, the exclusion of the agreements of supply of goods and services between public authorities and private sector is criticiwed in doctrine especially by mean of contradiction to the preamble (Atamer & Nilsson, 2013 s. 64; Yatağan, 2011, s. 100; Ayan, 2012, s. 733, dn. 40).

The provisions of the referred Directive about the sales with the retention of title do not take a place in the Turkish Commercial Code. According to Article 9 of the referred Directive; "*1. Member States shall provide in conformity with the applicable national provisions designated by private international law that the seller retains title to goods until they are fully paid for if a retention of title clause has been expressly agreed between the buyer and the seller before the delivery of the goods. 2. Member States may adopt or retain provisions dealing with down payments already made by the debtor.*"

In accordance with Article 10 of the Directive 2011/7/EU of EU; "*Member States shall ensure that an enforceable title can be obtained, including through an expedited procedure and irrespective of the amount of the debt, normally within 90 calendar days of the lodging of the creditor's action or application at the court or other competent authority, provided that the debt or aspects of the procedure are not disputed. Member States shall carry out this duty in accordance with their respective national laws, regulations and administrative provisions. 2. National laws, regulations and administrative provisions shall apply the same conditions for all creditors who are established in the Union. 3. When calculating the period referred to in paragraph 1, the following shall not be taken into account: (a) periods for service of documents; (b) any delays caused by the creditor, such as periods devoted to correcting applications. 4. This Article shall be without prejudice to the provisions of Regulation (EC) No 1896/2006.*" The exclusion of this provision which is one of the most important regulations of the supply of goods and services among the ones that protect the supplier is not up to the purpose. Since the recovery of debts occur after a long period of judiciary in our country, the regulation in the referred Directive of EU shall take place in the Turkish Commercial Code Code No. 6102.

Conclusion

The special regulations on the agreements of supply of goods and services made by the Turkish Commercial Code No. 6102 may be encouraging by means of the reduction of the problems that the SMEs face with in practice. However, despite the regulations made on the basis of the referred Directive of EU, the differing parts from the mentioned one is contradictory to the aim to protect the weak ones. Within this scope, especially two aspects have importance.

First is the provision about the default interest rate that is enacted in Article 1530/7 of the Code. It is possible to say that the doctrine has an agreement on the issue that the expression *"plus 8 eight points"* of the referred directive is stated as *"plus 8%"* in our Code.

The second aspect is that a proper regulation to Article 10 of the referred Directive about the applied procedure shall be made with the Turkish Commercial Code. Such a regulation shall be up to the purpose of the protection of SMEs which have a weak position by reducing the judiciary period.

As a consequence we consider that the review of the mentioned regulation by the legislative in frame of the referred Directive will be up to purpose.

Research List

Atamer Y. & Okutan Nilsson G. (2013). Para Alacaklısının Geç Ödemelere Karşı Korunmasına İlişkin Yeni TK. M. 1530 Düzenlemesi ve Uygulama Alanı. *BATİDER, C. XXIX, Sa. 3.*

Ayan, S. (2010). 6102 sayılı Türk Ticaret Kanunu'nun 1530. maddesi Gereğince Borçlunun Temerrüdü. *Dokuz Eylül Üniversitesi Hukuk Fakültesi Dergisi Cilt: 12, Özel S., 2010, s.717–793* (Basım Yılı: 2012).

Aydoğdu, M. & Ayan, S. (2013). *Türk Borçlar ve Türk Ticaret Hukukunda Yer Alan Faiz İle İlgili Düzenlemeler*. Adalet Yayınevi.

Ayhan R. & Özdamar M. & Çağlar H. (2015). *Ticari İşletme Hukuku Genel Esaslar*. Ankara. Yetkin Yayınları.

Helvacı M. & Kaya A. (Ülgen H. & Kendigelen A. & Nomer Ertan F. (2014). *Ticari İşletme Hukuku,* İstanbul, 12 Levha Yayıncılık.

Kendigelen, A. (2011). *Yeni Türk Ticaret Kanunu, Değişiklikler, Yenilikler ve İlk Tespitler*. İstanbul. 12 Levha Yayıncılık.

Münchener Kommentar zum Bürgerlichen Gesetzbuch/Ernst, Band 2, Schuldrecht Allgemeiner Teil § 241, 432, 6. Aufl, München, 2012.

Yatağan Ç. (2011). *2011/7/EU Sayılı Topluluk Yönergesi ve 6102 Sayılı TTK'nın 1530. Maddesi Çerçevesinde Mal ve Hizmet Tedarikinde Geç Ödemenin Sonuçları.* Ankara Üniversitesi sosyal Bilimler Enstitüsü Özel Hukuk Anabilim Dalı, Yüksek Lisans Tezi, Ankara.

www.ingramcontent.com/pod-product-compliance
Ingram Content Group UK Ltd.
Pitfield, Milton Keynes, MK11 3LW, UK
UKHW041825100926
8556IPUK00002B/24

9 783631 681077